Towards a Worldwide Index
of Human Freedom

www.freetheworld.com · www.fraserinstitute.org · Fraser Institute ©2012

TOWARDS A

Worldwide Index
of Human Freedom

Edited by Fred McMahon

Fraser Institute • Liberales Institut • 2012

Printed and bound in Canada

Editing: Kristin McCahon

Cover design and artwork: Bill C. Ray

Cite this book: McMahon, Fred (ed.) (2012). *Towards a Worldwide Index of Human Freedom*. Fraser Institute.

National Library of Canada Cataloguing in Publication Data

Towards a Worldwide Index of Human Freedom / edited by Fred McMahon

Includes bibliographical references.

ISBN 978-0-88975-259-7.

Contents

About the co-publishers

Fraser Institute

The vision of the Fraser Institute is a free and prosperous world where individuals benefit from greater choice, competitive markets, and personal responsibility. Our mission is to measure, study, and communicate the impact of competitive markets and government interventions on the welfare of individuals. Founded in 1974, we are an independent research and educational organization with locations throughout North America and international partners in nearly 90 nations and territories. Our work is financed by tax-deductible contributions from thousands of individuals, organizations, and foundations. In order to protect its independence, the Institute does not accept grants from government or contracts for research.

Website: http://www.fraserinstitute.org.

Liberales Institut

The *Liberales Institut* is the think tank of the Friedrich-Naumann-Foundation for Freedom, based in Potsdam, Germany. It spreads liberal and free-market ideas through publications, the analysis of political trends, and the promotion of research. It aims to promote the goal of making freedom valid for the dignity of all people and in all areas of society, both in Germany and abroad. Its policies work towards promoting the rule of law, democracy, and the world-wide liberalization of all markets: information, technology, goods and services, as well as currency and capital markets. The Institute organizes conferences and workshops to stimulate an intellectual exchange among liberals around the world.

Website: http://www.libinst.de.

Acknowledgments

This publication has been generously supported by the Lotte & John Hecht Memorial Foundation, and by the sponsors of the seminars out of which the book arose: the first, in Atlanta, sponsored by Liberty Fund; two, in Potsdam, sponsored by the Liberal Institute of the Friedrich Naumann Foundation for Freedom; and one, in Washington, DC, sponsored by the Cato Institute.

Overview

The quest

People have been seeking freedom for millennia, but not freedom for all. Slaves, serfs, women, outsiders, and the defeated were not included. That changed in the last few centuries as the circle of those considered deserving of freedom expanded. Evolution continues. Two centuries ago, slavery was alive in the world in many nations, not just the United States; a century ago, women everywhere lacked full citizenship and the freedoms that go with it; more recently, sexual orientation is being removed as a barrier to freedom.

The analysis

A rigorous debate on freedom and what it is did not fully blossom until the Enlightenment when the thinkers of the time made clearer both the nature of freedom and the universal right to it. They also understood and developed the relationship between economic freedom, including property rights, and other freedoms. Key analytical advances (Berlin, 1958 and MacCallum, 1967) have been even more recent.

The measure

Yet efforts to measure freedom have only emerged in the last quarter century or so. Unfortunately, these efforts have been flawed: blurring various definitions of freedoms (despite Berlin's and MacCallum's analytical work), confusing "other good things" with freedom, using subjective rather than objective measures, and either failing to account for economic freedom or focusing exclusively on it.

The project

This project focuses on creating a comprehensive index of human freedom, which includes economic freedom and is based on the "negative" definition of freedom—in other words, the absence of barriers or coercion that prevent individuals from acting as they might wish. (This concept is discussed at more length in the McMahon, chapter two in this volume.)

We have held four seminars to explore the concept and develop a way to proceed: the first in Atlanta, sponsored by Liberty Fund; two in

Potsdam, sponsored by the Liberales Institut (Liberty Institute) of the Friedrich Naumann Foundation; and one in Washington, DC, sponsored by the Cato Institute.

Contents

understand the difference between "actions" that individuals can undertake and obstacles to them, on the one hand, and the range of rights granted to individuals by culture, society, or law, on the other.

5 A Compact Statement of a Cost-based Theory of Rights and Freedom: Implications for Classifying and Measuring Rights

Michael A. Walker

The author draws a distinction between two types of rights or freedoms: those that are costless or low cost for a society to provide and those that require the expenditure of resources to provide. The first set simply requires government to refrain from acting. It includes, among others, freedoms like non-interference with families, most elements of economic freedom, non-discrimination by government, and no prohibition of religions, clubs, newspapers, or other modes of communication. Costly rights include security of property and persons, and some aspects of freedom of speech, the latter because government needs to actively protect those who say unpopular things. He argues the initial freedom index should include only low cost rights which are equally available to all nations to provide whether wealthy or not, thus establishing a "level playing field" for international comparisons.

6 Conditions for Freedom: A Few Theses on the Theory of Freedom and on Creating an Index of Freedom

Andrei Illarionov

The author builds a "zikkurat" of freedom, showing how far different aspects of freedom are from the human core, which he labels "the decision-taking-center of human beings." After an analysis of a number of different aspects of freedom—its supply and demand, evolution, and divisibility, among others—he concludes that it will be difficult to construct a freedom index based on individual preference, since that varies so broadly among humans. Nonetheless, he argues that it is possible to measure the conditions in a society that are conducive for freedom, mainly a tolerant (the author's word is "mild") legal, cultural, and political climate. And, while a measure of freedom based on individual preferences may be problematic, the author suggests that a broad index may be possible, which includes at least four components: the level, spread, inequality, and volume of freedom.

7 Evolution and Freedom

Paul H. Rubin

The author argues that evolution has created two opposing human forces: one that values freedom, and one that strives for dominance, where individuals and groups seek to impose their will on others, limiting freedom.

Freedom thus requires the establishment of strong freedom-supporting institutions to restrain the dominance urge. However, the institutions, which are designed to limit "dominance" (i.e., freedom-suppressing actions) must be properly balanced to protect freedom without the institutions themselves unnecessarily suppressing freedom.

8 Liberty in Comparative Perspective: China, India, and the West

Erich Weede

The author argues that freedom is not the product of human planning but of political evolution. Turbulence and rivalry in Europe led to checks and balances on the power of the state that were required to allow economic and military growth. India and China faced less external and internal rivalry and thus needed to allow lower levels of freedom since the imperative to grow to compete was not as strong. More recently, competition with the West and other rivals has lead China, and to a lesser extent, India, to increase economic freedom to add dynamism to their economies. Weede leaves the reader with a question: Will China be able to continue to growth with only economic freedom in place, or will it need to expand the sphere of freedom to avoid stagnation?

9 The Evisceration of Liberty in Canadian Courts

Karen Selick, Derek From, and Chris Schafer

The authors argue that Canadian courts have "eviscerated" liberty in Canada by interpreting Canada's Charter of Rights and freedoms as protecting only "a degree of autonomy in making decisions of fundamental importance," to quote a Supreme Court decision. Aside from the limited nature of protecting only "a degree of autonomy," the authors also note several problems with distinguishing fundamentally important decisions from other decisions: the dividing line is subjective; many minor violations of liberty together can become a fundamentally important violation; how can individuals ever acquire the wisdom and experience to make decisions of fundamental importance if they can be prevented from making minor decisions; and what justifies politicians in making minor decisions for the whole community?

10 From Fighting the Drug War to Protecting the Right to Use Drugs

Doug Bandow

The author argues that to "have meaning, liberty must protect the freedom to act in ways which may offend individuals and even majorities. So it is with 'drugs' currently banned by the US and other governments." This should apply whether or not legalization produces bad results, but the author argues that a well-structured legalization will reduce harms, not increase them. More importantly, the author argues that the "war on drugs" has sideswiped and reduced a range of other freedoms. For these and other reasons, the paper argues that drug use should be treated as "a protected liberty."

—*Fred McMahon, editor*

References

Berlin, Isaiah (1958). Two concepts of liberty. In Isaiah Berlin (author) and Henry Hardy (ed.) (2002), *Liberty: Incorporating Four Essays on Liberty* (Oxford University Press): 166-217.

MacCallum, G.C., Jr. (1967). Negative and positive freedom. *Philosophical Review* 76: 312-34.

Towards a Worldwide Index of Human Freedom

www.freetheworld.com • www.fraserinstitute.org • Fraser Institute ©2012

CHAPTER ONE

Why Do We Measure Freedom?

Detmar Doering *

"Freedom is so valuable that we must be prepared to sacrifice everything for it; even prosperity and opulence when economic freedom constrains us do so. To our great and undeserved fortune, however, a freedom-based economic order which general freedom cannot do without, has an incomparable material superiority over an economic order based on force," the German liberal economist Wilhelm Röpke wrote in 1959 (S. 286).

Indeed, it is perfectly legitimate and appropriate to define freedom in moral terms as a purpose in itself and to disregard any "consequentialist" argument in its favour (that is, that the consequences of freedom are the ultimate basis by which to judge its rightness). But to explain the causes behind the emergence of free societies (and why they have often remained quite stable), does call for empirical and, therefore, necessarily consequentialist arguments. A whole school of classical liberal thought, ranging from Hume to Hayek, has maintained that a spontaneous free order evolved only because it was more successful than any planned order that consciously used centralized coercive power to achieve its various goals.

But how do we know? We all somehow (and probably rightly) think that free South Korea does much better than unfree North Korea in almost every respect, just as West Germany did better than communist East Germany during the Cold War. Even China's partial and incomplete

---

* Dr. Detmar Doering is Director of the Liberales Institut (Liberty Institute) of the Friedrich-Naumann-Foundation in Potsdam, Germany. He studied philosophy and history at Cologne University, where he earned a Ph.D. in Political Philosophy in 1990, and at University College London. He has published several books. Among them are *Kleines Lesebuch über den Liberalismus* (ed. Translated into 18 languages. English translation: *Readings in Liberalism*, published by the Adam Smith Institute) (1992); *Frédéric Bastiat: Denker der Freiheit* (1997); *The Political Economy of Secession* (ed., with Jürgen Backhaus) (2004); *Globalisation: Can the Free Market Work in Africa?* (2007); and *Freedom, the Rule of Law, and Market Economy* (2011). He has also published numerous articles in German and international academic journals and daily newspapers on economic, political, and historical subjects. Since 1996, Dr. Doering has been a member of the Mont Pelerin Society.

freedom now seems to be a very significant advancement compared to the Stone Age Communism in place during Mao's "Great Leap Forward" of the late '50s and early '60s, which cost tens of millions lives. However, it is more difficult to distinguish between less striking examples. For example, the distinction is less clear to most people whether today's US or Sweden, Portugal or Greece, or Singapore or Taiwan enjoy more freedom or do better or worse than each other. To settle these questions we need more than just a rough intuitional guess; we need more precise measurement.

The economic aspects of freedom,[1] which Röpke mentioned, have already been dealt with quite intensely. Specifically, since the mid-1990s, *Economic Freedom of the World* has been published annually. It has equipped us with strong, long-term evidence that free-market-oriented economic policy leads to an overall better economic performance (as measured by growth rates, income, etc.) and also improves non-economic aspects of life (such as life expectancy, health, literacy, etc.).

But is what has been measured in *Economic Freedom of the World* also related to freedom beyond the pure economic sphere? Opponents of liberalism like to claim that economic freedom can also flourish in otherwise objectionable regimes including Singapore or Chile in the time of the Pinochet dictatorship. Sometimes they give the argument a positive spin: successful economic transformation can best be accomplished under authoritarian control. The success of authoritarian China as opposed to the negative outcomes from Russia during the democratic reform period of the Yeltsin era seem to demonstrate that political liberalization can be harmful to successful economic transformation. One hears this view more and more.

Much of the "evidence" that economic freedom flourishes well or even better under dictatorships does not stand the empirical test. All statistical evidence shows quite clearly that economically free dictatorships are the exception rather than the rule. Correlations between *Economic Freedom of the World* and human rights indices, such as *The Freedom House Report,* suggest a very strong link between economic freedom on the one hand, and democracy and human rights on the other.

Nevertheless, in order to produce any clear statements about the effects of an overall free society, more than its economic aspect must be measured. The assumption that other freedoms, such as the freedom of science, or artistic creativity, contribute a lot to human well-being borders on common-sense. Other freedoms (such as the right to use or abuse

---

1 Freedom here is defined as the absence of constraint. Nobody should be subjected to the will and coercive power of other individuals. Freedom is, therefore, not a matter of lone individuals acting in isolation, but rather pertains to the relationship that individuals have to one another. That is, it concerns the demarcation of individual rights so that freedom does not endanger similar freedoms for others.

drugs, etc.) are, however, often seen as harmful—though the hypothesis of harm is often supported with disputable empirical evidence. But are they really that harmful? And how do those freedoms relate to economic freedom? What do they contribute to society? We can only know the answers if we have empirical evidence.

There is one problem here and it is also the basis for our attempt to develop a genuine freedom index: a comprehensive freedom index does not yet exist. What can we expect from such an effort? We cannot yet know, but at least there are individual indices that already allow a certain rough overview.

A better insight is supplied by the Cingranelli-Richards Human Rights Dataset (CIRI) from the American Binghamton University. This index lists the various official human rights acknowledged by the international community and has a rating scale. The rights are broken up into various categories (fairness in judicial systems, democratic rights, etc.). For our purposes, the "Physical Integrity Index" is of particular interest as it comprises only human rights abuses that violate the most basic liberties, e.g., torture, detention as a political prisoner, arrest without legal process, or the "disappearing" of individuals.

Figure 1 shows the CIRI-Dataset on "physical integrity" (7 to 8 in the rating points equals a good human rights situation, 0-2 points equals a bad situation correlated with GDP per capita. The findings are clear: Once the most basic freedoms are realized, people also derive an economic advantage. Even beyond the fact that freedom is also an insuperable blessing, free human beings are better off!

Figure 1: Human rights and economic performance

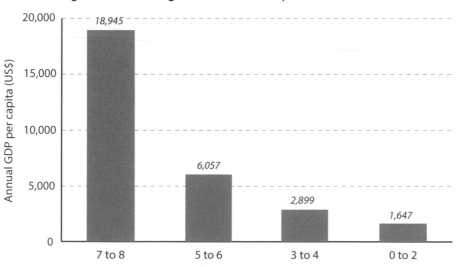

Rating points on the Cingranelli-Richards human rights dataset
(where 8 is high and 0 is low)

There might be an argument to be made that the measurement of freedom goes beyond academic discourse to the political arena. At a time when freedom in the world is receding rather than advancing (due to the financial crisis and other events), the forces of freedom should not be divided, but united between economic liberals and human rights activists.

People often treat the market economy with suspicion. It appears to represent an aspect of freedom with which not everyone feels secure. In political discussion, we often hear the claim that there is a contradiction between political freedoms or civil rights on the one hand, and market freedom on the other. This distinction seems to be becoming more and more pronounced and should be considered both factually wrong and politically harmful for the cause of freedom. Many civil rights liberals see market economics as a non-essential (if not harmful) part of personal freedom; some market economists in turn believe that civil rights are a luxury of limited relevance. Civil rights are often considered to be a concern of the "left," whilst market freedom is seen as "right wing." More and more, freedom is being divided into "good" and "bad" freedoms. The number of individuals who unreservedly embrace freedom does not seem to be particularly large.

An index that could provide us with sound empirical evidence about the state of freedom and its beneficial consequences could do a lot to bridge the gap that has divided the friends of freedom for long time. Or, as was established as early as 1896 by Eugen Richter, a leading liberal in the years before World War I: "Economic freedom is not safe without political freedom and political freedom finds its safety only in economic freedom" (1896, Vol. II: 114).

References

Richter, Eugen (1986). *Im alten Reichstag. Erinnerungen.* 2 volumes. Berlin.

Röpke, Wilhelm (1959). Erziehung zur wirtschaftlichen Freiheit. In A. Hunold (ed.), *Erziehung zur Freiheit*, Zürich.

CHAPTER TWO

Human Freedom from Pericles to Measurement

Fred McMahon *

1 Introduction

The idea of freedom is one of the most contested in political and philosophical discourse and one of the most vital. The contests run along several fronts, which can be transposed to the following questions: Q1) What is freedom? Q2) Who has freedom? Q3) Is freedom always good? Is more freedom always better? Q4) More generally, what are the consequences of freedom in different areas of human endeavor? Q5) How is freedom achieved? Q6) How is it made stable and secure? Q7) How is it defeated?

All subsequent questions depend upon the answer to the first question: What is freedom? Those who would argue that people are "free" in nations like the United States will have very different answers to this question than those who believe, for example, that Venezuela is on a path to socialist freedom, liberating people from the tyranny of markets. Such views are prevalent today, as they were in the past. John Somerville once argued that "in the Communist world, there is more freedom from the power of private money, from the influence of religious institutions, and from periodic unemployment" (Carter, 1999: 1).

A number of societies have spent and are spending much blood and treasure to export their version of freedom, most famously the Soviet and free market blocs during the Cold War. This contest continues, with various latter day versions of socialist freedom, theocratic freedom, and

---

* Fred McMahon holds the Dr. Michael A. Walker Chair in Economic Freedom Research at the Fraser Institute. He manages the *Economic Freedom of the World* Project and examines global issues, such as development, trade, governance, and economic structure. The Centre coordinates the Economic Freedom Network, an international alliance of independent think tanks in nearly 90 nations and territories.

Roadmap to the sections

1. Introduction
   a. This section reviews the literature on human freedom
   b. The opening sub-sections examine the conceptual tools that key 20th century philosophers developed to describe and analyze differing ideas of freedom. They anticipate later sections of the paper by describing what "type" of freedom would be most appropriately measured.
   c. The latter part of the discussion uses these tools to analyze, back to the classical era, the historical depth of modern ideas of freedom; it traces later writers on freedom beginning with the enlightenment.
2. Section 3 then examines various ideas of "freedom" that have entered into popular consciousness and tests to see whether these are consistent with classical ideas of freedom and the rigorous definitions of freedom developed in the last century.
3. This section applies the same tests to the various charters and measures of freedom now available.
4. The final section looks forward to developing an index that is consistent with a rigorous definition of freedom.

others replacing the Soviet version. Yet the few existing freedom indexes are problematic or incomplete or both, as will be discussed later. In other words, leaders and societies, including those in the "free" world, don't have clear definition of freedom or an operational measure of what they claim to be supporting.

This means it is difficult to answer Q2, at least in a comparative sense, regardless of the version of freedom chosen. This, in turn, means that Q3 and Q4 cannot be answered reliably, since there is no objective measure of freedom that could be used to test against outcomes. Although many would argue that freedom has intrinsic value, the task of determining whether it produces positive outcomes is also important.

Measurement is important for another reason. Since a number of versions of "freedom" are mutually exclusive, it means that if some produce positive results, others are likely to produce harms. Much debate rages over the question of which version of freedom benefits people (and which people, for that matter[1]). A reliable measure of any one of the various versions of freedom would help clarify the debate. Answers to these questions also would help determine whether those nations that spend blood

---

1   For example, a socialist might claim that "negative freedom," particularly in the economic realm, provides benefits for only the richest. An objective measure of this version of freedom could provide authoritative answers: i.e., are the poor worse off, or better off, in negative freedom nations? The work on economic freedom (Gwartney and Lawson, 2008) suggests the answer is better off, but more research is required on overall freedom.

and treasure to promote freedom see results that are worth the expenditures in increased freedom (or at least the version of freedom being measured) and improved outcomes.[2]

Measurement is also required for Q5, Q6, and Q7. Without an objective measure of freedom, it is impossible to determine in any quantitative way whether action X leads to increases or decreases in freedom; whether it lends stability to freedom or causes instability. Given a) that many nations have made great sacrifices to spread their versions of freedom and b) the possibility that some version(s) of freedom creates better lives for people than others, answering Q5, Q6, and Q7 becomes highly significant, in conjunction with Q3.

2 Concepts of freedom

This literature review will, by necessity, discuss broad themes. Hundreds of pages of densely-argued work have been written over the smallest details in the debate and cannot be dealt with in a review of this scope. The paper also will assume an informed readership that is already familiar with basic concepts, so these will not be discussed at length in this essay.

Berlin

Isaiah Berlin's 1958 essay, "Two Concepts of Liberty," provides an important conceptual tool to examine notions of freedom, so we will begin there and then move backward to look at earlier views of freedom, before examining more current literature. Following Berlin, this paper will treat the terms "freedom" and "liberty" as being interchangeable, though it typically will speak of "freedom." Some thinkers have tried to distinguish between liberty and freedom, but such efforts appear forced and hinge on idiosyncratic definitions of the two—distinctions without differences. None have caught on.

Berlin's two concepts were "negative" and "positive" freedom. The negative concept of freedom concerns lack of humanly imposed barriers to action. "By being free in this sense I mean not being interfered with by others. The wider the area of non-interference, the wider my freedom" (Berlin, 1958: 170). Positive freedom, on the other hand, involves freeing oneself from whatever constraints one imposes on oneself. This enables the person to find his or her true self. It implies some sort of higher and lower plane of being with the higher plane freeing itself from constraints imposed by the lower plane. For example, class consciousness would have been perceived by many communists as part of a lower self, blocking the release and freedom one experiences under the higher form of socialist liberty.

---

2 Granted, much international maneuvering is for geopolitical reasons, but, at least for some nations, the question of whether the lives of people are improved is important.

Berlin distinguishes between two manifestations of positive freedom. The first is benign, where individuals themselves choose a course they find liberating—for example, by voluntarily joining a religious order, which they can also voluntarily leave. The other is an attack on negative freedom. This is where positive freedom is imposed by some powerful group, for example communist re-education camps supposed to "liberate" people from class consciousness so they can find true Marxist freedom.

Berlin was not the first to discuss negative and positive freedom. However, his essay came at the right time, when increasing claims for positive freedom were contesting the essentially negative view of freedom that had emerged from most Enlightenment thinkers. Both the recently-defeated Nazis and the communists in the then-ongoing Cold War contained strong strains of non-benign positive freedom. Both opposed negative freedom in practice, if not in word.[3] Berlin brought clarity to the contest and, for that reason, his essay became highly influential.

Jumping ahead

The concepts of negative and positive freedom will be developed more fully later in the paper. But to provide context for the reader of the discussion ahead and how it relates to developing a measure of freedom, here we will briefly anticipate the last section of the paper on what "type" of freedom should be measured.

Positive freedom cannot be measured outside of some ideology, one that has a version of true freedom. Positive freedom has very different meanings for an evangelist, an Islamist, a Marxist, a supporter of Robert Mugabe, and so on. Yet, we are looking for a measure of freedom that transcends particular ideologies and has a universal application.

Unlike positive freedom, negative freedom comes in only one flavor—lack of constraint imposed on the individual. Constraint investigation happily lends itself to empirical measurement based on third party data, and thus the creation of an objective measure. Negative freedom is also universal and prior to positive freedom in that it enables individuals to explore, without constraint, various versions of benign positive freedom. Thus, this paper argues that negative freedom is the appropriate "type" of freedom to measure for this project.

MacCallum

Although less essential for reviewing early ideas on freedom, it also is worth jumping the gun a bit to bring in what is arguably the second most influential modern analysis of freedom, Gerald C. MacCallum's 1967 *Negative and Positive Freedom*. He argues that there is only one concept of freedom,

---

3   The wording of the constitutions of communist regimes was often quite liberal.

though it may have several "conceptions."[4] MacCallum bases his argument on his triadic analysis of freedom[5]: x, an actor, who is free or not free to do z (a certain action, state of mind, etc.), depending on restraints created by y.

MacCallum put it this way: "'x is (is not) free from y to do (not do, become, not become) z,' x ranges over agents, y ranges over such 'preventing conditions' as constraints, restrictions, interferences, and barriers, and z ranges over actions or conditions of character or circumstance. When reference to one of these three terms is missing in such a discussion of freedom, it should be only because the reference is thought to be understood from the context of the discussion" (1967: 314).

Depending on the nature of x, y, and z, this formulation can capture both positive and negative freedom, MacCallum argues. Thus, for him, positive and negative freedoms are different "conceptions" of the core concept of freedom, which is formally described by the triadic relationship. The various conceptions involve differing ideas of what x, y, and z are. To give a simple example (considering the complex literature that has developed) focusing on y, negative freedom is denied when the blocking agent, y, is a human being; positive freedom is denied when, in effect, "x" is divided into two—x itself representing some true higher plane of self while y, the other part of self, is some lower plane of being (such as the addict, y, trapping x in desire and blocking a clean life; class consciousness, imposed by y, blocking x from joining the revolution) that is the blocking agent that prevents the higher plane of being, x, from something that would be desired by this higher plane of self freed from the restraints imposed by y. Positive freedom is the Jekyll-and-Hyde version of freedom.

Much debate has concerned the nature of each variable, x, y, and z. For example, again focusing on y for consistency, does the blocking agent, y, in the negative version of freedom, have to limit x's options *intentionally*, as Hayek (1960/1978) claimed, for this relationship to count as a reduction of freedom for x? Does y have to be human, as Hayek also claimed? (See, for example, Hayek, 1960/1978: 12-13.) These issues will be discussed later.

---

4 See, for example, Gray, 1990, for the concept/conception distinction. MacCallum does not use the "concept/conception" terminology but it is consistent with his thought. MacCallum uses phrases like "the ranges of the term variables" (1967: 312), to capture the idea that varying "conceptions" of freedom are actually based on a single "concept" of freedom, with the "conceptions" differing based on what constitutes each of the variables in the triadic relationship.

5 Interestingly, just as Berlin did not originate the analytical tool he made famous in "Two Concepts," MacCallum specifically refers to Oppenheim (and others) as being prior to him in developing the triadic concept, though with the proviso that Oppenheim "limits the ranges of the term variables so sharply as to cut one off from many issues I wish to reach" (1967: 314, fn. 2). In effect, Oppenheim's limits on the terms restricted the relationship to one essentially of negative freedom (Oppenheim, 1961).

Now turning to history before coming back to Berlin and MacCallum, this review will argue that the idea of both negative and positive[6] freedom can be traced back at least to the classical world, though many argue that modern concepts of freedom did not exist in the ancient world (Constant (1816), for example). Such voices claim that a new understanding of at least negative freedom emerged only later in the Western world, reaching first maturity in the Enlightenment. However, this paper argues that the ideas of negative and positive freedoms that are very close Berlin's go back at least to the classical world, but will agree with those commentators who argue that neither the idea of freedom *for all* nor the connection between commerce (economic freedom) and other freedoms were found (or at least were prevalent) in the ancient world, but instead were only fully introduced during the Enlightenment.

Carrying forward the review into modern times, the paper will show that an early emphasis on economic freedom (in the negative sense) is now almost entirely absent from the current philosophical literature and, moreover, that economic freedom has been decoupled from overall freedom in existing measurements. Supposedly "broad" measures of freedom either exclude economic freedom or, perversely, define state economic coercion as economic freedom. Both the absence of economic freedom and the perversion of economic freedom in most freedom measures is an important gap and problem in our understanding of important issues.

In fact, a key goal of the project for which this review is being written is to develop a truly broad-based measure of freedom that appropriately deals with economic freedom.

Finally, any paper, even a literature review, will by necessity be selective. This paper, for example, has chosen a broad sweep to put things into perspective. Unlike many reviews of the state of the freedom literature, such as Carter (1999) or Gray (1990), this paper will not focus on the minutiae of the debate over the precise meaning of negative or positive freedom, nor on the various possible meanings of MacCallum's x, y, and z and their possible relationships to each other. This is not to disparage either Carter or Gray, both of whom are quoted liberally, but instead to recognize the limits of a paper compared to books of many pages, and to gain a broader historical sweep than either of those books is able to provide.

Even given a broad sweep, choices not to everyone's liking have to be made. For instance, Hobbes, Locke, and Rousseau are discussed, but J.S. Mill is mentioned only in passing and Kant is largely ignored, even though his views on "universal" and fundamentally negative freedom along with his emphasis on property and contracting rights well fit the

---

6 Albeit, given space considerations, the argument for positive freedom in history will be mostly by assertion since this proposition is little contested.

themes developed in the paper. Surprising for a paper that has a strong focus on economic freedom, Adam Smith is also not discussed, largely because his views on what we would now call economic freedom are well known and because he bases his discussion largely, though not exclusively, on utilitarian grounds, at least in *Wealth of Nations*. The only defense for this selectivity is that the key points for the purposes of this paper will already have been made with the thinkers selected and that piling on more thinkers would do little to advance the paper.

The ancients and their modern interpreters

It is important in a literature review of this sort to go back to the early origins of the ideas being discussed. This sheds light on the following discussions and on whether the ideas are culture-based and non-universal, or have a wider draw. Aside from arguing that freedom, even in its modern form, is not merely a modern concept, this review will show that the idea of economic freedom has been intertwined with overall freedom and appears to be a necessary condition for other freedoms, an insight developed by Enlightenment thinkers and supported by modern empirical research, as will be discussed.

Many thinkers believe that the "Western" concept of freedom is not merely unique to the West, but is also of recent vintage. Illustrative thinkers here are Stark (2006) and Constant (1816). Both argue that the ancients (both Greek and Roman) had a fundamentally different version of freedom—either in concept or extent—than the one that evolved in the Enlightenment, though they disagree on why.

Constant allows that the ancients knew "collective freedom," in effect the limited forms of democracy found in some Greek states. However, he argues that "you find among them [the ancients] almost none of the enjoyments which we have just seen form part of the liberty of the moderns. All private actions were submitted to a severe surveillance. No importance was given to individual independence, neither in relation to opinions, nor to labor, nor, above all, to religion…. Individual liberty, I repeat, is the true modern liberty" (Constant, 1816). I will argue that the ancients did have the concept of individual liberty, just not individual liberty for all.

Stark's is the more interesting claim. He does not contest or much discuss whether the ancients' concept(s) of freedom matched more modern concepts. Instead, he claims, correctly I think, that the ancients (both Greek and Roman) extended freedom, where it was available, only to elite members of society. He contrasts this with Christianity's focus on the moral equality of the individual, regardless of background. "Jesus asserted a revolutionary conception of moral equality, not just in words but in deeds. Over and over again he ignored major status boundaries and associated with stigmatized people…" (2006: 76).

Although the early church clearly accepted slavery and some church members owned slaves, Stark argues that the moral weight of Christian beliefs, over the centuries, ultimately triumphed over older social patterns, just as, to switch times and authors, Martin Luther King (1983) would with some success call on Americans to "live out the true meaning of its creed: 'We hold these truths to be self-evident, that all men are created equal…'" which in turn had a theological origin.

Stark is focused on Christianity but his arguments would be better served if he referred to the Judeo-Christian tradition. The ideas Stark stresses, like respect for work, are all clearly present in both the Old and the New Testament, which is predominately a Jewish book, written by Jews, and reflective of the Jewish culture of the time, though there are obviously some differences between the two. But, it is the commonalities that lie at the heart of Stark's arguments rather than the differences. To go a step further to broaden the argument beyond the Judeo-Christian tradition, MacNeill (1992) argues that major "new" religions, like Christianity, Islam, and Buddhism, initially grew because they offered some form of salvation to all—in other words, the same type of universality that Stark shows is found in Christainity.

Stark is clearly right that the extension of freedom was limited in the ancient world, but the core individual concept was not absent, as Constant claims. In his famous funeral oration as represented in Thucydides' *Histories,* Pericles addresses Constant's arguments so clearly it might seem to be a direct debate between the two. "[I]n our private business we are not suspicious of one another, nor angry with our neighbor if *he does what he likes*; we do not put on sour looks at him which, though harmless, are not pleasant…. *[W]e are thus unconstrained in our private business …*" (Hooker, 1996, emphasis added).

This is surely a statement of "negative" individual freedom, with neither the state nor social pressure constraining individuals, albeit for a limited set of free male citizens. It may be that in practice Athenians did not have the same level of negative freedom as residents of the freest nations today, but clearly the concept was alive. In fact, the concept of negative freedom was so alive that it repelled many of the philosophers of the time. Palmer quotes a question Socrates asks in *The Republic* to show this:

> "In the first place, then, aren't they free? And isn't the city full of freedom and free speech? And isn't there license in it to do whatever one wants?
>
> "That is what is said, certainly," he said.
>
> "And where there's license, it's plain, that each man would organize his life in it privately just as it pleases him." (Plato, quoted in Palmer, 2008: 3)

Palmer then shows that, while Plato understood the concept of negative freedom, and thus it existed in Athenian culture, the idea of negative freedom created a "litany of horrors" for him. As will be briefly noted later, Plato's idea of freedom was positive freedom.

To return to Pericles, Thucydides goes on to have Pericles say that despite this freedom, Athenians are "prevented from doing wrong by respect for the authorities and for the laws" (Hooker, 1996). This is no different than Hayek's speculation that "it is probably true that a successful free society will always in large measure be a tradition-bound society" (1960: 61) where respect for law and custom is high and maintains social cohesion even as people go their own way (1960: 63 contains this extension of Hayek's thinking).

Early in his essay, Constant allows that Athens might at least appear to be an exception to his supposition. Later he on, he writes, "Athens, whose example might be opposed to some of my assertions, but which will in fact confirm all of them." Through a number of examples, he argues that "that the individual was much more subservient to the supremacy of the social body in Athens, than he is in any of the free states of Europe today." Whether Constant was right or not is an empirical question that, short of time travel, we will never be able to resolve, but clearly the concept of individual negative freedom lives in the words Thucydides puts in Pericles's mouth and in Plato's horror at the concept.[7]

The classicist Victor Davis Hanson argues convincingly that negative freedom (he does not employ the word "negative" though that is effectively what he means) enjoyed by the Greek city states was crucial to their ability to defend themselves from the Persians. Free men, he claims, fight better and conduct wars better than unfree men. He also details many instances where Greek writers explicitly say the Greeks are fighting for their freedom. Hanson describes four types of freedom valued by the Greeks:

> If one were to ask a Greek sailor at Salamis, "what is the freedom you row for?" he might have provided a four-part answer. First, freedom to speak what he pleased.... Second, the Greek rowers at Salamis also fought with the belief that their governments in Athens, Corinth, Aegina, Sparta and other states of the Panhellenic alliance were based on the consent of their citizenry.... Third, the Greeks at Salamis freely had the right to buy and sell property, pass it on, and improve or neglect it as they found fit.... Finally, the Greeks at Salamis

---

7 Straumann (2009), also argues that Constant is wrong to believe the ancients lacked modern concepts of freedom. He claims that Groitus' views of natural rights were based on Roman law.

entertained a freedom of action .... Throughout the campaign refugees, soldiers, and onlookers came and went ... as they saw fit. (Hanson, 2002: 51-53)

While it would be beyond the scope of this paper to recite in detail Hanson's arguments and evidence for these claims, they can be quickly alluded to: 1) he notes the well-recorded and unrestrained argument and debate not just in the Greek city forums of the time, but even on the battlefield between generals over tactics and strategy; 2) Hanson is right about proto forms of democracy in the Greek world, but he weakens his point by failing, by and large, to distinguish democracy from freedom (a distinction that will be discussed latter in this paper); 3) he notes that the Greeks had the security of *property rights* to feel confident to leave their most valued possessions at home "trusting in the law to protect the private capital of the free citizen" (p. 52); and 4) along with the example of free action in the above quote, he notes that many free Athenians simply decided not to evacuate Attica despite the assembly's order to do so. It is worth noting this runs directly counter to Constant's arguments, since Athenians were clearly ready to disobey community authority, and this disobedience was not even strongly proscribed.

Hanson's claims about property rights should not be extended to commerce in general in the Greek world. Property rights may well have been respected even when commerce was considered an unseemly profession. Stark argues convincingly that commerce was despised by the elites in the Greco-Roman world. Constant provides now outdated statistics to argue that the commerce of the ancients was extremely limited compared to the commerce of his day, but he does not much explore why this is so, other than his claim that the culture of the ancients created a warlike (or confiscatory) concept of commerce, limiting its emergence, while new technology, such as the compass, encouraged it in his time.

Whatever the true data on ancient commerce, the Greeks, particularly the Athenians, were traders. Yet, while comments praising (or deploring) negative freedom are fairly common in ancient literature, there are few, if any, ancient quotes that praise what today we would call economic freedom. It is only in the debate of the last few centuries that economic freedom was seen as crucial to other freedoms, a connection that seems lost again in most modern freedom indexes, as will be argued later.

Although Hanson lists property rights as a central element of freedom, both Stark and Constant claim that private commerce is not just a freedom, but also the basis of other freedoms.[8] Constant, for example,

---

8   Constant also claims that the size of the polity also affects freedom, with small polities exercising more social control over the citizens. He opposes direct democracy with freedom.

states, "[C]ommerce inspires in men a vivid love of individual independence. Commerce supplies their needs, satisfies their desires, without the intervention of the authorities…. [N]ot only does it emancipate individuals, but, by creating credit, it places authority itself in a position of dependence." Despite the earlier quote, he credits the commerce of Athens for allowing a somewhat higher level of individual freedom than other Greek states.[9]

Constant, Stark, and Hanson are on to something that all too often has gotten lost in the recent philosophical literature on freedom, and that is the link between property rights and commerce, or economic freedom, and other freedoms. This will be discussed later.

It goes virtually without saying that the ancients did have versions of positive freedom, as is evidenced in Plato's *Republic,* for example, or in sects like the Pythagoreans. As this is not contested, to my knowledge, nothing further will be added.

This section has suggested that the concepts of both negative and, less controversially, positive freedom were alive in the classical world, though it agrees with Stark about the lack of universality in the concept of freedom. One could go further and suggest that the much earlier *Epic of Gilgamesh* reveals a very human joy in being unconstrained in free action and even a version of positive freedom when Gilgamesh understands and accepts his mortality. It is beyond the scope of this review to explore other cultures, though this would be an important endeavor. Nonetheless, the evidence presented strongly suggests that the ideas of both negative and positive freedom are not simply modern constructs.

The Enlightenment

The Enlightenment thinkers were not mere theorists: they had a world to remake. Thomas Hobbes, the first great English theorist of the Enlightenment, saw a continental European world that had virtually collapsed into flames and blood. Then the relatively calm England of his youth fell into civil war in as the Roundheads fought to remove Charles I, the bloodiest internal conflict since Henry VII seized the English throne almost 150 years earlier. This is important context to understanding not just Hobbes, but the political thinking of all early and perhaps all Enlightenment thinkers.

This section focuses on three thinkers: Hobbes, Locke, and Rousseau. With the possible exception of Rousseau, these are not unusually vague thinkers. Yet, for each, there is considerable dispute over what they actually meant, how they tied their premises to their logic and then to their

---

9 Constant is perhaps too optimistic about the stability and impact of commerce: "Hence it follows that an age must come in which commerce replaces war. We have reached this age."

conclusions, and whether they actually succeeded in doing this for a number of their arguments. This review will tread the surface of these matters, rather than mining deeply. It will instead try to explore the meaning of their conclusions relevant to freedom, which are typically fairly clear, while only sketching the sometimes tortuous routes taken to reach these conclusions. (See Walker for one theory of the development of freedom.)

Hobbes

After fleeing first to Holland during the English civil war, Thomas Hobbes huddled in Paris writing the *Leviathan*, published in 1651. This was just three years after the Peace of Westphalia in 1648 brought an official close to a much bloodier and vicious period of warfare on the continent than was found in England during the civil war.[10]

With the old political order destroyed by a tide of hate and violence, both the theorists and peacemakers at Westphalia (and later the English peacemakers) strove to find a new or revived order that would preserve the peace and bring stability. The *Leviathan* was a very conscious attempt to do just that.

Hobbes starts with the state of nature, which he interprets as a state of full (negative) freedom, which he elsewhere describes as "the absence of external impediments" (Hobbes, 1651: ch. XIV, 2.)[11] However, there are also no impediments on the ability of individuals or groups to suppress the freedom of others. This ends up not just destroying freedom, but creating brutal chaos, certainly reminiscent of, in Hobbes time, the recent state of affairs on continental Europe.

However, individuals are endowed with rationality, a law of nature. Hobbes theorized that such individuals would come together in a social contract to protect themselves, given that humans' first priority is their survival, the right of nature. The most effective and appropriate "social contract" would be to construct an absolutist state, with a firm monopoly on violence, reflecting Hobbes abhorrence of the troubles that were so common prior to and during much of his own lifetime.

---

10 Those who casually claim the problem with today's Islam is that it has not undergone a "reformation" should remind themselves of the carnage the actual Reformation wreaked in Europe, which arguably was much bloodier than anything found in the Islamic world today.

11 Hobbes' "state of nature" is a fictional state. Early humankind was extremely social and bound by tribal norms (Fukuyama, ch. 2). However, for an intellectual examination of individual freedom, it is an appropriate place to start—a status of full freedom—just as Rawls' fictional "veil of ignorance" is an appropriate place for him to start his examination of the nature of justice.

Hobbes believed that a monarchy would best achieve this state of absolutism,[12] but he was willing to accept other forms of government, including some form of democracy, so long as the government was absolute. Thus, having begun at with a state of freedom, Hobbes moves to a state that has no *right* of individual liberty, except in one circumstance. Survival is a right of nature and individuals may rebel against the sovereign to protect their existence.[13]

Regardless of the laws, individuals should obey them with only that one exception. However, the sovereign has a motive for good rule: to maintain consent and the monopoly of power. Thus, individuals might be allowed a sphere of freedom: "The liberty of a subject, lies only in those things which the sovereign has praetermitted in regulating their actions. That is the liberty to buy and sell, and otherwise contract with one and another; to choose their own abode, their own diet, their own trade of life, and institute their children as they themselves think fit; and the like" (ch. 21, 146). Hobbes also gives a practical reason for allowing some liberty; he argues that creating rules to govern all aspects of individuals' life: "To try to do this would be impossible" (ch. 21, 146).

Three things become apparent. Hobbes held a "negative" view of freedom: "[L]iberty refers to the man himself. This liberty consists in that he finds no stop to doing what has the will, desire or inclination to do" (ch. 21, 145), though he believed it should be largely constrained by the sovereign. Men have created the absolutist and "artificial" commonwealth through assent to the social contract: "they made artificial chains for themselves by mutual covenants, which are called civil laws. They are fastened the chains at one end, to the lips of the man, or assembly, to whom they have given sovereign power; and at the other end to their own ears" (ch. 21, 145).

Second, the freedom that Hobbes says could (and perhaps should) be allowed would now be defined primarily as economic freedom, something that will be picked up again in the discussion of current measures of freedom.

Third, Hobbes views all individuals as equal in the state of nature and in developing the social contract. His concern is focused on the individual's relationship to Leviathan.

Locke

There are many parallels between John Locke and Hobbes. As will be noted, both often begin at the same starting point, but then Locke moves in a different direction. Locke, like Hobbes, tries to develop a theory of

---

12   However, his dispensing with divine right did not make him popular with the monarchies of the time, including Charles II.

13   Hobbes in *Leviathan* writes a great deal about religion, but I do not review it. Most discussions argue that Hobbes' religious commentary is not well connected to his overall argument.

government that will work. Although the two overlap, he is somewhat further away in time from the continental horrors, though he experienced England engaged in civil war in his youth. Nonetheless, perhaps because of the peaceful resolution of the civil war with the restoration of the Stuarts, he feared revolution less and valued liberty more than Hobbes.

Locke, again like Hobbes, brings together ideas on the state of nature and the social contract. Locke begins roughly where Hobbes does. Individuals find the state of nature unsatisfactory and to improve their situation they enter into a social contract, but he does not paint the state of nature as being as dismal as Hobbes.

He replaces the "Right of Nature," the fundamental right to survival, with a "Law of Nature." Nonetheless, like Hobbes, Locke bases natural law on the right to existence, a gift from God that cannot be violated except in opposition to the Law of Nature, but Locke does not stop there. Survival is the end; the means to the end are life, liberty, and property. Since these are the means for survival, individuals have a natural right to life, liberty, and property just as they have to survival. Thus, Locke is able to expand the idea of a right to survival into other rights and, importantly, expand the idea of individual freedom to a universal concept, since all are under the law of nature.

Since these rights are also present in the state of nature, Locke's social contract is much different than Hobbes's. The sole imperative of the contract is no longer survival, for which absolutism provides the best, though not certain, guarantee; instead, the other imperatives, the other natural rights, need to be taken into account. Thus, the goal of government is not mere stability; it extends to protecting these rights.

Perhaps surprisingly, Locke, once more like Hobbes, proclaims himself willing to accept a monarchy, oligopoly, or democracy. However, just as Hobbes places the same burden—absolutism—on government, whatever its nature, so does Locke, though of course the nature of the burden, protecting freedom, differs from Hobbes's burden. For Locke, government actions must be consistent with the protection of the rights that Locke deduces. Moreover, since these are natural rights, if government violates them, citizens in turn have the natural right to overthrow that government.[14]

---

14 Locke also wrote one of the crucial arguments on religious freedom, *Letter Concerning Tolerance*. He notes that there is no example in the Bible of Jesus or his followers using coercion to bring others to faith. He develops three philosophical arguments that reach beyond Christianity to universal application: neither God nor the social contract gives sovereignty over individuals' souls to government since this would be a violation of liberty gained under natural law; since religion is an inward state, force is ineffective in imparting true belief; and since the magistrate is as prone to error as others, giving the state coercive power over religion would not reduce error.

Like Hobbes, Locke argues that everyone in the state of nature is equal and holds equal rights and freedoms. However, unlike Hobbes, he argues that these freedoms and rights should be preserved under a just magistrate. He thus, at least predominately, is a supporter of negative liberty and equality.

> To understand political power right, and derive it from its original, we must consider what state all men are naturally in, and that is, a state of perfect freedom to order their actions, and dispose of their possessions, and persons as they think fit, within the bounds of the law of nature, without asking leave, or depending on the will of any other man. (Locke, 1691, *The Second Treatise*: ch. II, 218, para 4)

His version of freedom, as noted, is also, at least predominately, negative, within a sphere of law with a stress on property ownership, quite similar to Hayek's later concepts of law and freedom:

> [T]he end of law is not to abolish or restrain, but to preserve and enlarge freedom: for in all the states of created beings capable of laws, "where there is no law, there is no freedom;" for liberty is to be free from restraint and violence from others; which cannot be where there is not law: but freedom is not, as we are told, "a liberty for every man to do what he lists:" (for who could be free, when every other man's humour might domineer over him?) but a liberty to dispose, and order as he lists, his person, actions, possessions, and his whole property, within the allowance of those laws under which he is, and therein not to be subject to the arbitrary will of another, but freely follow his own. (Locke, 1691, *The Second Treatise*: ch. VI, 241-2, para 57)[15]

However, he also wrote: "But though this be a *State of Liberty,* yet it is not a *State of Licence,* though men in that state have an uncontrollable Liberty, to dispose of his Person or Possessions, yet he has not Liberty to destroy himself [given the prior natural law of survival] or so much as any Creature in his Possession…" (*The Second Treatise*: ch. II, 270-1, para 6). The significance of "the state of licence" will become clear later.

Locke's development of property rights is also worth emphasizing. In the above quote, Locke makes property an extension of the person. Without the fruit of one's labors, whether they be through manual work, investment, or invention, negative freedom becomes an impossibility.

---

15 Interestingly, in the next paragraph, 58 (p. 242), Locke begins an argument that parents have a "… duty … to take care of their offspring during the imperfect state of childhood." The argument has similarities to Hayek's on parents' responsibility to children.

Not only is an individual's effort alienated from that individual, but material existence is threatened. If property is not secure, then neither is the ability to obtain, through property exchange, even the essentials of life. Therefore, the extension of the person to his or her property is appropriate since property is necessary for survival. Without property rights, the individual becomes dependent on whomever or whatever controls property.

Locke also provides a specific rationale for the extension of the person to property:

> [E]very man has a property in his own person: this nobody has any right to but himself. The labour of his body, and the work of his hands, we may say, are properly his. Whatsoever then he removes out of the state that nature hath provided, and left it in, he hath mixed his labour with, and joined to it something that is his own, and thereby makes it his…. (Locke, 1691, *The Second Treatise*: ch. V, 270-1, paragraph 27).

Thus property rights, the foundation of negative economic freedom, are a necessary condition for overall negative freedom. This will also become important in the later discussion of "claim" freedoms and the distinction between opportunity and freedom.

Rousseau

Jean-Jacques Rousseau was born almost a decade after Locke's death. Though Rousseau overlaps the Enlightenment period, he is often considered more of a Romantic thinker. This well suits the purpose of this paper since it introduces concepts that have been influential (and, to some views, dangerous) ever since.

Like both Hobbes and Locke, Rousseau introduces the idea of a state of nature and a social contract leading out of this state of nature. However, he added on the fuzzy concept of "general will." How this arises or relates to the individual's will is far from clear. Moreover, while, according to Rousseau, the social contract reached by the free individuals in the state of nature must be in accord with the general will, it is unclear how this is to be accomplished or carried out.

Nonetheless, the general will (whatever it is, however it is articulated, wherever it comes from, etc.) is always for the public good and thus must not be violated. The individual is only free when in accord with the general will.

> These clauses, properly understood, may be reduced to one – the total alienation of each associate together with rights to the whole community… Moreover the alienation is without reserve, the union is as perfect as it can be, and no associate has anything more to demand: for,

if the individuals retained certain rights, as there would be no common superior to decide between them and the public, each being on one point his own judge, would ask and so on all: the state of nature would thus continue... *'Each of us puts his person and all his power in common under the supreme direction of the general will, and, in our capacity, we receive each member as an indivisible part of the whole.'* (Rousseau, 1762, Book 1: ch. 6, 14-15. Italics and internal quote in the original.)

This is clearly a statement of positive freedom: the individual is liberated by conformity to and belief in the direction set by the "general will." Then in Book IV, when Rousseau considers voting, he explains the state of those in the minority who lose a vote and must conform:

But, it is asked how can a man be both free and forced to conform to the wills that are not his own? How are the opponents both free and subject to laws they have not agreed to?

I retort that the question is wrongly put. The citizen gives his consent to all the laws including those which are passed in spite of his opposition... [T]he general will is found by counting votes. When therefore the opinion that is contrary to my own prevails, this proves neither more nor less than that I was mistaken, and that what I thought to be the general will was not so. If my particular opinion had carried the day I should have achieved the opposite of what was my will; and it is in that case that I should not have been free. (Book IV, ch. 2, 106)

This might appear at first glance to be benign. After all, all democracies require the minority to accept the will of the majority. But, there are three important differences. First, those who support a liberal version of democracy argue that the constitution of liberty (to borrow Hayek's title) creates a sphere into which the state cannot intrude. This seems absent from Rousseau's formulation. Second, liberal democracies do not require the losers to change their mind; citizens of the United States were not all required to become supporters of the Democratic Party after the 2008 elections. Third, no liberal democracy claims that its citizens can only be free when they have seen the error of their ways and accept the majority opinion as their own, reflecting a higher self, in this case, the one embodied in the general will.

The last point again moves Rousseau's thinking into positive liberty territory, but with the malign twists discussed by Berlin. Positive liberty does not, in Berlin's view, become a dangerous concept until it is wedded with the idea that society or government has the right to force you to accept positive freedom for your own benefit and that of the larger society. This idea emerges in Rousseau's thought.

Rousseau may be the first influential example of a coercive *political* version of positive freedom versus coercive religious, semi-religious, or philosophical schools of positive freedom. In the ancient world, positive freedom was limited to these categories.[16] Obedience to secular power was typically just that, obedience in the visible world. No claim was made, for example, that obedience to the emperor liberated you to do what some higher self would freely want to do, as obedience to the "general will" did in Rousseau's thought.

Although the New Testament talks of positive liberty in Christ, people were not forced to this liberty by other Christians. That changed as Christianity developed, particularly in the centuries following the official adoption of Christianity by the Roman empire, and reached horrific levels during the wars of the Reformation. Early Muslim states, at least for the time, practiced high levels of tolerance, but that too changed over time for some sects of Islam (Lewis, 2003; and Jenkins, 2010.)[17]

Nonetheless, Rousseau was the first influential thinker to develop the idea of, and justification for, coercive positive liberty in the political sphere. It is a small step from liberty in conformity to the common will to, for example, Marxist liberty in communism, where the "general will" is replaced by the dictates of the science of history revealed by an infallible seer. "Rousseau's formulations, twisted and modified, have been used to justify everything from the despotisms of Marx, Lenin, Hitler, Mussolini, and Castro, who are on record as repeatedly and sincerely insisting their movements were 'democratic' in a much higher sense than our own" (Gairdner, 1999).

Mills

One more thinker will be briefly considered before moving on. Arguments for freedom had been based largely on either natural rights or a social contract. Neither was entirely satisfactory. None of the theorists were able to

---

16   There is a lively debate over whether someone who voluntarily submits to a constrained order remains free. Although the subject will not be pursued here, the consensus answer is "yes," so long as that person retains the ability to leave the order.

17   The distinguished historian of Christianity, Philip Jenkins, argues that intolerance leading to sectarian violence in Roman Christianity and particularly the church's condemnation of monophysitism (that Christ was totally divine with no human component) and related beliefs, highly popular in the Christian Middle Eastern heartland, led to alienation of Christians. this reduced resistance to Muslim invaders, who were tolerant of Christianity and did not differentiate between various Christians beliefs, and thus to the easy conquest of the old heartland. According to Jenkins, the "Muslim … invaders promised (and practiced) tolerance for diverse Christian sects … [Alienated Christians saw them] as a clean break from the historic cycle of violence and persecution that had so disfigured late-antique Christianity" (Jenkins, 2010, ch. 1: 1-33).

develop a comprehensive theory of natural law from first principles. Nor were the theorists entirely clear as to whether they believed the social contract an actual thing, or some sort of logical metaphor to explain and justify a particular construct.

John Stuart Mill, using ideas developed by Jeremy Bentham, produced a utilitarian justification for freedom (Mill, 1863/2002). Although Mill explored empiricism deeply, his freedom views were based largely on argument: best to allow free debate since no one knows *a priori* what the most successful ideas will be and, since the individual knows best his or her capacities, potentials, and desires, each person is in the best position to determine what is best for him- or herself and should be free to follow this self-determined course to find the greatest happiness and thus utility.

Utilitarianism will pose an interesting test for negative and positive freedom. Supporters of various forms of *positive* freedom claim they know better than the individual how the best life is to be lived, and that the greatest utility is thus to be found in their version of positive freedom, imposed, if necessary, to create the greatest level of utility. Supporters of negative freedom may argue the reverse—either that negative freedom in itself is a value that trumps utility and/or that negative liberty also produces the most utilitarian results. In the end, utilitarian arguments are ultimately empirical arguments—what does, in reality, produce the greatest happiness?—and for this an empirical index is required, as was discussed in the introduction and as will be discussed later.

The other interesting idea to note is that Mill appears to have initially supported what here is called economic freedom. However, he moved to a version of socialism that was based on something similar to A. Sen's capacity approach to freedom (Sen, 1999). Mill came to argue that freedom and happiness were limited by a person's capacity to take advantage of freedom and follow their chosen path to happiness. To more equally share resources, he proposed a variety of socialist ideas in his later writings.

Conclusion

Through representative thinkers, this section has attempted to examine the rise of the concept of freedom "for all" and its ties to economic freedom (and particularly property rights) which were either absent or uncommon in writings on freedom prior to the Enlightenment.

Recent writings on freedom

Before returning to the debates engendered by Berlin and MacCallum, we shall look at another great thinker on freedom, or rather negative freedom, since his thoughts on this are more systematic than Berlin's, and his views also shed light on measurement questions.

Hayek

Hayek (1960) does not explicitly refer to negative or positive freedom but he is clearly on the negative side. While Hayek's complex and insightful writings cannot be fully explored here, it is worth looking briefly at his views on the nature of "negative" freedom, how they fit in with the ideas of Berlin and other thinkers, and, in particular, how freedom is essentially a social concept.

He sums up his overall point on freedom, and makes clear he has a "negative" view of freedom, while not using that word. "The task of a policy of freedom must therefore be to minimize coercion or its harmful effects, even if it cannot eliminate it completely.... [Liberty] describes the absence of a particular property—coercion by other men" (Hayek, 1960/1978: 12 and 19). It is interesting to note that Hayek's description in effect describes the triadic relationship—the implied sentence is: x suffers "coercion by other men" (y) not to do/become z.

According to Hayek, freedom is a social concept and can only be limited by a human agency, again in a description that follows the triadic relationship:

> [F]reedom refers solely to the relation of men to other men, and the only infringement on it is coercion by men. This means, in particular, that the range of physical possibilities from which a person can choose at a given moment has no direct relevance to freedom. The rock climber on a difficult pitch who sees only one way out to save his life is unquestionably free, though we would hardly say he has any choice.... Whether [x] is free or not does not depend on the range of choice but on whether he can expect to shape his course of action [to do/become z] in accordance with his present intentions, or whether someone else has power so to manipulate the conditions [y, preventative conditions] as to make him act according to that person's will rather than his own. (1960/1978: 12-13)[18]

The restriction that "y" must be caused by an intentional human agency for a restriction on freedom to occur is in accord with what other thinkers on freedom, including Berlin, conclude. "If I say that I am unable to jump more than ten feet in the air, or cannot read because I am blind, or cannot understand the darker passages of Hegel, it would be eccentric to say that I am to that degree enslaved or coerced. Coercion implies the deliberate interference of other human beings within the area that I would otherwise act" (Berlin, 1958: 169). The word "deliberate" indicates

---

18 Interestingly, this passage also anticipates and responds to what would become Amartya Sen's version of capacity-freedom.

intention and moral responsibility. Carter says much the same thing: "Freedom is a social *concept*—that is, 'freedom' expresses a relationship between *persons*—so that mere natural obstacles as such do not constrain a person's freedom" (1999: 173).

That "freedom is a social concept" is an important point for the idea of measuring freedom, or at least negative freedom. It not only clarifies what is needed; it simplifies the task.

Unresolved questions: Berlin and MacCallum

Two key 20th century treatises on freedom, by Berlin and MacCallum, have already been introduced. Interestingly, both were relatively brief essays, though they have spawned many books. Alfred North Whitehead may not have been quite right when he remarked that "The safest general characterization of the European philosophical tradition is that it consists of a series of footnotes to Plato,"[19] but it is fairly safe to say that the that the vast majority of writings on freedom since the appearance of these essays have been footnotes to Berlin and MacCallum.

Gray (1990) carries out an in-depth analysis of MacCallum's triad, which he believes captures the central concept of freedom, and the seven "conceptions" of freedom that arise depending on how x, y, or z are defined. He claims that the variations of x, y, and z he examines are all conceptions of freedom because they share the formal triadic relationship. The book is genuinely interesting and often insightful, but its central contention on the definition of freedom fails. Gray makes freedom a formula concept defined by the triad relationship.

However, while the triadic relationship may be a necessary condition for the description of a freedom, it is clearly not a sufficient condition. For example, as discussed above, it is generally accepted that y, the blocking agent, must be human and must intend the consequences of the blocking action for freedom to be reduced under negative "conceptions" of freedom. The triadic relationship remains in place when the blocking agent is not human, but according to most thinkers it no longer concerns an issue of freedom. What about J.S. Mill's argument that if you physically stop a person from walking on an unsafe bridge, you are not limiting that person's freedom? Here again, the triadic relationship is in place, but questions arise about x's intentions (does he really want to walk on a bridge about to collapse?) and the unintended consequences of those actions. But in many cases, our actions create unpleasant, unintended consequences, and yet it

---

19 It all depends on where you start. Elizabeth Anscombe characterized Plato as "Parmenides's footnote" (http://philosophysother.blogspot.com/2007_12_01_archive.html). For the Whitehead quote, see http://thinkexist.com/quotes/alfred_north_whitehead/4.html, both accessed on November 28, 2011.

would clearly be an infringement of freedom for y to stop those actions. So why would the triadic relationship describe freedom in one instance and something else in another instance, even when the formal relationship is the same? This weakens the formal power of the triadic relationship since extra machinery has to be bolted onto the concept to determine where the relationship describes an issue relating to freedom and where it does not.

Thus, the triadic relationship does not appear to be a "sufficient" condition for the suppression of freedom, but it does appear to be a "necessary" condition. Like MacCallum, I cannot imagine any suppression of freedom happening outside the triadic relationship, with the above discussion of Hayek designed to show how the relationship is present even when it is not explicit.

Nonetheless, such difficulties with the triadic formula may be why, as Carter (2007) notes, "Despite the utility of MacCallum's triadic formula and its strong influence on analytic philosophers, however, Berlin's distinction continues to dominate mainstream discussions about the meaning of political and social freedom."

Whichever thinker is dominant, virtually all subsequent thinkers base arguments on Berlin's positive/negative dichotomy and/or MacCallum's recasting of the dichotomy as two versions or conceptions of the same thing. These fundamental distinctions have not been altered by the debate of the last 50 years since Berlin's essay first appeared, or the last 40 years since MacCallum's essay.

Nor have they successfully clarified a paradox both Berlin and MacCallum noted: that many thinkers hold views on freedom that encompass both positive and negative versions. "The trouble is not merely that some writers do not fit too well where they have been placed; it is rather that writers who are purportedly the very models of membership in one camp or the other (for example, Locke, the Marxists) do not fit very well where they have been placed—thus suggesting that the whole system of dichotomous classification is futile and, even worse, conducive to distortion of important views on freedom" (MacCallum, 1967: 322).

In a footnote, MacCallum draws out this idea referring to John Locke and a quote we considered above: "Locke said: 'liberty . . . is the power a man has to do or forbear doing any particular action according . . . as he himself wills it' (*Essay Concerning Human Understanding*, Bk. II, ch. xxi, sec. 15). He also said, of law, 'that ill deserves the name of confinement which hedges us in only from bogs and precipices,' and 'the end of law is, not to abolish or restrain, but to preserve and enlarge freedom' (*Second Treatise of Government*, sec. 57). He also sometimes spoke of a man's consent as though it were the same as the consent of the majority. Why doesn't all this put him in the camp of 'positive' freedom vis-à-vis at least points (2) and (3) above?" (1967: fn. 9).

This is, of course, an argument that the paradox can be solved by acknowledging that there is only one form of freedom, defined by the triadic formula, as MacCallum would have it, but that there are various "conceptions" of it. Surely, this just begs the question. How can the same writer hold two differing "conceptions" of freedom when these conceptions themselves produce very different analysis, as Gray acknowledges.

The literature contains very little, if any discussion, of an important link between negative and positive freedom that appears to exist despite the sometimes fuzzy boundary between the two: it can be argued that negative freedom is a necessary condition for any true form of benign— i.e., unforced— positive freedom.

As noted earlier, Berlin draws a distinction between benign positive freedom and malignant forms of positive freedom. The first involves individuals voluntarily finding freedom in, say, religion. The second involves being forced to find freedom in, say, communism. The second of these in effect allows freedom only for those who first and voluntarily accept their version of positive freedom and then force it on others, some of whom will be converted, others of whom will fake conversion and thus will have neither positive nor negative freedom.

On the other hand, negative freedom allows individuals to seek their own version of positive freedom if they so wish. In a society marked by negative freedom, all are able to avail themselves of their version of positive freedom.

Where are we? The need for a proximate measure

An empirical measure, or at least a first proximate empirical measure, could help define the fuzzy boundary between negative and positive freedom. Similarly, Carter (1999) rightly argues that empirical input is required to further clarify the debate. His recommended method is "reflective equilibrium" reached by a back-and-forth process between theory and evidence. Insights empirically derived feed back into theoretical discussions which are then developed into new insights which feed back into the empirical investigation. This makes sense. It is an aspect of scientific investigation. A useful comparison is the process by which, for example, biological families are classified. Yet, this method first requires a proximate empirical measure.

3 "False" freedoms and the distinction between rights and freedoms

Having examined the historical roots of the idea of freedom and the conceptual tools developed to analyze it, we now turn to examine what might be called "false freedoms": that is definitions of "freedom" that fall outside the classical tradition of freedom and fail the analytical tests that define freedom.

These "false" freedoms are motivated by a number of confusions:

1. A confusion between freedom and "other good things," to use Hayek's phrase (quoted at greater length later in this section).

2. A confusion between things that "enhance" freedom and freedom itself—this largely overlaps the first confusion since things that enhance freedom are usually thought of as "good."

3. A confusion between things that help develop, support, or maintain freedom and freedom itself.

Claim-freedom

First we will look at a "third" concept of freedom, one that is often confused with positive freedom. These are the "claim" rights or freedoms, to use Hardy Bouillon's (2004) insightful phraseology. These are material claims, such as "freedom to have a job" or "freedom from want." Even when they appear not to describe material things, they lead back to material things. For example, "freedom from disease" actually means access to health care, clean water, and so on. As will be discussed below, various forms of claims involve the confusion of "other good things" with freedom and/or the enhancement of freedom with freedom.

We need to glance briefly here at the differences between rights and freedoms. Freedoms may be considered rights, but all human rights may not be freedoms. In other words, freedom is a subset of rights. Humans may have a right to democratic governance, but democratic governance is not a freedom, something that will be discussed below. Because this paper is concerned about freedom, it has not, and will not below, discuss whether humans have rights outside of freedom, but rather whether a number of "claims" represent freedom using the analytical tools described earlier.

This is relevant because many such claims are no longer merely labeled as "rights"; they have been recast as freedoms. Instead of the claim that people have a "right" to work, the claim becomes that people have a "freedom" to work, in other words, a "claim-freedom". Democracy is no longer a "right," according to Freedom House, it is a freedom. To clarify succinctly: things which may or may not be human rights have been with little logic defined as freedoms.

This raises several questions. Hayek (1960/1978), like Berlin, McCallum, and Carter, argues convincingly that for freedom to be limited, there must be an "intention" to limit it. The free market allocates goods and services according to the freely made choices of a number of individuals. It creates "spontaneous order" that does not involve the intention of depriving one person of x in favour of another person.[20] This means that because an individual may not have the resources to buy x, his freedom is not being reduced since no intention to reduce freedom is involved. Under this analysis, "claim-freedoms" do not exist, at least as negative freedoms.

Moreover, claim-freedoms involve something by *necessity* that other freedoms do not—violating another person's freedom by violating property rights. It is true that for virtually all freedoms, in some cases my exercise of freedom may violate yours. Most accept that the limit of individual freedom is where the exercise of freedom by one person limits the identical freedoms of others, and this constrains some sub-set of actions. But, for claim-freedom, a violation of freedom is necessary in every case and not simply to protect someone else's freedom, but rather to limit others' freedom—to coerce A to undertake actions that favor B, typically to the disadvantage of A. To successfully make a claim on something that normally would not be provided, it is necessary to force its provision. Thus, individuals, through the tax code for example, may in effect be forced to work for a portion of each year without pay, something they would not freely do. Once again, this analysis suggests that "claim" freedoms cannot be classified as freedoms, at least in the classical sense described earlier in this chapter.

Still, many of the "claim" freedoms involve "good" things that might enhance freedom—by expanding choice or opportunity—and this relationship to freedom has been used by some to try to blur the distinction between what enhances freedom and what actually is freedom. A metaphor might help: that, say, cosmetics enhance beauty, does not create an identity between cosmetics and beauty. Both have their own distinct meanings. In other words, that more choice or capacity, for example, enhances freedom does not create an identity between freedom and capacity, as Sen's "capacity" version of freedom, discussed below, for example, would have it.

Somewhat remarkably, one of the most influential recent philosophers, John Rawls, whose "Theory of Justice" stands clearly on the left of the political spectrum, and who supports redistributive efforts, rejects such identities between freedom and various claims, as in effect a confusion between freedom and "other good things." He gets at this by arguing that what is being considered is not freedom itself, but the value or worth of freedom. "The inability to take advantage of one's rights and responsibilities as a result of poverty and ignorance, and a lack of means generally, is

---

20 Of course, collusion among market participants or the aims of a specific participant may be intended to deprive x of some good or service, and this would be a violation of freedom. But this does not counter Hayek's larger point.

sometimes counted among the constraints definitive of liberty. I shall not, however, say this but rather I shall think of these things as affecting the worth of liberty, the value to individuals of the rights that the first principle defines.... Thus liberty and the worth of liberty are distinguished as follows: liberty is represented by the complete system of the liberties of equal citizenship, while the worth of liberty to persons and groups is proportional to their *capacity* to advance their ends within the framework the system defines" (1971: 204, italics added).

Thus, according to Rawls, "claim-freedoms" are not in fact freedoms, though they may enhance freedom. While Rawls doesn't fall into the trap of equating other good things with freedom, his theory of justice nonetheless requires a redistributive effort. "[T]he basic structure is to be arranged to maximize the worth [of freedom] to the least advantaged of the complete scheme of equal liberty shared by all" (1971: 205). For example, in discussing the political realm, he favours distribution of wealth to individuals, so they can more effectively make their voices heard and thus obtain an equal value of freedom. "[I]nequalities will enable those better situated to exercise an ever larger influence... [I]n a society allowing private ownership of the means of production, property and wealth must be widely distributed and government monies provided on a regular basis to encourage free public discussion" (1971: 225).

Perhaps the best known of the claim-freedoms is Amartya Sen's capacity version of freedom—roughly speaking, the idea that the greater the individual's capacity, choices, opportunity, education, health care, etc., the greater the freedom. This is very close to the concerns that motivated Mill in his later career as discussed above. Hayek and Berlin get right to the point of the confusion that muddles analysis like Sen's. As Hayek says, interestingly in an argument that is very close to Rawls' argument, "These two words [liberty and freedom] have been also used to describe many other good things in life" (1960/1978: 11). Sen is actually talking about capacity and calling it freedom. This can be clearly seen when he talks about "the freedom to live long" (Sen, 1999: 291). Interestingly, in the quote above, Rawls explicitly distinguishes "capacity" from freedom.

Berlin goes further than Hayek and acknowledges that in some cases he might accept limits of freedom for "other good things," but argues that calling these things freedom is a confusion of terms.

> [N]othing is gained by a confusion in terms. To avoid glaring inequality or widespread misery I am ready to sacrifice some or all of my freedom: I may do so willingly and freely; but it is freedom I am giving up for the sake of justice or equality or the love of my fellow man.... Everything is what it is: liberty is liberty, not equality or fairness of justice or culture, or human happiness or a quiet conscience. (Berlin, 1958: 172)

Berlin also talks of "the natural tendency of all but a very few thinkers to believe that all the things they hold good must be intimately connected, or at least compatible, with one and other" (1958: 175, fn). This is increasingly seen in writings on freedom, with Sen as the most prominent example.

The reader will have noticed that "claim" freedoms are expressed in a number of terms: opportunity, capacity, and redistribution, among others. As "claim" freedoms, what they all have in common is that they reduce someone else's freedom to increase "the worth of liberty,"[21] but not liberty itself.

Having described "claim" freedoms, we now turn to seeing whether they meet definitions of freedom. They fail the negative concept of freedom in that they do not involve lifting humanly imposed, intentional barriers to some action. In fact, to supply the claims, other individuals are forced to do and supply things they would not otherwise do.

As noted, "claim" freedoms are often expressed in terms of opportunity, choice, and capacity. In an important way, as in a Venn diagram, these concepts overlap with negative freedom, even though they are conceptually distinct. When a blocking agent—say, a government—prevents one taking advantage of an opportunity, choice, or capacity that is otherwise within an individual's reach, then negative freedom has been violated. However, when an opportunity, choice, or capacity is outside an individual's reach, because of physical or material limitations, then no violation of negative liberty has occurred.

To remind the reader of Berlin's quote a few pages earlier: "If I say that I am unable to jump more than ten feet in the air… it would be eccentric to say that I am to that degree enslaved or coerced" (Berlin, 1958: 169). It would be equally "eccentric to say that I am… enslaved or coerced" if I am unable to generate the material resources to buy a new car, given that, as argued earlier, the ability to acquire and securely own material possessions is an extension of the individual. As Rawls notes above, "The inability to take advantage of one's rights and responsibilities as a result of poverty and ignorance" is separate from freedom.

"Claim" freedoms might be conceived of as positive freedom in a very narrow sense. Since the claim freedoms involve material acquisitions, some version of positive freedom would have to be described in an equally material manner for the two to be equated. Whether or not positive freedom is subject to such a narrow interpretation, and it likely is not, claim freedom can, at best, define a very limited idea of positive freedom.

Finally to the triadic relationship, as discussed, claim freedoms involve no humanly intended blocking, so claim freedoms fail this test too.

---

21 To use Rawls' previously quoted phrase, but, while it is beyond the scope of this paper, many of these efforts in fact decrease both liberty and the worth of what liberty remains, even for the supposed beneficiary.

Democracy as freedom

Democracy, itself, is not a freedom, at least from negative rights point of view, as both Hayek and Berlin argue. As Berlin notes, "Just as a democracy may, in fact, deprive the individual citizen of a great many liberties which he might have in some other form of society, so it is perfectly conceivable that a liberal-minded despot would allow his subjects a large measure of personal freedom.… [T]here is no necessary connection between individual liberty and democratic rule. The answer to the question 'Who governs me?' is logically distinct from the question 'How far does government interfere with me?'" (1958: 176-7).

However, certain political systems and aspects of systems are likely to be conducive to the development and maintenance of freedom while other systems are not. As Berlin says, "Self-government may, on the whole, provide a better guarantee of civil liberties than other regimes" (1958: 177). This may also apply to finer structures of government. For example, limits on the chief executive's power, even in a democracy, may be more conducive to the development and maintenance of freedom than unchecked executive power. However, as noted above, we need to avoid the common confusion that equates freedom definitionally with something that promotes freedom. Democracy may promote freedom, but it is separate from freedom and is represented by its own word.

Thus, while the equation (democracy = political freedom) does not hold, it is probable that some systems are more conducive to the development and maintenance of freedom. In other words, democracy <—> freedom, where the double arrow indicates causality running in both directions. This argument has relationship to the claims freedom argument. By that argument, something that may enhance freedom is confused with freedom itself and a false identity is established. In the case of democracy, the argument is similar. Democracy enhances the development of freedom, and this is then turned into a false identity. The vast majority of thinkers on freedom, including some on the left (Rawls), the right (Hayek), or the middle (Berlin), do not confuse democracy, a power relationship, with freedom.

The argument that democracy enhances freedom (and the wide acceptance of this argument) provides yet another important motivation for finding a successful measure of freedom. Once freedom is measured it will be possible to test such propositions rigorously and empirically.

However, there a sidelight to this discussion on democracy and freedom. An interesting argument has been developed by the "republican" or "neo-Roman" school of thought to include a measure of democracy into a measure of freedom. But we will see this breaks down again to something similar to the "enhancement" argument.

The innovative part of the argument is that proponents do not confuse democracy with freedom but they argue that known threats to freedom in the future reduce freedom today by constraining actions for fear of future retribution. Therefore, to be free, one must be sure of "resiliently realized" non-interference in the future. Only democratic forms provide this, the argument goes. It is worth emphasizing again that republican philosophers are not claiming democracy is freedom; only that democracy "ensures" today's freedom by lifting the threat of retribution in the future for things said or done today which in turn acts as a coercive agent which causes us to curtail our freedom today.

The "neo-Roman's" two key assumptions also need examining. First, it is true that if my actions today may cause retribution in the future, I will constrain my actions, but if threats to future freedom do not necessarily involve retribution, they therefore would not reduce today's freedom. Thus, for the argument to hold, one needs to make assumptions about future retribution in both democratic and non-democratic societies.

Second, the assumption that freedom is best protected by democracy is not theoretical a question but an empirical one. Certainly, one could argue the future of freedom is more in danger in Hugo Chavez's Venezuela, even though democratic forms are being maintained, than it was in Hong Kong under British rule, at least for the period that British rule endured. This simply shows that there is clearly no one-to-one relationship between democracy and "resiliently realized" non-interference.

Moreover, empirical research suggests that democracies that lack institutions and, even more importantly, public attitudes supportive of "liberal" democracy, have proved unstable and a threat to freedom. (The key empirical research can be found in Inglehart and Welzel, 2005. See also Collier, 2009; Zakaria, 2003; and Chua, 2004.) In other words, if one accepts neo-Roman arguments about resilience, then democracy, under circumstances where supportive institutions and attitudes are lacking, reduces freedom if the investigations cited prove correct. This in turn means that the neo-Roman argument cannot be applied to democracy in general, but only to a subset of democracies.

One of the key advantages of producing a measure of freedom is that it will allow testing of the neo-Roman hypothesis and related hypotheses, such as those that point to institutions and attitudes as providing a stable, socio-political platform for freedom. An empirical measure may provide (or reject) the empirical argument for including some measures of democracy and/or institutional structure and/or attitudes into a measure of freedom not on the grounds that democracy is freedom, since even the neo-Romans reject this, but on the grounds that future threats to freedom reduce freedom today—another hypothesis that can be tested once empirical measures are developed.[22] In this case, democracy becomes a proxy for freedom rather than freedom itself.

We now turn to whether or not democracy meets definitions of freedom. In a negative sense, clearly not. My actions, as Berlin and Hayek both note, can be blocked in a democracy as well as under other forms of government. That this blocking may be less likely in democracy does not itself create an identity between democracy and the lack of blocking since, again, it may well occur under a democracy. This also means democracy fails the triadic test.

As with claim freedoms, democracy might be conceived of as positive freedom in a very narrow sense: for individuals who consider themselves only truly liberated when they live in a democracy and can vote—i.e., when their sense of liberation is democracy. Whether or not positive freedom is subject to such a narrow interpretation, and it likely is not, democracy, like claim freedom, can at best define a very limited idea of positive freedom.

Conclusion

The strong conclusion is that "claim-freedoms" are not freedoms; instead, they are an excuse to limit freedom. The argument for claim-freedom is nothing other than "confusing other good things with freedom," a point, as noted, made from the right by Hayek, for instance, and from the left by Rawls, for example, and more-or-less from the middle by Berlin, for one. The argument that democracy is a freedom suffers from similar flaws, though at least one line of thought has found a way to associate democracy directly with freedom.

So the philosophical debate over the last 40 to 50 years has not only failed to clarify issues surrounding negative and positive freedom, it has seen the increasing introduction of claim-freedom and other confusions. These thoughts will be picked up again in the conclusion, but first, it is worthwhile to look at how the differing "flavors" of freedom have been addressed in various freedom charters in order to supplement the philosophic debate with some insight on how these arguments have been translated into the political realm.

4 Freedom, charters and indexes

So far we have examined the history of the concept of freedom and the rise of "false" freedoms. Now we turn to the charters and indexes of freedom available today. We will use the tools developed earlier in this paper to see what "types" of freedom are found in indexes and charters.

---

22 For example, through Ian Carter's reflective equilibrium.

The development of freedom discussed in this paper, from the predominately negative views found in the early Enlightenment thinkers to the emergence of claim-freedoms can be seen in the charters that have been written to protect rights and freedoms.

The United States *Bill of Rights* and France's *Declaration of the Rights of Man* are the best known of the early freedom charters. Nine of the 10 amendments of the Bill of Rights are "rights" that do not fit clearly into any of the freedom types discussed. However, the first amendment clearly reflects "negative" freedom. "Congress shall make no law respecting an establishment of religion, or prohibiting the free exercise thereof; or abridging the freedom of speech, or of the press; or the right of the people peaceably to assemble, and to petition the Government for a redress of grievances" (United States Constitution).

Most clauses of France's *Declaration of the Rights of Man* also discuss rights other than freedom. However, Articles 10 and 11 reflect the negative view of freedom, at least for the most part, though the latter parts of both paragraphs might raise some concerns.

> 10. No one shall be disquieted on account of his opinions, including his religious views, provided their manifestation does not disturb the public order established by law.

> 11. The free communication of ideas and opinions is one of the most precious of the rights of man. Every citizen may, accordingly, speak, write, and print with freedom, but shall be responsible for such abuses of this freedom as shall be defined by law. (Avalon Project)

However, many of the paragraphs of the *Declaration of the Rights of Man* directly or indirectly reflect Rousseau's view on the general will, opening the door to positive freedom. Articles 1 and 6 are particularly interesting.

> 1. Men are born and remain free and equal in rights. Social distinctions may be founded only upon the *general good* ....

> 6. Law is the expression of the *general will*. Every citizen has a right to participate personally, or through his representative, in its foundation. It must be the same for all, whether it protects or punishes. All citizens, being equal in the eyes of the law, are equally eligible to all dignities and to all public positions and occupations, according to their abilities, and without distinction except that of their virtues and talents. (Avalon Project, italics added)

Both "general good" in 1 and "general will" in 6 involve potential sources of imperatives that could and would be misused in the Republic.

Interestingly, some of the first appearances of claim-freedoms come from unexpected sources in the United States. Franklin Roosevelt's famous four freedoms of 1941 involved a combination of negative and claim-freedoms: "freedom of speech and of religion; freedom from fear and from want" (Amnesty International, 2007: 1).

Skipping ahead, in July 1953, President Dwight Eisenhower "signed a Declaration of Freedom drawn up by the National Association of Evangelicals and based on 'seven divine freedoms' found in the 23rd Psalm" (*Time*, 1953). As the reader can determine, these turn out to be a mix of positive and claim-freedoms, showing just how confused the idea of freedom was becoming. They are:

¶ Freedom from Want: "The Lord is my shepherd; I shall not want."

¶ Freedom from Hunger: "He maketh me to lie down in green pastures."

¶ Freedom from Thirst: "He leadeth me beside the still waters."

¶ Freedom from Sin: "He restoreth my soul: he leadeth me in the paths of righteousness for his name's sake."

¶ Freedom from Fear: "Yea, though I walk through the valley of the shadow of death, I will fear no evil: for thou art with me; thy rod and thy staff they comfort me."

¶ Freedom from Enemies: "Thou preparest a table before me in the presence of mine enemies." (*Time*, 1953)

The United Nations *Universal Declaration of Human Rights* dates from 1948. It has a number of clauses to protect negative freedom, perhaps the most notable being articles 18 to 20, though for brevity I will quote only the first of these. "Everyone has the right to freedom of thought, conscience and religion; this right includes freedom to change his religion or belief, and freedom, either alone or in community with others and in public or private, to manifest his religion or belief in teaching, practice, worship and observance" (United Nations, 1948).

Starting with Article 23, a number of claims are listed as *rights*, not freedoms, with the partial exception of 23.1: "Everyone has the right to work, to *free choice of employment*, to just and favorable conditions of work and to protection against unemployment" (United Nations, 1948, emphasis added). "Free choice of employment" is ambiguous; it could mean free choice of what is on offer, but the phrase "protection against unemployment" implies that the state is obliged to offer work. Later articles appear to veer into positive freedom territory, especially 29.1: "Everyone has duties to the community in which alone the free and full development of his personality is possible" (United Nations, 1948).

I will not review other similar charters, such as the Organization of American States' *Declaration of the Rights and Duties of Man*, *African Charter on Human and Peoples' Rights*, or the Council of Europe's *Convention for the Protection of Human Rights and Fundamental Freedoms*. They have about the same mix as the UN *Declaration*.

Despite the absence of claim-freedoms from these charters, today such claim-freedoms seem increasingly common. The United Nations' (2000) *Human Development Report: Human Rights and Human Development* is a prime example. This report comes up with the remarkable discovery of seven essential freedoms, printed on the cover page, the inside cover page, and described inside:

> Today, with impressive achievements and a significant unfinished agenda in human rights and human development, the struggle continues for realizing and securing human freedoms in seven areas:
>
> - Freedom from discrimination—for equality
> - Freedom from want—for a decent standard of living
> - Freedom for the realization of one's human potential
> - Freedom from fear—with no threats to personal security
> - Freedom from injustice
> - Freedom of participation, expression and association
> - Freedom for decent work—without exploitation
> (United Nations, 2000)

The first, fifth, and the sixth areas are related to negative freedom, or at least the conditions required for negative freedom,[23] the third appears to reflect a positive freedom, and the rest are claim-freedoms. Many of the classic examples of negative freedom—assembly, for example—are missing.

This leaves public discourse, as represented by the world's most important charters of rights and freedoms, with a mish-mash of negative, positive, and claim-freedoms, mixed together as if they were all birds of a feather. This creates real confusion and enables just about any interest group to declare that the key points of its ideology represent freedom, and to be able to take that message to the public.

---

23 Hayek (1960) throughout his work emphasizes the need for an impartial justice system, or "freedom from injustice," as a necessary support for freedom. The problem with the United Nations formulation is that justice is, in fact, justice, not freedom, though it may be a necessary condition for freedom.

Measures of freedom

This confused situation found in charters and indexes calls out for a measure of freedom, clearly defined. The debate and understanding on the part of the public and policymakers would be improved, regardless of which version of freedom a measure represented, so long as the measure provided clarity and consistency as to what was being measured. This would enable the testing of at least that version of freedom against other variables of interest and allow researchers to work toward a reflective equilibrium on the definition and measure of that flavour of freedom. Unfortunately, no such measure is now available.

In the philosophical literature, Carter has done the most exploration of measurement issues, as reflected in the title of his book, *A Measure of Freedom*. In the realm of negative freedom, he considers what counts as a constraint on freedom, even after one accepts that only human beings can constrain freedom. He helps clarify a challenge from Hillel Steiner, who argues that only physical impossibility counts as a constraint on freedom (Carter, 1999: ch. 8). Thus, according to Steiner, if you are physically able to demonstrate against the regime but will be shot afterwards, you are free to demonstrate. Only if you are shot before you demonstrate are you unfree to demonstrate.

Carter agrees that you maintain your *specific* freedom to demonstrate in the first case, but that your overall freedom—to demonstrate and then do other things—has been limited. Thus, any measurement of freedom could accept Steiner's central argument and still calculate reductions in overall freedom. In the same chapter, Carter also presents a neat solution to the idea of costs: you can demonstrate, but you will have to pay the police, cleaners, etc. Again, there is no physical impossibility, but the payments increase the probability that you will not be free (or have the resources) to undertake some activities in the future.

Nonetheless, Carter is frank in saying that he sees "the practical problems involved in measuring freedom as lying outside the scope of this book…. This book is… a book on political philosophy…. Is it not the job of the social scientist to tell us… what practical steps can be taken in order to estimate the actual extents of overall freedom?" (1999: 270). In fact, it is very difficult to understand how Carter's measure, regardless of how philosophically correct, could be operationalized, at least as a first approximation of a freedom measure.

So we turn now to see what "social scientists" have been doing to create a measure of freedom.

Freedom House

The best of the guides, Freedom House's *Freedom in the World*, suffers from including things it shouldn't and omitting things it should include, and its subjective manner of measurement.

Its Civil Liberties index reflects a negative concept of freedom. Like its Political Rights index, it is based on the subjective judgments of Freedom House's experts. This of course means that no one can duplicate the measurements and it also opens the possibility of political manipulation and bias, though it should be emphasized that Freedom House is well respected and to my knowledge such a charge has never convincingly been made.

The Political Rights index is confusingly named since it seems to claim to be a freedom index and scores countries as unfree to free. It is actually a democracy index. Freedom House simply seems to assume the identity between freedom and democracy. It does not, for example, make the neo-Roman argument or any other argument supporting the identity of freedom and democracy, which is not to say that a democracy index is without value. In fact, it is extremely important and a genuine contribution by Freedom House, but it is not a freedom index.

Freedom House's omission of any measure of "negative" economic freedom is even more glaring. The stress that early thinkers and more recent ones like Hayek put on economic freedom has already been discussed. In fact, a strong argument can be made that economic freedom is prior to other freedoms. Without economic freedom, when a government has the power to determine the ability of individuals to feed, clothe, house, and educate their families, hold a job and get a promotion, and restrict their ability to move ahead in other ways, government has all the tools it needs to suppress other freedoms, at least until life becomes unbearable and recourse is made to violence. When economic freedom is lacking, individuals and families must depend on the kindness of government to get ahead. Economic freedom gives people economic independence and lessens dependence on government, opening the way for increases in other freedoms. Empirical studies support the connection between economic freedom, other freedoms, and democracy (see, for example, Griswold, 2004; and Dawson, 1998). No nation that lacks economic freedom has ever supported stable political and civil freedoms. (Here, political freedoms are not defined as democracy, but rather the freedom to express political views, write or broadcast them, assemble for political reasons, and so on.) On the other hand, no nation that has adopted economic freedom has ever failed to evolve towards civil and political freedoms, with only two possible exceptions: Singapore and Hong Kong. But even here, while democracy is limited or non-existent, relatively good levels of others freedoms exist compared to jurisdictions that lack economic freedom. (See Gwartney and Lawson (various editions), and Freedom House (various editions), to examine relationships between economic freedom what Freedom House labels "civil liberties," and "political rights.") Of course, the great question for the future is whether this pattern will be maintained in China; will market reforms ultimately lead to other freedoms in China, as they did in South Korea and Taiwan, though with a considerable lag?

Measurements matter and may even affect policy decisions. The US democracy push by President George Bush following 9/11 seemed to mix up the ideas of freedom and democracy, and failed to understand that while freedom can and should be advanced in virtually any set of conditions, democracy is unlikely to be stable or even desirable until the appropriate set of institutions are in place. These include not just building economic freedom, as noted above with references, but also building other freedoms. Only when these are in place at an acceptable level can democracy thrive (see also Zakaria, 2003; and Inglehart and Welzel, 2009). It can be unhelpful if a key index confuses the issues, depriving policymakers of appropriate information on sequencing and results among other matters.

Charles Humana

Charles Humana produced editions of his *World Human Rights Guide* in 1983, 1986, and 1992.[24] A version of the report was also included in the United Nations *Human Development Report* for 1991. This index, like Freedom House's, is troubled by subjective judgment. It also excludes economic freedom. Finally, its 40 variables contain a mix of various sorts of freedom, such as free legal aid, freedom from execution or even corporal punishment, and differing variables on democracy.

The discussion of the index in the UN development report, not apparently written by Humana, though surely he approved the text, has a very muddy idea of freedom; it contains an element of negative freedom but it is mostly about "claim-freedom." It goes on to say, "These are freedoms to do something—to take part in the community's life, to organize opposition parties or trade union groups, or go about without being 'ashamed to appear in Publick', as Adam Smith expressed it some 200 years ago" (United Nations, 1991: 18-19). This appears to be a reference to a quote on customs and needs from the *Wealth of Nations*. Adam Smith, the United Nations to the contrary, did not define a freedom as the "ability to appear in socially acceptable clothes"—a "claim" freedom and perhaps an enhancement of freedom in Rawls' sense, but not a freedom itself.

The Humana index was discontinued after 1992 and was not particularly useful in any event for the reasons discussed above: subjective judgments and a muddy definition that conflates "claim freedom" with negative freedoms.

---

24 It is also often referred to as a "freedom index," another example of the common confusion of the ideas of rights and freedoms. For example: "It is a *human freedom* index" (United Nations, 1991: 19, italics in the original).

Fraser Institute

First, a disclaimer: I am not an unbiased observer and am directly involved in the *Economic Freedom of the World*, the annual report prepared by the Fraser Institute and co-published by institutes in nearly 90 nations and territories. It takes a "negative" view of economic freedom.

The Fraser Institute's report on economic freedom is obviously incomplete as a full measure of human freedom. However, it arguably takes the appropriate approach to measurement. It uses only third party data for its 40-plus variables. Thus, the subjective opinions of the authors and publishers cannot affect the scores, which can be reproduced by anyone with the same data. Reproducibility is a key requirement in science and should be in social science as well, because it allows scientific scrutiny.

There are also a number of indexes on various other aspects of freedom, such as freedom of the press and religious freedom, but these also suffer from incompleteness and typically use subjective judgments.

Conclusion

Thus the various measures of freedom today are an odd mix of "negative," "positive," and "claim" freedoms, along with "other good things." None provide an appropriate empirical measure of freedom that is internally consistent and consistent with a rigorous definition of freedom.

5 Going forward

The ideas of negative and positive freedom go back at least to the classical world. They are separated from modern notions less by definitional issues than by questions as to who holds a right to freedom: that is, how broadly freedom is spread within a society.

The modern *broad-based* idea of freedom, shared across the full population, emerged most forcefully in the early Enlightenment, inspired at least in part to find a new political order that would avoid the disasters which had recently befallen Europe. The early Enlightenment writers held a predominately "negative" view of freedom, but with positive elements mixed in. Rousseau shifted the focus to positive views of freedom and was the first major writer to push positive views of freedom into the political realm.

Isaiah Berlin brought clarity to the ideas of positive and negative freedom, considering both to be legitimate—but opposing—ideas of freedom. Gerald MacCallum further illuminated the debate with his triadic concept of freedom. However, his analysis has not been fully successful in clarifying the issues, and debate still rages over whether positive or negative or both versions of freedom are real freedom. More recently, the issue of freedom has been confused further by the emergence of claim-freedoms in a number of guises. Perhaps more problematic, the question of economic freedom has been detached from other freedoms.

Research on freedom would be greatly facilitated by a measure of freedom, as Ian Carter argues (1999: ch. 10). This would allow for a process of "reflective equilibrium," where theory and empirical evidence inform each other in a back-and-forth process that ultimately reaches an equilibrium close to the correct answer, as discussed earlier.

What would a measure of freedom look like?

Unfortunately, no acceptable empirical measure of human freedom is now available for this process. What would such a measure look like and what type of freedom should it attempt to measure? That is the purpose of the project for which this review is being written.

Consistency

The measure should choose one definition of freedom and consistently stick to it. Fifty years after Berlin's article, no argument is going to convince an advocate of some version of, say, positive freedom, that it is not THE real freedom. But clarity in measurement at least allows other researchers and the public to understand what is being measured, even if some disagree with the label. After that, a process of reflective equilibrium can be put in place to work towards a stronger definition of the particular version of freedom involved.[25]

This also has the advantage of providing a measurement of that version of freedom to determine whether it is correlated with positive outcomes, the utilitarian version of freedom developed by John Stuart Mill.

What type of freedom should be measured?

Positive freedom

Positive freedom involves freeing oneself from whatever constraints some lower form of self imposes on one's higher self. This freedom enables the person to find his or her true self. For example, class consciousness would have been perceived by many communists as part of a lower self, blocking the release and freedom one experiences under the higher form of socialist liberty. Positive freedom can be benign (where, for example, people are urged non-coercively to find "freedom in God.") It can be dangerous (for example, Communist re-education concentration camps to help free people from class consciousness).

It goes virtually without saying that positive freedom cannot be measured outside of some ideology, one that has a version of true freedom. Positive freedom has very different meanings for an evangelist, an Islamist, a Marxist, a supporter of Robert Mugabe, and so on. Yet, we are looking

---

25 As in most matters of human endeavor, definitions likely fade into each other at the margins. That is all the more reason to begin measurement to clarify such ambiguities.

for a measure of freedom that transcends particular ideologies and has a universal application. It may be that others will develop an index of one of the many (infinite?) versions of positive freedom.

Claim-freedoms

"Claim-freedoms" are mislabeled as freedom and at best seem to represent redistributive welfare functions. Claim-freedoms are such things as "freedom to have a job," or, most prominently today, Amartya Sen's "capacity" version of freedom. Many of the "claim" freedoms involve things that would enhance freedom, but enhancement does not create an identity. Interestingly, even a strong redistributionist like John Rawls has been able to see through the linguistic sleight-of-hand that confuses redistributionist claims with freedom.[26]

Like positive freedom, "claim-freedom" comes in many forms, but all involve some sort of large-scale redistribution or economic control (i.e., limits on economic freedom) to provide the "claims." In short, a measure of claim-freedom is not a measure of freedom, though others might want to develop an index based on their version of the ideal welfare function.

Negative freedom

Isaiah Berlin argued that both negative and positive freedom were legitimate forms of freedom that had long intellectual histories. Berlin, with qualifications, favored negative freedom. This is also the appropriate type of freedom to measure for several reasons.

Unlike positive and claim freedom, negative freedom comes in only one flavor—lack of constraint imposed on the individual. Constraint investigation happily lends itself to empirical measurement based on third party data, the model followed by the *Economic Freedom of the World Annual Report*. For that reason, it is also consistent with building a comprehensive measurement of freedom that includes economic and non-economic freedoms.

Despite the fact that our measure should focus on negative freedom, it has implications for benign forms of positive freedom in that it enables individuals to explore, without constraint, various versions of positive freedom.

Empirically based on third-party data

For reasons already discussed, the measure should be based on objective third party data to separate the researcher's subjective judgment from

---

26 Rawls, however, would support redistribution and other "capacity-enhancing" type measures, not to increase freedom itself but to increase the "worth" of freedom to the most disadvantaged. While I would disagree with Rawls on this, I applaud the clarity of thought that sees through false identities.

the results and to allow replicability. The measure should also cover all important aspects of freedom, including economic freedom, and exclude non-freedoms, such as democracy and "claim-freedoms."

Final thoughts

As noted, a measure of negative freedom will not be to everyone's taste, but it will enable empirical investigation of the consequences for human well-being of negative freedom and those factors that promote the establishment and stability of negative freedom. It creates a consistent answer to Q1, which began this paper: "What is freedom?" Focusing on a consistent version of freedom, then allows us to move on to objective, measurement criterion to answer Q2) "Who has freedom?" (See Vásquez and Štumberger, this volume.)

The measurement in turn will ultimately provide for negative freedom the tools needed to answer the other questions that began this essay: Q3) Is freedom always good? Is more freedom always better? Q4) More generally, what are the consequences of freedom in different areas of human endeavor? Q5) How is freedom achieved? Q6) How is it made stable and secure? Q7) How is it defeated?

Others may well attempt to establish a measure of positive freedom based on their particular ideology or claim-freedom based on their view of optimal welfare functions. This would provide the empirical means of testing the consequences for human well-being of negative freedom versus these differing concepts of claims and freedoms.

Overall human freedom presents a tougher measurement challenge than economic freedom. However, a huge number of data sources are now available, giving some prospect of success, or at least moving towards ever better measures if this approach is taken. Appendix A explores some of the challenges.

Appendix A: Developing a Measurement Taxonomy and Other Puzzles

This appendix has a limited goal: simply to lay out some of the challenges faced in developing a freedom measure. It makes no claim to being a full menu of these challenges. It merely aims to develop a partial menu of some important items.

Taxonomy

An important step in developing a taxonomy of freedom is to clear up a confusion found almost everywhere in discussing freedom. Policy papers, leaders, and even thinkers talk about freedom of the press, freedom of religion, political freedom, freedom of speech, and so on, as if they are talking similar about similar things.

These are not similar things. There are two distinct, logical dimensions of freedom being confused here, labeled, arbitrarily, "spheres" and "actions" of freedom. By sphere, I mean differing aspects of behavior; for example, political versus religious versus civic or personal activities. By actions, I simply mean actions in these spheres. Here I have in mind things like freedom of speech, freedom of assembly, freedom of the press, and so on. These are the traditional negative freedoms.

A simple matrix for 'Country X' makes clear why these are separate:

		Freedom Actions			
		Speech	*Assembly*	*Press*	*Etc.*
Spheres of Freedom	*Personal*	4.7	3.6	2.1	...
	Political	4	1	4.5	...
	Religious	1	3.5	0.9	...
	Etc.	...	...	...	...

In the above matrix, Country X allows moderately good freedom of speech in religion, but suppresses religious assemblies and press discussions of religion. X's security forces are much more tolerant of political discussions than they are of politically-oriented assembly or journalism.

Thus, for example, it does not make sense to talk about religious freedom and freedom of the media as if they were similar creatures. A free media can explore political, social, religious issues, etc. However, religious freedom can be expressed in the media, association, speech, etc.

Once the link between democracy and political freedom is broken, the question arises as to whether political freedom is a specific sphere of freedom or whether it falls under personal freedom. The former would appear to be the most appropriate. For example, it is easily possible to imagine a regime that does not restrict assembly for personal or religious activities—for example, marriage or religious festivals—but does restrict assembly for political purposes.

The above table is meant to be simply illustrative and not comprehensive. Other freedom actions would include, for example, association and movement. Another sphere could be scientific investigation. Moreover, not all cells in the matrix will be relevant. For example, "freedom to worship" may be a component of freedom, but may be relevant only to religious freedom.

Coercion

This section, following Hayek, will suggest that we are seeking to measure coercion (or restraints) as limits on freedom applied by human beings. This immediately raises the question: which set of human beings doing the blocking are of interest—those running the state, the religion, the setters of social conventions?

Initially, any freedom index would have to be limited to restrictions applied by government. This is where the data and where most thinking on freedom has concentrated. Moving beyond government restriction initially would probably prove too ambitious a task.

But the question remains: what human agencies can limit freedom? First, we can eliminate voluntary organizations. Virtually every religion limits some freedoms, but so long as the individual voluntarily gives these up on joining the religion, and can leave the religion at will, there is no restriction on freedom since such decisions themselves are freely made.

What about society? Can it impose restrictions on freedom? Hayek (1960/1978) makes a number of important comments on this, with several brought together below.

> Paradoxical as it may appear, it is probably true that a successful free society will always in large measure be a tradition-bound society (p. 61).… It is this flexibility of voluntary rule which in the field of morals makes gradual evolution and spontaneous growth possible. Such an evolution is possible only with rules which are neither coercive more deliberately imposed—rules which, though observing them is regarded as merit and though they will be observed by the majority, can be broken by individuals who feel that they have strong enough reasons to brave the censure of their fellows (p. 63).… Liberty is an opportunity for doing good, but it is only so when it is also an opportunity for doing wrong. The fact [is] that a free society will function successfully only if the individuals are in some measure guided by common values (p. 79).… On the whole, these conventions and

norms of social intercourse and individual conduct do not constitute a serious infringement of individual liberty but secure a certain minimum uniformity of conduct that assists individual efforts more than it impedes them (p. 147).

This would argue against trying to measure societal limits on freedom. But surely society can be coercive. In the 1950s, in many parts of the United States, there were no legal restrictions on serving Negroes, but a black person would have difficulty getting a room in a "white" hotel. Hayek discusses this in a general sense: "We should be very dependent on the beliefs of our fellows if they were prepared to sell their products to us only when they approved of our end and not for their own advantage" (1960/1978: 144).

When the civil rights law passed, federal officials worried about massive disobedience through the south. Instead, thousands of businesses quietly opened their doors to black customers. The speedy, quiet acceptance suggests that many business owners would have voluntarily accepted black customers earlier were it not for social constraints—and that these social restraints limited their economic freedom to accept black customers.[27]

Despite—and because of—these complications, the tentative recommendation is to set aside social restrictions on freedom. There are intense conceptual and measurement problems here. It seems reasonable to first tackle government-imposed restrictions on freedom. This was clearly the central concern of the enlightenment writers on freedom and remains the central concern in most current commentary on freedom. However, devising such a measure will ultimately help in clarifying whether social restrictions are enduring without government support and whether such restrictions can ultimately be measured.

Official versus unofficial limits on freedom

The annual report, *Economic Freedom of the World*, focuses on official limits on freedom and this seems appropriate for a broader freedom index at first blush, particularly if the index limits itself to government restrictions on freedom, but the index does have a weakness.

First, even if we limit our measure of freedom to government coercion, it is important to note that unofficial limits may be sanctioned by government. Thus, a newspaper may be bombed or a journalist killed without the perpetrators facing any legal threat, and perhaps with the encouragement of government officials. The perpetrators may even be security officials.

---

27 This is a debatable point since owners were coerced by the new law to accept black patrons, and maybe would not have done so if they had been economically free.

Such unofficial limits on freedom would cover a broad spectrum, from active government involvement to backroom sanctioning. Where on this spectrum would the line be drawn between "official" freedom limits and "unofficial" ones? This demarcation would be particularly difficult for limits on the freedom of women and minorities. Recall that most nations now have laws that officially support freedom and equality even if the government unofficially suppresses women and/ or minorities.

My sense is that governments are more open about official restrictions on economic freedom than non-economic freedom, making it easier to use official measures for restrictions on economic freedom than for restrictions on non-economic freedoms. Socialism and publicly acknowledged limits on economic freedom remain fashionable, at least in some quarters. On the other hand, non-economic freedoms are "officially" supported across a broad spectrum, even in nations actively involved in "unofficially" suppressing such freedom.

For example, could female literacy serve as one indication of whether freedom extends equally to females? Proxy measures will pick up both official and unofficial limits on freedom, and problematically, given the above, societal restrictions on freedom.

In fact, if appropriate proxy measures could be found, then, despite the recommendation above, a measure of freedom could incorporate societal restrictions on freedom, though this would raise some difficult conceptual issues: i.e., the idea, only briefly explored above, that societal pressures cannot really be considered limits on freedom.

Possible proxy measures: law and responsibility

Hayek argues that "general and equal laws" are a necessary and, he seems to indicate, a sufficient condition for freedom. His comments speak for themselves: "It is often not recognized that general and equal laws provide the most effective protection against the infringement of liberty..." (1960/1978: 210). "The conception of freedom under the law... rests on the contention that when we obey laws, in the sense of general abstract rules laid down irrespective their application to us, we are not subject to another man's will and are therefore free.... This, however, is only true if by 'law' we mean the general rules that apply equally to everybody" (1960/1978: 153). "Under a reign of freedom the free sphere of any individual includes all actions not explicitly restricted by general law" (1960/1978: 216).

This, of course, does not equate "general and equal laws" with freedom, but it suggests a possible source of proxy measures.

Hayek also argues that freedom is impossible without responsibility. This is in some ways related to the law, which forces people to take responsibility for at least a subset of their actions. We are not attempting to measure personal responsibility, but if we found such measures, they may be potential proxies for freedom.

Weighting schemes

Many weighting schemes are possible, and not simply weighted addition. It may be that freedoms are more than their sum. For instance, having both freedom of speech and freedom of assembly in religion may create more (or less) than twice the value of having only one of the freedoms. Freedoms may be multiplicative and/or they may be non-linear, so that one freedom is worth "1," two are worth "2," and three are worth "4," and so on. We need a better understanding of what freedom is, how it should be measured, and what measures are available before this issue can be addressed.

Scale

We have not addressed the question of scale: can A be *slightly* freer to do X than B? Franco's Spain was not free, but it was freer than Stalin's Russia. Can such gradations be captured? Carter (1999: 220) notes constraint variables: physical impossibility, threats, and difficulty, though the list could easily be made longer. He also argues that at a conceptual level, a measure of freedom should consider only "physical impossibility" supplemented by knowledge of the probability of future restraints on freedom, like being sent to a concentration camp for certain speech. That speech is not physically impossible, but has a high probability of reducing freedom in the future. Whether one accepts this or not, developing a freedom scale will be difficult.

It is also unclear whether a cardinal or only an ordinal measuring system will be possible.

Race, etc.

Governments can restrict freedom based on race, gender, ethnicity, etc. However, this can also involved a complicated interplay between government coercion and society. Measuring this will be a great challenge. This also complicates weighting. If a minority of, say, 20 percent of the population lacks a certain freedom, does this mean that the measure is weighted by 20 percent?

References

Amnesty International (2007). *The State of the World's Human Rights*. The Alden Press.

Avalon Project (n.d.). *Declaration of the Rights of Man—1789*. Yale Law School. <http://avalon.law.yale.edu/18th_century/rightsof.asp>, as of October 31, 2011.

Berlin, Isaiah (1958). Two concepts of liberty. In Isaiah Berlin (author), Henry Hardy (ed.) (2002), *Liberty: Incorporating Four Essays on Liberty* (Oxford University Press): 166-217.

Bouillon, Hardy (2004). *What are Human Rights?* The Liberal Institute of the Friedrich Naumann Foundation. <http://www.fnf.org.ph/downloadables/What%20are%20Human%20Rights.pdf>, as of October 31, 2011.

Carter, Ian (1999). *A Measure of Freedom*. Oxford University Press.

Carter, Ian (2007). Positive and negative liberty. In Edward N. Zalta (ed.), *The Stanford Encyclopedia of Philosophy (Winter 2007 edition)* (Stanford University). <http://plato.stanford.edu/archives/win2007/entries/liberty-positive-negative/>, as of October 31, 2011.

Chua, Amy (2004). *World on Fire: How Exporting Free Market Democracy Breeds Ethnic Hatred and Global Instability*. Anchor Books.

Collier, Paul (2009). *War, Guns, and Votes*. HarperCollins.

Constant, Benjamin (1816). *The Liberty of the Ancients Compared with that of the Moderns*. Institute for Humane Studies. <www.uark.edu/depts/comminfo/cambridge/ancients.html>, as of October 31, 2011.

Dawson, John W. (1998). Institutions, investment, and growth: New cross-country and panel data evidence. *Economic Inquiry* 36 (October): 603-19.

Freedom House (2008). *Freedom in the World Report*. Freedom House. <www.freedomhouse.org/template.cfm?page=363&year=2008>, as of March 12, 2009.

Fukuyama, Francis (2011). *The Origins of Political Ordeer: From Prehuman Times to the French Revolution*. Farrar, Straus, and Giroux.

Gairdner, William (1999). Jean-Jacques Rousseau and the Romantic roots of modern democracy. *Humanitas* XII(1). <www.williamgairdner.com/rousseau-and-the-romantic-root/>, as of October 31, 2011.

Gray, Tim (1990). *Freedom*. Macmillan.

Gwartney, James, and Robert Lawson (2008). *Economic Freedom of the World: 2008 Annual Report*. The Fraser Institute.

Gwartney, James, and Robert Lawson (2006). *Economic Freedom of the World: 2006 Annual Report*. The Fraser Institute.

Griswold, Daniel T. (2004). Trading tyranny for freedom: How open markets till the soil for democracy. *Trade Policy Analysis* 26 (January 6). Cato Institute.

Hanson, Victor Davis (2002). *Carnage and Culture*. Anchor Books.

Hayek, Friedrich A. (1960/1978). *The Constitution of Liberty*. University of Chicago Press.

Hobbes, Thomas (1651/1996). *Leviathan*. (Marshall Missner, ed.) Pearson Longman.

Hooker, Richard (1996). *Thucydides, Pericles' Funeral Oration*. University of Minnesota Human Rights Library. <www.umn.edu/humanrts/education/thucydides.html>, as of October 31, 2011.

Inglehart, Ronald, and Christian Welzel (2009). How development leads to democracy. *Foreign Affairs* 88(2) (March/April).

Inglehart, Ronald, and Christian Welzel (2005). *Modernization, Cultural Change, and Democracy: The Human Development Sequence*. Cambridge University Press.

Jenkins, Philip (2010). *Jesus Wars*. HarperOne.

King, Martin Luther Jr. (August 28, 1983). *I Have a Dream*. Speech delivered at the Lincoln Memorial in Washington, DC. <http://www.writespirit.net/inspirational_talks/political/martin_luther_king_talks/i_have_a_dream/index.html>, as of November 28, 2011.

Lewis, Bernard (2003). *What Went Wrong? The Clash Between Islam and Modernity in the Middle East*. Harper Perennial.

Locke, John (1690/1960). *Two Treatises of Government*. In the Online Library of Liberty: The Works of John Locke, vol. 4, Economic Writings and Two Treatises of Government. Liberty Fund. <http://oll.libertyfund.org/index.php?option=com_staticxt&staticfile=show.php%3Ftitle=763&Itemid=27>, as of August 12, 2012.

MacCallum, G.C., Jr. (1967). Negative and positive freedom. *Philosophical Review* 76: 312-34.

MacNeill, William (1992). *The Rise of the West: A History of the Human Community*. University of Chicago.

Mill, John Stuart (1863/2002). *The Basic Writings of John Stuart Mill: On Liberty, the Subjection of Women and Utilitarianism*. The Modern Library.

Oppenheim, Felix E (1961). *Dimensions of Freedom*. St. Martin's Press.

Palmer (2008). *Freedom Properly Understood*. Occasional Paper 48. Liberal Institute, Friedrich Naumann Stifung.

Plato (n.d./1968). *The Republic* (Alan Bloom, trans.) Basic Books.

Rawls, John (1971). *A Theory of Justice*. Harvard University Press.

Rousseau, Jean-Jacques (1762/1950). The social contract. In G.D.H. Cole. (trans.), *The Social Contract and Discourses* (E.P. Dutton and Company), pp. 4-134.

Sen, Amartya (1999). *Development as Freedom*. Anchor Books.

Somerville, J. (1962). Towards a consistent definition of freedom and its relation to value. In C. J. Friedrich (ed.), *Liberty* (Atherton Press). Quoted from Carter, 1999.

Stark, Rodney (2005). *The Victory of Reason: How Christianity Led to Freedom, Capitalism, and Western Success.* Random House.

Straumann, Benjamin (2009). Is modern liberty ancient? Roman remedies and natural rights in Hugo Grotius' early works on natural law. *Law and History Review* 27(1) (Spring): 55-85.

Time (1953, July 13). The seven freedoms. *Time.* <www.time.com/time/magazine/article/0,9171,806723,00.html>, as of October 31, 2011.

United Nations (1948). *The Universal Declaration of Human Rights.* United Nations. <www.un.org/Overview/rights.html>, as of October 31, 2011.

United Nations (1991). *Human Development Report.* pp. 18-21. New York: United Nations.

United Nations Development Program (2000). *Human Development Report: Human Rights and Human Development.* United Nations.

United States Constitution (1787). *US Constitution Online* web page. <www.usconstitution.net/const.html>, as of October 31, 2011.

Walker, Michael A (2010). A Compact Statement of a Cost-based Theory of Rights and Freedom: Implications for Classifying and Measuring Rights. In Fred McMahon (ed.), *Towards a Worldwide Index of Human Freedom* (Fraser Institute): 137–52.

Zakaria, Fareed (2003). *The Future of Freedom: Illiberal Democracy at Home and Abroad.* Norton.

CHAPTER THREE

An Index of Freedom in the World

*Ian Vásquez and Tanja Štumberger**

Using available data, we have created an index that we believe is a reasonable, early attempt at measuring freedom around the world. As a result of the Fraser Institute's decades-long work to define and measure economic freedom, a tremendous amount of progress has been made in understanding the concept of economic freedom and its contribution to human well-being.[1] Building on that work, this paper attempts to devise a broader measure of human liberty that also includes indicators of civil and other liberties.

No such index currently exists, at least not one that is comprehensive and consistent with a classical liberal perspective. The purpose for engaging in this exercise is to more carefully explore what we mean by freedom, and to better understand its relationship to any number of social and economic phenomena. Just as important, this research could improve our appreciation of the way in which various freedoms—economic, civil, and political—relate to one another. To the extent possible, we will be able to observe those relationships through time, even if at first the time frame is limited.

We are under no illusion that this is an ideal index of what it purports to measure (league tables rarely are), but it helps us get closer to our goal. Our hope is that the current paper will stimulate a more focused discussion about the suitability of the data and about a sensible approach to their use. The paper is organized as follows: a description of the concept measured and methodology; a justification and description of the data used; results and preliminary findings.

---

* Ian Vásquez is director of the Center for Global Liberty and Prosperity at the Cato Institute. Tanja Štumberger is a senior fellow at the Atlas Economic Research Foundation.

1 The culmination of that work is the annual *Economic Freedom of the World* report published by the Fraser Institute and co-authored by James Gwartney and Robert Lawson (and now also by Joshua Hall); the report has spawned an extensive research literature. For a more comprehensive view on the economic freedom research, see <www.freetheworld.com>.

Overall concept and approach

In constructing this index, we use indicators that are as consistent as possible with the concept of negative liberty: the absence of coercive constraint on the individual. We do not attempt to measure positive freedom, however desirable such may be, nor do we measure so-called "claim freedoms," which often become government-imposed attempts at realizing positive freedoms (e.g., the "right" or freedom to a have job or housing).[2] As Isaiah Berlin, Friedrich Hayek, and others have noted, calling other good or desirable things such as wealth "freedom" merely causes confusion.[3]

This index of freedom also does not incorporate measures of democracy or "political freedom." The reason is that democracy describes a "power relationship," to use Fred McMahon's term, in which freedom may increase or decrease depending on the collective decisions of the elected government. Democracy may be more consistent than other forms of government at safeguarding freedom, but it is not freedom, nor does it necessarily guarantee freedom.[4] The relationship between democracy and freedom is of crucial interest to all advocates of liberty, which is all the more reason to establish an independent measure of freedom. In the final section of this paper, we look at the correlation of our index of freedom with democracy.

Our criteria in selecting data for the index follow that used by the Economic Freedom of the World Project. The data come from credible third-party sources and are not generated by the authors; the index is as transparent as possible on methodology and on sources; and the report covers as large a number of countries over as long a time period as was possible given the data available. In general, we measure official restrictions on freedom, although some measures capture social or non-official violations of liberty (e.g., violence or conflict measures).

The index of freedom is constructed as follows. We combine economic freedom measures from the *Economic Freedom of the World* (EFW) index with measures of what we somewhat imprecisely call civil or personal freedoms. The economic freedom index and the personal freedom index we devise each receive half the weight in the overall index. A description of the EF ratings and EF index methodology

---

2   This topic, and the justification for relying on the concept of negative freedom, is discussed at length in McMahon, 2010.

3   See McMahon, 2010. See also Palmer, 2009, especially chapter 2 (pp. 13-32), "Freedom Properly Understood," in which he critiques Amartya Sen's capability approach to defining freedom; and Chauffour, 2009, ch. 2.

4   See again McMahon, 2010, for a fuller discussion of this point.

can be found in the EFW annual reports (Gwartney, Hall, and Lawson, 2010). The following is a description of the personal freedom measure and methodology.

For the personal freedom sub-index, we use 34 variables covering 123 countries for the year 2008, and for a minority of variables we use a more recent year if earlier data were not available. In selecting the countries we limited ourselves to those that are presented in the EFW. In selecting time periods, we would have liked to have used data from at least two periods separated by five or more years to track changes in the level of freedom over time (as we did in a preliminary index that used less extensive data (Vásquez and Štumberger, 2011)), but doing so would be of limited value since almost half of the data we use in the current index was not available for most countries prior to 2008, the earliest year for which we felt we could produce a robust enough index.

The index is divided into four categories: 1) Security and Safety; 2) Freedom of Movement; 3) Freedom of Expression; and 4) Relationship Freedoms. Table 1 outlines the categories and the subcategories. Each indicator is rated on a 0 to 10 scale, with 10 representing the most freedom. We average the variables in each category to produce an average for each of the four categories. We then average the category ratings to produce a final rating on the personal freedom index. To produce the overall freedom index we then average final country ratings of the economic and the personal freedom indexes. The overall freedom index is thus derived from a total of 76 distinct variables (42 from the EF index and 34 from the personal freedom index).

What we measure

We have tried to capture the degree to which people are free to enjoy the major civil liberties—freedom of speech, religion, and association and assembly—in each country in our survey. In addition, we include indicators of crime and violence, freedom of movement, and legal discrimination against homosexuals. We also include six variables pertaining to women's freedom that are found in various categories of the index. (For an overview of the sources of our data, see the table in Appendix A.) We would have liked to have included other important variables, such as drug and alcohol prohibition, but we found no reliable data sources. In the case of drug use and alcohol consumption restrictions, we discovered that constructing our own such data set would be an especially ambitious and rather complex task better left for the future. The following is a brief description and justification of the data we use. For a more detailed description of the data sources, what they measure, and their methodology, see appendix B.

Table 1: Structure of the Personal Freedom Index

I. Security and safety
  A. Government's threat to a person
    1. Extrajudicial killings
    2. Torture
    3. Political imprisonment
    4. Disappearances
  B. Society's threat to a person
    1. Intensity of violent conflicts
    2. Level of organized conflict (internal)
    3. Female genital mutilation
    4. Son preference
    5. Homicide
    6. Human trafficking
    7. Sexual violence
    8. Assault
    9. Level of perceived criminality
  C. Threat to private property
    1. Theft
    2. Burglary
    3. Inheritance
  D. Threat to foreigners

II. Movement
  A. Forcibly displaced populations
  B. Freedom of foreign movement
  C. Freedom of domestic movement
  D. Women's freedom of movement

III. Expression
  A. Press killings
  B. Freedom of speech
  C. Laws and regulations that influence media content
  D. Political pressures and controls on media content
  E. Dress code in public

IV. Relationship freedoms
  A. Freedom of assembly and association
  B. Parental authority
  C. Government restrictions on religion
  D. Social hostility toward religion
  E. Male-to-male relationships
  F. Female-to-female relationships
  G. Age of consent for homosexual couples
  H. Adoption by homosexuals

Security and Safety

Personal safety and physical security from harm is a basic indicator or condition of freedom.[5] The provision of domestic and national security is also a service that most classical liberals consider a proper function of government. We mainly try to measure the degree to which people who have not violated the equal rights of others are in their body or property physically threatened, assaulted, imprisoned, kidnapped or killed, or are otherwise insecure in their safety.

The first component of this category—government's threat to a person—is composed of indicators of the following human rights violations: extrajudicial killings, torture, political imprisonment, and disappearances. The first two regard violations by government officials or by "private individuals at the instigation of government officials." The last measure refers to politically motivated disappearances.

The next component—society's threat to a person—rates armed conflicts and crime. Nine indicators make up this component. The first two indicators measure the extent to which war or armed conflict with internal or external aggressors impinges on personal freedom in observed countries. For each country, we calculate battle-related deaths per one million people as a measure of the intensity of violent conflict. For the level of organized conflict indicator, we use a "qualitative assessment of the intensity of conflicts within" each country used by the *Global Peace Index*, but derived by the Economist Intelligence Unit (EIU).

A high level of crime in society reduces personal freedom. The remaining seven indicators in this component mainly measure transgressions resulting in bodily harm or loss of life. Here we ignore a possible valid objection to the use of crime statistics (that there is no standardized reporting of crime, nor do the statistics necessarily reflect the true level of crime due to under- or mis-reporting). We also ignore optimal-level-of-crime considerations or any account of the use of public resources to provide a public good intended to enhance freedom, but that by its nature (taxation) represents a reduction in freedom. This concern applies to our entire index.[6]

Female genital mutilation measures the prevalence of such among the population of women in a given country. Son preference is an indicator of the number of "missing women" in a country, typically due to

---

5 The rule of law can be considered as supportive of, consistent with, or even as a proxy of, safety and security or other components of the personal freedom index. We do not include it, however, as a measure of rule of law is already included in the economic freedom index.

6 Fred McMahon brings up the problem of "how restrictions on freedom that are designed to enhance freedom should be measured" in the brief, "Some Issues Concerning the Scope of a Freedom Measure," presented in a colloquium in Potsdam, Germany, June 2010 organized by the Friedrich Naumann Foundation.

sex-selective abortions and infanticide of females. Homicide is calculated as murders per 100,000 population. Human trafficking gauges the rate per 100,000 population of "the recruitment, transport, transfer, harboring or receipt of a person by such means as threat or use of force or other forms of coercion, of abduction, of fraud or deception for the purpose of exploitation."[7] The sexual violence indicator refers to rape and sexual assault, while the assault measure refers to all other forms of assault that result in bodily harm short of death. Finally, we use an indicator from the EIU that provides a qualitative assessment of the level of perceived criminality.

The final two components in this category are the threat to private property and the threat to foreigners. The first of the two components includes indicators of theft and burglary, which are self-explanatory, and inheritance, which measures whether the practice favors male heirs. The last component is a qualitative assessment by the EIU that measures "societies' and governments' attitude to foreigners and their investments," an indicator of the level of freedom not just of foreigners but also of nationals who wish to peacefully interact with them.

One indicator we did not include because of a lack of agreement rather than a lack of data was capital punishment. One of us—Tanja Štumberger—believes that it should be included; one of us—Ian Vásquez—does not. The argument in favor of its inclusion is that the government should never be given the power to take away a person's life, at least not in the case of a crime for which a judicial process was held and the defendant convicted (a national military killing in the case of legitimate self-defense is a different matter). State power exercised in this way is itself a huge transgression of rights. The other view opposes capital punishment as a poor policy because the judicial process cannot be counted on even in the most civilized countries to always avoid making mistakes that result in the death penalty being imposed on an innocent person. However, that efficiency argument is different from one that claims that it is unjust to take away one's life as punishment for committing a most heinous crime. Because this index attempts to measure the extent of negative liberty and actual transgressions against it— rather than merely good or bad policy—capital punishment should not be included here according to this view. We have looked for guidance in the classical liberal literature and among contemporary liberal thinkers and it is not clear that there is any settled liberal opinion on the matter. We have thus left this indicator out of the index for the time being

---

7   United Nations Office on Drugs and Crime. This data refers to the country in which trafficking is detected. Note that this definition does not include human smuggling, which involves consent.

and encourage a vigorous discussion about whether capital punishment, meted out as a result of due process, is in and of itself an infringement of liberty, the latter consideration being a criterion both authors agree all indicators in this study must meet.

Movement

Here we attempt to capture government impositions or restrictions on people's freedom to move about their country or to leave it. The first indicator, forcibly displaced populations, takes into account the country source of refugees and the number of internally displaced persons in the same country. Data from the *World Refugee Survey* was used to calculate the rating in the following way: If 10 percent or more of the population was displaced, then the country scored 0. If no persons were displaced, then the country scored 10; other countries are in between.

The next two indicators measure freedom of domestic and foreign movement (i.e., freedom to leave the country), while the last indicator in this category, women's freedom of movement, measures the extent to which women can "move freely outside of the house."

Expression

Five indicators make up the Freedom of Expression category of the index. Press killings refer to murders of journalists "in retribution for, or to prevent, news coverage or commentary" and journalists killed on dangerous assignments as documented by the Committee to Protect Journalists. The number of killings per country was converted into a 0-10 scale, where 5 was a cut-off (meaning that every country that documented 5 or more killings that year received a rating of 0, while the countries with 0 killings received a rating of 10; the countries with 1 through 4 killings received corresponding values on a 0-10 scale). The freedom of speech indicator measures the extent to which speech or expression, including the press, music, and art, are affected by government ownership of the media or censorship. It is based on an evaluation by the *CIRI Human Rights Data Project*.

The third indicator, laws and regulations that influence media content, is an assessment by Freedom House of the legal environment that governments can use to "restrict the media's ability to operate." The next measure is a Freedom House assessment of the political environment's influence on the media, namely, political pressure over news and editorial content. It also evaluates "the vibrancy of the media and the diversity of news available within each country," and indicators of violence against journalists. There is some overlap of coverage among the above four components of this category. Lastly, the dress code in public variable gauges the extent to which women are obligated to wear a veil in public.

Relationship freedoms

Here we measure what we broadly categorize as freedoms to have relationships with others and of the kind not covered above. Nine indicators make up this category. The first measure refers to the standard understanding of freedom of association and assembly, including the freedom to form political parties, trade unions, and to organize public demonstrations. Parental authority refers to the extent to which women have equal rights based in law and custom regarding "legal guardianship of a child during a marriage and custody rights over a child after divorce."

The next two indicators on freedom of religion are drawn from *the Pew Forum on Religion and Public Life*. The first measures government restrictions on religion (practices and beliefs) and the second measures non-official or social hostility "that effectively hinder the religious activities of the targeted individuals or groups." This second measure probably does reduce the liberty of certain people to practice religion, but its inclusion in the index is debatable depending on what is meant by a "hostile act" according to Pew; some acts may deter people from behaving in a certain way but may be consistent with freedom of expression, for example. Note also that we've slightly modified the Pew index, excluding two categories that did not measure actual freedoms or would have been redundant in our own index.[8]

The last four indicators measure the freedom of homosexuals to establish relationships. The male-to-male relationship indicator gauges the extent to which sexual relationships between men are legal; the female-to-female indicator gauges the same for relationships between women. The age of consent indicator measures whether such laws are equal for heterosexual and homosexual couples. Lastly, we measure the extent to which it is legal for homosexual couples to adopt children.

Results and preliminary findings

Table 2 gives the ratings of the personal freedom index for 2008. The table includes the economic freedom ratings and the ratings and rankings of the overall freedom index. For the ratings for all countries of all categories and measures that make up the personal freedom index, see appendix C.

The resulting personal freedom index and overall freedom index looks about right in that most countries fall into the spectrum of freedom that would be generally expected. The top three jurisdictions in the freedom

---

8   The two Pew categories our index excludes are: a) government restrictions on religion question #1: "Does the constitution, or law that functions in the place of a constitution (basic law), specifically provide for 'freedom of religion' or include language used in Article 18 of the United Nations Universal Declaration of Human Rights?" and b) social hostility question #4: "Were religion-related terrorist groups active in the country?"

Table 2: Freedom Index and Sub-Indexes

		Personal Freedom	Economic Freedom	Freedom Index
1	New Zealand	9.2	8.22	8.73
2	Netherlands	9.5	7.45	8.47
3	Hong Kong	7.8	9.02	8.39
4	Australia	8.8	7.83	8.33
5	Canada	8.7	7.92	8.33
6	Ireland	9.0	7.68	8.33
7	United States of America	8.7	7.93	8.30
8	Denmark	8.9	7.71	8.30
9	Japan	9.2	7.38	8.28
10	Estonia	8.9	7.65	8.28
11	Switzerland	8.6	7.96	8.26
12	Norway	9.2	7.34	8.26
13	Finland	8.8	7.54	8.16
14	Austria	8.7	7.59	8.13
15	Luxembourg	8.7	7.53	8.12
16	Chile	8.2	7.99	8.12
17	Iceland	9.0	7.16	8.10
18	United Kingdom	8.4	7.78	8.08
19	Slovakia	8.6	7.57	8.07
20	Costa Rica	8.8	7.35	8.05
21	El Salvador	8.5	7.58	8.04
22	Uruguay	9.4	6.67	8.03
23	Spain	8.8	7.19	8.00
24	Albania	8.6	7.38	7.98
25	Portugal	8.9	7.08	7.97
26	Bahamas	8.8	7.08	7.94
27	Malta	8.8	7.06	7.94
28	Panama	8.5	7.32	7.92
29	Sweden	8.6	7.26	7.91
30	Mauritius	8.1	7.61	7.88
31	Hungary	8.4	7.39	7.87
32	Belgium	8.5	7.14	7.83
33	France	8.4	7.20	7.78
34	Czech Republic	8.7	6.88	7.78
35	Germany	8.0	7.47	7.75
36	Guatemala	8.3	7.15	7.73
37	Poland	8.6	6.88	7.73
38	Peru	8.0	7.36	7.68
39	Singapore	6.6	8.75	7.67
40	Italy	8.5	6.75	7.62
41	Lithuania	8.2	7.03	7.61
42	Bulgaria	8.0	7.18	7.60

		Personal Freedom	Economic Freedom	Freedom Index
43	Slovenia	8.5	6.61	7.56
44	Korea, Republic of	7.7	7.33	7.53
45	Cyprus	7.6	7.50	7.53
46	Jamaica	8.0	6.97	7.48
47	Taiwan	7.4	7.56	7.48
48	Latvia	7.9	6.98	7.44
49	Papua New Guinea	7.8	6.94	7.39
50	Brazil	8.5	6.18	7.35
51	Haiti	8.0	6.68	7.34
52	Honduras	7.5	7.12	7.31
53	Nicaragua	7.8	6.85	7.30
54	Paraguay	7.9	6.62	7.27
55	Ghana	7.3	7.17	7.23
56	Argentina	8.4	6.01	7.22
57	Croatia	7.9	6.54	7.20
58	Thailand	7.3	7.06	7.17
59	Guyana	7.6	6.74	7.16
60	Trinidad and Tobago	7.5	6.78	7.13
61	Fiji	7.7	6.56	7.11
62	Namibia	7.6	6.61	7.10
63	Belize	7.5	6.72	7.09
64	Bolivia	8.0	6.15	7.07
65	Greece	7.1	6.92	7.03
66	Romania	7.6	6.43	7.03
67	Philippines	7.3	6.76	7.02
68	Mexico	7.1	6.88	7.00
69	South Africa	7.3	6.55	6.94
70	Madagascar	7.5	6.28	6.88
71	Botswana	6.8	6.89	6.85
72	Dominican Republic	7.5	6.22	6.84
73	Ecuador	7.6	6.04	6.80
74	Bahrain	6.3	7.23	6.74
75	Oman	6.0	7.50	6.74
76	Barbados	7.4	5.97	6.68
77	Mali	7.2	6.15	6.66
78	Zambia	6.1	7.27	6.66
79	Ukraine	7.5	5.46	6.49
80	Rwanda	6.3	6.61	6.44
81	Colombia	6.6	6.24	6.41
82	Jordan	5.6	7.18	6.38
83	Turkey	5.8	6.91	6.37
84	Indonesia	6.2	6.49	6.36
85	Kuwait	5.2	7.50	6.35
86	United Arab Emirates	5.2	7.45	6.31

		Personal Freedom	Economic Freedom	Freedom Index
87	Benin	7.1	5.49	6.27
88	Malawi	6.6	5.95	6.27
89	Russia	5.9	6.57	6.25
90	Guinea-Bissau	7.4	4.93	6.15
91	Kenya	5.2	7.00	6.12
92	India	5.6	6.48	6.06
93	Morocco	5.8	6.29	6.04
94	Uganda	4.9	7.15	6.00
95	Tanzania	6.0	5.94	5.96
96	Egypt	5.0	6.82	5.93
97	Nepal	6.3	5.44	5.89
98	Senegal	6.2	5.56	5.88
99	Malaysia	5.0	6.71	5.84
100	China	5.1	6.44	5.76
101	Congo, Republic of	6.7	4.77	5.73
102	Niger	6.1	5.35	5.71
103	Sierra Leone	6.0	5.37	5.68
104	Nigeria	5.4	5.93	5.68
105	Israel	4.4	6.86	5.60
106	Togo	5.5	5.62	5.54
107	Gabon	5.4	5.64	5.54
108	Cote d'Ivoire	5.3	5.67	5.48
109	Venezuela	6.5	4.35	5.42
110	Tunisia	4.7	6.00	5.36
111	Bangladesh	4.7	5.95	5.31
112	Central African Republic	5.2	5.16	5.18
113	Chad	4.8	5.35	5.07
114	Cameroon	4.2	5.86	5.03
115	Burundi	5.2	4.65	4.93
116	Iran	3.6	6.08	4.83
117	Algeria	4.5	5.02	4.77
118	Congo, Democratic Republic of	4.7	4.84	4.76
119	Syria	4.3	5.07	4.67
120	Sri Lanka	3.4	5.89	4.64
121	Pakistan	3.1	5.80	4.47
122	Burma	4.0	3.49	3.72
123	Zimbabwe	3.2	3.57	3.38
	Average	**7.1**	**6.7**	**6.9**
	Median	**7.5**	**6.9**	**7.1**

index are New Zealand, the Netherlands, and Hong Kong, in that order. The bottom three are Pakistan (121), Burma (122), and Zimbabwe (123). The following are the rankings of selected countries in the freedom index: Australia (4); Canada (5); United States (7); Japan (9); Estonia (10); Switzerland (11); Chile (16); United Kingdom (18); Germany (35); Singapore (39); Brazil (50); Ghana (55); Greece (65); Turkey (83); United Arab Emirates (86); Russia (89); India (92); Egypt (96); China (100); Venezuela (109); Cameroon (114); Iran (116).

The average rating of the Freedom Index for all countries was 6.9, with the average personal freedom rating (7.1) being higher than the average economic freedom rating (6.7). The correlation between the economic freedom ratings and personal freedom ratings was 0.60. That there would be at least that level of correlation was not a surprise given theory and cruder but indicative previous attempts to discover such a relationship.

Among the categories that make up the personal freedom index, freedom of movement exhibited the highest rating (8.6), while freedom of expression had the lowest rating (6.4). See figure 1.

Regional levels of freedom varied widely. The average rankings on the freedom index by region were highest for North America (Canada and the United States), Northern Europe, and Western Europe in that order, and lowest for the Middle East, sub-Saharan Africa, and North Africa in descending order (see figure 2). The regions that had greater overall levels of freedom exhibited higher ratings in personal freedom than in economic freedom, while the less free regions (Asia, Middle East, sub-Saharan Africa, and North Africa) tended to have higher levels of economic freedom than of personal freedom (see figure 3).

Figure 1: Freedom Index Categories

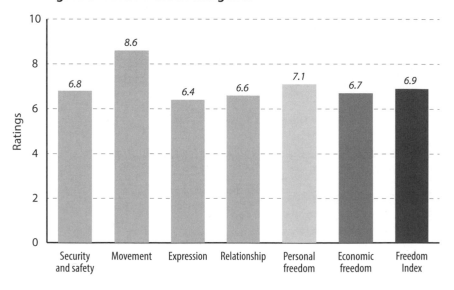

Figure 2: Average Freedom Index Ranking by Region

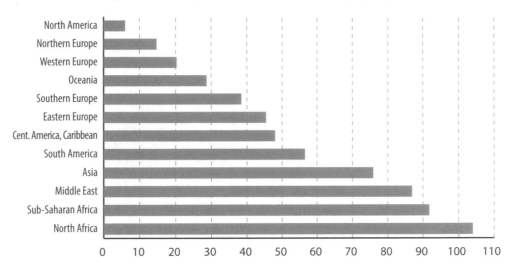

Figure 3: Average Freedom Ratings by Region

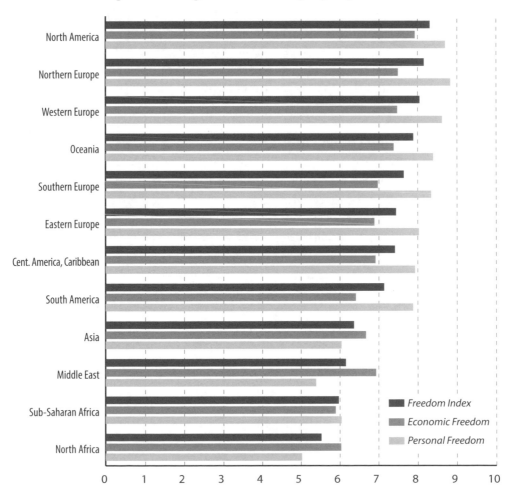

We present the above findings as tentative and subject to revision. These limited findings are also presented to see if they suggest any especially puzzling or problematic features about the way we have chosen to measure freedom. To our mind, the overall findings conform to expectations.

Freedom and democracy

What is the relationship between freedom and democracy? A well constructed freedom index can help to answer that question. We use our index and the Economist Intelligence Unit's *Democracy Index 2008* to see how political freedom and freedom relate. The EIU defines democracy broadly and thus constructs an index that produces a "wide" measure of democracy, as opposed to a more limited measure of the existence of free and fair elections. The EIU's *Democracy Index* covers five areas, of which we use the following four: electoral process and pluralism; functioning of government; political participation; and political culture. That index also measures civil liberties, but we leave that out of this exercise since that area is included in our freedom index. See appendix D for the resulting democracy ratings we construct based on the EIU data.

We find a strong correlation of 0.79 between freedom and democracy (see figure 4). Here again, the findings are not surprising, but if valid, they provide a good base from which to empirically examine a relationship that is surely more complex than what is suggested by a simple correlation.

Some conclusions

The freedom index we devise provides a proximate measure for the concept of negative freedom around the world. It relies on the most comprehensive databases on freedom to produce an index that covers the largest number of countries for which sufficient data are available. We believe the methodology, data, and outcomes are reasonable early attempts at creating an index that we hope can be useful in exploring and demonstrating the value of freedom.

A sensible question may be, "If a freedom index merely confirms what we already expected or could otherwise observe about freedom, does it really add anything to our knowledge?" To which there are probably a number of valid answers. One such answer was provided by Milton Friedman upon the publication of the first edition of *Economic Freedom of the World*, which supported previous theory and observation about the importance of economic freedom to growth and prosperity: "We have not in a sense learned any big thing from this book that we did not know before. What we have done is to acquire a set of data that can be used to explore just how the relation works, and what are the essential connections, and that will enable skeptics to test their views objectively" (Friedman, 1996: vii).

Figure 4: Freedom and Democracy

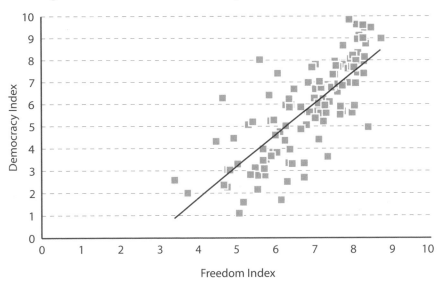

Indeed, *Economic Freedom of the World* has served just that purpose and more, producing a rich literature on the link between economic freedom and phenomena as diverse as foreign aid, armed conflict, and happiness. A broad freedom index has the potential to do as much and looks increasingly important in the wake of a global financial crisis that has reduced economic freedom in the world and at a time when hybrid forms of authoritarianism are being sold as viable alternatives to liberalism. Over time, a proper index can track not only specific gains and losses of freedom; it can also help to see what links may exist between the assortment of freedoms and other variables. What is the relationship between personal freedom, economic freedom, and democracy at different levels of development? Are some types of freedom, economic or personal, more conducive to the spread and sustenance of other freedoms? What is the relationship between various measures of human well-being (including income) and changes in personal freedom? Under what conditions are increases or decreases in freedom likely to come about? Delving into those and innumerable other questions that the data may help us to answer will surely lead to a better understanding of the role of freedom in human progress.

References

Chauffour, Jean-Pierre (2009). *The Power of Freedom: Uniting Human Rights and Development*. Cato Institute.

Friedman, Milton (1996). Foreword. In James Gwartney, Robert Lawson, and Walter Block, *Economic Freedom of the World: 1975-1995*. Fraser Institute.

Gwartney, James, Joshua Hall, and Robert Lawson (2010). *Economic Freedom of the World: 2010 Annual Report*. Fraser Institute.

McMahon, Fred (2010). *Literature Review: The Fraser Institute Human Freedom Project*. Discussion paper presented at a colloquium in Potsdam, Germany, organized by the Friedrich Naumann Foundation (June).

Palmer, Tom (2009). *Realizing Freedom: Libertarian Theory, History and Practice*. Cato Institute.

Vásquez, Ian, and Tanja Štumberger (2011). *A Prototype Index of Freedom in the World*. Paper presented at Freedom Index Seminar, Cato Institute, co-sponsored by the Fraser Institute and Friedrich Naumann Foundation, Washington, DC, May 25-27.

Appendix A: Data Sources for Freedom Index

Category	Source	Data Available for Years	Number of Countries
Extrajudicial Killing	CIRI Human Rights Data Project	1981–2010	195
Torture	CIRI Human Rights Data Project	1981–2010	195
Political Imprisonment	CIRI Human Rights Data Project	1981–2010	195
Disappearance	CIRI Human Rights Data Project	1981–2010	195
Battle-related Deaths	Uppsala Conflict Data Program	1989–2010	195
Level of organized conflict (internal)	Economist Intelligence Unit	2000–2010	149
Female Genital Mutilation	OECD	2009	122
Son Preference	OECD	2009	122
Homicide	UN Office on Drugs and Crime	2003–2008	207
Human Trafficking	UN Office on Drugs and Crime	2003–2008	67
Sexual Violence	UN Office on Drugs and Crime	2003–2008	104
Assault	UN Office on Drugs and Crime	2003–2008	106
Level of perceived criminality in society	Economist Intelligence Unit	2000–2010	149
Theft	UN Office on Drugs and Crime	2003–2008	104
Burglary	UN Office on Drugs and Crime	2003–2008	92
Inheritance	OECD	2009	122
Hostility to foreigners & their private property	Economist Intelligence Unit	2000–2010	149
Forcibly Displaced Populations	U.S. Committee for Refugees & Immigrants	since 1964	166
Freedom of Foreign Movement	CIRI Human Rights Data Project	1981–2010	195
Freedom of Domestic Movement	CIRI Human Rights Data Project	1981–2010	195
Women's Freedom of Movement	OECD	2009	122
Press Killings	Committee to Protect Journalists	since 1992	207
Freedom of Speech	CIRI Human Rights Data Project	1981–2010	195
Laws and regulations that influence media content	Freedom House	since 1980	194
Political pressures and controls on media content	Freedom House	since 1980	194
Dress code in public	OECD	2009	122
Freedom of Assembly and Association	CIRI Human Rights Data Project	1981–2010	195
Parental Authority	OECD	2009	122
Religion - Government Restrictions	Pew Forum on Religion & Public Life	2009, 2011	198
Religion - Social Hostility	Pew Forum on Religion & Public Life	2009, 2011	198
Male to Male Relationship	International Lesbian & Gay Association	2008–2011	195
Female to Female Relationship	International Lesbian & Gay Association	2008–2011	195
Age of Consent for Homosexual Couples	International Lesbian & Gay Association	2008–2011	195
Adoption by Homosexuals	International Lesbian & Gay Association	2008–2011	195

Appendix B: Description and Methodology of Data Sources, Freedom Index

Note The source descriptions are taken from the original texts.

Security and Safety

Extrajudicial killing
by CIRI Human Rights Data Project

Description Killings by government officials without due process of law. They include murders by private groups if instigated by government. These killings may result from the deliberate, illegal, and excessive use of lethal force by the police, security forces, or other agents of the state whether against criminal suspects, detainees, prisoners, or others.

Source The primary source of information about human rights practices is obtained from a careful reading of the annual United States Department of State's Country Reports on Human Rights Practices. In addition, coders of this index also use a second source, Amnesty International's Annual Report. If there are discrepancies between the two sources, coders are instructed to treat the Amnesty International evaluation as authoritative.

Score 0 indicates that extrajudicial killings were practiced frequently in a given year;
1 indicates that extrajudicial killings were practiced occasionally; and
2 indicates that such killings did not occur in a given year.

Pro's 195 countries; annually since 1981

Con's —

Torture
by CIRI Human Rights Data Project

Description Purposeful inflicting of extreme pain, whether mental or physical, by government officials or by private individuals at the instigation of government officials. Torture includes the use of physical and other force by police and prison guards that is cruel, inhuman, or degrading. This also includes deaths in custody due to negligence by government officials.

Source The primary source of information about human rights practices is obtained from a careful reading of the annual United States Department of State's Country Reports on Human Rights Practices. In addition, coders of this index also use a second source, Amnesty International's Annual Report. If there are discrepancies between the two sources, coders are instructed to treat the Amnesty International evaluation as authoritative.

Score 0 indicates that torture was practiced frequently in a given year;
    1 indicates that torture was practiced occasionally; and
    2 indicates that such torture did not occur in a given year.

Pro's 195 countries; annually since 1981. For 33 of these countries, added in December 2004, data only exist for 2001 and 2003 and beyond.

Con's —

Political imprisonment
by CIRI Human Rights Data Project

Description The incarceration of people by government officials because of: their speech; their non-violent opposition to government policies or leaders; their religious beliefs; their non-violent religious practices including proselytizing; or their membership in a group, including an ethnic or racial group.

Source The primary source of information about human rights practices is obtained from a careful reading of the annual United States Department of State's Country Reports on Human Rights Practices. In addition, coders of this index also use a second source, Amnesty International's Annual Report. If there are discrepancies between the two sources, coders are instructed to treat the Amnesty International evaluation as authoritative.

Score 0 indicates that political imprisonment was practiced frequently in a given year;
    1 indicates that political imprisonment was practiced occasionally; and
    2 indicates that such imprisonment did not occur in a given year.

Pro's 195 countries; annually since 1981

Con's —

Disappearance
by CIRI Human Rights Data Project

Description Cases in which people have disappeared, political motivation appears likely, and the victims have not been found. Knowledge of the whereabouts of the disappeared is, by definition, not public knowledge. However, while there is typically no way of knowing where victims are, it is typically known by whom they were taken and under what circumstances.

Source The primary source of information about human rights practices is obtained from a careful reading of the annual United States Department of State's Country Reports on Human Rights Practices. In addition, coders of this index also use a second source, Amnesty International's Annual Report. If there are discrepancies between the two sources, coders are instructed to treat the Amnesty International evaluation as authoritative.

Score 0 indicates that disappearances have occurred frequently in a given year;
     1 indicates that disappearances occasionally occurred; and
     2 indicates that disappearances did not occur in a given year.

Pro's 195 countries; annually since 1981

Con's —

Battle-related deaths

by Uppsala Conflict Data Program

Description Counted as battle-related deaths is armed conflict behavior between warring parties in a conflict dyad, be it state-based or non-state-based. In state-based conflicts the violence must be directly related to the incompatibility, i.e., carried out with the purpose of realizing the goal of the incompatibility and result in deaths. In non-state-based conflicts the violence does not have to be related to an incompatibility (since incompatibilities are not used in such conflicts), but has to take place between warring parties and result in deaths. Typically, battle-related deaths occur in what can be described as "normal" warfare involving the armed forces of the warring parties. This includes traditional battlefield fighting, guerrilla activities (e.g., hit-and-run attacks or ambushes) and all kinds of bombardments of military units, cities and villages, etc. The targets are usually the military itself and its installations, or state institutions and state representatives, but there is often substantial collateral damage in the form of civilians killed in crossfire, indiscriminate bombings, etc. All deaths—military as well as civilian—incurred in such situations, are counted as battle-related deaths.

Source The general rule for counting battle-related deaths is moderation. All battle-related deaths are based on each coder's analysis of the particular conflict. Each battle-related death has to be verified in one way or another. All figures are disaggregated as much as possible. All figures that are not trustworthy are disregarded as much as possible in the coding process. Sometimes there are situations when there is lack of information on disaggregated battle-related deaths. When this occurs, the coder may rely on sources that provide already calculated figures either for particular incidents, or for the total number of deaths in the conflict. The UCDP incorporates such death figures for particular incidents and for an entire armed conflict if they are coherent with the definition. If they are not, or if there is no independent verification of the figure, it cannot be accepted.

Score Number of battle-related deaths.

Pro's 195 countries; annually since 1989.

Con's —

Level of organized conflict (internal)
by Economist Intelligence Unit

Description Qualitative assessment of the intensity of conflicts within the country.

Score Ranked 1 to 5 (very low to very high) by EIU analysts.

Pro's 149 countries; annually since 2004.

Con's Access to the EIU is expensive. Hence, we used data provided by the Global Peace index, a project of the Institute for Economics and Peace, which does not specify the EIU's sources.

Female genital mutilation
by OECD

Description Measurement of the percentage of women who have undergone female genital mutilation.

Source Social Institutions and Gender Index (SIGI) country notes.

Score Prevalence of female genital mutilation (values are between 0 and 1), where

0 indicates none

1 indicates all

Pro's 122 countries

Con's no OECD country

Son preference
by OECD

Description The coding of countries regarding gender bias in mortality or "missing women."

Source The coding was done based on the following information: 1) Existing precise estimates of gender bias in mortality for a sample of countries (e.g., Klasen and Wink, 2003) and 2) examination of the sex ratios of young people and adults; if these sex ratios were abnormally high given the state of overall mortality (i.e., differences could not be explained by biological and/or socioeconomic factors such as sex-biased international migration), the score reflects the excess masculinity in these two age groups.

Score   Scale 0, 0.25, 0.5, 0.75, and 1 where
  0 indicates that missing women is no problem at all
  1 indicates a severe incidence of excess female mortality or missing women

Pro's   122 countries.

Con's   no OECD country.

Homicide
by UN Office on Drugs and Crime

Description   Intentional homicide is defined as unlawful death purposefully inflicted on a person by another person.

Source   National police statistics.

Score   Count and rate per 100,000 population

Pro's   207 countries; annually since 2003.

Con's   —

Human trafficking
by UN Office on Drugs and Crime

Description   Measurement of the recruitment; transportation; transfer; harboring or receipt of persons; by means of threat or use of force or other forms of coercion; of abduction; of fraud; of deception; of abuse of power or position of vulnerability or of giving or receiving payments or benefits to achieve the consent of a person having control over another person; for the purpose of exploitation. Reference may be made to the provisions of the Protocol to prevent, suppress, and punish trafficking in persons; supplementing the United Nations Convention against Transnational Organized Crime. Data on smuggling of migrants should be excluded.

Score   Police-recorded offences (count and rate per 100,000 population).

Source   United Nations Survey of Crime Trends and Operations of Criminal Justice Systems (UN-CTS).

Pro's   Annually since 2003.

Con's   67 countries

Sexual violence
by UN Office on Drugs and Crime

Description Sexual intercourse without valid consent.

Source United Nations Survey of Crime Trends and Operations of Criminal Justice Systems (UN-CTS).

Score Police-recorded offences (count and rate per 100,000 population).

Pro's 104 countries; annually since 2003.

Con's —

Assault
by UN Office on Drugs and Crime

Description Measurement of physical attack against the body of another person resulting in serious bodily injury; excludes indecent/sexual assault, threats, and slapping or punching. "Assault" leading to death should also be excluded.

Source United Nations Survey of Crime Trends and Operations of Criminal Justice Systems (UN-CTS).

Score Police-recorded offences (count and rate per 100,000 population).

Pro's 103 countries; annually since 2003.

Con's —

Level of perceived criminality in society
by Economist Intelligence Unit

Description Qualitative assessment of perceived criminality.

Score Ranked 1 to 5 (very low to very high) by the Economist Intelligence Unit's Country Analysis team.

> 1 indicates "very low": The majority of other citizens can be trusted; very low levels of domestic security.
> 2 indicates "low": An overall positive climate of trust with other citizens.
> 3 indicates "moderate": Reasonable degree of trust in other citizens.
> 4 indicates "high": High levels of distrust in other citizens; high levels of domestic security.
> 5 indicates "very high": Very high levels of distrust in other citizens; people are extremely cautious in their dealings with others. There are a large number of gated communities, high prevalence of security guards.

Pro's 149 countries; annually since 2004.

Con's Access to the EIU is expensive. Hence, we used data provided by the Global Peace index, a project of the Institute for Economics and Peace, which does not specify the EIU's sources.

Theft
by UN Office on Drugs and Crime

Description Measurement of depriving a person or organization of property without force with the intent to keep it. "Theft" excludes burglary, housebreaking, robbery, and theft of a motor vehicle, which are recorded separately.

Source United Nations Survey of Crime Trends and Operations of Criminal Justice Systems (UN-CTS).

Score Police-recorded offences (count and rate per 100,000 population).

Pro's 104 countries; annually since 2003.

Con's —

Burglary
by UN Office on Drugs and Crime

Description Gaining unauthorized access to a part of a building, dwelling, or other premise, including by use of force, with the intent to steal goods (breaking and entering). "Burglary" should include, where possible, theft from a house, apartment, or other dwelling place; from a factory, shop, or office; from a military establishment; or by using false keys. It should exclude theft from a car, a container, a vending machine, a parking meter, or from a fenced meadow or compound.

Source United Nations Survey of Crime Trends and Operations of Criminal Justice Systems (UN-CTS).

Score Police-recorded offences (count and rate per 100,000 population).

Pro's 92 countries; annually since 2003.

Con's —

Inheritance
by OECD

Description Measurement based on the legal code available and divided into two indicators: 1) inheritance rights of spouses, and 2) inheritance rights of daughters. The final scoring of this indicator can also be driven by the actual application of the law (or the lack thereof).

Source Social Institutions and Gender Index (SIGI) country notes.

Score Inheritance practices in favor of male heirs: 0, 0.5, and 1

   0 indicates that women have equal rights of inheritance

   0.5 indicates that (some) women have (some) rights of inheritance, but less than men

   1 indicates that women have no rights of inheritance.

Pro's 122 countries.

Con's no OECD country.

Hostility to foreigners and private property
by Economist Intelligence Unit

Description Measures societies' and governments' attitude to foreigners and their investments.

Score Ranked 0 to 4 (very low to very high) by EIU analysts.

Pro's 149 countries; annually since 2004.

Con's Access to the EIU is expensive. Hence, we used data provided by the Global Peace index, a project of the Institute for Economics and Peace, which does not specify the EIU's sources.

Movement

Forcibly displaced populations
by US Committee for Refugees and Immigrants

Description Documenting refugees ("SOURCE" - Number of Refugees (x1000) Originating in the Named Country at the end of the Designated Year) and internally displaced persons ("IDP" - Number of Internally Displaced Persons (x 1000) in the Named Country at the end of the Designated Year).

Source *World Refugee Survey* series by the US Committee for Refugees and Immigrants is an annual, cross-national, time-series data: numbers of "source" refugees and internally displaced persons (IDPs). Data on internally displaced persons is now provided separately by the Internal Displacement Monitoring Centre.

Score Number of refugees (SOURCE) and internally displaced persons (IDP).

Pro's 166 countries; annually since 1964.

Con's —

Freedom of foreign movement
by CIRI Human Rights Data Project

Description Citizens' freedom to leave and return to their country.

Source The primary source of information about human rights practices is obtained from a careful reading of the annual United States Department of State's *Country Reports on Human Rights Practices*. [NOTE: This indicator is new for 2007 and will be back-coded for years 1981-2006 as quickly as resources allow.]

Score Ranked 0 to 2

        0 indicates that this freedom was severely restricted

        1 indicates the freedom was somewhat restricted

        2 indicates unrestricted freedom of foreign movement

Pro's 195 countries; annually since 1981

Con's —

Freedom of domestic movement
by CIRI Human Rights Data Project

Description Citizens' freedom to travel within their own country.

Source The primary source of information about human rights practices is obtained from a careful reading of the annual United States Department of State's *Country Reports on Human Rights Practices*. [NOTE: This indicator is new for 2007 and will be back-coded for years 1981-2006 as quickly as resources allow.]

Score Ranked 0 to 2

        0 indicates severely restricted freedom of domestic movement

        1 indicates somewhat restricted freedom of domestic movement

        2 indicates unrestricted freedom of domestic movement

Pro's 195 countries; annually since 1981

Con's —

Women's freedom of movement
by OECD

Description Measurement of the freedom of women to move outside the home. The following elements were considered: freedom to travel; freedom to join a club or association; freedom to do grocery (and other types of) shopping without a male guardian; freedom to see one's family and friends.

Source Social Institutions and Gender Index (SIGI) country notes.

Score Scale 0, 0.5, and 1

0 indicates no restrictions of women's movement outside the home

0.5 indicates (some) women can leave home sometimes, but with restrictions

1 indicates women can never leave home without restrictions (i.e., they need a male companion, etc.)

Pro's 122 countries.

Con's no OECD country.

Expression

Press killings
by The Committee to Protect Journalists

Description Documenting attacks on the press.

Source Each case identified as a violation of press freedom is corroborated by more than one source for factual accuracy, confirmation that the victims were journalists or news organizations, and verification that intimidation was the probable motive. The Committee to Protect Journalists defines journalists as people who cover news or comment on public affairs in print, in photographs, on radio, on television, or online. Writers, editors, publishers, producers, technicians, photographers, camera operators and directors of news organizations are all included.

Score Number of Individuals Killed – Murdered in retribution for, or to prevent, news coverage or commentary. Also includes journalists killed in crossfire or while covering dangerous assignments.

Pro's Coverage of a wide number of countries.

Con's —

Freedom of speech and press
by CIRI Human Rights Data Project

Description The extent to which freedoms of speech, press, or expression are affected by government censorship, including ownership of media outlets. Expression may be in the form of art or music.

Source The primary source of information about human rights practices is obtained from a careful reading of the annual United States Department of State's *Country Reports on Human Rights Practices*.

Score 0, 1, and 2

0 indicates that government censorship and and/or ownership of the media (including radio, TV, Internet, and/or domestic news agencies) is "complete"

1 indicates that there was "some" government censorship and and/
or ownership of the media

2 indicates that there was "no" government censorship and and/
or ownership of the media (including radio, TV, Internet, and/or
domestic news agencies) in a given year

"Some" censorship means the government places some restrictions, yet
does allow limited rights to freedom of speech and the press. "No" censorship means the freedom to speak freely and to print opposing opinions
without the fear of prosecution. It must be noted that "None" in no way
implies absolute freedom, as there exists in all countries some restrictions
on information and/or communication. Even in democracies there are
restrictions placed on freedoms of speech and the press if these rights
infringe on the rights of others or in any way endangers the welfare of
others. Finally, in practice, if the government owns all of any one aspect
of the media, such as all radio stations or all television stations, then that
country receives a 0.

Pro's 195 countries; annually since 1981

Con's —

Laws and regulations that influence media content
by Freedom House

Description Survey of media independence. The index assesses the degree of print,
broadcast, and internet freedom in every country in the world, analyzing the events of each calendar year.

Source Twenty-three methodology questions divided into three subcategories.
The legal environment category of "freedom of the press" encompasses
an examination of both the laws and regulations that could influence
media content and the government's inclination to use these laws and
legal institutions to restrict the media's ability to operate. We assess the
positive impact of legal and constitutional guarantees for freedom of
expression; the potentially negative aspects of security legislation, the
penal code, and other criminal statutes; penalties for libel and defama-
tion; the existence of and ability to use freedom of information legislation; the independence of the judiciary and of official media regulatory
bodies; registration requirements for both media outlets and journalists; and the ability of journalists' groups to operate freely.

Checklist of Methodology Questions for 2010

1. Does the constitution or do other basic laws contain provisions
designed to protect freedom of the press and expression, and are they
enforced? (0–6 points)

2. Do the penal code, security laws, or any other laws restrict reporting, and are journalists punished under these laws? (0–6 points)

3. Are there penalties for libeling officials or the state, and are they enforced? (0–3 points)

4. Is the judiciary independent, and do courts judge cases concerning the media impartially? (0–3 points)

5. Is freedom of information legislation in place, and are journalists able to make use of it? (0–2 points)

6. Can individuals or business entities legally establish and operate private media outlets without undue interference? (0–4 points)

7. Are media regulatory bodies, such as a broadcasting authority or national press or communications council, able to operate freely and independently? (0–2 points)

8. Is there freedom to become a journalist and to practice journalism, and can professional groups freely support journalists' rights and interests? (0–4 points)

Score Countries are given a total score from 0 (best) to 30 (worst). Assigning numerical points allows for comparative analysis among the countries surveyed and facilitates an examination of trends over time. The degree to which each country permits the free flow of news and information determines the classification of its media as "Free," "Partly Free," or "Not Free."

Pro's 195 countries and territories; annually since 1980

Con's —

Political pressures and controls on media content
by Freedom House

Description Survey of media independence. The index assesses the degree of print, broadcast, and internet freedom in every country in the world, analyzing the events of each calendar year.

Source Twenty-three methodology questions divided into three subcategories. Under the political environment of "freedom of the press" category, we evaluate the degree of political control over the content of news media. Issues examined include the editorial independence of both state-owned and privately owned media; access to information and sources; official censorship and self-censorship; the vibrancy of the media and the diversity of news available within each country; the ability of both foreign and local reporters to cover the news freely and without harassment; and the intimidation of journalists by the state or other actors, including arbitrary detention and imprisonment, violent assaults, and other threats.

Checklist of Methodology Questions for 2010

1. To what extent are media outlets' news and information content determined by the government or a particular partisan interest? (0–10 points)
2. Is access to official or unofficial sources generally controlled? (0–2 points)
3. Is there official or unofficial censorship? (0–4 points)
4. Do journalists practice self-censorship? (0–4 points)
5. Do people have access to media coverage that is robust and reflects a diversity of viewpoints? (0–4 points)
6. Are both local and foreign journalists able to cover the news freely? (0–6 points)
7. Are journalists or media outlets subject to extralegal intimidation or physical violence by state authorities or any other actor? (0–10 points)

Score Countries are given a total score from 0 (best) to 40 (worst). Assigning numerical points allows for comparative analysis among the countries surveyed and facilitates an examination of trends over time. The degree to which each country permits the free flow of news and information determines the classification of its media as "Free," "Partly Free," or "Not Free."

Pro's 195 countries and territories; annually since 1980

Con's —

Dress code in public
by OECD

Description "Freedom of dress" measures women's obligation to follow a certain dress code, e.g. to cover a part or the entire body when in public (i.e., voluntary use of a certain dress code is not considered).

Source Social Institutions and Gender Index (SIGI) country notes.

Score Scale 0, 0.5, or 1:

0 indicates that less than 50% of women are obliged to follow a certain dress code

0.5 indicates that more than 50% of women are obliged to follow a certain dress code

1 indicates that all women are obliged to follow a certain dress code, or it is punishable by law not to follow it

Pro's 122 countries.

Con's no OECD country.

Relationships

Freedom of assembly and association
by CIRI Human Rights Data Project

Description   Indicates the extent to which the freedoms of assembly and association with other persons in political parties, trade unions, cultural organizations, or other special-interest groups are subject to actual governmental limitations or restrictions (as opposed to strictly legal protections).

Source   The primary source of information about human rights practices is obtained from a careful reading of the annual United States Department of State's *Country Reports on Human Rights Practices.*

Score   When coding "freedom of assembly and association," the *actual practices* of governments are being coded, not what legal protections exist. For the purposes of coding this variable, it is possible that a citizen or group of citizens (e.g., political party, trade union, minority group, the media as a whole) restrict their own activities *a priori* because of fear of government reprisal for these public activities. Any such reported cases of self-restriction DO count towards government restrictions on freedom of assembly and association. There are many other types of self-restriction, several of which one may encounter in the United States State Department (USSD) reports. These include, but are not limited to, self-restriction in exchange for bribes by public officials and self-restriction as a means to guarantee continued employment (where a self-restricting individual's superiors are not under government orders to engage in this practice). Such cases DO NOT count against the government, as they are self-invoked for reasons not related to government activity.

Score   Scored as 0, 1, or 2:

> 0 indicates severely restricted or denied completely to all citizens
> 1 indicates limited for all citizens or severely restricted or denied for select groups
> 2 indicates virtually unrestricted and freely enjoyed by practically all citizens

> *More detailed explanation of the coding: What a "2" means*
> A country receiving a "2" provides for the freedom of assembly and association of virtually all its citizens. Instances where government respect for these rights is described as "full," "unimpeded," "unrestricted," or likewise, should be coded as a "2." It must be noted that this in no way implies absolute freedom to assemble and associate. Even in the freest democracies there are minor prohibitions or restrictions imposed on these rights, particularly if they credibly

threaten national security, public safety and/or order, or if the exercise of these rights infringes unduly on the rights of others. An example of a minor prohibition in a country receiving a "2" would be the requirement that a permit be obtained for public demonstrations and assemblies. For example, in the United States, permits are required for public demonstrations as groups cannot block traffic. The government can also restrict demonstrations according to time, place, and manner. Organizers of large demonstrations are often required to inform government officials of the time and place of their demonstration and their planned route.

A country should be coded a "2" if the following conditions are met:

a) There is government respect for the rights of peaceful assembly and association for virtually all citizens. Government respect for these rights entails that public meetings, including those of political parties and opposition groups, are generally held unimpeded. Professional, academic, trade, and political associations are also allowed to operate without government interference unless the activities of these associations threaten public safety or public order. Citizens are allowed to freely protest government decisions and actions. Permits to demonstrate are routinely granted to both opponents and supporters of the government.

b) The government uses transparent and non-discriminatory criteria in evaluating requests for permits to associate and/or assemble. That is, the requirements for obtaining a permit or organizing a public gathering or meeting are usually published in an ordinance, statute, or other legally binding document. Citizens are permitted to know of these requirements and these requirements are applied consistently to everyone on a non-discriminatory basis. If the process for approving or denying the registration of an assembly or association is non-transparent, but there are no reports that a government has discriminated unfairly against certain groups or individuals, a government receives a score of "2."

More detailed explanation of the coding: What a "1" means
A government receiving a "1" typically places some restrictions on assembly and association for all citizens, or severely restricts or denies these rights to particular groups. Also, instances where government respect for the right of assembly and association is described as "limited," "restricted," "partial," or likewise, should be coded as a "1." An example of a moderate restriction is the denial of permits to outlawed groups. For instance, the German government generally respects all citizens' rights to free assembly and association, but also routinely bans rallies and marches by neo-Nazi groups and right-wing radical groups. In this instance, Germany would be coded a "1," as some groups are

targeted for prohibition of enjoyment of these rights. Another example of a score of "1" would be government denial of permits to even non-violent political opposition groups or requiring certain groups to go through burdensome registration procedures in order to be allowed to legally exist or gather. Some restrictions may be backed by laws stating vague justifications such as the potential undermining of democratic order or necessity to maintain the integrity of the state.

What a "0" means

A government receiving a "0" routinely denies or severely restricts all citizens' freedom of assembly and association, or restricts this right for a significant number of citizens based on their gender, race, religion, or other criteria. For example, there are countries that legally bar women from participating in public assemblies or from freely associating with other persons in political associations, trade unions, cultural organizations, and other groups. In this instance, a country should receive a "0" because half the population cannot freely exercise their right to freedom of assembly and association. Instances where political associations or political parties are not allowed to exist as a rule, or members of political associations or political parties are banned from exercising their right to assembly and association, should be counted as a severe restriction and coded as a "0." A country should receive a score of "0" in this instance even if civic associations and government-sanctioned political associations are allowed to exist and to assemble and associate. Instances where government respect for the right to assembly and association is described as "severely restricted," "severely curtailed," "significantly limited," "frequently denied," or likewise, should be coded as a "0." Examples of severe restrictions or denials of freedom of assembly and association include:

1 Using official intimidation, harassment, or threats of retaliation to prevent citizens from exercising the right to assembly and association. Examples include arbitrarily arresting, detaining, and imprisoning peaceful demonstrators; using excessive or unnecessary force (severely beating, maiming, or killing demonstrators); firing or threatening to fire supporters of opposition movements from their jobs; intimidating or threatening protestors' family members; and various other retaliatory measures.
2 Prohibiting the right of citizens to join political parties, trade unions, professional associations, human rights organizations, religious associations, and similar types of groups.
3 Prohibiting the existence of political associations or political parties and/or prohibiting members of political associations or political parties from exercising the right to assembly and association.

4 Permitting only government-sanctioned or official party organizations to exist and/or assemble.

5 Compelling citizens to join government-backed organizations or official political parties as a formal requirement for access to influential positions. In some instances, the government stipulates that access to positions of authority in government, academia, the media, and similar institutions are contingent upon citizens' membership in the official party organization.

Pro's   195 countries; annually since 1981
Con's   —

Parental authority
by OECD

Description   Measurement is based on legal and customary practices regarding (1) legal guardianship of a child during a marriage and (2) custody rights over a child after divorce.

Source   Social Institutions and Gender Index (SIGI) country notes.

Score   Both indicators are scored (0, 0.5, or 1) as follows:
    0 indicates equal rights for women and men
    0.5 indicates that (some) women have (some) rights, but less than men
    1 indicates that women have no rights

Pro's   122 countries.
Con's   no OECD country.

Religion—government restriction
by Pew Forum on Religion and Public Life

Description   Assesses the level of restrictions on religious practices or beliefs by government.

Source   Based on 20 questions to assess whether governments, including at the local or provincial level, restrict religious practices or beliefs. The questions are intended to gauge the extent to which governments try to control religious groups or individuals, prohibit conversions from one faith to another, limit preaching and proselytizing, or otherwise hinder religious affiliation by means such as registration requirements and fines. The Pew Forum's staff combed through 16 published sources of information, including reports by the US State Department, the United

Nations, and various nongovernmental organizations, to answer the questions on a country-by-country basis. The questions are:

1. Does the constitution, or law that functions in the place of a constitution (basic law), specifically provide for "freedom of religion," or include language used in Article 18 of the United Nations Universal Declaration of Human Rights?

2. Does the constitution or basic law include stipulations that appear to qualify or substantially contradict the concept of "religious freedom"?

3. Taken together, how do the constitution or basic law and other national laws and policies affect religious freedom?

4. Does any level of government interfere with worship or other religious practices?

5. Is public preaching by religious groups limited by any level of government?

6. Is proselytizing limited by any level of government?

7. Is converting from one religion to another limited by any level of government?

8. Is religious literature or broadcasting limited by any level of government?

9. Are foreign missionaries allowed to operate?

10. Is the wearing of religious symbols, such as head coverings for women and facial hair for men, regulated by law or by any level of government?

11. Was there harassment or intimidation of religious groups by any level of government?

12. Did the national government display hostility involving physical violence toward minority or non-approved religious groups?

13. Were there instances when the national government did not intervene in cases of discrimination or abuses against religious groups?

14. Does the national government have an established organization to regulate or manage religious affairs?

15. Did the national government denounce one or more religious groups by characterizing them as dangerous "cults" or "sects"?

16. Does any level of government formally ban any religious group?

17. Were there instances when the national government attempted to eliminate an entire religious group's presence in the country?

18. Does any level of government ask religious groups to register for any reason, including to be eligible for benefits such as tax exemption?

19. Did any level of government use force toward religious groups that resulted in individuals being killed, physically abused, imprisoned, detained, or displaced from their homes, or having their personal or religious properties damaged or destroyed?

20. Do some religious groups receive government support or favors, such as funding, official recognition or special access?

Score The index is divided into four ranges from very high restrictions to low restrictions:

> Very high (the top 5% of scores) have intensive restrictions on many or all of the 20 measures
>
> High (the next highest 15% of scores) restrictions have intensive restrictions on several of the 20 measures, or more moderate restrictions on many of them
>
> Moderate (the next 20% of scores) have intensive restrictions on a few measures, or more moderate restrictions on several of them
>
> Low (the bottom 60% of scores) generally have moderate restrictions on few or none of the measures

[North Korea Note that the sources clearly indicate that the government of North Korea is among the most repressive in the world with respect to religion as well as other civil liberties. But because North Korean society is effectively closed to outsiders, the sources are unable to provide the kind of specific and timely information that the Pew Forum coded in this quantitative study. Therefore, the report does not include a score for North Korea.]

Pro's The study covers 198 countries and self-administering territories, representing more than 99.5% of the world's population.

Con's This is not an annual index. The first edition of this index was published in 2009, covering two-year period from mid-2006 to mid-2008. The second edition was released in 2011.

Religion—social hostility
by Pew Forum on Religion and Public Life

Description Measuring concrete, hostile actions that effectively hinder the religious activities of the targeted individuals or groups. Restrictions on religion can result not only from the actions of governments, but also from acts of violence and intimidation by private individuals, organizations, or social groups.

Source The Social Hostilities Index is based on 13 questions used to gauge hostilities both between and within religious groups, including mob or sectarian violence, crimes motivated by religious bias, physical conflict over conversions, harassment over attire for religious reasons, and other religion-related intimidation and violence, including terrorism and war. The Pew Forum's staff combed through 16 published sources of information, including reports by the US State Department, the United Nations and various non-governmental organizations, to answer the questions on a country-by-country basis. The questions are:

1. Were there crimes, malicious acts, or violence motivated by religious hatred or bias?
2. Was there mob violence related to religion?
3. Were there acts of sectarian or communal violence between religious groups?
4. Were religion-related terrorist groups active in the country?
5. Was there a religion-related war or armed conflict in the country?
6. Did violence result from tensions between religious groups?
7. Did organized groups use force or coercion in an attempt to dominate public life with their perspective on religion, including preventing some religious groups from operating in the country?
8. Did religious groups themselves attempt to prevent other religious groups from being able to operate?
9. Did individuals or groups use violence or the threat of violence, including so-called honor killings, to try to enforce religious norms?
10. Were individuals assaulted or displaced from their homes in retaliation for religious activities, including preaching and other forms of religious expression that were considered offensive or threatening to the majority faith?
11. Were women harassed for violating religious dress codes?
12. Were there incidents of hostility over proselytizing?
13. Were there incidents of hostility over conversions from one religion to another?

Score   The index is divided into four ranges from very high social hostilities to low social hostilities:

>Very high social hostilities (the top 5% of scores) countries have severe levels of violence and intimidation on many or all of the 13 measures
>
>High social hostilities (the next highest 15% of scores) countries have severe levels of violence and intimidation on some of the 13 measures, or more moderate levels on many of them
>
>Moderate social hostilities (the next 20% of scores) countries have severe levels of violence and intimidation on a few of the 13 measures, or more moderate levels on several of them
>
>Low social hostilities (the bottom 60% of scores) countries generally have moderate levels of violence and intimidation on a few or none of the 13 measures

[North Korea   Note that the sources clearly indicate that the government of North Korea is among the most repressive in the world with respect to religion as well as other civil liberties. But because North Korean society is effectively closed to outsiders, the sources are unable to provide the

kind of specific and timely information that the Pew Forum coded in this quantitative study. Therefore, the report does not include a score for North Korea.]

Pro's The study covers 198 countries and self-administering territories representing more than 99.5% of the world's population.

Con's This is not an annual index. The first edition of this index was published in 2009, covering the two-year period from mid-2006 to mid-2008. The second edition was released in 2011.

Male-to-male relationship
by International Lesbian and Gay Association (ILGA)

Description The extent to which male-to-male sexual relationships are legal.

Source Surveys of participating LGBTI (lesbian, gay, bisexual, trans, and intersex) organizations.

Score "Legal," "Legal in only some areas," and "Not legal."

Pro's 195 countries; annually since 2008

Con's —

Female-to-female relationship
by International Lesbian and Gay Association (ILGA)

Description The extent to which female-to-female sexual relationships are legal.

Source Surveys of participating LGBTI (lesbian, gay, bisexual, trans, and intersex) organizations.

Score "Legal," "Legal in only some areas," and "Not legal."

Pro's 195 countries; annually since 2008

Con's —

Age of consent laws for homosexual couples
by International Lesbian and Gay Association (ILGA)

Description Measures whether age-of-consent laws treat heterosexual and homosexual couples equally.

Source Surveys of participating LGBTI (lesbian, gay, bisexual, trans and intersex) organizations.

Score "Equal for heterosexual and homosexual couples" and "Different for heterosexual and homosexual couples."

Pro's 195 countries; annually since 2008

Con's —

Adoption by homosexual couples

by International Lesbian and Gay Association (ILGA)

Description	Measures whether same-sex couples can adopt children together.
Source	Surveys of participating LGBTI (lesbian, gay, bisexual, trans and intersex) organizations.
Score	"Legal," "Legal in only some areas," and "Not legal."
Pro's	195 countries; annually since 2008
Con's	—

Appendix C: Freedom Index 2008

	1	2	3	4	5	6	7	8	9	10
	New Zealand	Netherlands	Hong Kong	Australia	Canada	Ireland	United States	Denmark	Japan	Estonia
SECURITY & SAFETY	7.7	8.8	9.5	7.5	7.1	8.3	6.8	7.8	8.9	7.9
Extrajudicial Killing	10	10	—	10	5	10	5	10	10	10
Torture	10	10	—	5	5	0	5	10	5	5
Political Imprisonment	10	5	—	10	10	10	10	10	10	10
Disappearance	10	10	—	10	10	10	10	10	10	10
Intensity of the Violent Conflicts	10	10	10	10	10	10	9.9	10	10	10
Level of organised conflict	10	7.5	—	10	10	7.5	10	10	10	10
Female Genital Mutilation	—	—	10	—	—	—	—	—	—	—
Son Preference	—	—	7.5	—	—	—	—	—	—	—
Homicide	9.4	9.6	9.8	9.5	9.3	9.5	8.0	9.6	9.8	7.9
Human Trafficking	10	—	—	10	9.9	—	—	—	9.9	9.3
Sexual Violence	0.9	—	—	—	0.0	—	—	—	9.0	6.1
Assault	9.5	—	—	—	6.5	—	4.6	5.9	9.1	9.8
Level of perceived criminality	7.5	7.5	—	7.5	7.5	7.5	7.5	7.5	7.5	5.0
Theft	0.0	—	—	0.0	2.6	—	0.8	0.0	5.3	2.7
Burglary	0.0	—	—	0.0	3.7	—	2.9	0.0	8.8	—
Inheritance	—	—	10	—	—	—	—	—	—	—
Hostility to foreigners & private property	10	10	—	7.5	10	10	7.5	10	10	7.5
MOVEMENT	10	10	10	10	10	10	10	10	10	10
Forcibly Displaced Populations	10	10	—	10	10	10	10	10	10	10
Freedom of Foreign Movement	10	10	—	10	10	10	10	10	10	10
Freedom of Domestic Movement	10	10	—	10	10	10	10	10	10	10
Women's Freedom of Movement	—	—	10	—	—	—	—	—	—	—
EXPRESSION	9.5	9.4	6.9	9.0	9.2	9.3	9.1	8.4	9.0	9.3
Press—Killings	10	10	—	10	10	10	10	10	10	10
Freedom of Speech	10	10	—	10	10	10	10	5	10	10
Laws & regulations that influence media content	9.3	9.3	6.3	8.0	8.7	8.7	8.3	9.3	9.3	8.7
Political pressures & controls on media content	8.8	8.3	7.5	8.0	8.0	8.5	8.0	9.3	6.8	8.5
Dress code in public	—	—	10	—	—	—	—	—	—	—
RELATIONSHIPS	9.8	9.7	4.7	8.9	8.7	8.3	8.8	9.4	8.9	8.4
Freedom of Assembly and Association	10	10	—	10	10	10	10	10	5	10
Parental Authority	—	—	10	—	—	—	—	—	—	—
Religion—Government Restriction	9.6	9.5	8.7	9.0	8.6	9.0	8.3	7.7	9.6	9.3
Religion—Social Hostility	9.1	8.5	9.4	8.0	8.4	9.2	8.2	7.9	8.6	9.2
Male to Male Relationship	10	10	0	10	10	10	10	10	10	10
Female to Female Relationship	10	10	0	10	10	10	10	10	10	10
Age of Consent for Homosexual Couples	10	10	0	10	—	10	10	10	10	10
Adoption by Homosexuals	—	10	—	5	5	0	5	10	—	0
PERSONAL FREEDOM	9.2	9.5	7.8	8.8	8.7	9.0	8.7	8.9	9.2	8.9
ECONOMIC FREEDOM	8.2	7.5	9.0	7.8	7.9	7.7	7.9	7.7	7.4	7.7
FREEDOM INDEX	8.7	8.5	8.4	8.3	8.3	8.3	8.3	8.3	8.3	8.3

	11	12	13	14	15	16	17	18	19	20	21	22	23	24	25
	Switzerland	Norway	Finland	Austria	Luxembourg	Chile	Iceland	United Kingdom	Slovakia	Costa Rica	El Salvador	Uruguay	Spain	Albania	Portugal
	8.0	7.5	7.1	9.1	6.9	6.1	7.1	6.4	8.7	8.8	6.9	9.2	7.0	8.7	7.8
	10	10	10	10	10	5	10	10	10	10	5	10	10	10	10
	5	5	10	5	10	5	10	5	5	5	0	10	0	5	5
	10	10	5	10	10	5	10	10	10	10	10	10	10	10	10
	10	10	10	10	10	10	10	10	10	10	10	10	10	10	10
	10	10	10	10	10	10	10	10	10	10	10	10	10	10	10
	10	10	10	10	7.5	10	10	10	10	10	7.5	10	7.5	10	10
	—	—	—	—	—	—	—	—	—	10	10	10	—	10	—
	—	—	—	—	—	—	—	—	—	10	10	10	—	5.0	—
	9.7	9.8	9.1	9.8	9.0	8.5	9.9	9.5	9.4	5.5	0.0	7.6	9.6	8.8	9.5
	—	5.0	9.5	—	—	9.3	8.4	9.7	—	—	—	—	0.0	10	8.0
	—	3.1	2.2	—	0.0	2.3	0.0	0.0	—	—	—	—	6.3	9.7	7.0
	7.6	8.6	0.0	—	0.4	0.0	2.2	0.0	9.0	—	—	—	6.7	9.6	3.7
	7.5	7.5	7.5	7.5	7.5	5.0	7.5	5.0	7.5	7.5	5.0	5.0	5.0	5.0	7.5
	3.0	0.0	0.1	—	4.0	7.7	0.3	0.0	8.4	—	—	—	8.6	9.6	5.9
	2.6	5.4	6.5	—	4.2	0.4	1.3	0.0	7.2	—	—	—	6.1	10	5.0
	—	—	—	—	—	—	—	—	—	10	10	10	—	10	—
	10	10	10	10	7.5	7.5	10	10	7.5	7.5	5.0	7.5	7.5	5.0	7.5
	10	10	10	10	10	10	10	10	10	8.8	10	10	10	10	10
	10	10	10	10	—	10	—	10	10	10	10	10	10	10	10
	10	10	10	10	10	10	10	10	10	10	10	10	10	10	10
	10	10	10	10	10	10	10	10	10	5	10	10	10	10	10
	—	—	—	—	—	—	—	—	—	10	10	10	—	10	—
	8.1	9.6	9.6	7.6	9.5	7.2	9.6	7.8	7.7	7.8	8.0	8.5	8.8	7.7	9.3
	10	10	10	10	—	10	—	10	10	10	10	10	10	10	10
	5	10	10	5	10	5	10	5	5	5	10	10	10	10	10
	8.3	9.0	9.3	7.3	9.3	6.7	9.7	8.0	8.0	8.0	6.7	6.7	8.3	4.7	8.7
	9.3	9.3	9.3	8.0	9.3	7.0	9.0	8.3	7.8	8.3	5.5	7.5	6.8	6.0	8.5
	—	—	—	—	—	—	—	—	—	10	10	10	—	10	—
	8.1	9.7	8.3	8.0	8.4	9.7	9.5	9.3	7.9	9.7	9.1	9.8	9.5	7.9	8.4
	10	10	10	10	10	10	10	10	10	10	5	10	10	10	10
	—	—	—	—	—	—	—	—	—	10	10	10	—	5	—
	8.9	8.8	9.2	7.2	9.1	9.1	7.7	7.7	7.1	8.2	9.2	9.4	8.0	8.6	9.3
	8.1	9.2	9.2	8.7	9.9	9.2	8.8	7.5	8.1	9.6	9.7	9.4	8.3	9.7	9.4
	10	10	10	10	10	10	10	10	10	10	10	10	10	10	10
	10	10	10	10	10	10	10	10	10	10	10	10	10	10	10
	10	10	10	10	10	—	10	10	10	10	10	10	10	10	10
	0	10	0	0	0	—	10	10	0	—	—	—	10	0	0
	8.6	9.2	8.8	8.7	8.7	8.2	9.0	8.4	8.6	8.8	8.5	9.4	8.8	8.6	8.9
	8.0	7.3	7.5	7.6	7.5	8.0	7.2	7.8	7.6	7.4	7.6	6.7	7.2	7.4	7.1
	8.3	8.3	8.2	8.1	8.1	8.1	8.1	8.1	8.1	8.1	8.0	8.0	8.0	8.0	8.0

Appendix C: Freedom Index 2008, continued

	26	27	28	29	30	31	32	33	34	35
	Bahamas	Malta	Panama	Sweden	Mauritius	Hungary	Belgium	France	Czech Republic	Germany
SECURITY & SAFETY	6.7	7.8	8.0	6.3	8.1	8.1	6.5	6.8	8.0	6.5
Extrajudicial Killing	5	10	10	10	10	10	10	5	10	5
Torture	5	5	5	5	0	5	5	5	5	10
Political Imprisonment	10	10	10	10	10	10	10	10	10	10
Disappearance	10	10	10	10	10	10	10	10	10	10
Intensity of the Violent Conflicts	10	10	10	10	10	10	10	10	10	10
Level of organised conflict	—	—	10	10	—	7.5	10	7.5	10	10
Female Genital Mutilation	—	—	9.5	—	10	—	—	—	—	—
Son Preference	—	—	10	—	10	—	—	—	—	—
Homicide	0.0	9.6	1.4	9.6	8.3	9.4	9.3	9.4	9.6	9.7
Human Trafficking	—	8.8	—	8.8	6.5	9.5	—	—	8.6	5.4
Sexual Violence	—	7.2	—	0.0	5.4	9.3	2.4	4.5	3.6	0.1
Assault	—	—	—	0.0	9.8	7.5	0.0	3.9	6.5	0.0
Level of perceived criminality	—	—	5.0	7.5	—	5.0	7.5	5.0	10	7.5
Theft	—	1.3	—	0.0	4.8	4.8	1.1	5.7	3.8	0.0
Burglary	—	6.4	—	0.0	8.1	5.7	1.5	5.2	4.8	5.4
Inheritance	—	—	—	—	10	—	—	—	—	—
Hostility to foreigners & private property	—	—	7.5	7.5	—	10	7.5	7.5	10	7.5
MOVEMENT	10	10	10	10	10	10	10	10	10	10
Forcibly Displaced Populations	—	—	10	10	10	10	10	10	10	10
Freedom of Foreign Movement	10	10	10	10	10	10	10	10	10	10
Freedom of Domestic Movement	10	10	10	10	10	10	10	10	10	10
Women's Freedom of Movement	—	—	10	—	10	—	—	—	—	—
EXPRESSION	8.8	9.0	6.2	8.3	7.8	7.8	8.3	8.9	9.2	7.9
Press—Killings	—	—	10	10	10	10	10	10	10	10
Freedom of Speech	10	10	5	5	5	5	5	10	10	5
Laws & regulations that influence media content	9.0	9.0	4.0	9.3	8.0	8.3	9.3	8.0	8.7	8.0
Political pressures & controls on media content	7.5	8.0	5.8	8.8	8.0	7.8	9.0	7.8	8.3	8.5
Dress code in public	—	—	10	—	10	—	—	—	—	—
RELATIONSHIPS	9.7	8.4	9.9	9.7	6.7	7.5	9.3	7.7	7.5	7.7
Freedom of Assembly and Association	10	10	10	10	10	5	10	10	5	5
Parental Authority	—	—	10	—	10	—	—	—	—	—
Religion—Government Restriction	8.9	9.0	9.1	9.0	8.7	9.5	6.2	6.7	8.8	6.7
Religion—Social Hostility	9.6	9.8	10	8.9	8.5	8.1	8.5	6.9	8.7	7.5
Male to Male Relationship	10	10	10	10	0	10	10	10	10	10
Female to Female Relationship	10	10	10	10	10	10	10	10	10	10
Age of Consent for Homosexual Couples	—	10	10	10	—	10	10	10	10	10
Adoption by Homosexuals	—	0	—	10	0	0	10	0	0	5
PERSONAL FREEDOM	8.8	8.8	8.5	8.6	8.1	8.4	8.5	8.4	8.7	8.0
ECONOMIC FREEDOM	7.1	7.1	7.3	7.3	7.6	7.4	7.1	7.2	6.9	7.5
FREEDOM INDEX	7.9	7.9	7.9	7.9	7.9	7.9	7.8	7.8	7.8	7.7

36	37	38	39	40	41	42	43	44	45	46	47	48	49	50
Guatemala	Poland	Peru	Singapore	Italy	Lithuania	Bulgaria	Slovenia	Korea, Rep of	Cyprus	Jamaica	Taiwan	Latvia	Papua New Guinea	Brazil
7.3	8.5	7.5	9.2	8.7	8.2	8.2	8.1	7.3	7.9	6.9	8.2	7.3	6.4	7.2
5	10	5	10	10	10	10	10	10	10	0	10	10	5	0
5	5	5	10	5	5	5	10	5	5	5	10	5	0	0
10	10	10	5	10	10	5	10	0	10	10	10	5	10	10
10	10	5	10	10	10	10	10	10	10	10	10	10	10	10
10	10	9.8	10	10	10	10	10	10	10	10	10	10	10	10
7.5	10	7.5	10	10	10	10	7.5	7.5	7.5	5.0	5.0	7.5	10	10
10	—	9.5	10	—	—	—	—	—	—	10	10	—	10	10
10	—	10	10	—	—	—	—	—	—	10	5.0	—	2.5	10
0.0	9.5	7.9	9.8	9.6	7.0	9.2	9.8	8.8	9.3	0.0	8.6	8.1	4.8	0.9
—	9.2	—	—	—	7.4	6.3	7.8	—	0.0	—	—	3.1	—	—
—	8.8	—	—	—	8.4	8.6	9.2	7.1	—	—	—	7.4	—	—
—	10	—	—	—	9.8	9.2	7.9	6.4	9.6	—	—	8.8	—	—
5.0	5.0	5.0	5.0	3.8	5.0	5.0	7.5	7.5	5.0	5.0	7.5	5.0	2.5	7.5
—	7.8	—	—	—	6.5	7.8	3.8	8.0	9.3	—	—	5.4	—	—
—	6.7	—	—	—	—	—	2.6	9.9	7.0	—	—	8.8	—	—
10	—	10	10	—	—	—	—	—	—	10	5	—	10	10
5.0	7.5	5.0	10	10	7.5	10	7.5	5.0	10	7.5	7.5	7.5	2.5	7.5
10	10	9.9	7.5	10	10	10	10	8.3	6.7	10	8.8	10	10	10
10	10	9.5	10	10	10	10	10	10	0.0	10	10	10	10	10
10	10	10	5	10	10	10	10	5	10	10	5	10	10	10
10	10	10	5	10	10	10	10	10	10	10	10	10	10	10
10	—	10	10	—	—	—	—	—	—	10	10	—	10	10
7.0	7.5	6.4	4.0	7.3	7.9	7.2	7.6	7.3	9.0	8.1	7.7	7.8	8.9	7.8
10	10	10	10	10	10	10	10	10	10	10	10	10	10	10
10	5	5	0	5	5	5	5	5	10	5	5	5	10	10
4.3	7.3	5.0	2.0	6.7	8.3	6.7	8.0	7.0	8.3	9.0	7.7	8.0	8.7	5.0
3.8	7.8	5.5	4.0	7.5	8.3	7.0	7.5	7.0	7.8	8.5	8.3	8.0	6.8	6.0
10	—	10	10	—	—	—	—	—	—	10	10	—	10	10
9.0	8.2	8.3	5.7	8.0	6.7	6.7	8.3	8.1	6.6	7.0	4.9	6.6	6.1	9.2
5	10	10	5	10	0	5	10	0	10	10	5	0	5	10
10	—	10	10	—	—	—	—	—	—	10	10	—	10	10
8.9	9.0	8.0	5.1	7.7	8.1	5.0	9.1	8.4	8.4	9.1	9.5	7.5	9.1	9.3
8.7	8.5	9.7	10	7.9	8.7	7.1	9.0	10	8.1	9.9	10	8.8	8.5	8.9
10	10	0	0	10	10	10	10	10	10	0	0	10	0	10
10	10	10	10	10	10	10	10	10	10	10	0	10	10	10
10	10	10	—	10	10	10	10	10	0	—	0	10	—	10
—	0	—	0	0	0	0	0	—	0	0	—	0	0	5
8.3	8.6	8.0	6.6	8.5	8.2	8.0	8.5	7.7	7.6	8.0	7.4	7.9	7.8	8.5
7.1	6.9	7.4	8.7	6.8	7.0	7.2	6.6	7.3	7.5	7.0	7.6	7.0	6.9	6.2
7.7	7.7	7.7	7.7	7.6	7.6	7.6	7.6	7.5	7.5	7.5	7.5	7.4	7.4	7.3

Appendix C: Freedom Index 2008, continued

	51 Haiti	52 Honduras	53 Nicaragua	54 Paraguay	55 Ghana	56 Argentina	57 Croatia	58 Thailand	59 Guyana	60 Trinidad & Tobago
SECURITY & SAFETY	7.1	6.3	7.5	7.4	6.8	7.5	8.8	6.5	6.4	6.9
Extrajudicial Killing	5	5	5	5	5	5	10	0	5	5
Torture	5	5	5	0	0	5	10	5	5	5
Political Imprisonment	5	5	5	10	10	5	10	5	5	10
Disappearance	10	5	10	10	10	10	10	5	10	10
Intensity of the Violent Conflicts	10	10	10	10	10	10	10	9.8	10	10
Level of organised conflict	7.5	7.5	7.5	7.5	7.5	7.5	10	5.0	10	7.5
Female Genital Mutilation	10	10	10	10	8.0	10	10	10	—	10
Son Preference	10	10	10	10	10	10	10	10	—	7.5
Homicide	7.2	0.0	4.7	5.4	3.7	7.8	9.6	7.9	2.6	0.0
Human Trafficking	—	—	—	—	—	—	9.1	—	—	—
Sexual Violence	—	—	—	—	—	—	7.5	—	—	—
Assault	—	—	—	—	—	—	9.5	—	—	—
Level of perceived criminality	2.5	5.0	5.0	5.0	5.0	5.0	5.0	5.0	2.5	5.0
Theft	—	—	—	—	—	—	7.2	—	—	—
Burglary	—	—	—	—	—	—	6.0	—	—	—
Inheritance	5	10	10	10	5	10	10	10	—	5
Hostility to foreigners & private property	7.5	2.5	7.5	6.3	7.5	5.0	5.0	5.0	7.5	7.5
MOVEMENT	10	10	10	10	10	10	9.7	10	10	10
Forcibly Displaced Populations	9.8	10	10	10	10.0	10	8.8	10	10	10
Freedom of Foreign Movement	10	10	10	10	10	10	10	10	10	10
Freedom of Domestic Movement	10	10	10	10	10	10	10	10	10	10
Women's Freedom of Movement	10	10	10	10	10	10	10	10	—	10
EXPRESSION	6.1	6.1	5.3	5.7	7.5	6.5	5.3	4.3	7.4	7.6
Press—Killings	10	10	10	10	10	10	2.6	8.7	10	10
Freedom of Speech	5	5	0	5	5	5	5	0	5	5
Laws & regulations that influence media content	5.0	5.0	5.3	3.7	7.3	6.3	7.0	4.3	8.0	8.0
Political pressures & controls on media content	4.3	4.5	5.8	4.3	7.5	4.8	6.8	4.0	6.5	7.5
Dress code in public	10	10	10	10	10	10	10	10	—	10
RELATIONSHIPS	8.9	7.6	8.3	8.5	4.9	9.7	7.7	8.4	6.6	5.4
Freedom of Assembly and Association	10	0	0	5	5	10	5	5	10	10
Parental Authority	5	5	10	10	5	10	10	10	—	10
Religion—Government Restriction	8.7	8.9	8.3	8.8	9.1	8.5		6.5	9.3	9.3
Religion—Social Hostility	8.7	9.6	9.4	9.2	5.3	9.1	7.6	7.1	10	8.5
Male to Male Relationship	10	10	10	10	0	10	10	10	0	0
Female to Female Relationship	10	10	10	10	10	10	10	10	10	0
Age of Consent for Homosexual Couples	10	10	10	10	—	10	10	10	—	—
Adoption by Homosexuals	—	—	—	5	0	10	0	—	0	0
PERSONAL FREEDOM	8.0	7.5	7.8	7.9	7.3	8.4	7.9	7.3	7.6	7.5
ECONOMIC FREEDOM	6.7	7.1	6.8	6.6	7.2	6.0	6.5	7.1	6.7	6.8
FREEDOM INDEX	7.3	7.3	7.3	7.3	7.2	7.2	7.2	7.2	7.2	7.1

	61	62	63	64	65	66	67	68	69	70	71	72	73	74	75
	Fiji	Namibia	Belize	Bolivia	Greece	Romania	Philippines	Mexico	South Africa	Madagascar	Botswana	Dominican Rep	Ecuador	Bahrain	Oman
	8.2	6.7	6.7	7.0	6.9	7.4	5.6	5.6	4.2	7.4	7.9	6.9	6.5	6.9	8.5
	5	10	5	5	5	5	0	0	0	5	5	0	5	10	10
	5	5	5	5	0	0	0	0	0	5	5	0	0	5	10
	5	5	10	5	5	10	0	5	0	5	10	10	5	5	5
	10	10	10	10	10	10	5	5	10	10	10	10	10	10	10
	10	10	10	10	10	10	9.5	10	10	10	10	10	10	10	10
	—	7.5	—	5.0	7.5	10	2.5	7.5	2.5	2.5	10	10	5.0	7.5	10
	10	10	—	10	—	—	10	—	10	10	10	10	10	10	—
	10	7.5	—	10	—	—	10	—	10	10	10	10	10	5.0	5.0
	8.9	3.1	0.0	6.4	9.6	9.3	7.8	2.8	0.0	6.8	4.2	0.0	2.7	9.8	9.7
	—	—	—	—	8.2	0.0	—	9.8	—	—	—	—	—	—	—
	—	—	—	—	—	9.0	—	—	—	—	—	—	—	6.8	9.1
	—	—	—	—	—	9.1	—	—	—	—	—	—	—	0.6	8.5
	—	5.0	—	5.0	7.5	5.0	5.0	3.8	2.5	5.0	7.5	5.0	5.0	5.0	10
	—	—	—	—	6.7	9.2	10.0	—	—	—	—	—	—	5.7	9.1
	—	—	—	—	6.0	9.5	—	10	—	—	—	—	—	9.8	—
	10	0	—	10	—	—	10	—	0	10	5	10	10	5	5
	—	7.5	—	2.5	7.5	7.5	2.5	7.5	5.0	10	7.5	7.5	5.0	5.0	7.5
	8.8	10	10	10	10	10	8.6	10	8.8	10	8.8	7.5	10	8.8	8.8
	10	10	—	10	10	10	9.5	10	10	10	10	10	10	10	10
	5	10	10	10	10	10	5	10	10	10	10	5	10	10	10
	10	10	10	10	10	10	10	10	10	10	5	5	10	10	10
	10	10	—	10	—	—	10	—	5	10	10	10	10	5	5
	5.5	7.5	6.7	5.9	7.2	6.7	6.3	6.0	8.7	6.4	5.8	7.0	6.5	3.8	3.7
	10	10	—	6.4	10	10	9.5	9.7	10	10	10	10	10	10	10
	0	5	5	5	5	5	5	5	10	5	0	5	5	0	0
	6.3	7.3	7.3	6.7	7.0	5.7	6.3	5.7	7.7	5.3	7.3	7.7	5.3	2.0	1.7
	5.5	7.5	7.8	5.5	6.8	6.0	4.3	3.8	7.0	5.3	5.8	5.3	5.8	3.3	3.3
	10	10	—	10	—	—	10	—	10	10	10	10	10	5.0	10
	8.2	6.2	6.5	9.0	4.5	6.5	8.6	6.9	7.7	6.1	4.8	8.5	7.2	5.6	2.9
	0	5	10	5	0	5	5	0	0	5	10	0	0	0	5
	10	10	—	10	—	—	10	—	5	0	5	10	10	0	0
	9.5	9.7	8.8	9.0	5.1	5.4	8.7	6.0	9.2	7.9	9.1	9.5	8.7	6.1	5.6
	8.0	8.7	10	9.3	6.2	4.9	6.6	4.9	7.5	9.5	9.7	10	9.3	7.4	9.7
	10	0	0	10	10	10	10	10	10	10	0	10	10	10	0
	10	10	10	10	10	10	10	10	10	10	0	10	10	10	0
	10	—	—	10	0	10	10	10	10	0	—	10	10	—	—
	—	0	0	—	0	0	—	8	10	—	0	—	0	—	0
	7.7	7.6	7.5	8.0	7.1	7.6	7.3	7.1	7.3	7.5	6.8	7.5	7.6	6.3	6.0
	6.6	6.6	6.7	6.2	6.9	6.4	6.8	6.9	6.5	6.3	6.9	6.2	6.0	7.2	7.5
	7.1	7.1	7.1	7.1	7.0	7.0	7.0	7.0	6.9	6.9	6.8	6.8	6.8	6.7	6.7

Appendix C: Freedom Index 2008, continued

	76	77	78	79	80	81	82	83	84	85
	Barbados	Mali	Zambia	Ukraine	Rwanda	Colombia	Jordan	Turkey	Indonesia	Kuwait
SECURITY & SAFETY	7.6	5.6	5.8	7.5	6.3	4.1	6.1	5.4	6.1	7.2
Extrajudicial Killing	10	5	5	5	5	0	5	0	5	10
Torture	5	5	0	0	5	0	0	0	0	5
Political Imprisonment	5	5	5	5	0	0	0	0	0	5
Disappearance	10	10	10	10	10	0	10	10	10	10
Intensity of the Violent Conflicts	10	9.5	10	10	10	9.5	10	9.3	10	10
Level of organised conflict	—	2.5	10	7.5	7.5	2.5	10	1.3	7.5	10
Female Genital Mutilation	—	0.6	10	10	10	10	—	—	9.0	10
Son Preference	—	10	10	10	10	10	5.0	—	10	5.0
Homicide	5.5	6.8	0.0	8.1	3.2	0.0	9.3	8.7	6.8	9.1
Human Trafficking	—	—	—	6.5	—	—	—	9.5	—	—
Sexual Violence	—	—	—	9.4	—	—	—	9.6	—	—
Assault	—	—	—	9.8	—	—	—	5.8	—	—
Level of perceived criminality	—	7.5	5.0	5.0	2.5	2.5	5.0	3.8	5.0	7.5
Theft	—	—	—	9.0	—	—	—	9.3	—	—
Burglary	—	—	—	—	—	—	—	8.5	—	—
Inheritance	—	0	0	10	5	10	5	—	5	5
Hostility to foreigners & private property	—	5.0	5.0	5.0	7.5	5.0	7.5	0.0	5.0	0.0
MOVEMENT	10	8.8	8.8	8.8	8.5	7.8	6.3	7.8	8.7	5.0
Forcibly Displaced Populations	—	10	10	10	9.1	1.3	10	8.5	9.9	10
Freedom of Foreign Movement	10	10	10	5	10	10	0	10	10	0
Freedom of Domestic Movement	10	5	5	10	5	10	10	5	10	5
Women's Freedom of Movement	—	10	10	10	10	10	5	—	5	5
EXPRESSION	7.2	7.4	5.6	6.4	3.4	5.8	4.3	4.6	6.0	4.7
Press—Killings	—	10	10	10	10	10	10	10	10	10
Freedom of Speech	5	5	5	5	0	5	0	0	5	0
Laws & regulations that influence media content	9.0	6.7	3.3	5.3	2.0	5.7	3.0	3.3	4.3	4.0
Political pressures & controls on media content	7.5	7.8	4.0	5.3	1.5	2.5	4.0	5.0	4.5	4.8
Dress code in public	—	10	10	10	10	10	5.0	—	5.0	5.0
RELATIONSHIPS	4.8	7.0	4.0	7.4	6.8	8.6	5.7	5.5	4.2	3.9
Freedom of Assembly and Association	10	0	0	5	5	5	0	0	5	5
Parental Authority	—	0	0	10	5	10	0	—	5	0
Religion—Government Restriction	9.2	9.1	8.2	7.2	7.9	7.8	4.7	3.5	3.0	5.0
Religion—Social Hostility	9.7	9.9	10	7.2	10	7.2	5.6	4.9	2.0	7.2
Male to Male Relationship	0	10	0	10	10	10	10	10	0	0
Female to Female Relationship	0	10	10	10	10	10	10	10	10	10
Age of Consent for Homosexual Couples	—	10	—	10	0	10	10	10	—	—
Adoption by Homosexuals	0	—	0	0	—	—	—	0	—	0
PERSONAL FREEDOM	7.4	7.2	6.1	7.5	6.3	6.6	5.6	5.8	6.2	5.2
ECONOMIC FREEDOM	6.0	6.1	7.3	5.5	6.6	6.2	7.2	6.9	6.5	7.5
FREEDOM INDEX	6.7	6.7	6.7	6.5	6.4	6.4	6.4	6.4	6.4	6.3

86	87	88	89	90	91	92	93	94	95	96	97	98	99	100
United Arab Emir	Benin	Malawi	Russia	Guinea-Bissau	Kenya	India	Morocco	Uganda	Tanzania	Egypt	Nepal	enegal	Malaysia	China
8.1	7.5	6.1	6.4	5.8	5.4	4.5	7.3	6.1	6.1	6.4	5.5	7.2	7.2	5.4
10	10	5	5	5	0	0	10	5	5	5	0	5	5	0
5	0	0	0	5	0	0	0	0	0	0	0	5	5	0
10	10	5	5	5	5	0	0	0	5	0	0	5	0	0
10	10	10	5	10	5	0	10	10	10	5	10	10	10	5
10	10	10	9.7	10	10	9.9	10	9.8	10	10	10	10	10	10
10	—	7.5	5.0	—	2.5	5.0	5.0	5.0	7.5	10	7.5	7.5	10	10
7.0	8.3	8.2	10	5.0	6.0	10	10	9.5	8.5	1.0	10	7.2	—	10
5.0	10	10	10	10	10	2.5	7.5	10	10	5.0	5.0	10	10	0.0
9.7	4.0	0.0	5.5	1.9	2.0	8.6	9.4	0.0	0.2	9.5	8.9	6.5	9.1	9.6
—	—	—	9.8	—	—	—	—	10	—	—	—	—	—	—
—	—	—	8.3	—	9.0	—	8.8	—	—	10	—	—	—	—
—	—	—	—	—	9.4	—	8.0	8.7	—	10	—	—	—	—
7.5	—	5.0	2.5	—	2.5	5.0	7.5	5.0	7.5	7.5	7.5	7.5	7.5	2.5
—	—	—	5.9	—	9.9	—	8.9	9.5	—	9.8	—	—	—	—
—	—	—	—	—	—	—	9.9	9.6	—	9.9	—	—	—	—
5	5	5	10	0	5	5	5	0	5	5	5	5	5	10
7.5	—	7.5	5.0	—	5.0	7.5	6.3	5.0	5.0	5.0	2.5	7.5	7.5	7.5
6.3	7.5	8.7	7.5	10	6.0	7.5	8.8	5.7	8.8	7.5	8.7	8.6	6.3	5.0
10	10	9.9	9.9	10	9.0	10	10	8.0	10	10	9.8	9.5	10	10
0	10	10	10	10	5	5	5	0	10	0	10	5	5	0
10	0	10	0	10	0	10	10	10	5	10	10	10	5	0
5	10	5	10	—	10	5	10	5	10	10	5	10	5	10
4.1	6.0	6.1	3.7	6.1	5.7	6.9	4.1	4.6	6.4	4.5	4.5	6.2	4.1	3.0
10	10	10	9.9	10	10	10	10	10	10	10	10	10	10	10
0	0	5	0	5	5	5	0	0	5	0	0	5	0	0
2.3	6.3	4.3	3.0	5.0	3.0	6.7	2.0	3.3	5.0	3.0	5.0	4.7	2.0	0.7
4.3	7.5	5.0	1.8	4.3	4.8	6.0	4.3	5.0	5.5	5.0	3.0	5.0	4.3	1.3
5.0	10	10	10	10	10	5.0	10	10	10	5.0	10	10	5.0	10
2.2	7.3	5.5	6.2	7.6	3.8	3.7	3.1	3.0	2.7	1.7	6.6	2.8	2.4	6.9
0	5	0	0	5	0	0	0	0	0	0	0	0	0	0
0	0	10	10	0	5	0	10	5	5	5	5	0	5	10
5.9	9.6	9.6	3.6	9.0	6.9	4.6	4.7	7.4	7.1	2.2	6.3	9.5	2.9	2.2
9.6	9.1	8.6	5.8	9.5	4.9	1.3	7.1	8.7	6.8	3.1	5.0	10	8.7	8.3
0	10	0	10	10	0	10	0	0	0	0	10	0	0	10
0	10	10	10	10	10	10	0	0	0	—	10	0	0	10
—	—	—	10	10	—	—	—	—	—	—	10	—	—	10
0	—	0	0	—	0	0	0	0	0	0	—	0	0	5
5.2	7.1	6.6	5.9	7.4	5.2	5.6	5.8	4.9	6.0	5.0	6.3	6.2	5.0	5.1
7.4	5.5	5.9	6.6	4.9	7.0	6.5	6.3	7.2	5.9	6.8	5.4	5.6	6.7	6.4
6.3	6.3	6.3	6.3	6.1	6.1	6.1	6.0	6.0	6.0	5.9	5.9	5.9	5.8	5.8

Appendix C: Freedom Index 2008, continued

	101	102	103	104	105	106	107	108	109	110
	Congo, Rep of	Niger	Sierra Leone	Nigeria	Israel	Togo	Gabon	Cote d'Ivoire	Venezuela	Tunisia
SECURITY & SAFETY	5.5	6.7	6.6	4.4	3.6	6.6	7.0	5.4	5.8	6.2
Extrajudicial Killing	5	5	10	0	5	10	10	5	0	5
Torture	0	5	5	0	0	0	5	0	0	0
Political Imprisonment	5	5	5	0	0	5	5	5	5	0
Disappearance	10	5	10	10	10	10	10	5	10	10
Intensity of the Violent Conflicts	10	9.7	10	10	0.9	10	10	10	10	10
Level of organised conflict	5.0	—	—	5.0	2.5	—	7.5	5.0	10	7.5
Female Genital Mutilation	—	9.8	1.5	8.1	—	8.8	10	5.5	10	10
Son Preference	10	7.5	10	7.5	—	10	10	10	10	7.5
Homicide	0.0	8.5	4.0	5.1	9.2	5.6	4.5	0.0	0.0	9.6
Human Trafficking	—	—	—	—	—	—	—	—	—	—
Sexual Violence	—	—	8.4	—	0.9	—	—	9.5	—	—
Assault	—	—	2.9	—	0.0	—	—	9.0	—	—
Level of perceived criminality	2.5	—	—	0.0	2.5	—	5.0	2.5	2.5	5.0
Theft	—	—	9.2	—	4.5	—	—	—	—	—
Burglary	—	—	9.9	—	3.9	—	—	9.6	—	—
Inheritance	5	5	0	5	—	0	0	5	10	5
Hostility to foreigners & private property	7.5	—	—	2.5	7.5	—	7.5	0.0	2.5	5.0
MOVEMENT	7.3	7.5	6.2	7.5	2.0	6.2	3.8	6.7	8.8	6.3
Forcibly Displaced Populations	9.3	10	9.7	10	6.1	9.9	10	7.0	10	10
Freedom of Foreign Movement	0	5	5	10	0	5	0	10	5	0
Freedom of Domestic Movement	10	5	0	5	0	0	0	0	10	5
Women's Freedom of Movement	10	10	10	5	—	10	5	10	10	10
EXPRESSION	6.3	4.2	5.8	6.2	4.9	5.0	4.1	4.1	3.5	3.4
Press—Killings	10	10	10	10	5.1	10	10	10	10	10
Freedom of Speech	5	0	5	5	0	5	0	0	0	0
Laws & regulations that influence media content	4.3	2.7	4.0	5.3	8.0	2.3	2.0	3.3	1.3	1.0
Political pressures & controls on media content	5.8	4.0	4.3	4.5	6.5	2.8	4.3	3.3	2.8	2.5
Dress code in public	10	10	10	5.0	—	10	10	10	10	10
RELATIONSHIPS	7.7	6.0	5.4	3.6	6.9	4.0	6.9	4.9	7.9	3.1
Freedom of Assembly and Association	10	0	5	0	0	5	10	0	0	0
Parental Authority	5	5	5	10	—	5	0	0	10	10
Religion—Government Restriction	9.4	8.3	9.6	6.2	5.5	8.0	8.6	7.8	6.6	4.7
Religion—Social Hostility	9.7	8.3	8.1	4.0	2.6	10	9.8	6.2	8.6	6.9
Male to Male Relationship	10	10	0	0	10	0	10	10	10	0
Female to Female Relationship	10	10	10	5	10	0	10	10	10	0
Age of Consent for Homosexual Couples	0	0	—	—	10	—	0	0	10	—
Adoption by Homosexuals	—	·	0	0	10	0	—	—	—	0
PERSONAL FREEDOM	6.7	6.1	6.0	5.4	4.4	5.5	5.4	5.3	6.5	4.7
ECONOMIC FREEDOM	4.8	5.3	5.4	5.9	6.9	5.6	5.6	5.7	4.3	6.0
FREEDOM INDEX	5.7	5.7	5.7	5.7	5.6	5.5	5.5	5.5	5.4	5.4

	111	112	113	114	115	116	117	118	119	120	121	122	123
	Bangladesh	Cent. African Rep	Chad	Cameroon	Burundi	Iran	Algeria	Congo, Dem Rep	Syria	Sri Lanka	Pakistan	Burma	Zimbabwe
	5.1	4.9	3.1	5.4	4.3	5.5	6.1	4.2	6.3	4.2	3.5	4.9	3.7
	0	0	0	0	0	0	5	0	0	0	0	0	0
	0	0	0	0	0	0	5	0	0	0	0	0	0
	0	5	5	5	0	0	5	0	0	5	0	0	0
	5	10	5	10	5	0	10	5	5	0	0	0	0
	10	10	3.5	10	7.5	9.8	9.0	9.1	10	0.0	8.1	9.9	10
	5.0	7.5	0.0	5.0	2.5	10	5.0	2.5	5.0	1.3	2.5	2.5	1.3
	10	6.0	6.4	8.0	10	10	10	9.5	10	10	9.5	10	9.5
	5.0	10	10	10	10	7.5	5.0	10	5.0	10	2.5	7.5	10
	8.9	0.0	3.7	2.1	1.3	8.8	9.4	1.3	8.8	8.2	7.1	5.9	4.3
	—	—	—	—	—	—	—	—	—	—	—	—	—
	—	—	—	—	—	—	—	—	9.9	—	—	—	—
	—	—	—	—	—	—	—	—	9.9	—	—	—	1.8
	5.0	0.0	0.0	2.5	2.5	7.5	2.5	2.5	5.0	2.5	5.0	5.0	0.0
	—	—	—	—	—	—	—	—	9.9	—	—	—	6.8
	—	—	—	—	—	—	—	—	10.0	—	—	—	6.2
	5	5	0	5	5	5	5	10	5	5	5	10	5
	7.5	5.0	3.8	7.5	7.5	7.5	2.5	0.0	7.5	8.8	2.5	7.5	0.0
	7.5	4.9	6.9	3.8	7.9	5.0	6.3	4.1	5.7	4.2	4.5	4.4	1.9
	9.8	4.7	7.8	10	6.6	10	10	6.3	7.9	6.9	8.2	7.6	2.5
	5	5	5	0	10	0	5	0	0	0	5	0	0
	10	0	5	0	5	5	5	0	5	0	0	0	0
	5	10	10	5	10	5	5	10	10	10	5	10	5
	5.0	4.5	3.7	4.3	3.9	3.0	4.2	3.4	3.0	3.2	3.8	2.6	3.0
	10	10	10	10	10	10	10	10	10	6.7	9.2	10	10
	5	0	0	0	0	0	0	0	0	0	0	0	0
	2.7	3.7	2.3	3.3	3.0	0.3	2.7	1.7	0.3	3.7	3.3	0.0	0.3
	2.5	4.3	2.5	4.0	2.8	1.5	4.3	2.0	1.8	2.3	2.8	0.3	1.8
	5.0	10	5.0	10	10	0.0	5.0	10	5.0	5.0	5.0	10	10
	1.1	6.5	5.4	3.3	4.7	0.9	1.4	7.1	2.0	1.9	0.7	4.0	4.2
	0	5	0	0	5	0	0	0	0	0	0	0	0
	0	0	0	5	10	0	0	5	5	5	0	10	5
	5.4	7.2	5.9	9.3	9.7	1.5	4.0	8.2	4.8	5.9	3.2	2.1	6.8
	2.3	6.9	6.5	8.5	8.3	4.6	6.0	6.4	4.3	2.7	1.7	6.0	7.8
	0	10	10	0	0	0	0	10	0	0	0	0	0
	0	10	10	0	0	0	0	10	0	0	0	10	10
	—	—	—	—	—	—	—	10	—	—	—	—	—
	0	—	—	0	0	0	0	—	0	0	0	0	0
	4.7	5.2	4.8	4.2	5.2	3.6	4.5	4.7	4.3	3.4	3.1	4.0	3.2
	6.0	5.2	5.3	5.9	4.7	6.1	5.0	4.8	5.1	5.9	5.8	3.5	3.6
	5.3	5.2	5.1	5.0	4.9	4.8	4.8	4.8	4.7	4.6	4.5	3.7	3.4

Appendix D: Freedom and Democracy Indexes, 2008

	Freedom Index	Democracy Index*
Albania	7.98	5.62
Algeria	4.77	3.05
Argentina	7.22	6.24
Australia	8.33	8.87
Austria	8.13	8.34
Bahrain	6.74	3.34
Bangladesh	5.31	5.07
Belgium	7.83	7.85
Benin	6.27	5.96
Bolivia	7.07	5.70
Botswana	6.85	6.98
Brazil	7.35	6.88
Bulgaria	7.60	6.57
Burma	3.72	2.00
Burundi	4.93	4.46
Cameroon	5.03	3.30
Canada	8.33	8.84
Central African Republic	5.18	1.59
Chad	5.07	1.10
Chile	8.12	7.44
China	5.76	3.51
Colombia	6.41	5.98
Congo, Democratic Republic of	4.76	2.27
Congo, Republic of	5.73	2.80
Costa Rica	8.05	7.70
Cote d'Ivoire	5.48	3.13
Croatia	7.20	6.75
Cyprus	7.53	7.35
Czech Republic	7.78	7.88
Denmark	8.30	9.48
Dominican Republic	6.84	5.69
Ecuador	6.80	5.06
Egypt	5.93	3.83
El Salvador	8.04	5.94
Estonia	8.28	7.40
Fiji	7.11	4.41
Finland	8.16	9.13

* Source: I-IV categories from the Economist Intelligence Unit.

	Freedom Index	Democracy Index*
France	7.78	7.81
Gabon	5.54	2.79
Germany	7.75	8.67
Ghana	7.23	5.22
Greece	7.03	7.81
Guatemala	7.73	5.68
Guinea-Bissau	6.15	1.69
Guyana	7.16	5.59
Haiti	7.34	3.63
Honduras	7.31	5.96
Hong-Kong	8.39	4.96
Hungary	7.87	7.02
Iceland	8.10	9.63
India	6.06	7.40
Indonesia	6.36	6.24
Iran	4.83	3.03
Ireland	8.33	8.76
Israel	5.60	8.02
Italy	7.62	7.70
Jamaica	7.48	6.80
Japan	8.28	7.96
Jordan	6.38	3.96
Kenya	6.12	4.75
Korea, Republic of	7.53	7.95
Kuwait	6.35	3.35
Latvia	7.44	6.76
Lithuania	7.61	6.91
Luxembourg	8.12	8.96
Madagascar	6.88	5.64
Malawi	6.27	5.01
Malaysia	5.84	6.41
Mali	6.66	5.87
Malta	7.94	8.06
Mauritius	7.88	7.63
Mexico	7.00	6.27
Morocco	6.04	3.82
Namibia	7.10	6.04
Nepal	5.89	3.66
Netherlands	8.47	9.49
New Zealand	8.73	8.99
Nicaragua	7.30	5.61
Niger	5.71	3.09

	Freedom Index	Democracy Index*
Nigeria	5.68	3.46
Norway	8.26	9.60
Oman	6.74	2.70
Pakistan	4.47	4.32
Panama	7.92	6.98
Papua New Guinea	7.39	6.11
Paraguay	7.27	5.95
Peru	7.68	5.90
Philippines	7.02	5.37
Poland	7.73	6.85
Portugal	7.97	7.71
Romania	7.03	6.69
Russia	6.25	4.36
Rwanda	6.44	3.31
Senegal	5.88	5.24
Sierra Leone	5.68	3.97
Singapore	7.67	5.53
Slovakia	8.07	6.96
Slovenia	7.56	7.75
South Africa	6.94	7.68
Spain	8.00	8.22
Sri Lanka	4.64	6.28
Sweden	7.91	9.85
Switzerland	8.26	9.01
Syria	4.67	2.36
Taiwan	7.48	7.35
Tanzania	5.96	5.28
Thailand	7.17	6.75
Togo	5.54	2.16
Trinidad and Tobago	7.13	7.03
Tunisia	5.36	2.82
Turkey	6.37	5.86
Uganda	6.00	4.60
Ukraine	6.49	6.69
United Arab Emirates	6.31	2.51
United Kingdom	8.08	7.98
United States of America	8.30	8.15
Uruguay	8.03	7.68
Venezuela	5.42	5.20
Zambia	6.66	4.87
Zimbabwe	3.38	2.58
Correlation		0.79

Comments on "An Index of Freedom in the World"

Joshua Hall and Robert Lawson

Although is has taken a number of years and several conferences to reach this point, this latest Index of Freedom in the World (IFW) by Vásquez and Štumberger represents a great job. Unlike the Economic Freedom of the World (EFW) index, that comes primarily from a few obvious (at least now) data sources, Vásquez and Štumberger had to scour the globe for these data sources and evaluate them not only for their internal consistency but for their consistency with their conception of personal freedom. Too many scholars would look at a job like this and see that it is too daunting and go back to running regressions on the same old tired data sets. Vásquez and Štumberger deserve praise for taking this project on and doing it so well. That being said, there are several areas for improvement in this paper.

We think a more complete discussion about the blurry line between economic freedom and civil liberties is warranted. While some issues are clearly one or the other, often in practice there is much overlap. One of Michael Walker's examples has been a prohibitive tariff on newspaper ink, which appears on the surface to be merely an economic restriction, but may have significant implications for freedom of the press (at least in the age before electronic media) as well.

In the discussion about the criteria for selecting variables, we would emphasize one additional issue. The data not only need to be from third-party sources (to ensure replicability and transparency) and cover a large number of countries and time periods, they need to be easily updateable. If a dataset is created as a one-time thing, or is only sporadically updated, it may not be useable in a project like this no matter how conceptually appealing it may be.

People frequently will ask, "Why don't you include [fill in the blank]?" The answer is often that the many great datasets we can imagine simply do not exist, do not cover many countries, cannot be acquired for much of the past, will not be updated regularly, or cannot be easily acquired with our limited time and money. Yet, with all these limitations in mind, we are reminded of Walter Block's admonition some years ago to not let the perfect be the enemy of the good. A good, if imperfect index, can still yield valuable insight.

While their data appendix is very thorough in describing the sources of the data and the pros and cons, it says nothing about how Vásquez and

Štumberger transform each variable into a score on a zero-to-ten scale. It is very hard to evaluate some of these variables without that knowledge. For example, for variables that are numerical in question (see homicide), how they are benchmarked (max and min) in the current year is important not only in determining the initial distribution of countries across the 0-10 spectrum but also in how we evaluate change over time. This is important not only for good feedback but also for transparency, which is a key value of the EFW project and should be of this project as well.

There are a lot of blanks in the "Security and Safety" variable for a large number of countries and so we are worried about coverage. Guyana, for example, has 10 out of 18. The Bahamas has just 7 out of 18! Obviously, complete coverage is impossible, but having countries with fewer than 50 percent of the variables in any one area is problematic. Our suggestion to deal with this is to create a composite variable that either is aggregated from multiple sources, such as "Burglary and Theft," or use one variable to fill in holes in another variable. The idea is to combine several of these data series into one component that captures very well the essence of what you are getting at. Some testing to be sure the variables being combined are sufficiently collinear would be helpful.

Several of the variable titles were too terse for our tastes. For example, the titles "Son Preference," "Inheritance," and "Parental Authority" left us wondering what they meant. In reading the details, all of these variables are okay conceptually (they all deal with equality of gender under the law) though the simple titles were hard to decipher. Each variable title should confer the basic meaning of the variable. So "Equality of Legal Treatment of Daughters and Sons" (or some such) is better than "Son Preference."

There needs to be a discussion in the main text regarding the women's freedom and homosexuality variables to point out that these are not about women or homosexual activity per se, but are instead trying to get at the extent certain groups are discriminated against under the law. Equality before the law is a key component of the classical liberal tradition. By the same token, the freedom to speak, denounce, and even privately discriminate against people is also a part of the classical liberal tradition. An expanded discussion of this nuance would be helpful. The bottom line from the classical liberal tradition is that private inequality of treatment is allowable but the government and legal system, which is based on force, must treat people equally.

We liked the honest internal debate on the issue of capital punishment, but suggest the authors add a similar internal debate about another issue of contention amongst us, namely, the right to bear arms. We have had a vigorous debate about this among the conferees over the years, with most representatives of the Western Hemisphere arguing for the inclusion of such a measure in the index whilst most representatives of the Eastern Hemisphere arguing against inclusion. For the record, we would include a variable measuring the right to bear arms if it was up to us.[1]

Finally, we suggest that a series of statistical robustness checks be conducted. For example, the Freedom House's Civil Liberties index is very well known as a measure of personal liberty. That index fails to live up to some of our methodological standards especially as related to transparency and replicability. Nevertheless, it would be comforting to know that the personal liberties side of the IWF correlated well with the Freedom House measure. Likewise, we are curious about how closely this index correlates with the so-called State of World Liberty index (an amalgam of EFW index, Heritage's index, Freedom House's indexes, etc.)

In the final analysis, we are very pleased with this effort and think it should be quickly revised and published. There is always time to improve the index in subsequent editions, as we have done with the EFW index, but we believe it is time to get this project out into the hands of a wider audience.

---

1   *Editor's note*: Subsequent to these comments, the authors explained that they would still wish to include an indicator on the right to bear arms. They removed an indicator on weapons from an earlier version of their paper only because it proved not to be an accurate measure of the right to bear arms. A standardized measure of such across countries does not appear to exist, but as soon as one is created or discovered the authors intend to include it in their overall index.

Comments on "An Index of Freedom in the World"

Fred McMahon

I congratulate Ian Vásquez and Tanja Štumberger for an excellent proto-index and agree with their general approach and methodology. These comments will focus on some future directions and specific issues. They will not provide solutions but instead suggest areas for further research and study.

Weighting: minorities and women

Weighting is a virtually intractable puzzle in developing many indexes. Here it will likely become even more problematic as the index becomes more finely tuned. For example, "Women's freedom of movement" is one variable in the "Movement" area.

When a variable refers to the population in general, there are no obvious *general a priori* reasons to give one variable a different weight than another, though their may be specific arguments with some variables.

However, when a variable measures one part of the population, there is a clear *a priori* reason *not* to give it an equal weighting with other variables. One might argue, on one hand, that a women's freedoms variable should be half weighted to represent roughly the weight of women in the population. Or perhaps better, one could argue that to the extent the variable directly represents broad freedoms for half the population and/or is a proxy for women's broad freedoms, the variable should be used to downward grade all other variables, since the women's variable indicates that these broad freedoms are not available to the full population.

Here the specific question would concern the overall "Movement" area, but it would also apply to minorities: for example, the "Threat to Foreigners" under the area "Security and Safety" and the various variables for homosexual relationships under the area "Relationship Freedoms."

Here is a numerical example meant only to demonstrate the above, not to suggest the type of weighting used in the example. Let's say the women's variable gives 5 out of 10 for a particular nation. Now, should the weight of this be cut in half? Or alternatively, should the available variables on women's freedoms be taken as a proxy for the overall freedom of women? Say a nation gets an 8 generally, but the variables on women only score an average of 4. In this case, could we assume that while men get an 8, women are likely to get only a 4, so that the nation gets a score of 6?

Proxies

It is highly likely that useful proxies could be found for many difficult areas, a prime example again being women's freedoms.

Two examples: The difference in birth rates between males and females may be a good proxy, at least in some nations, for women's freedom. Differences in literacy rates may also be a good proxy.[1]

Given there are many areas of freedom (for example with minorities) where direct measures will be difficult, further focus on finding good proxies is warranted. Arguably the proto index already uses proxies, for example "Perceived Criminality."

A finer grained matrix

There is every reason to believe that freedoms vary across what could be called spheres (religion, civic, political speech, etc.) and actions (assembly, media, etc.). So, for example, the media may be able to discuss political issues quite freely while political assembly is suppressed. (This was more or less the situation in Egypt under Mubarak.) Or a nation may allow religious assemblies but suppress religious speech. (Again, something like this was the case in Egypt under Mubarak for Copts who could assemble but faced great violence for proselytizing.)

Ultimately, a full index will capture these finely tuned differences in a matrix like the one below.

Country X

		Freedom Actions			
		Speech	*Assembly*	*Press*	*Etc.*
Spheres of Freedom	*Personal*	4.7	3.6	2.1	…
	Political	4	1	4.5	…
	Religious	1	3.5	0.9	…
	Etc.	…	…	…	…

In the above matrix, Country X allows moderately good freedom of speech and press for political issues but suppresses political assemblies. It is fairly liberal on religious assemblies but suppresses freedom of speech and press in discussions of religion.

Building this sort of matrix would require considerably more information that is available today, though proxies may in the end provide further information.

---

1   It may be that in some nations, women have a higher degree of literacy than males. This could actually reflect prejudice against men in the school system or an innate ability, on average, for girls to do better in school. This points to a weakness of using any proxy measure, but does not prove they are unfeasible in general.

Individual variables

Drug access

Restrictions on "recreational" drugs, whether a good or a bad thing, are freedom limiting and should be included in the index. The authors in our discussions agree with this but have been unable to find variables on access/restrictions on recreational drugs.

Relationships

Under "relationships," the freedom to form a homosexual relationship may be over weighted, representing one half of all the variables for this section.

Foreigners

In almost all nations (Gulf states being notable outliers), the percentage of foreigners in a population is quite small, so why does hostility to foreigners get its own variable?[2] Obviously "hostility" towards internal ethnic or religious groups will be much more important in most nations. Perhaps the only motivation for including this variable would be as a proxy that is likely to pick up hostility towards other minorities, otherwise we are picking "foreigners" as a privileged minority. More generally, what does "hostility" mean?

Perceived criminality

Perception of criminality is a poor marker of actual criminality. Perceived criminality has gone up in the United Kingdom, for example, while criminality has declined. Is it, then, rather than a proxy for criminality, actually a proxy for people limiting their actions because of perceived danger?

---

2 The property rights aspect of this variable is presumably picked up in the economic freedom index.

CHAPTER FOUR

Measuring Individual Freedom

Actions and Rights as Indicators of Individual Liberty

Peter Graeff [*]

Introduction—the problem of measuring freedom

The problem with measuring individual freedom begins on the theoretical level. After centuries of debating, theorists still do not agree about what freedom actually is. There are at least two distinct theoretical streams—positive and negative freedom, as discussed later—that claim to provide theoretical foundations for measurement. The measurement problem is becoming more acute as there is also a gap between theory and empirical operationalization, partly because scholars tackling the issue of freedom are mostly interested in theoretical approaches and do not construct their theories or ideas with regard to empirical conditions. Empirical issues also restrict the theory-operationalization fit by the fact that data are not producible for all theoretical ideas. From a measurement perspective, this could be taken as a drawback. In theory, these aspects make theoretical propositions irrefutable.

[*] Peter Graeff is Assistant Professor of Sociology in the Department of Social Sciences, Goethe-University Frankfurt am Main. He obtained a Ph.D. from the University of Bonn. His research interests focus on the analysis of negative and positive social capital and freedom. He is also interested in the methodology of measurement and on statistical methods for the analysis of social science data. He has coedited several books and has published in the discipline's major journals including the *Journal of Mathematical Sociology*, the *European Sociological Review*, and *Quality and Quantity*.

A previous version of this paper was presented to the International Colloquium on Freedom organized by the Friedrich-Naumann Foundation in Potsdam, June 2010. I'm grateful for helpful comments from the conference participants. The comments by Ian Carter, Jim Gwartney, and Bob Lawson have proven particularly valuable in improving the paper.

As opportunities to act freely or restrictions on acting freely unfold, the question remains open as to whether subjective data about freedom opportunities or restrictions can contribute to the measurement of freedom. It seems obvious that replies to interview questions such as, "How free do you feel?" or "Do you think that you are a free person?" produce self-reported issues that might not correlate with recognizable states of freedom outside the interviewee. Likely most authors would prefer to have "objective" (or non-personal) data with which to test their theoretical propositions about freedom as long they do not have to commit themselves to just psychological ideas about subjective liberty. Their notion of freedom is related to an actual restriction or shaping of freedom, not only to a perceived one. Even if it is assumed that the perception of freedom is positively related to actual freedom, a person's assessment of freedom will necessarily rely on other psychic factors.

While it hardly seems possible to measure and test propositions of classical theories about freedom using self-reported data, it is also hardly conceivable that we could fully measure restrictions on or opportunities for individual freedom. Moreover, even if indicators or proxies for restrictions and opportunities would be more suitable for an empirical transfer of theoretical freedom propositions, there are, however, no "objective" indicators that would capture the pure content of freedom but nothing else. Measurement theory in the social sciences would demand exactly this for an optimal measurement process, namely, that the indicator or proxy "… measures what it is supposed to measure" (Bollen, 1989: 184) (validity) with a consistent measurement process (reliability). Measuring social phenomena according to these criteria presupposes that their theoretical conceptualization is well-founded. Otherwise, the measurement process is already hindered on the theoretical level.

Theories of freedom could not only be assessed according their logical consistency, but could also be evaluated in their contribution to measuring freedom. A valid measurement presupposes a clear cut, convincing theoretical approach that provides hints for operationalization. A valid and reliable tool to measure freedom must reveal congruence between the theoretical ideas and their measurement, even if the analyzed construct is rather broad and general. Some factors might spoil the theory-operationalization fit in general. First of all, if freedom is defined in such a broad way that its content is mixed up with non-relevant aspects, the development of a reliable measurement is already hindered on the theoretical level (Neumann and Graeff, 2010). As mentioned before, this is likely to happen if indicators or proxies are used to gauge the degree of freedom, which brings in other content as well. Variables or indicators that are derived from vague theoretical concepts typically come up with inappropriate measurement features and do not work properly in empirical testing. Consider, as an example, that freedom is equated with political conditions such as democratic structures or aspects of wealth (Hanke and Walters, 1997).[1] In this vein, measuring the number of democratic structures in a country could be seen as an attempt to measure political freedom. If indicators of democratic structures are taken as measures of freedom it is no longer possible to empirically separate effects of democracy and effects of freedom from each other. Since the theoretical debate about the notion of freedom was mostly conducted with regard to affairs of the state and the law, it is not unusual in literature to mix up theoretically different things. And because freedom is often considered as a value of great importance for modern societies, theoretical propositions sometimes imply conflicts between values, such as the tradeoff between security and freedom. Take, as a practical example, a situation of national danger brought about by an impending military attack from another state. In such an emergency caused by an outside threat, the government might reduce civil rights in order to improve the national readiness to defend. For sorting out these conflicts between values, normative preferences must be applied. Typically, ideological or political ideas are associated with those and might cause a bias. For the measurement of freedom, the relevance of a political or ideological bias should not be underestimated, as it might suppress relevant content in the measurement process so that necessary information is not taken into account or is misinterpreted. Measurements attempts would then remain incomplete and comparisons with other measurement tools become complicated due to their theoretical differences inherent in their construction (Hanson, 2003). An ideological bias could also lead to an overestimation of the importance or effect of sources that restrict or provide the opportunity to act freely. This problem is closely linked to the well-known fact that freedom is often confused with other positively evaluated things (Carter, 1999: 274).

Even if some of these pitfalls cannot be avoided completely,[2] the measurement of individual freedom must stick to a theoretical foundation, which means that one has to use one of the theoretical approaches

---

1 As both Berlin and Hayek argue, democracy and freedom are not the same thing.

2 Researchers who want to apply a theoretical approach for deriving hypotheses and develop measurement tools must opt for one of the existing theories of freedom. The major theories of freedom largely exclude each other. There is no theoretical criterion that would allow one to prefer one theory or another. Deciding upon one theoretical approach is essentially a matter of preference or opportunity for measurement. Normative assumptions and preferences about values will also enter the analysis, even if the researchers are not interested in ideological or political propositions. This set of assumptions and value preferences should be made explicit in order to avoid confusion about the implications of measurement results.

and derive a valid and reliable measure from it. For this, freedom should not be considered as a value, or as Palmer puts it, "Let us not, then, confuse freedom with ability, capability, knowledge, virtue, or wealth. Let us hold up a standard of freedom, expressed in clear and precise terms…. But as we enjoy the blessings of freedom, let us not confuse those blessings with freedom itself, for on that path we are led to lose both freedom and its blessings" (2008, 16). Depending on the intention of applicability, a measure should also come relatively culture-free. At least, it should fulfill the criterion that it is (potentially) applicable to every society in order to measure freedom (see Jackman, 1985, for the issue of comparability).

Besides these demands, there is also a group of conditions that a measurement tool for freedom should accomplish (see, for example, Carter, 2004; McMahon, 2010). The aim of this paper is provide an overview of a suggestion to construct a measurement index of individual freedom with regard to these conditions. For this, classic and newer theoretical approaches to freedom and their operationalization are briefly described in the first and second sections. The theoretical implications of these approaches are discussed in the next section. For theoretical and empirical reasons, a "negative freedom" approach is chosen for further examination. In contrast to existing measures, actions (and their restrictions) are considered to be the point of departure for constructing an index of individual freedom, which is dealt with in the next section. The second source for the index consists of liberty rights. The implications of this approach are analyzed in the following section, which also provides some reasons why this measurement is a potential improvement on previous ones. The last section presents the conclusion.

Theories of freedom

In scientific literature, two theoretical approaches to freedom, the so-called "positive" and "negative" concepts of freedom, dominate the debates (Berlin, 1969; Carter, 2004; Silier, 2005). Even if both approaches can be taken as a theoretical point of departure, they are inherently incompatible and lead to different (practical) consequences. They also need different ways of being operationalized, as will be explained further on.

Positive freedom (or positive liberty) denotes the possibility of acting itself and refers in its broader sense to the fact that actors can realize their goals. It also involves conditions of granting the opportunity to realize the goals. Therefore, it presupposes the existence or presence of situations in which actors can behave in a self-determined and autonomous manner.

In contrast to the positive understanding of freedom, negative freedom (or negative liberty) refers to the absence of obstructions that hinder actors in realizing their actions. Contrary to positive freedom, this approach does not assume the existence of conditions for providing opportunities for self-realization. Rather, it stresses the point that actors are not hindered in whatever they want to do.

When referring to the "negative" understanding of freedom, scholars plead for restrictions of governmental actions in order to minimize the probabilities of action constraints upon citizens. In contrast to this, adherents of "positive" freedom accept governmental intervention in order to enable people to act according to their own will (given that the people are able to behave in a self-determined way). The different "camps" emphasize different aspects of the freely acting person. Scholars preferring the negative understanding of liberty focus on the degree by which actors or groups face obstruction from external forces (such as a government imposing restrictions); scholars who like the positive understanding of freedom bring more attention to the degree by which actors or groups act autonomously, even if there is a third party that enables them to act.

The biggest theoretical gap between these camps emerges from the assumption that the understanding of negative freedom implies the incapability of a third party (such as the state) of procuring positive freedom. For scholars adhering to the positive liberty camp, the state is able to create conditions for citizens that result in positive liberty, even if there are inherent problems with action rights (Gwartney and Lawson, 2003: 407). If, for instance, all people have the same "positive right" to do something, such as get a medical treatment, then a third party or another person or group that granted this right can be held responsible for procuring it. This is contradictory to the rationale of scholars belonging to the negative freedom camp who say that people or groups are only in charge of their own actions and are not allowed to coerce others (which would mean a violation of their freedom, accordingly). In a strict interpretation of negative freedom, "invasive" rights are therefore considered as not being compatible with the ideas of this concept.

Since both approaches refer to different facets of human life, to obstructing actions or fulfilling self-determination, many attempts have been made in the literature to reconcile these contradicting ideas. MacCallum (1967) made the most prominent effort to do so; he argued that both dimensions of freedom are part of each situation in which freedom is considered. If, for example, one desires to do something, then it is necessary that he or she has the freedom to do it without being obstructed. In this vein, aspects of freedom refer to the absence of prevention measures on the possible actions of a person. However, freedom is only conceivable for people if they have the opportunity to act according to their will, regardless of any obstruction that may get in the way. Therefore, even if the approaches of negative and positive freedom differ substantially in their political and social consequences, their weaknesses can be partly mended in theory, provided they are combined with each other. According to MacCallum, scholars from the two different camps differ from each other to the degree by which they stress the three variables: "actor," "freedom preventing conditions," and "action opportunities."

In the (philosophical) literature that deals with the general distinction between positive and negative freedoms, recent publications and attempts to measure freedom still distinguish between the objective element of (non-) liberties, such as legal restrictions, and cognitive (partly "psychological") elements such as attitudes. However, measurement ideas that refer to positive freedom are usually developed and applied in accordance with Social Choice Theory. Those authors call attention to both MacCallum's integrative view and to postulations by Sen (1988, 1991). This literature deals with axiomatic measures of the availability of choices and seeks to find ranking scores for individual liberties while at the same time making use of measurement issues for negative freedom. Bavetta, for instance, applied MacCallum's triadic concept to situations in which people have freedom of choice and reviewed the literature according the correspondence between conceptions of liberty and their measures. He found that the measures used in the freedom of choice literature consist of many dimensions of liberty (such as availability of choices or autonomy) and suffer from a lack of validity, accordingly. His main criticism is directed toward the measurement of individual freedom: "In each and all cases constraints are defined in terms of unavailability of the relevant opportunities. In the literature, they do not provide independent information about how a measure of freedom of choice should be constructed" (Bavetta, 2004: 47). Adherents of Social Choice Theory focus on a person's capability, which identifies the person's freedom to be useful and create useful things. In doing so, they explicitly refer to value-based underpinnings of liberty that correspond with several positively evaluated states for people (such as well-being) (see Olsaretti, 2005).

For the negative freedom concept, and in contrast to the value-based measurement attempts of positive freedom adherents, the ongoing debate about the issue of whether this concept can be applied in a value-free manner continues to persist. Recently, Dowding and van Hees made an attempt to partly circumvent a value-laden concept of negative freedom by arguing for an intention-based conception that "… reduces the normative problem that a person can increase his own freedom simply by changing his preferences. Moreover, it is less likely to be the case—although it still cannot be precluded—that a person increases the collective freedom by a mere change of preferences. Hence we conclude that the intention based account of negative freedom satisfies the normative criterion in a more satisfactory manner than the 'pure negative accounts' that we have taken as our starting point" (2007: 158). In specific aspects, their

Table 1: Dimensions of freedom

Freedom as	Content	Similar to
Opportunity concept	Availability of opportunities	Negative freedom
Exercise concept	Way people act	Positive freedom
Intention-based concept	Intentions of constraining actors become relevant	Freedom as social relation (Oppenheim, 2004)
Non-intention-based concept	Ignore intentions of constraining actors	Freedom as social relation (Oppenheim, 2004)

ideas counter the arguments made by Carter (2004) and Kramer (2003) (see also Carter and Kramer, 2008; and Dowding and van Hees, 2008). This discussion is not pursued in detail here as it only marginally pertains to methodological or measurement issues but more so to semantic and (philosophically) logical arguments.

However, Dowding and van Hees provided different "dimensions of freedom" (2007: 143) which could be used as a framework in analyzing indices also in accordance with the distinction between positive and negative freedom, even if it is impossible to separate these dimensions in a rigorous way (see table 1).

If freedom is defined within an opportunity concept, attention is given to the availability of opportunities, not to the course of action itself. Usually, there must be some kind of criterion defining options as opportunities and determining their values, too. A working approximation may count relevant opportunities as only those that others do not interfere with. The interpretation of freedom as the absence of common restraints in societies (e.g., legally prohibited actions) also refers to this concept. Opportunity concepts are pertinent to many approaches of negative freedom (Taylor, 1979).

Freedom as an exercise concept, capturing most ideas of positive freedom, touches on the way in which people act. Usually, it is implied that a person's action is not caused by others, suggesting that there is congruence between the person's aims and actions. Obviously, problems with the distinction of opportunity and exercise concepts occur if mental states of a person are identified as inherently unfree (which might happen in situations of addictions).

The second dimension of freedom suggested by Dowding and van Hees (2007) is the distinction between intentions of actors. Others can constrain a person's freedom intentionally or unintentionally. Given that an actor performs an action intentionally and not accidentally, the scope of freedom widens from the person who experiences free and unfree situations to the people who influence these situations. In this sense, a prisoner in a state prison is made unfree intentionally, but a child that has been unintentionally locked in her parents' home is not unfree, even if the child might not be able to leave the house. As Dowding and van Hees put it: "Whatever one's judgment about such cases, bringing in intentions underlying actions—and inactions or omissions—becomes an important element in assessing freedom, though it also makes the assessment messier than conceptions of freedom that ignore intentions" (2007: 146). The mess is partly caused because the theoretical integration of intentions results in regarding the social relationship between actors. Oppenheim (2004) maintains (by referring to theoretical ideas by MacCallum (1967)) that it is hardly possible to measure "social freedom" that is defined as a relationship between actors. Judged by specific parameters, it could be possible to specify the degree to which an actor is free in respect to another person as long as subjective assessment of the persons could be quantified.

Dowding and van Hees (2007) also introduce a third dimension not listed in table 1: the distinction between value-free and value-laden conceptions of freedom. Since all existing freedom indices necessarily bring in value-based assessments, this idea will not be continued here.

Empirical attempts to measure freedom

With reference to the theoretical approaches, freedom has been scrutinized in different areas of human life, particularly in the economic area (economic freedom), the media (press freedom), and the law (civil liberties). There are also some new measures that capture freedom from a seldom analyzed point of view, such as religion or time.

The indices exemplarily presented in table 2 fulfill, at least, the criterion that they are (potentially) applicable to every society in order to measure elements of freedom. The indices were developed, however, with different aims and applied under different empirical circumstances.

The *State of the World Liberty Index* is the broadest of all freedom indices presented here. It provides country scores that are combined from three sources: the Fraser Institute's economic freedom index, Freedom House's assessments of individual freedom (civil liberties and political rights), and the sizes of governments and their taxes. As an overall measure, the *State of the World Liberty Index* is partly realized as an (inverted) opportunity concept in the sense of negative freedom. Given that the state is perceived as the (negative) opposite to citizens, interfering with their freedom (to spend their own money) by imposing taxes and "crowding out" their consumption opportunity in markets (indicated by the size of government), the intentions of this actor are assumed to be negative for citizens. The remaining two sub-components of the index, "economic freedom" and "individual freedom," however, have to be evaluated differently and are discussed in greater detail below.

Table 2: Cross-country indices of freedom

Area	Index	Some topics or sub-indices
Global Index (2006)	State of the World Liberty Index	1. Economic Freedom (Fraser) 2. Individual Freedom (civil liberties, press freedom) 3. Government Size and Tax
Economic Freedom (1970-ongoing)	Economic Freedom of the World (The Fraser Institute)	Area 1: Size of Government: Expenditures, Taxes, and Enterprises Area 2: Legal Structures and Security of Property Rights Area 3: Access to Sound Money Area 4: Freedom to Trade Internationally Area 5: Regulation of Credit, Labor, and Business
Economic Freedom (1995-ongoing)	Index of Economic Freedom (Heritage Foundation)	1. Business freedom 2. Trade freedom 3. Fiscal freedom 4. Government size 5. Monetary freedom 6. Investment freedom 7. Financial freedom 8. Property rights 9. Freedom from corruption 10. Labor freedom
Civil Liberties (1972-ongoing)	Civil Liberty Index (Freedom House)	1. Political rights 2. Civil liberties
Freedom of media (2006-ongoing)	Worldwide Press Freedom Index 2008	
Religious Freedom (2001)	International Religious Freedom Data	Government Regulation of Religion Government Favoritism of Religion Social regulation of Religion
Time (ca. 2005)	Discretionary time (temporal autonomy)	

Economic freedom is a frequently analyzed phenomenon in macro data research. Two broad indices are used the most: one developed by the Fraser Institute (which is also a component in the *State of the World Liberty Index*) and one developed by the Heritage Foundation. The Fraser Institute's economic freedom index is divided into five "areas" that reflect freedom, again regarding the absence of economic restraints. The term "economic freedom" is defined in the classical libertarian sense as presented on the home page of the Fraser Institute's Free the World web site (http://www.freetheworld.com/background.html): "One would like a definition that says that economic freedom is the voluntary allocation of resources subject to as few constraints as possible—other than those imposed by nature, and those imposed by voluntary, non-coercive associations of others." All areas of economic freedom reflect the idea of a negative opportunity concept. But the role of government is not only assumed to be aversive for the citizens. The government also ensures that property rights are secure and that the meeting of business commitments between private parties is guaranteed. The operationalization is, however, only in the negative sense, e.g., it is registered if there is a lack of property rights or flaws in the legal structure.

The authors of the Heritage Foundation's economic freedom index define economic freedom as "… individuals are free to work, produce, consume, and invest in any way they please, and that freedom is both protected by the state and unconstrained by the state" (http://www.heritage.org/research/features/index/faq.cfm). This index is, again, referring to an opportunity concept, still applying an ambivalent intention of state actions. On the conceptual level, the relationship between citizens and the government or state is blurred by such subcomponents as corruption, because corruption sometimes allows citizens to advance their particular interests at the expense of universal ones. In general, one can have reservations about these kinds of composite indices which mix different phenomena in order to measure yet another phenomenon. They typically do not regard the causal links between the variables and are not useful in clarifying the influences between each other.

Freedom House's *Civil Liberty Index* is a composite measure divided into subcomponents of political rights and civil liberties. Political rights pertain to the electoral process and the rights to participate politically. They also refer to the degree of an abuse of administrative positions by corruption. The subcomponents of civil liberties consist of elements like the freedom of expression and beliefs, or the rule of law. The subindices mix exercise and opportunity conceptions because they focus both on the availability of action opportunities and on procedural forms of conduct. The *Civil Liberty Index* is based on surveys that do not explicitly ask who the restraining actor for restrictions of freedom is, rendering this index a non-intentional concept.

Several cross-country indices exist that attempt to measure freedom of the press. Only the *Freedom of Media Index* is presented here, because it is the most influential one and is often used as subcomponent for other composite macro indices (it is also a subcomponent of the *State of the World Liberty Index*). The *Freedom of Media Index* is available in several languages and for several countries. The index is constructed, following a negative opportunity concept with non-intentional features, by summing up (extreme and less extreme) restrictions on journalistic work. It records how often journalists are hindered from doing their work. The survey asks not only about the restraints placed upon journalists by public officials, but also by private citizens, too. Many items deal with state censorship.

The *International Religious Freedom Index* gives information about social and governmental regulations of religious issues (Grim and Finke, 2006). This index consists of three subcomponents that measure governmental or social regulation of religion and how much government favors religion. The authors' aim was to develop an index that reflects specific forms of religious persecution and discrimination. In its construction, the index is non-intentional, focusing on opportunity, not on exercise conceptualization of freedom elements.

The *Index of Temporal Autonomy* tries to view freedom from a different perspective (Goodin et al., 2008). Since time is (different to monetary resources or objects) universal in every society, and because time budgets are comparable across individuals on the same scale, it suggests that in modern societies, temporal autonomy as an indicator of freedom can be measured by the hours people are free to spend as they please. The authors provide "discretionary time" measures for some countries and imply that personal well-being and aggregated welfare are inherently connected to it. Conceptually, these measures are basically non-intentional and refer to the (positive) availability of opportunities, even if, on the measurement level, restrictions come into play.

In sum, there are examples of freedom measurements that apply an opportunity concept and refer to theoretical ideas of negative liberty and to some of the political ideas connected to this concept. Those indices assume that state interventions are more or less negative for citizens if the government does more than necessary in order to create a stable environment for people, firms, and markets. These indices measure the availability of opportunities by counting the restrictions that actions, people, and firms usually face.[3] Only rarely do freedom indices consider

---

3   It is important to distinguish "opportunity" from "freedom," as noted in other words in the previous quotation from Palmer. Here, we are not talking about describing an "opportunity" that otherwise would not be available as a freedom, but rather about an agent blocking an opportunity that is available—the blocking is the restriction on freedom in the negative sense.

elements of positive freedom. In general, the indices presented here do not aim to put both positive and negative ideas of freedom into practice; the *Human Freedom Index* is the only exception. The indices differ in the way they refer to freedom and the degree to which they address contemporary topics such as terrorism (freedom of religion) or issues of gender (time autonomy).

In their methodologies, all indices come up with aggregated country scores that are weighted or averaged. These scores are designed to be comparable across different countries.

Theoretical implications and previous measurement attempts

Despite their political and social ramifications, classical and new approaches to freedom consider individual freedom as the interplay between individual actors and the opportunities or obstacles in their social environment. Both the positive and negative classical theoretical camps make use of the assumption that this social environment is relatively stable and that decisions, aspirations, or capabilities could fit to the opportunities provided by the environment. While this social environment is taken as an encouraging force in the positive freedom approach because the degree of freedom varies with the reinforcements given by third parties (such as the state), it is mostly considered a source for hindering actions in the negative freedom approach because freedom belongs solely to the individual and in no way depends on the support of others.

The role of the state as the factor of greatest general influence on the social environment has been discussed extensively in the literature. Adherents of positive freedom usually consider the state to be a positive factor influencing freedom. Theorists who approve of the idea of negative freedom usually plead for the existence of a small (minimum) state, e.g., a minimal amount of normative regulation. In the special area of economic freedom, Gwartney and Lawson put it this way: "Institutions and policies are consistent with economic freedom when they provide an infrastructure for voluntary exchange, and protect individuals and their property from aggressors seeking to use violence, coercion, and fraud to seize things that do not belong to them" (2003: 408). While this idea might earn merit in economic areas given previous empirical results, it must be scrutinized further in other areas of freedom. Even theorists who adhere to the precepts of the negative freedom camp accept violations of freedom in certain situations, such as when national threats or global crises arise. In a strict sense, they accept interference by a third party that is not compatible with the ideal conditions of negative freedom, as coercion implies the absence of freedom. But in some situations, coercion (e.g., by the state) seems to be justified when other values that are more highly regarded (such as human life) are in jeopardy. Then, "invasive" interventions are considered compatible with negative freedom. Then, the matter of freedom becomes a matter of values.

For the measurement of freedom that refers to more than just economic freedom, those observations imply that a measurement tool for freedom should not contain the idea that the state is a threat to freedom *per se*. The state is only one of many potential parties in the social environment. For operationalization, it would be best to separate and to name these parties (such as the state or social groups) that are able to restrict or reinforce individual freedom. Whether these parties support or restrict certain areas of freedom is ultimately an empirical issue.

So far, the theoretical background and the ramifications of negative and positive freedom approaches have been discussed together. For a specific measurement, though, these approaches cannot be combined because negative freedom does not contain any theoretical contribution about the preferences and aims of individuals that are at the center of positive freedom. The measurement of positive freedom involves assumptions about aims and preferences so that theoretical inconsistencies do not occur. Otherwise, it seems possible that "… a person can increase his own freedom simply by changing his preferences. Moreover, it is less likely to be the case—although it still cannot be precluded—that a person increases the collective freedom by a mere change of preferences" (Dowding and van Hees, 2007: 158).

In the following sections, I will therefore focus on the measurement conditions for negative freedom concepts. By doing this, necessary assumptions about preferences and aims for maintaining theoretical consistency can be avoided. Furthermore, a suitable theory-measurement fit becomes more likely if theoretical propositions clearly indicate which content should be measured and which should not. By choosing a negative freedom approach, several aspects associated with positive freedom can be removed from the agenda, such as possible becomings (such as becoming rich and independent), obstacles for which no agent is responsible (such as external shocks or natural disasters) or indicators of self-realization (see Carter, 2004).

Freedom as an individual feature

What can be learned from both classic approaches to freedom (and the attempts to combine them theoretically) is that freedom is associated in the first degree with real persons only. What might appear as trivial at first sight is actually important for operationalizing and measuring. The classic theories of freedom pick up the assumption that freedom belongs to individuals, not to collective or amorphous entities such as nations or organizations. As such, freedom is linked to the *actions* of individuals which can be observed, assessed, and hindered. In this vein, freedom is neither a personality trait, nor merely a thought, nor a state. Freedom refers to the conducting of actions, committed by individuals.

The implication of measuring freedom is evident: ideally, the measurement of individual freedom starts with actions of people. For negative freedom, the free processing of actions, or the degree of their hindrance, could count as indicative information.[4] Freedom is present as long as actions are not hindered. This concept of freedom becomes explicitly visible if obstacles occur that block opportunities for action. Regarding actions as the basis for measuring freedom is in accordance with Carter's proposition to measure freedom as a "non-specifically valuable quantitative attribute" (2004: 68). The previous attempts to measure freedom that have been presented earlier demonstrate that there is no uniform basis for constructing a freedom index. But without that uniform basis there might be no certain criterion for choosing the ingredients of a tool for measuring freedom.

If individuals act in situations in which they relate to others or in which others relate to them, an action has an effect on the actions of others. Due to this, actions of people (or their hindrance) are typically regulated by other people, communities, or the state. Consider, as an example, drinking alcohol in public. According to Berlin, this action becomes relevant in terms of freedom if restrictions are imposed by others that affect one's liberty to consume alcoholic beverages in public (1969: 121). By their nature, such social regulatory mechanisms (and other laws or norms) exist separately from the specific action itself. In this special example, one might think of a norm or law that prohibits drinking alcohol in the public sphere. Here, a norm might be established to ensure that drinkers do not become role models for children (among other reasons). Children's well-being might be considered to have a higher value than the individual pleasure that comes from consuming alcohol in public.

Even if all actions that affect others can be linked to social values, and even if it is necessary to make assumptions about values if freedom issues are considered, it is questionable whether certain values must be taken as a prerequisite for freedom. Take the idea of property rights as an example. Adherents of negative freedom, economists for example, would assume that the existence of property rights (and their protection) is a necessary condition for the existence (and restriction) of individual freedom. While this assumption earns some merit when it comes to the explanation of the efficiency of economic processes, freedom is equated with other (political) ideas on the theoretical level. The idea of freedom is "moralized" which has theoretical implications (that also affect the measurement

---

4 For positive freedom concepts, capturing positive features would mean that elements of self-determination and the fulfilling of aims must be applied.

of freedom). Carter puts it this way: "By 'moralizing' the notion of freedom—by making the meaning of freedom depend wholly on that of another good—one indeed disposes completely of the need to talk about freedom in any literal sense" (2004: 71).

There is no doubt that theoretical assumptions and assessments always enter the construction of a measurement tool for freedom. But if one is interested in a measure of freedom but not in a measure of a political idea about freedom and some other prerequisites and consequences, the measurement tool should reduce the dependence of other political and ideological assumptions.

On closer inspection, it is obvious that a lot of actions happen in almost every society without restrictions. This is particularly true if these actions refer to the functioning of society, such as in the area of economics or religion. In accordance with the theoretical approaches mentioned above, the measurement of freedoms should focus first and foremost on actions *as they are realizations of freedom.*

In many cases, actions are not available for quantification. The *space* for freedom opportunities (regarding actions) is (theoretically) infinite, while the *experience* of freedom is very real for people, and involves more than the absence of obstacles. For the conceptualization of freedom measures (concerning choices between actions), real world examples correspond to the experience of liberty in people's lives (Rosenbaum, 2000). A theoretical distinction that implies a separation of experiences and constraints artificially cuts a good part of freedom out. If one accepts that freedom is always and necessarily from restraint (McCallum, 1968), action opportunities and restrictive incidents are interrelated. For measurement, this leads to the suggestion that external and internal obstacles erected by responsible agents are a complement of actions. It turns out that we get complementing results when we measure real freedoms in the way an action is conducted, or the way it is constrained. Take, for example, the prominent economic freedom category, "starting a business." This action opportunity is usually measured on a scale ranging from "0 days" to "x days." Higher values indicate less freedom.[5] Increasing restraints correspond to less freedom.

Treating of the degree of restraint as a corresponding restriction on possible freedom allows the operationalization of freedom areas that can be summarized to an overall freedom score. By this, overall freedom "... 'generalized comparisons' purely in terms of empirical freedom are meaningful given that overall freedom is an attribute of agents and given that it has non-specific value" (Carter, 1999: 274).

---

5   It is debatable what a general prohibition around starting a business means. If a country does not allow anyone to start a business, the number of days would become infinite.

The indices presented earlier partly consist of quantification of action. Since they list those as one indicator among others, they are not able to separate the actions from other operationalizations of freedom (e.g., rights).

Rights as measurement indicators

Theories of freedom have been primarily developed and discussed in philosophy and political science. In discussions about rights, freedom does play an important role, if only because formal law does not prohibit all actions and leaves some residuum, which includes opportunities to act freely. One might, however, posit that there is necessarily a loss of freedom whenever law is imposed (Brenkert, 1991: 71). In accordance with the arguments made earlier, this point underlines the fact that law is required in situations of social coordination or (potential) conflict. There remains, however, an unregulated public space. If smoking in public is not prohibited, one might feel free to have a cigarette anywhere. One might consider this unregulated social space as a (rightfully claimed) liberty that derives its existence from formal regulations that do not affect this space. There are also rights that provide action opportunities by guaranteeing that no one is allowed to interfere. If some religious practices, such as attending mass on Sunday, are protected by freedom of worship laws, these rights provide the basis for one to act freely.

These scientific roots become evident if one looks at attempts to measure liberty. The actual measurement of liberties that produce indices (such as those coming from Freedom House or the Heritage Foundation) do not rely on the assumption that freedom belongs only to human beings. On the contrary, freedom is only seldom related to actions; it is rather connected to *rights* (Hanke and Walters, 1997: 120). In fact, confusion about the applicability of the terms "freedom" and "rights" exists in the literature. As McMahon puts it: "Humans may have a right to democratic governance, but democratic governance is not a freedom.... However, many such claims are no longer merely labeled as 'rights'; they have been recast as freedoms" (2012: 30). Even on the theoretical level, rights are distinguishable from freedom (Jones, 1994), particularly when it comes to the measurement of freedom (Carter, 2004). In contrast to this, existing rights are often treated as indicators of freedom.

For reasons of measurement, there might be a simple explanation for this: rights are more easily observable than individuals' actions and are, more or less, valid for all citizens. Another reason might be that the field of discussion in which classic theories were developed was related to political matters, that is, freedom was scrutinized particularly in its theoretical implications for people living under certain political conditions, such as democratic or autocratic regimes. Beside this, depicting the content of freedom as rights comes with the interesting feature that rights usually exist and are valid for all citizens in a country. In practice, this assumption might often be violated as rights necessarily need an institution that provides, supports, and maintains them. Rights are similar to norms as they coordinate social action, but differ from them in that their enforceability depends on the actual presence of the providing institution. A state may grant the right to vote, but might not be able to enforce this right in all areas of the country.

Another drawback of rights as indicators of freedom is their potential to interfere with each other. Typically, rights guarantee a person or organization's specific claim. But, for instance, libel laws intended to enable the prosecution of corrupt actors usually interfere with the right of social integrity. One may justify the application of libel laws on the basis of the more highly regarded benefit of curbing corruption, but doing so contradicts other rights that are commonly held in Western societies. Since the assessment of the ordinal order of rights (and norms) is a political and social matter of jurisdictional and public negotiation, rights are sometimes changed quickly as a result of circumstances (Döring, 2009: 32). The temporal stability of rights might be stronger the more basic the rights become. Among all others, human rights can be considered fairly stable, at least in Western nations. This argument is only partly true for matters of freedom, as areas where people freely conduct their social lives typically touch upon facets other than human rights, for instance, upon specific issues of education or communication.

However, the relationship between rights and free actions is a close one, both in theoretical and empirical research. Existing freedom scales (such as the Fraser Institute Index of Economic Freedom) usually confuse rights and actions, that is, treat them as equal sources for scale construction. In situations of social interdependence, rights constitute a social sphere in which action takes place. By this, action presupposes a social environment regulated by rights and norms. For social coordination, rights and norms can be considered as having a supply and a demand, implying that there is an optimum situation in which both meet each other (Coleman, 1990; Walker, 2012). A measurement tool for freedom that refers to actions or their obstacles can take advantage of this information. A freedom measurement consisting of rights necessarily reflects other factors that are not directly related to freedom. Usual aspects of the political system (democratic, autocratic), the quality of the governmental infrastructure, and a country's development level are more or less part of the measurement score. This mix-up implies a high correlation between the freedom scale and variables or indicators that measure political or economic aspects (such as the degree of democracy) and it also implies collinearity in multivariate approaches (Xu and Haizheng, 2008: 183). One may also state that the theory-operationalization link must be weaker compared to the scales dealing with actions because making rights amenable to empirical research comes only at the expense of bringing other aspects in as well. The validity of such a rights measure can be assumed to be lower, accordingly (Neumann and Graeff, 2010).

Methodological implications

Up to this point in the argument, suggestions have been aimed at criteria that allow for the construction of a valid and reliable instrument for measuring negative freedom. Actions and obstacles by responsible agents constitute the core meaning of freedom. Rights augment this meaning insofar as they reflect the social environment that is relevant for liberty.

The different ways the term "freedom" can be defined implies that different concepts are associated with it. Instead of concept, we could also use the term "construct" (Cronbach, 1971). Typically for the social sciences, these constructs are not directly measurable. In the words of Nunnally and Durham: "… words that scientists use to denote constructs, for example, 'anxiety' and 'intelligence,' have no real counterpart in the world of observables; they are only heuristic devices for exploring observables" (1975: 305). If, for instance, the term "freedom" is understood in its negative sense, several items measuring actions or obstacles could operationally define the construct "negative freedom." Freedom is called a "latent construct" or "latent variable" here because it is not directly observed—only its items on the measurement level are observed.

The application of latent variable approaches for measurement happens differently in social sciences, such as sociology or psychology, than in econometrics. While in economic approaches, unobserved component models or dynamic factor models (Lüdkepohl, 2005) predominate, structural equation models or factor analysis (or multidimensional scaling) are most prominent in other social sciences (which do typically make use of cross-unit information but only seldom use cross-time information).

A statistical advantage of the latent variable approach is that it can be used to assess how tenable the assumed theory-operationalization fit is. A prerequisite for a good fit is a close connection between the latent construct and the items by which it is measured (usually this connection is determined by a correlation between items and latent construct). Furthermore, one would expect, for example, that a straightforward construct derived from theory, such as negative freedom, does in fact measure freedom, but no other constructs such as democracy or wealth. Therefore high correlations between other (valid) measures of freedom are desirable and likely (convergent validity). But low correlations between measures of freedom and, for instance, political or economic indicators, are also necessary (divergent validity).

From this methodological point of view, to be useful, the construct of freedom should not be too general, that is, it should avoid including other variables (such as political conditions). If it does so, factor analysis (or its statistical relatives) will reveal that the components of the freedom measure are contributing to the same latent factor.

Keeping a measurement pure from other influences is not an end in itself. If a construct is used in a multivariate analysis (such as a multiple regression analysis) as an explanatory variable, collinearity is inevitable and typical statistical problems such as endogeneity are harder to tackle (Faria and Montesinos, 2009: 103).

Conclusion

The attempt of this contribution is to reduce the gap between theoretical ideas of freedom (in the negative sense) and operationalization. The empirical input is clearly derived from theory, which allows for a distinction between rights and actions/obstacles on the theoretical level. By doing so, it fits with the idea of "consistency" as McMahon proposes: "The measure should choose one definition of freedom and consistently stick to it" (2010: 30).

On the individual and the aggregated (cross-country) levels, most of the previous attempts in the literature to explicitly measure freedom do not consider action (or obstacles as their counterparts) and liberty rights as separate entities. This is hardly surprising, as for many areas of human life in which freedom was measured (such as the media or the law), actions for citizens do not exist. These areas might be important parts of society, but actions can be conducted in such areas only by special persons (such as journalists or lawyers). It is debatable whether such an area should be integrated into a measure of individual freedom. If it becomes part of these measures, it is at the expense of the idea of freedom as an individual feature, which gets lost.

If a measurement index is developed which makes use both of actions (or obstacles) and (corresponding) liberty rights, a measurement tool with regards to individual freedom (of every citizen) is warranted. Some of the previous freedom indices were developed with the ulterior motive of their being useful for policymakers (Hanke and Walters, 1997). There is also an open question as to how well an index of actions and rights would work here. In contrast to other measurement tools, the relative comparison of different areas of actions (or rights) could be an informative feature. Consider a fictional example of a country in which it is possible to enjoy freedom in economic activities but at the same time have communication activities restricted. This difference must be judged as particularly revealing if the rights of neither freedom area are subject to extensive interference. The actual communication restriction might be a result of social suppression, which exists outside of the jurisdictional sphere.

This example clearly shows that before the index is generated, it must be determined which areas of social life are to be integrated into it. If these are found, and actions and obstacles and rights are quantified, it is furthermore possible to determine which of these areas are relevant for explaining, for example, democratic stability or social unrest. Here it becomes evident once again how important it is that the explanatory variables simultaneously measure features of freedom (but not of democracy).[6]

The proposed measurement procedure here rests on a micro-macro link, starting from the individuals on the micro-level, but allowing for increasing aggregate measures for countries or nations as well (Coleman, 1990; Wippler and Lindenberg, 1987). In a certain sense, (aggregated) collective freedom is derived from individual freedom (deHaan and Sturm, 2000: 218). As individual actions and rights remain separate parts of the index, these sources of freedoms are still clearly distinguishable.

---

6 In multivariate regressions, "diluted" indices appear as highly collinear with other explanatory variables. Typically, variance inflation factors become very high which indicates that variables overlap in their explanation of the dependent variable. Usually, test statistics are negatively affected, accordingly.

References

Alchian, A.A. (1965). Some economics of property rights. *Il Politico* 30: 816-829.

Bavetta, Sebastiano (2004). Measuring freedom of choice: An alternative view of the recent literature. *Social Choice Welfare* 22: 29-48.

Berlin, Isaiah (1969). *Four Essays on Liberty*. Oxford University Press.

Boko, Sylvain H. (2002). Institutional reform and economic growth in Africa. *Journal of African Finance and Economic Development* 5(2): 57-76.

Bollen, Kenneth A. (1989). *Structural Equations with Latent Variables*. Wiley.

Brenkert, George G. (1991). *Political Freedom*. Routledge.

Carter, Ian (2004). *A Measure of Freedom*. Oxford University Press.

Carter, Ian, and Matthew H. Kramer (2008). How changes in one's preferences can affect one's freedom (and how they cannot): A reply to Dowding and van Hees. *Economics and Philosophy* 24: 81-96.

Coleman, James (1990). *Foundations of Social Theory*. Harvard University Press.

Cronbach, Lee J. (1971). Test validation. In R.L. Thorndike (ed.), *Educational Measurement* (2nd ed.), (American Council on Education): 443-507.

deHaan, J., and J.E. Sturm (2000). On the relationship between economic freedom and economic growth. *European Journal of Political Economy* 16: 215-241.

Dowding, Keith, and Margin van Hees (2007). Counterfactual success and negative freedom. *Economics and Philosophy* 23: 141-162.

Dowding, Keith, and Martin van Hees (2008). Counterfactual success again: Response to Carter and Kramer *Economics and Philosophy* 24: 97-103.

Döring, Detmar (2009). *Traktat über Freiheit*. Olzog.

Dreier, James (2006). *Contemporary Debates on Moral Theory*. Blackwell.

Faria, Hugo J., and Hugo M. Montesinos (2009). Does economic freedom cause prosperity? An IV approach. *Public Choice* 141: 103-127.

Gwartney, James, and Robert Lawson (2003). The concept and measurement of economic freedom. *European Journal of Political Economy* 19: 405-430.

Goodin, Robert E., James Mahmud Rice, Antti Parpo, and Lina Eriksson (2008). *Discretionary Time: A New Measure of Freedom*. Cambridge University Press.

Grim, Brian J., and Roger Finke (2006). International religion indexes: Government regulation, government favoritism, and social regulation of religion. *Interdisciplinary Journal of Research of Religion* 2(1): 3-40.

Hanke, S., and S. Walters (1997). Economic freedom, prosperity, and equality: A survey. *Cato Journal* 17 (Fall): 117-46.

Hanson, John R. (2003). Proxies in the new political economy: Caveat emptor. *Economic Inquiry* 41: 639-46.

Jackman, Robert W. (1985). Cross-national statistical research and the study of comparative politics. *American Journal of Political Science* 29(1): 161-182.

Jones, Peter (1994). *Rights*. Palgrave Macmillan.

Kramer, Matthew H. (2003). *The Quality of Freedom*. Oxford University Press.

Lutkepohl, H. (2005). *New Introduction to Multiple Time Series Analysis*. Springer.

Mangahas, Mahar (1977). The Philippine social indicators project. *Social Indicators Research* 4: 67-96.

MacCallum, G.C., Jr. (1967). Negative and positive freedom. *Philosophical Review* 76: 312-34.

McMahon, Fred (2012). Human Freedom from Pericles to Measurement. In Fred McMahon (ed.), *Towards a Worldwide Index of Human Freedom* (Fraser Institute): 7-54.

Neumann, Robert, and Peter Graeff (2010). A multitrait-multimethod approach to pinpoint the validity of aggregated governance indicators. *Quality and Quantity*, 44: 849-864.

Nunnally, J.C., and R.L. Durham (1975). Validity, reliability, and special problems of measurement in evaluation research. In E.L. Struening and M. Guttentag (eds.), *Handbook of Evaluation Research* (Vol. 1) (Sage Publications): 289-352.

Olsaretti, Serena (2005). Endorsement and freedom in Amartya Sen's capability approach. *Economics and Philosophy* 21: 89-108.

Oppenheim, Felix E. (2004). Social freedom: Definition, measurability, valuation. *Social Choice and Welfare* 22(1): 175-185.

Palmer, Tom G. (2008). *Freedom Properly Understood*. Occasional Paper 48. Paper presented at the International Colloquium *Global Freedom? The Future of International Governance* (November 9-11). Friedrich Naumann Foundation.

Parsons, Talcott (1953). Some comments on the state of the general theory of action. *American Sociological Review* 18(6): 618-631.

Rosenbaum, Eckehard F. (2000). On measuring freedom. *Journal of Theoretical Politics* 12(2): 205-227.

Sen, Amartya (1988). Freedom of choice: Concept and content. *European Economic Review* 32: 269-294.

Sen, Armatya (1991). Welfare, preference and freedom. *Journal of Econometrics* 50: 15-29.

Sharif, Mohhamed (2003). A behavioral analysis of the subsistence standard of living. *Cambridge Journal of Economics* 27: 191-207.

Silier, Yildiz (2005). *Freedom: Political, Metaphysical, Negative and Positive*. Ashgate.

Taylor, Charles (1979). What's wrong with negative liberty? In Alan Ryan (ed.), *The Idea of Freedom* (Oxford University Press): 175-194.

Veenhoven, Ruut (2004). Happy life years. A measure of gross national happiness. In Karma Ura and Karma Galay (eds.), *Gross National Happiness and Development*. Proceedings of the First International Seminar on Operationalization of Gross National Happiness (Center for Bhutan Studies): 287-318.

Walker, Michael (2012). A Compact Statement of a Cost-based Theory of Rights and Freedom: Implications for Classifying and Measuring Rights. In Fred McMahon (ed.), *Towards a Worldwide Index of Human Freedom* (Fraser Institute): 137-152.

Wippler, Reinhard, and Siegwart Lindenberg (1987). Collective phenoma and rational choice. In Jeffrey C. Alexander, Bernhard Giesen, Richard Münch, and Neil J. Smelser (eds.), *The Micro-Macro Link* (University of California Press): 135-152.

Xu, Zhenhui, and Haizheng Li (2008). Political freedom, economic freedom, and income convergence: Do stages of economic development matter? *Public Choice* 135: 183-205.

CHAPTER FIVE

A Compact Statement of a Cost-based Theory of Rights and Freedom

Implications for Classifying and Measuring Rights

Michael Walker *

This is my third attempt to sort out my own thinking about rights and freedom as part of our project to develop an index of all human rights, both those related to what we call economic activities and the broader range of human activities.[1] In the course of reactions by others to my first two attempts I have been introduced to a veritable smorgasbord of thinking about human nature, evolved norms, the economic foundations of government, and other elements that should be reflected in a theory of rights measurement. This chapter attempts to distill from my earlier papers and reactions to them a compact statement of what I think is our understanding about freedom and rights. It also explores the implications of that understanding for the project to devise an index to comprehensively consider, and measure, human rights.

1 The origins of rights

Paul Rubin's book, *Darwinian Politics,* summarizes a wide body of literature that leads to a coherent view of the nature of man as an evolved social creature. The implication of the literature is that political behavior is bred

---

* Michael Walker is president of the Fraser Institute Foundation and a Senior Fellow of the Fraser Institute. He was the executive director of the Fraser Institute from its inception in 1974 until September 2005 and is the co-founder, with Milton and Rose D. Friedman, of the Economic Freedom of the World project, which is now a collaboration of institutes in 85 countries and produces the annual index published in *Economic Freedom of the World.*

1 The first attempt to create a definition of economic and civil freedom was *Freedom as Behavior toward Uncertainty*, presented at the Friedrich Nauman Foundation Conference on Freedom in Berlin, December 12, 2008 (revised May 27, 2009). The second attempt was *A Theory of Freedom: The Supply of and Demand for Negative Rights*, a paper presented at the Friedrich Naumann Foundation Conference on Freedom, May 10, 2010.

in the bone and is a result of fitness-sorting amongst competing homi-nids in the Pleistocene period of human development. During that phase of evolution, the tribal/community groups were composed of between 50 to 100 individuals; according to Rubin's synopsis, the attitudes, cop-ing mechanisms, and sense of entitlement that modern humans manifest reflect that social structure.

The principal implication of Rubin's theory about how we got to be the way we are is that "human nature" has evolved, and so the departure point of any analysis of rights must be that there is a hard-wired set of prefer-ences that will be expressed in the political structures that emerge. (This is distinct from the notion that every generation is born as barbarians, or as blank slates, which have to be instructed and formed in a particular way to be compatible with effective social living.) As Rubin points out, it is clear that social norms and political conduct emerged in apes before the split that produced chimpanzees and humanoids as separate species because we observe complex political behavior in chimps.[2]

The taste for rights and the sense of justice are part of evolved human nature. The "shoulds" that play a key role in shaping human action are genetically imparted. A child is not born as a blank slate, but rather as an individual with pre-conceived notions of what "should be," and therefore compatible with only a limited range of actual social structures.[3]

As economists, we take tastes as given. The implication of Rubin's book is that the framework of tastes about rights are "given" in a genetic sense and not just presumed to be given as an analytical convenience in presenting complex behavior in three-dimensional spatial models.

Freedom and the exchange model of rights

In the second of my two papers, I started with the premise developed by Fred McMahon and Tom Palmer that freedom was a bundle of rights

---

2 In his 2002 book, *The Blank Slate*, Steven Pinker explores extensively the notion of human nature from the point of view of evolutionary psychology and convincingly synopsizes a vast body of research pointing to the existence of a genetically based human nature.

3 It follows as a corollary of this model that it is possible that evolved tastes might differ somewhat over time as groups are exposed to different environmental challenges. The "shoulds" that prove to have superior fitness in northern climates might well be different from those amenable to moderate climes. While neither Rubin nor the authors he cites seem to suggest this, it difficult to understand why it would not be true.

A particular feature of the pre-hominids who preceded both chimps and humans in the evolutionary chain was that they lived in benign climates, as far as we know. No pre-hominid fossils have yet been discovered outside the tropical zones of climatic variation and chimps, the principal co-existing ape to display complex political behavior, live only in tropical zones. The successful migration of the pre-hominids out of Africa to the rest of the world would sug-gest that perhaps some modification of social norms would have been necessary in the process.

and attempted to work out the implications of that concept for our index-building enterprise. I suggested that we consider rights as part of the basket of things that consumers seek to acquire to maximize their utility, subject to the constraint of the total resources available to them. A key factor leading to this approach is the notion that while the aspiration or inbred preference for certain rights is given, the acquisition of these rights requires the expenditure of resources. As distinct from the *aspiration* to have certain rights, the *acquisition* of rights is not costless.

I therefore proposed that we had to conceive of a rights market in which the demand for rights emerged from a joint maximization process. In this process, rights and other desirable commodities are traded off, reflecting preferences for rights and other things. In turn, the quantity of the different kinds of rights demanded would reflect the total resources available and the "price" of rights.

I did not realize it at the time, but the model I was suggesting was similar in approach to one proposed by Randy Holcombe in his wonderful book, *The Economic Foundations of Government.* There, Holcombe proposes what he calls an "exchange model of rights" in which individuals will have the rights that they can bargain for either individually or collectively (1994: 11-71). As he notes, "There are no implications in this analysis regarding what rights individuals should have. The model considers only what rights individuals would be expected to be able to exercise as result of the bargaining process under various conditions. One might want to draw some normative implications for the type of rights societies should have, but to do so first requires an understanding of the underlying process of social interaction" (Holcombe, 1994: 71).

Holcombe comes to his understanding by considering the model of government and its constraints. I come to my understanding by regarding rights as just another of the features of the good life that individuals would like to have and which they will have to use a portion of their resources to acquire. The rights we observe are the product of this trade-off process of preferences subject to the constraint of limited resources.

Acknowledgment and the supply of rights

The granting process and the production process comprise the supply of rights. The granting process is essentially the political activity that decides who will have what rights, or, to state it more precisely, who can legitimately lay claim to what rights. The articulation of the rights-granting process consumes much of the Holcombe exchange model of rights and is something that, for our purposes, we are going to assume has already occurred. The only thing to note is that the granting of rights process itself is resource intensive and is, like the production of rights, an expensive activity.

A curious feature of rights is that while citizens may aspire to have them, and may expend the resources to acquire them, whether they are successful or not depends on the opinions and actions of their fellow citizens. The demand for rights is individual, but the supply is by its nature collective, since the only rights that any citizen can acquire are determined ultimately by the legal and political system in the jurisdiction in which they live. For example, in common-law jurisdictions, the law—and hence the rights system—is composed of three components: constitution laws, the statutes of government, and the decisions of the court system—especially the highest level of appeal court.

The development of the supply of rights reflects a variety of actions in each of these spheres. Many of the foundational or constitutional aspects of the Common Law countries emerged as a result of the direct effort of citizens to limit the sovereignty of the king. The *Magna Carta* in its various manifestations is one such example and emphasizes the role that private action to assert rights, with all of its attendant costs, has played in the evolution of rights.

The power of such agreements to establish rights has depended on their endorsement and acceptance by Parliaments and Congresses and their being upheld in the decisions of court systems. Each of these reinforcements of the initial rights required both private and public costs to achieve and relied upon the integrity of the system of laws, specifically, the systematic application of known rules in the determination of outcomes. One example of the systematic application of rules is that used by a Congress or Parliament in coming to a decision about whether to support or not to support a particular right—and to what extent.

The ubiquitous aspect of the rights granting process in all the jurisdictions where rights are found is that it is a collective activity. While individuals have an inbred taste for rights, the acquisition of these rights depends in part on the acknowledgement by fellow citizens that the individual is, in fact, entitled to them. While it is possible that this acknowledgement could occur under conditions of dictatorship, casual empiricism suggests that in general, rights acknowledgement occurs in jurisdictions having free political institutions. The exceptions, like Singapore and Hong Kong, are colonial states to which the rights apparatus was imported by the colonial rulers from their already developed systems at home.

The production of the supply of rights

The production function articulates the way in which resources, know-how, and effort are combined to produce goods, services, and, it is suggested here, rights. And there must be a production function. Even in jurisdictions where rights are acknowledged by some process, they still have to be produced—they don't just exist. Consider, for example, the right to personal security and the right to own property. Producing and providing both of those rights has clear resource costs. Furthermore, there are both individual and community costs associated with producing rights, with the relative burden varying with the sort of right considered.

Personal security

Every person wants the right to security of the person, that is, freedom from violence rendered by someone else. While the preference for this security is costless, the acquisition of the right is not. The right to security as distinct from the preference for it requires the actual provision of security and entails policing, a judiciary, and some method for incarcerating or punishing those who violate the right.

While in principle all of these functions could be provided privately subject to subscription, in practice they are almost exclusively provided in a collective process involving control by elected officials. In any event, it does not matter whether this right is effected by government or private providers; it is going to be costly to realize the right to security. [4]

Property rights

In 19th century United States, farmers could, in principle, own very large tracts of land in the mid-western and western states. However, when cattle and other animals foraged for food, it reduced the land's value to the extent that it was only possible to use land that had on it a sufficient number of

---

4   The history of the provision of security is interesting when we propose to construct an index comparing the rights to which citizens of different countries are entitled. The most important element in providing security is to deter people from engaging in violence. Historically, the way society did that was to maintain and enforce penalties sufficiently onerous to overwhelm the cost/benefit calculus of most would-be offenders. The more onerous the penalty compared to any benefit associated with the crime, the lower the incidence of the crime. In Canada during the 19th century, there were 123 crimes for which death was the punishment. They included theft, burglary, rape, homosexuality, bestiality, treason, and, for members of the military, cowardice and desertion. Typically the executions were by hanging and until after the 1870s the body was left hanging in a public place—sometimes covered in tar to protect it from the weather!

When viewed from the perspective of a modern, advanced, Western democracy, the penalties are horrific to contemplate, but they made the maintenance of security much cheaper than it would otherwise have been. In the pursuit of swift and brutal justice, the investigation and prosecution of the criminal often involved what would today be regarded as a miscarriage of justice. The gradual improvement in the administration of justice and the emergence of the notion of perpetrators' rights and the graduation of penalties to reflect the greater probability of apprehension had to await the availability of resources to support such an elaboration of the security apparatus. In many parts of the world today, neither the resources nor that elaboration have yet arrived.

trees to supply the required fencing to protect the crops. The invention of barbed wire in 1868 reduced the cost of fencing, and therefore made feasible the exertion of property rights where none could exist before. (For a history of this development and its implications see, Richard Hornbeck's "Barbed Wire, Property Rights and Agricultural Development .")

These examples illustrate the two different kinds of costs—private and public—involved in the production of rights. The right to security involves both the cost of self-protection (private) and the costs of maintaining the policing and justice system (public). The farmer's rights to his property could not be exerted until the cost of doing so fell to a level corresponding to the value of the rights that would be secured. In most jurisdictions, in addition to the farmer's private cost, there is the added cost of the courts, the land registry, and the police to enforce the property right that has been agreed is owned by the farmer.

In a modern context, that sort of calculus of the costs and benefits of rights is still very much a factor as business owners and householders decide whether it is worth their while to exert their rights. For example, a recording artist may find out that people have been stealing her tracks. They have, in effect, been violating her property rights. Whether she pursues the theft in court will depend on the cost of doing so compared to the money lost to the thief. While it is tempting to say that her rights exist and are being violated by the thieves, there is, in fact, a doctrine of property law in the Common Law that requires people to exert their rights or else lose them! That used to be the case with common trespass. Landowners who failed to make an adequate effort to prevent trespassers from using their land sometimes found that people traversing their land were awarded the right to continue to do so by the courts. (Statute law in many jurisdictions has now superseded this earned right of trespass.)

Even in mature pluralistic societies that have a full compliment of rights, the maintenance of the right to security continues to require private and public costs, as is reflected in the resources spent on policing, the courts, and the prison system, as well as the increasing amounts spent on private security firms, alarm systems, and their monitoring. (Private police forces, which in Canada, for example, outnumber public police by a wide margin, are engaged to protect the property of businesses and households by whom the public police force is found to be inadequate. In such instances, the demand for security rights is more readily observed as a service like any other and it seems less awkward to apply the standard economic model to its provenance.)

The evolution of the stock of rights

It is convenient when thinking about personal rights to imagine them as a stockpile. The aspirations of a country's citizens set the target for the pile's composition. The pile is added to as citizens acquire more rights by expending the resources to get them, and is diminished as rights are lost by a failure to defend them, or because they are eclipsed by the actions of government. The stockpile analogy is useful as we attempt to measure the comparative system of rights development in different countries with differing histories, different capacities for investing in the rights development process, and potentially different targets for their ultimate pile of rights.

The stockpile analogy is directly applicable in a consideration of the rights available to citizens in common law countries where precedent and case law build a stock of rights that are then available to all citizens of countries that rely on the common law. For example, Canada and the United States inherited a stock of ready-made law and court-decided rights that had been developed over the years in Britain, and now all three countries benefit from each other's discovery of legal principles which serve to extend and enrich the stockpile of rights available in all countries in the common law tradition.

The fact that the common law process of building precedents enables countries to learn from other countries means that the costs of establishing and protecting rights are thereby reduced. As noted by Tom Bingham in his masterful synoptic book, *The Rule of Law*, an American author writing in 1991 found that more than 900 federal and state courts in the United States had cited the *Magna Carta*, and in the period between 1940 and 1990, the Supreme Court had done so in more than 60 cases (Bingham, 2011: 13).

There is an interesting aspect to countries governed by the Common Law: when a wealthy person or a business decides to expend the resources to fight the rights-infringing actions of a government or another citizen or corporation, the results of the fight are potentially made available to every citizen of that and every other common law country by way of the precedent established. Thus, while the fact that resources are required to exert rights and cause them to exist means that the wealthy are likely in the first instance to acquire more rights than those without resources, the common law tradition ensures that they are then made immediately available to all at a much lower cost because of the tradition of precedent. It is less clear that this process works as well in Roman or Continental legal systems, but this is more in the nature of a question than an assertion.[5]

---

5   It may be that it is this feature of the common law compared to Roman law that explains some of the differential success of the colonies of continental European countries and the colonies of Britain. The existence of this differential, and an attempt to explain it in institutional terms, were the subject of a paper by Douglass North in the first symposium of the series that lead to the creation of the Economic Freedom of the World Index (North, 1987).

2 A taxonomy of rights

The use of the standard economic allocation model to analyze the development of rights suggests a taxonomy of rights, which ought to guide thinking about the development of rights, that is, a taxonomy based on the resource cost of establishing various kinds of rights. As a first approximation, we can simply group rights into two categories: rights that require modest or no expenditure of resources to achieve and rights that require a significant expenditure of resources to achieve.

As a way of making this taxonomic exercise crisper, we can further observe that enforcement of rights involves constraining two different kinds of actions by other actors that would affect the rights of citizens. The first sorts of actions are those taken by government against citizens. The second are actions taken by citizens against their fellow citizens.

Low-cost rights—constraining government actions that impair citizens' rights

Low-cost rights are those that are entirely of the negative rights kind. They involve the actions of government and essentially require government to desist from interfering in the activities of citizens. These rights essentially cost the government nothing to establish or preserve. They are rights that often are regarded as having existed in a state of nature.

The following is a list of some negative rights.

1. Don't interfere with families and their organization.

2. Don't interfere with economic activities of citizens as long as they are voluntarily undertaken

3. Don't subsidize (that is, interfere by means of financial interventions) in any activities of families or business.

4. Don't discriminate amongst citizens in the undertakings of government by race, gender, ethnicity, or in any other way.

5. Don't prohibit voluntary activities that don't affect uninvolved citizens.

6. Don't prohibit any religion, club, newspaper, internet site, or other mode of communication.

7. Don't steal from citizens by debasing the currency by clipping, sweating, or expanding the supply of fiat currency.

These sorts of rights are of the kind that every government, everywhere in the world, and at every point in history, could ensure to its citizens. There is no reason for citizens of any nation not to have these rights. Their provision does not require the use of resources; they only require that government not intervene in the affairs of its citizens.

High-cost rights—constraining people's actions when they interfere with the rights of others

The other kind of rights relate to actions by citizens that interfere with the rights of other citizens. These rights are referred to here as quasi-negative rights for the reason that they are not self-enforcing. In order for these rights to exist, there has to be an enforcement process that stops one citizen from interfering with the actions of another. That enforcement mechanism requires resources.

Thomas Jefferson wrote in the *Declaration of Independence of the American Colonies*, "and to ensure these rights we have created a government." Governments are the enforcement mechanism which ensures that the non-interference rights that the citizens acknowledge are actually enforced. Of course there is a subsidiary issue that arises once the citizens create a government and instruct it to ensure the realization of the rights which the citizens have acknowledged, and that is, how will the government be prevented from itself abusing these rights. In many of the world's jurisdictions that lack rights, government interferences are the core reason for that lack.

Personal security

The primary right of the quasi-negative kind that government must enforce is the right to personal security. Citizens have the right to be free from assault by other citizens and by citizens of other countries. It is possible that in some circumstances, this right can be acquired by citizens simply desisting from interfering with others, so that in principle, this could be a truly negative right. Such societies may employ religious beliefs or other forms of taboo to ensure that members conform to a code of conduct that eliminates much, if not all, of the threats to personal security.

However, in normal circumstances, reliance on mutual non-interference is not a reliable source of the right to personal security. Indeed, citizens rightly regard the preservation of their right to be not interfered with as one of the most important functions of government. This expectation implies the provision of policing. It also implies the provision of a mechanism for dealing with those who interfere with others, including a process for setting penalties to inhibit such behavior, an adjudication process, a system of prisons, etc.

Property security

In his book, *The Mystery of Capital*, Hernando de Soto notes that the most important features of property are its measurement and the acknowledgement of who owns it. In that sense, property is essentially bookkeeping and the transfer of ownership is the transfer of journal entries. But the system that keeps track of property, whether privately or publicly provided, is expensive. The mechanisms to protect property from theft, even if privately provided, rely on an enforcement mechanism. The most primitive form of private property security relies on the establishment of an adequate level of deterrence to theft and encroachment. The most sophisticated relies on intricate systems of contract that define the exact nature of rights, and the portion of them that are being extended or protected by certain actions, as in the articulation of intellectual property rights.

Freedom of speech

While in principle the right to speak publicly about any subject is a costless right, the defense of the right may be very costly, especially when the things that are to be spoken about are contentious. There are almost daily instances of speakers on one topic or another in this or that location being denied their right to speak—even in jurisdictions in which freedom of speech would normally be assumed to exist. Recently, the attempt by former US Vice-President Richard Cheney to speak in Vancouver, Canada, was interfered with by hooligans under the guise of a "peaceful demonstration." The demonstrators attempted to prevent people from getting into the venue where Cheney was speaking, choked one person, and jostled, pushed, and intimidated others.

Benjamin Netanyahu, trying to speak to a Concordia University audience in January 2003, was turned away because of the fear of violence at the demonstrations launched to prevent him from speaking on campus. His oppressors were Islamists of various affections who did not want the Israeli prime minster to have the opportunity to speak. The University, once a place where differences of opinion were encouraged and the right to express them fervently defended, caved in to the threat of violence and cancelled the speaking event.

The distinction between theoretical and actual rights: Implications for measurement

The failure of the government to intervene in these free speech cases resulted in impairment of the right to free speech—and in one case, the successful use of violence to silence people who should have been permitted to speak. In both cases, the presumption of a right of the protestors to demonstrate and express their views was permitted, by creating an atmosphere of intimidation or physical violence, to trump the right of the other two: the audiences and their speakers. In Canada in 2011, the *ideal* of the right to free speech is protected by our constitution, and yet the right to *actually* speak is not always protected.

In Canada, the reason there was in these and in many other cases a distinction between the actual and the theoretical right to free speech is not because of the costliness of providing the right due to a lack of resources. Rather, it reflects the fact that the well funded apparatus of the state is not acting to protect the rights which the constitution says it guarantees. It is a clear illustration of the fact that just because there is an undisputed, acknowledged right to free speech does not mean that the right actually exists in every instance, even in what is generally regarded as a free country.

As with the right to the security of the person and the right to own property, the actualization of the right to free speech depends on the active expenditure of resources by the state, and the effective channeling of the resources to ensure that the rights are upheld. In those instances where the state has the resources to do so but neglects to intervene to protect the rights of citizens, or actively contrives to prevent free speech (as in the celebrated case of Ezra Levant and his publication of the Danish cartoons in the *Western Standard* magazine[6]), the state can accurately be said to be depriving citizens of rights.

In simple terms: the Canadian state apparatus had the resources, yet either chose not to use them to protect the right to speech, or used them in ways to actively reduce the right to free speech. In an index measuring the protection of rights, Canada should receive demerit points for these illustrations of failure to act to protect the right to free speech.

The interesting question for the comparative measurement of free speech rights is, if we consider another context, a country, XYZ, with per capita income of only $1,000 per year. Were we to observe the same pattern of facts, what would we conclude about the action of the state? The right to free speech, or the right to personal security, or the right to own property, might be enshrined in the country's constitution, and we would say that on that ground, the country is free, since the key rights are acknowledged. We observe, however, that bullies frequently prevent others from speaking at political meetings or that the certain speakers cannot attend the university to speak because the bullies intimidate the administration by promising that they are going to create havoc. Assuming there is a minimalist government which consumes 10 percent of the nation's income, the government has $100 per capita to ensure the delivery of all of the rights to which the citizens are entitled by the constitution including the right to free speech.

While in both the Canadian case and the case of XYZ, we find that the right to free speech is not ensured; can we really with confidence say that both lack the right to free speech and both should be censured

---

6　The treatment of Ezra Levant by the so-called Alberta Human Rights Commission is chronicled on his website, www.ezralevant.com, and is a classic illustration of how the state, even when it acts with good intentions, can have an active and malevolent impact on rights in an otherwise free society.

to the same degree? Might the president of XYZ not effectively argue that she and her government are working to ensure that all rights are respected, but that they had to prioritize their use of the government's scarce resources? Security of the person and security of property, along with the costs of actually running the collective voice functions of government, had to come first because that is what the citizens wanted and expected, and there was consequently little money left for ensuring free speech. But notice, she adds, that there are many fewer violations of the right to free speech now than there used to be in her country when the per capita income was only $500.

No such explanation can be mounted by the authorities in Canada who permitted the violations of free speech noted above. There, the decision to give the bullies and demonstrators free reign to interfere with the rights of other citizens was presumably based on some short-term political calculus. For that, Canada should be censured for failing to provide and protect the free speech rights of Canadians.

The question is, should an index measuring the existence of the right to free speech give the same marks to Canada and to XYZ for having failed to produce the right to free speech? In both cases, the right to free speech is acknowledged to exist. In both cases, there is a failure of the government to ensure that it is realized. In one case, a decision is made to deny the right to hear and be heard to one group of citizens because of the political opprobrium which might attach to the suppression of the actions of the bullies. In the other case, the government wants to suppress the aggression of the bullies and allow free speech but does not have the resources to effect it. Should any measurement of the existence of rights treat these two situations the same?

Implications of the taxonomy

We have been persuaded, in papers by Fred McMahon and Tom Palmer, to use a sum-of-rights concept of freedom as the basis for extending our measurement of freedom beyond economic freedom. This approach is undoubtedly the most comprehensive and defensible approach. However, the fact that the wealth of a society will have a significant effect on the number and extent of costly rights that a country can provide suggests that there may be a reason not to include the costly rights in an index designed to measure and compare the existence of rights in countries that differ dramatically in their income levels and developmental stages.

Another way to pose the question is to consider a particular country and ask whether a certain measuring rod would have yielded the same indication of rights if applied during the several hundred years of the country's history? Take, for example, the United States. Would a comprehensive index including the costless and costly rights have recorded the same, a smaller, or a larger bundle of rights if applied serially in 1776, 1860, 1934, and 2011?

While undoubtedly the United States in each and every one of these years would have compared very favorably with the then-existing countries of the world in the level of freedom available, it is not as clear that the rating would have been uniform over time.

One response to this is to say, yes, societies change over time and the level of rights will increase or decrease, but that is just fine since we are measuring the actual rights that exist, and they either exist or they don't. So our index should—and does—simply measure what is.

The problem is that we do not typically have an absolute measure of rights. We have a comparative min/max grid into which we place the countries we measure. Every grid is epoch-specific and one designed for 1776 would not be a useful in measuring outcomes in 2011. That is true both for a single country measured across time and for a group of countries.

This criticism is not true of a grid used to measure the costless rights set. There is no particular reason to suppose that a grid designed to measure the freedom to trade in 1776 would have to be modified to correctly capture the range of behavior observed in 2011. Either the government leaves traders alone, or it does not. No resources are consumed to leave people alone to trade. Leaving them alone to trade neither increases nor decreases the ability of government to also leave them alone to decide which god to worship or in what way.

Of course, this is not to say that we should not also try to measure the provision of costly rights. Of course we should, but the publication of such measures must surely acknowledge the problems of applying 2011 yardsticks to societies and countries that are just emerging developmentally from the 1800s, as is currently the case with many of the world's countries. The measurement and presentation of an index of costly rights has to be treated differently because costly rights are different.

3   A proposed approach to measuring comprehensive rights

Reminding ourselves that what we are trying to measure is the extent to which governments acknowledge and produce rights, the implication of the approach to rights presented in this paper is that in the first attempt to comprehensively measure rights, we should confine our index to those rights which are costless to provide. All governments in all epochs of history have been able, and are able, to provide these rights. There is no confounding impact of resource constraints or other pre-existing inhibitors that would confuse the measurements.

To a great degree, the *Economic Freedom of the World* index is a measurement of costless rights. The sections on property rights and the size of government do not fit in this taxonomy, but the rest do. So the first segment of the index of costless rights ought to be subcomponents 3, 4, and 5 of the *Economic Freedom of the World* index.

The subsequent sections can deal with the following list of negative rights:

1. Don't interfere with families and their organization.

2. Don't subsidize (that is, interfere by means of financial interventions) in any activities of families or business.

3. Don't compete with private providers of goods or services.

4. Don't discriminate amongst citizens in the undertakings of government by race, gender, ethnicity, or in any other way.

5. Don't prohibit voluntary activities that don't have any effect on uninvolved citizens.

6. Don't prohibit any religion, club, newspaper, internet site, or other mode of communication.

Only after satisfactorily measuring these rights should we turn our attention to the broader and more complex issue of measuring those rights that are costly to produce.

References

Bingham, Tom (2011). *The Rule of Law*, Penguin Books.

de Soto, Hernando (2000). *The Mystery of Capital: Why Capitalism Triumphs in the West and Fails Everywhere Else*. Basic Books.

Holcombe, Randy (1994). *The Economic Foundations of Government*. New York University Press.

Hornbeck, Richard (2010). Barbed wire: Property rights and agricultural development. *Quarterly Journal of Economics* (May): 767-810. <http://www.economics.harvard.edu/faculty/hornbeck/files/Hornbeck_barbedwire.pdf>, as of November 9, 2011.

Jefferson, Thomas (1776). *Declaration of Independence of the American Colonies*. <http://oll.libertyfund.org/?option=com_staticxt&staticfile=show.php%3Ftitle=755&chapter=86068&layout=html&Itemid=27>, as of November 9, 2011.

North, Douglass (1987). Institutions, economic growth and freedom: An historical introduction. In Michael Walker (ed.), *Freedom, Democracy and Economic Welfare* (The Fraser Institute): 3-46.

Pinker, Steven (2002). *The Blank Slate*. Viking Penguin Books.

Rubin, Paul (2002). *Darwinian Politics: The Evolutionary Origin of Freedom*. Rutgers University Press.

CHAPTER SIX

Conditions for Freedom

A Few Theses on the Theory of Freedom and on Creating an Index of Freedom

Andrei Illarionov *

The following text presents an attempt to formulate a theoretical basis for constructing an overall index of freedom in which partial freedoms, such as individual, civil, legal, economic, politic, and national ones, might be included as its composite elements.

Introduction

Freedom is understood as of two types: positive and negative. Positive freedom is considered primarily to be the physical ability to do something, such as having physical control over ability, strength, resources, information, knowledge, technology, etc. Negative freedom is primarily a legalistic concept dealing with someone's rights, and involves the absence of subversion of a person's rights by somebody else. Isaiah Berlin gave a good philosophical definition of freedom (the words "freedom" and "liberty" are being used here mutually interchangeably):

* Dr. Andrei Nikolaievich Illarionov is a Senior Fellow at the Cato Institute's Center for Global Liberty and Prosperity in Washington, DC, and President of the Institute of Economic Analysis, an independent economic think tank in Moscow, Russia, which he founded in 1994.

In April 2000, Dr. Illarionov was invited to serve as Chief Economic Advisor to the newly-elected Russian President Vladimir Putin. From May 2000 to January 2005 he was also Putin's Personal Representative to the G-8. While serving in President Putin's administration, Dr. Illarionov was the driving force behind the adoption of a 13 percent flat income tax, the Russian government's creation of a stabilization fund for windfall oil revenues, and the early repayment of Russia's foreign debt.

Dr. Illarionov has co-authored several programs for Russian governments and has written three books and over 300 articles on Russian economic and social policies. He is a regular commentator on current events in Russia.

1. "… non-interference, which is the opposite of coercion, is good as such, although it is not only good. This is the 'negative' conception of liberty in its classical form" (Berlin, 1969). (The first definition of freedom.)

The rest of this essay is devoted primarily to developing a method for constructing an index built on negative understanding of freedom.

Human action

The very existence of human action suggests the existence of its several elements: a human actor (the subject of human action), a human act (the action itself), types of human actions, property rights over objects involved in human action, rules about how to use (or not to use) property rights while engaging in those actions.

Human actors

Actors are by definition human beings. Though the philosophy of classical liberalism insists that all people are born with legally equal rights, in real life different people in different societies, in different times, and under different circumstances do have different legal rights.

Those with different legal rights (capabilities) can be classified into a variety of different groups. People can be segregated by *age* (babies, children, teenagers, or adults). The number of rights they have tends to rise with age until it stabilizes in adulthood. People can also be divided by gender: men and women. Though modern societies recognize the legal equality of the sexes, historically in many societies men had more legal rights than women. People can also be divided by mental health: healthy or unhealthy. Mental illness has been associated with inappropriate or unacceptable behavior that has produced limitations on the affected people's legal rights; they are often considered to be partially or fully legally incapable. People can be classified by their different social groups, including race, ethnicity, tribe, kin, language, religion, class, caste, profession, conviction, experience, etc. In different societies members of those groups may have different legal rights.

Throughout the history of mankind, one of the most important differentiating factors among humans is the level of property rights they possess over themselves (self-ownership)—in other words, the amount of personal freedom they enjoy. Specifically, are they genuinely free people, or servants, or serfs, or slaves, etc.? Even in the freest of modern societies, the amount of freedom that healthy adults do have might differ notably, depending on circumstances.

Human action

Human actions differ first of all according to the free will of a subject. Actions (as well non-actions) might be free or performed under coercion.

For free actions there is an additional important criterion, namely, the existence or reward received in return for the actor's action. The judgment about whether or not a reward received can be considered as equivalent (more than equivalent, less than equivalent, without even any reward) can be made only by a free person. Free actions can be divided into two kinds: free exchange (that is, actions taken according to free will, for which the actor receives something of equivalent value) or free charity (an action taken by one of one's own free will, and for which one receives no reward).

For actions performed under coercion (under duress), where the actor can exercise no free will, the issue of equivalence of the reward is irrelevant, since the ability to judge the value of resources received in return is something only a free person can do. The very existence of coercion automatically excludes the notion of equivalent or non-equivalent value for any actions performed under coercion. Therefore, any human action made under coercion may be called involuntary charity, even if the resources provided to that actor are comparable to those provided in a similar situation to a free actor (see figure 1).

Types of human actions

Conscious individuals can engage in three main types of action: thought, speech, and physical acts. There is a vast difference between the physical and legal ability (of an individual, community, society, or state) to coerce human actions. Physical action is the easiest one to control (limit, regulate, or direct). It is possible, but much harder, to control human speech. To control human thought is even harder (though not completely impossible). For example, with the development of education curricula, propaganda, brainwashing, and psychological warfare one can seriously alter the ability of legally free people to think and speak independently.

Figure 1: Types of human action

Will Equivalent	Free will	No free will
Existence of equivalent	Voluntary exchange	--
Absence of equivalent	Free charity	Coercion

The decision-taking-centre-of-a-human-being (DTCOHB) is different in different circumstances. Though in the end a person's decision is probably made by their brain, many decisions can be significantly affected by signals sent by different systems in the human body: respiratory, digestive, thermoregulatory, reproductive, etc.

Human actions are performed according to a hierarchy of preferences. These actions take place in several main spheres that can be classified according to the importance of particular property rights for an actor. This importance may be measured by the "distance" of each particular sphere from the decision-taking-centre-of-a-human-being (DTCOHB).

Property rights in different areas

The crucial distinction between classes of different human actions comes from the amount of property rights an actor has, and an understanding of the borders between the actor's property rights and those of other actors. There are four main spheres of human activity (security, personal, private, public), each with its own sub-areas. People have property rights (or freedoms) in each of them (see figure 2).

In the security sphere, people execute property rights over their own bodies (self-ownership) that are strongly associated with their survival and reasonably good health. As a result, in many modern societies those rights are under no or very limited regulation. The most well-known exception is conscription imposed by governments and some quasi-state organizations. In this sphere, property rights may be reflected in the right to life (i.e., freedom from homicide) and the right to use one's own body (i.e., the freedom from physical intervention without one's clearly expressed consent, including for medical reasons). In most modern societies, executing property rights in the individual security sphere is recognized as inalienable human right and needs no regulation.

In the personal sphere, people execute property rights over their own bodies that are not necessarily intimately related to their survival or health. Such rights include the right to a choice of diet (i.e., freedom from a prescribed diet, such as from the prohibition of alcohol, drugs, kosher food, etc.); right to a choice of clothing; the right to physical movement (i.e., the freedom from illegal incarceration and from constraints or limits on an actor's movement locally, or within state borders, or internationally); the right to consciousness and independent thinking (i.e., the freedom from imposed views, indoctrination, propaganda, religion, ideology, etc.). In many modern societies, personal rights are relatively recently recognized as inalienable rights, and therefore are subjected to either no or only limited regulation.

In the private sphere, an actor's own property rights can collide with those of others who happen to be related to him or her either by common

Figure 2: Freedom's zikkurat and the importance of different areas

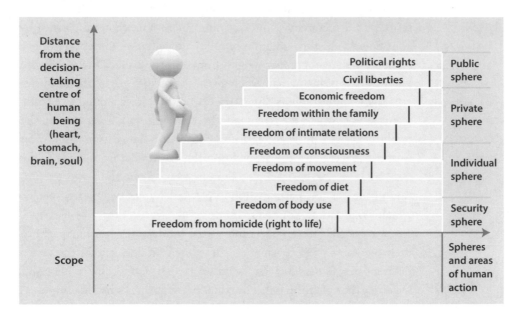

blood or by living in a shared household, or those with whom he or she has intimate relations. Rights in the private sphere include the right to non-coercive family relations (not intimate ones) (specifically, freedom from terror instigated by family members); rights over one's intimate relations (i.e., freedom from rape, coercion, arranged marriage, permissions from senior and/or male members of the family, restrictions on gender, etc.). In some societies this sphere of property rights is heavily regulated.

In the public sphere, an actor executes his or her property rights in areas where those rights meet (collide with) the property rights of others beyond the private sphere. Rights in the public sphere include rights to economic relations (i.e., economic property rights); rights on civil relations (i.e., non-economic, non-political property rights in a civil society); rights to political relations (i.e., property rights related to territory, including local, regional, national, and international polities). In all societies these property rights face very substantial and detailed regulations.

The relative importance (and thus value) for an actor of executing his or her property rights in different areas (and therefore the subjective relative weights he or she gives to different rights in different areas) in the overall group of rights he or she has (i.e., overall freedom) is a subject of individual choice. Relative importance of particular rights tends to diminish in proportion to the increased distance from the DTCOHB, with the most valuable rights being considered in the security sphere, then in the individual and private spheres, then in the public one. Nevertheless, there are many exceptions to this rule.

There is indirect confirmation that the importance of different rights varies according to their distance from the DTCOHB in the historic evolution of the hierarchy of human punishment. Punishment is generally considered to be the limitation or full removal (either temporary or permanent) of different property rights from those punished. Therefore, with gradual recognition in many societies of the natural origin of many property rights, punishments (limitations in rights) have shifted over time from the security to the personal sphere, then from the personal to the public sphere. Historically, punishments tend to evolve from capital punishment (execution), to corporal punishment (inflicting damage to the person's body), to enslavement, temporary incarceration, exile, prohibition of the person's participation in particular areas of activity, specific penalties, and moral condemnation.

As a general rule, one has the partial (and sometimes full) right to exchange one's property rights (or freedoms) in one area for those in a different area. Someone might decide to exchange part of his or her rights, including the right to his or her own life, for rights (freedoms) in other areas. Voluntary exchange of the most valuable right, namely, the right to life (or freedom from homicide) for any other good is traditionally called "sacrifice." There are many known examples where an actor sacrifices his or her right to life (or freedom from homicide) for rights and freedoms in other areas.

It might be said that Michael Jackson exchanged his right to life for the right to use his own body the way he wanted to; that Elvis Presley exchanged his right to life for the freedom to choose his own diet; that the Cuban Balseros people exchanged their right to life by risking drowning (and in many cases, by actually drowning) for their right to free movement and free consciousness; that Giordano Bruno gave up his right to life in exchange for freedom of conscience (translated into the rights to free thoughts and free speech); that Romeo and Juliette made the exchange of their rights to life for their rights to free intimate relations. Andrij (from the Nikolai Gogol's novel *Taras Bulba*) forfeits his right to life so that he can be free from family restrictions, while Sergey Magnitsky (who died in a Russian jail in November 2009) sacrificed his life for economic freedom. There are many historic personalities, including Jesus Christ and Martin Luther King, Jr., who gave up their right to life so that others could enjoy their civil rights (civil liberties), or who exchanged their right to life for political rights for their countrymen (as Mahatma Gandhi did) (see figure 3).

The legal aspects of freedom

The legal terms that correspond to the main types of human activity are as follows: *gift* refers to charity; contract is for exchange; and imposition is coercion. Particular rights and their volumes that are assigned to different

Figure 3: Freedom's staircase and the importance of different areas

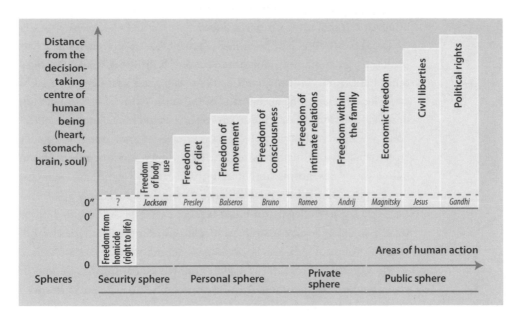

actors are determined by covenants. Covenants are either based on voluntary agreements (without coercion) between legally equal actors, or imposed by force using coercion.

Three types of regulations define how an actor can exercise his or her property rights: with permission (full property rights); via prescription (limited property rights); and prohibition (proscription, absence of property rights). These regulations lead to the second (legal) definition of freedom:

2. Freedom of human action is the freedom for an actor to exercise his or her property rights without legal or quasi-legal limitations.

Several serious problems exist with the actual execution of property rights: spheres of property rights are not well defined; borders that separate different actors' property rights are not well marked; protection of even well-defined property rights from violators can be difficult and costly, which leads to conflicts over property rights between different actors. Threats to individual property rights might come from a variety of different sources, legal and illegal: from members of family, community, neighborhood, clubs, associations, unions, society, government, from criminals (individual, groups, organizations, states).

The instruments regularly used for solving conflicts over property rights are legal ones: laws, instructions, and decisions of courts and judges. Laws, regulations, and instructions can be of several types: laws establishing, protecting or expanding property rights; laws limiting (reducing, violating, or taking) property rights; laws exchanging, distributing, or redistributing property rights.

Legal constraints may be ethically acceptable or unacceptable. Apart from the legal limitations on human actions, there are several quasi-legal ones: behavioral traditions and habits of the actor's family; social, ethical, religious traditions and norms of the actor's kin, tribe, ethnic, and/ or religious group. Though limitations such as tolerance, mutual respect, good manners, high style, political correctness, etc., are not directly coercive, they are still constraints, all be they indirect. Most people prefer to follow such rules, norms, and limitations in order to avoid sanctions that may not necessarily be legal, but may certainly be ethical.

Aside from the legal and quasi-legal constraints on human actions, there also exist illegal constraints, specifically, criminal activities of individuals, groups of individuals, organizations, and states.

The constraints on actions may be codified (according to religious or state laws) or non-codified. Among non-codified constraints are social, ethical, and cultural norms. There also exist constraints that violate state laws, but which enjoy widespread community support through habits and traditions as they are in line with prevailing social norms. (The Russian term for such illegal but socially acceptable constraints is "poniatia.") Finally, there are constraints that violate both laws and social norms (which in Russia is known as "bespredel," meaning that they are simultaneously illegal and socially unacceptable).

The absence of both legal and quasi-legal (social, ethical, cultural) constraints creates favorable conditions for executing individual property rights. The absence of legal bans, restrictions, regulations, or instructions creates the legal conditions conducive for realizing freedom. The absence of prohibitive cultural norms (quasi-legal constraints) creates the cultural conditions conducive for freedom. The absence of criminal activities committed by individuals or the state creates the security conditions conducive for freedom. The existence of a favorable legal framework creates instrumental conditions conducive for reducing the costs of conflict resolution over property rights.

That said, the security, legal, cultural, instrumental conditions conducive for freedom must not be confused with their actual execution. The connection between laws and regulations (conditions) and freedom (execution of these conditions) is intrinsic. As John Locke (1689) formulated it, "the end of law is not to abolish or restrain, but to preserve and enlarge freedom: for in all the states of created beings capable of laws, where there is no law, there is no freedom: for liberty is, to be free from restraint and violence from others; which cannot be, where there is no law." Benjamin Constant (1816/1988), too, noted, liberty "is the right to be subjected only to the laws, and to be neither arrested, detained, put to death or maltreated in any way by the arbitrary will of one or more individuals."

The economic aspects of freedom

Freedom is also an economic good. The utility of this good comes when an actor exercises his or her property rights. There are two types of property rights. In the case of private goods, property rights offer protection from actual or potential intruders. In the case of public goods, property rights are a suitable mechanism for allocating the private interests (shares) in public goods.

As with other goods, there is a demand for freedom and a supply of freedom (figure 4). The demand for freedom is being created both individually and collectively. It has individual and collective scales of preference. Therefore, it is highly subjective and therefore probably immeasurable.

On the contrary, the supply of freedom is produced only collectively (publicly), by the particular industry ("freedom-producing industry"). That industry's main producers are seniors in the family, elders, "wise people," priests, media, public opinion leaders, the state, etc., who produce habits, traditions, norms, rules, regulations, instructions, and laws related to the execution of individual rights in security, personal, private, and public spheres. These products are aimed at solving or facilitating the resolution of conflicts between actors over the execution of their property rights. Among the products of this industry are rules of conflict resolution including warfare, martial arts, queues, hierarchy, contracts (including marriage), negotiations, laws, ethical norms, and votes. Even if the fruits of this industry (conditions for freedom) might initially be produced

Figure 4: Supply and demand for freedom

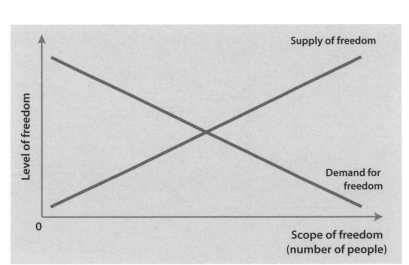

individually, to become widely acceptable and universal norms, they must be supported collectively. Therefore, the norms are objective and might be potentially measurable and comparable.

Conflicts are traditionally resolved through such mechanisms as warfare, courts, negotiations, media, or representative bodies. Historically, conflict resolution mechanisms evolved in several stages including the physical elimination of competing actors (i.e., killing them), to their enslavement, to the recognition of competing actors as legal entities, then recognizing some (later, all) of their rights, and finally, engaging them in mutually-agreed contracts. There was and is a permanent search for conflict resolution mechanisms that are increasingly more appropriate, more effective, less costly, and better adjusted to particular situations. The replacement of less effective rules with more effective ones enlarges and strengthens property rights, thereby enhancing the execution of freedom and so leading to an increase in the volume and variety of free human actions.

Neither the demand for freedom nor the supply of freedom is limited. The demand for freedom generally correlates with income, longevity, good health, education, experience, etc., and is increasing over time (see figure 5). Factors that influence the amount and variety of the supply of freedom are less evident and need more specific research. What is clear is that there is no positive or negative correlation between the availability of natural resources or level of income and the supply of freedom. In fact, the supply of freedom depends more on the sophistication and effectiveness of industries that produce conflict resolution mechanisms. For instance, comparisons of the Incan empire versus Iceland in the 15th century, present-day Equatorial Guinea versus Estonia, or Russia versus India produce an important observation. While in each pair the former country is richer

Figure 5: Supply of freedom and demand for freedom

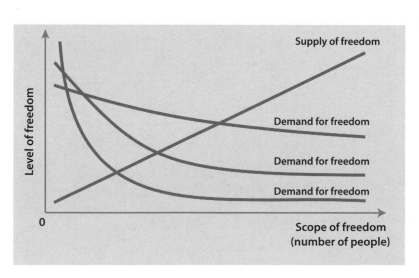

than the latter (in terms of average income per capita), at the same time the former has less effective conflict resolution mechanisms, and therefore has a lower supply of freedom than the latter.

Regulatory enhancements may decrease uncertainty, but won't necessarily increase freedom (see figure 6). Regulations that are either too limited or too pervasive lead to lower levels of freedom. The relationship between the amount of regulation and the amount freedom seems to follow an inverse U-curve (see figure 7). There is a permanent search for the optimal, freedom-maximizing amount of regulation. The upper point of the inverse U-curve may be shifted towards less rather than more regulation (figure 8).

Figure 6: Regulation and uncertainty

Figure 7: Regulation and freedom

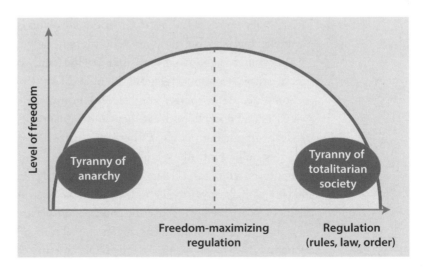

Figure 8: Regulation and freedom when freedom-maximizing regulations are increased

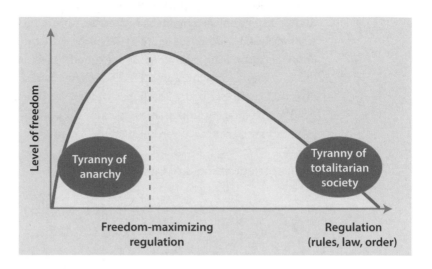

It looks similar to the curve for the growth-enhancing tax rate, which, as is well-known, is shifted towards a lower rather than a higher level of taxation.

Individual freedom and society

Conceptually, the discussion of individual freedom begins with a single person. However, "negative freedom" implies relations between at least two actors. Since negative freedom deals with the protection of one person's property rights from constrains, interventions, or regulations emanating from other actors, negative freedom can only be conceptualized for at least two persons, or a group of actors, or a community, or a society. Whenever negative freedom for one person is being considered, it is, in fact, about freedom within a society consisting of at least two persons. A society that consists of Robinson Crusoe alone on his island is an interesting intellectual exercise, but is not relevant to negative freedom.

Allocation of rights is a responsibility of the family, or community (territorial, social, economic, religious, ideological one), or state.

Some people in society are peaceful, non-violent, and non-aggressive, eager and ready to respect others' individual rights—in other words, freedom-supporting people. Others are aggressive, violent, predatory, including bullies, intruders, criminals, gangsters, bandits, killers, pirates, communists, NKVD and Gestapo officers (political police in Stalin's USSR and Hitler's Germany), or *silovikis* (security officials in present-day Russia), in other words, freedom-restricting and freedom-destroying people.

If they cannot constrain the aggressive actions of freedom-destroying people, the freedom-supporting people are not able to exercise their property rights. Therefore, freedom-supporting individuals must limit the actions of freedom-destroying people, or, more precisely, freedom-destroying criminal actions. (One of the most well-known documents providing justification for such activity is the United States *Declaration of Independence*). This goal can be achieved if freedom-supporters can work together and if they are able to apply force (coercion) to the freedom-destroyers. By limiting or restricting those who engage in freedom-destroying actions, by restricting their freedoms, the freedom of freedom-supporters will be expanded (figures 9 and 10).

Figure 9: Limitation of action in a free society

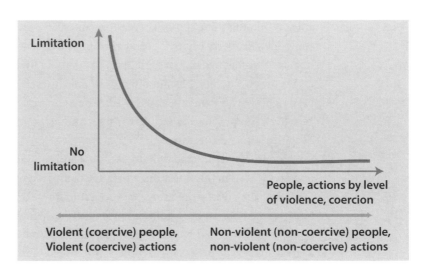

Figure 10: Freedom of action in a free society

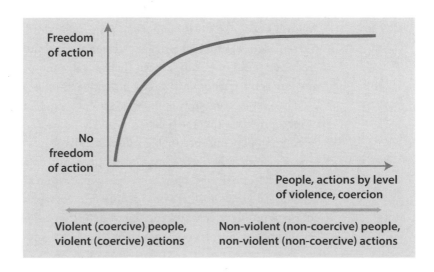

Freedom-destroying actors can be individuals, groups, organizations, or institutions that professionally specialize in the use of force, violence, and the application of coercion. Among such groups are bands of gangsters, the mafia, the police, the army, and the state. Therefore, limitations on the size and scope of those groups, organizations, and institutions can lead to expanded freedom.

This fact leads to the third definition of freedom:

3. Freedom of human action is the absence of some constraints (norms, laws, restrictions, regulations, instructions, prescriptions, prohibitions) and the presence of others.

The use of force and the application of coercion are not always unacceptable. While the initiation of aggression (initiation of coercion) against someone's property rights is considered to be unacceptable, using force to protect someone's property rights (i.e., coercion in response to intruders) is morally acceptable and often desirable. Therefore, free people do have rights to carry and use arms for their own protection, to protect their own lives and property as well as the lives and property of other victims of aggression and coercion.

Who in society has the right to use force and coercion? There are two main responses to this question: either specially designated people (such as police, the courts, the army, and government) exclusively; or everybody, with the possible addition of specially designated people. More freedom is associated with more widespread rights to use force against aggression given to as many people as possible (with the exception of criminals and others with legally constrained rights such as children and the mentally ill).

Political freedom as a negative freedom

Political freedom is a very important type of freedom. It should be considered as an example of a negative freedom and must be included in an overall index of freedom. Both theoretically and practically, political freedom is the freedom to exercise individual property rights in the public sphere. It is freedom from intervention by others into the individual property rights within the polity.

A group of people occupying some territory forms a polity. Since the time of Hammurabi and Solomon, regulations, instructions, and laws have been applied, for the most part, to people living within a particular territory. Territorial boundaries, therefore, identify the geographical area for the execution of property rights. According to Benjamin Constant (1816/1988), "Finally it [freedom] is everyone's right to exercise some influence on the administration of the government, either by electing all or particular offi-cials, or through representations, petitions, demands to which the author-ities are more or less compelled to pay heed." The measurement of the conditions for the execution of property rights as well as the level and amount of freedom can be calculated for the particular territory.

Legal and political systems are the main sources of supply for rights and freedoms. Different legal, political, and cultural systems do have dif-ferent productivity and do produce different types of conflict resolution mechanisms. The nature of legal, political and cultural systems is a crucial factor and an important predictor of the volume and quality of protected rights and executed freedoms.

Voting in an election can be considered an example of multilateral con-tract. There is a lot of commonality in the exercising of property rights in different types of contracts: marriages in interpersonal relations, business contracts, elections in civil associations, votes in political organizations. Citizenship may be considered as an example of a contract between an individual person and polity (state).

Politically free systems have several advantages over non-free systems. When other mechanisms turned out to be ineffective or unsuitable, politi-cal mechanisms of conflict resolution might be used. Political freedom in many cases is an ultimate guarantor of many other freedoms. It is not a coincidence that more politically free countries generally were and are more prosperous and more successful in many areas than less free coun-tries. It suggests that political freedom has played an important role in such an outcome.

The historical evolution of freedom

Freedom is a historical concept. Freedom may be considered as a particu-lar type of normative system that is identifying, protecting, and expanding property rights. Therefore, historically, the notion of freedom appeared later than the notion of property.

One widely known example of ethical norms that protect property rights comes from the last five of the *Bible's* Ten Commandments:

- You shall not murder.
- Neither shall you commit adultery.
- Neither shall you steal.
- Neither shall you bear false witness against your neighbor.
- Neither shall you covet your neighbor's wife. Neither shall you desire your neighbour's house, or field, or male or female slave, or ox, or donkey, or anything that belongs to your neighbour.

Over years, freedom has evolved in several dimensions: the number of actors whose property rights are being protected has increased and the areas of property rights being protected have widened. Similarly, the specific property rights being protected have increased, property rights protection has been strengthened (violators of property rights being punished), and mechanisms of conflict resolution over property rights have been created and developed.

The historical evolution of the spread of freedom through society may be seen as a movement beginning with freedom concentrated in the hands of one actor (such as an absolute monarch, tyrant, despot, secretary-general, fuehrer, national or supreme leader), to freedom held by a few actors (including members of a family, imperial court, security council, or government), to freedom enjoyed by many actors (a group of barons or other groups based on professional, ethnic, language, religious, racial, class, or gender criteria), to almost every adult citizen. Substantive rights have been recently been stretched to include non-citizens, illegal immigrants, children, and even animals.

The historical evolution of freedom also saw the gradual replacement of ethical, religious, and cultural regulations with legal ones, and a shift in the frontier between areas that are already legally regulated and those that are not yet, in the direction of those that are legally regulated (for example, prescribed paint colors for houses in California; or bans on cutting trees on privately owned plots in Maryland, or having an open fire in Virginia, or lighting fireworks in the District of Columbia).

The historic evolution of conflict resolution mechanisms has changed the sequence of actions from the immediate initiation of aggression (beginning of war) to something more nuanced and sophisticated (beginning with asserting claims and presenting arguments and counterarguments, through to pronouncing warnings of different kinds, then demonstrating threats, and finally to waging war, then signing peace treaties, agreements, or contracts). Lately it has become common for parties to adopt a more advanced scheme of negotiations without resorting to the use of force, application of coercion, or waging war.

The historic evolution of conflict resolution mechanisms (the protection of freedom) was and is proceeding along several dimensions: solidifying the legal equality of actors; strengthening the predictability of rules; increasing the predictability of mechanisms for changing existing rules; reducing the scope of the application of coercion and use of force; and finally, decreasing the brutality of laws that protect freedom.

Internationally, different societies have had no once-and-for-all sequence of stages in the historic evolution of conflict resolution mechanisms. Evidently, ethnic, religious, cultural, ideological, and political factors have played an important role in conceiving, sustaining, and developing the institutions that protect freedom. Different paths in the evolution of freedom can be seen in different cultural regions such as the Anglo-Saxon world, Germanic Europe, Scandinavia, Russia, Latin America, India, China, and the Muslim world, including its Arabic part.

It is important to note that even if an individual (or society) acquires a particular level of freedom, it does not give them an unlimited guarantee to keep that level of freedom forever. Equally true is that a low level of freedom does not prevent an individual (or society) from quickly increasing it. Also, cultural and other constraints can be so strong that they hinder the relatively quick acquisition of freedom. As numerous cases from world history have shown, it is extremely difficult to remove, ignore, avoid, or even just weaken those constrains. Overcoming cultural constraints turns out to be the most challenging problem for protecting, sustaining, and expanding freedom.

As a rule, freedom over the longer term is quite beneficial to those who have it. It gives a long-term advantage over those who do not have it, or have less of it. Nevertheless, the evolution of freedom is far from linear. Setbacks, recessions, and turnarounds on the path from serfdom to freedom happen regularly. Perhaps there is still no good theory to explain the temporal degradation of freedom.

Divisibility of freedom and its measurement

"Freedom is divisible." This statement is true for particular freedoms in each sphere, and for the freedom of an individual actor and of a whole society. Freedom can be increased, subtracted, multiplied, and divided. The volume of freedom can be expanded—or reduced—by family, tribe, community, neighbors, church, union, court, and state.

The measurement of freedom has at least three dimensions: level (i.e., freedom per person), spread (or scope) (i.e., diffusion or dissemination among the members of society), and volume (i.e., the amount of freedom in society as a whole). The volume of freedom is either the sum of individual freedoms or the multiplication of the average level of freedom per capita over the spread of freedom in a society (see figure 11).

Depending on the combination of the level and scope of freedom, political, social, legal, and economic regimes can be placed in different locations in figure 12. Most known societies are located along the diagonal line, somewhere between the lower right corner of the chart and its upper left one. The lowest levels of freedom per capita for most members of society and at the same time the widest spread of freedom can be found in societies ruled by violent anarchy. The model of totalitarianism suggests a very low level of freedom applied universally for all members of a society. In practice, totalitarianism gives an enormous amount of freedom to the totalitarian leader, who is effectively unrestricted in his or her actions, while the other members of the society are stripped of the

Figure 11: Three dimensions of freedom

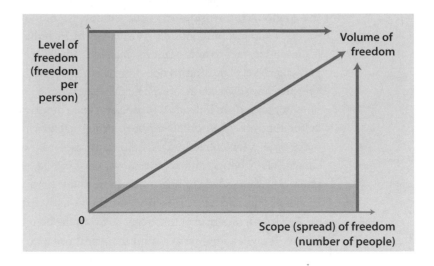

Figure 12: Level and scope of freedom vs. various regimes

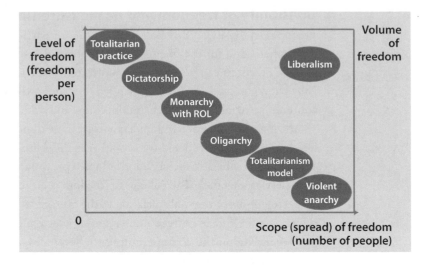

most basic freedoms. A dictatorship provides a very high (but not the highest) level of freedom for the dictator with low levels of freedom for other members of society. A monarchy with an effective rule of law (as in some European regimes at the time of the Enlightenment and in the 19th century) limits the monarch's level of freedom, but gives relatively more freedom (compared to the dictatorship) to the territory's general citizens. An oligarchy gives a relatively high level of freedom to the narrow circle of those who belong to the elite (but lower than that for the monarch) as well as middle level of freedom for the other members of the society. Finally, liberalism (a free society) provides the highest possible level of freedom per capita for most members of a society.

Figure 12 shows that there are both commonalities and differences between liberalism on the one hand, and violent anarchy and totalitarianism on the other. Free society (liberalism) and real totalitarianism are similar in that they provide the highest levels of freedom per capita. They are strikingly different in the spread of this freedom among the members of that society. Liberalism and anarchy are similar in that they provide equal or close to equal distribution of freedom per capita, but they are strikingly different in the absolute amount of freedom per capita.

Apart from the exceptions in extreme cases like violent anarchy, real totalitarianism, and liberalism, freedom in a society is neither evenly distributed among its all members nor totally concentrated in the hands of one actor. Therefore, the proper measurement of the scope of freedom may be supplemented with the measurement of freedom inequality, or differentiation of freedom.

Constructing an index of freedom

It is unlikely that an overall index of freedom (IF) can be constructed on the basis of individual preferences. Since human preferences are highly subjective and qualitatively different, it is probably next to impossible for anyone to measure, compare, and judge those personal priorities. What is nevertheless possible is to measure and compare the conditions that exist in different societies that are conducive for non-coercive human actions. Like natural climates that are neither too hot, nor too cold, neither too wet, nor too dry, but are warm and sufficiently damp, and thus create the most conducive conditions for the widest possible diversity of flora and fauna to flourish, so, too, a mild legal, cultural, and political climate (the optimal social climate) creates the most conducive conditions for the widest diversity of human activity to flourish.

The set of elements constituting an index of freedom includes at least four components: a *level of freedom per capita* in different spheres to measure the amount of freedom an individual person can possess; the *spread of freedom in society* to measure the number of a society's members that are enjoying freedom; *inequality in freedom* to measure how freedom is distributed among a society's members (and, conversely, the different levels of freedom among different members in that society); and the total *volume of freedom* in a society, which is a sum of per capita freedom for all members of that society. The proper indicator for measuring inequality in freedom might be a *degree of legal equality*, or *legal equality coefficient* (LEC, something similar to the Gini coefficient).

The formula of the overall index of freedom per capita might look as following:

4. IF = a*Fl*LECl + b*Fb*LECb + c*Fd*LECd + d*Fm*LECm + e*Fc*LECc
+ f*Fi*LECi + g*Ff*LECf + h*Fe*LECe + i*Fs*LECs + j*Fp*LECp),

where:

IF = overall index of freedom;

Fl, Fb, Fd, Fm, Fc, Fi, Ff, Fe, Fs, Fp = levels of freedom per capita in different spheres (life, use of one's own body, diet, movement, consciousness, intimate relations, family, economics, civil society, polity);

LECl, …, LECp = legal equality coefficients among members of society in the corresponding areas; and

a, b, …, j = weights for particular freedoms in each area of human action.

References

Berlin, Isaiah (1958). Two concepts of liberty. In Isaiah Berlin (1969), *Four Essays on Liberty* (Oxford University Press).

Locke, John (1689). Chapter VI: Of Paternal Power. *Second Treatise on Government*. Sec. 57.

Constant, Benjamin (1816/1988). The Liberty of the Ancients compared with the Liberty of the Moderns. In Biancamaria Fontana (ed.), *The Political Writings of Benjamin Constant* (Cambridge University Press): 309–28. <http://www.uark.edu/depts/comminfo/cambridge/ancients.html>, as of May 14, 2012.

CHAPTER SEVEN

Evolution and Freedom

Paul H. Rubin *

Thanks to the Economic Freedom of the World project, we know a good deal about economic freedom. Less is known about other forms of freedom. There is an ongoing effort to improve our knowledge of other forms of freedom, developed by the same organizations that originally developed the Economic Freedom index. (See, for example, Vasquez and Stumberger, 2012) In this paper I will explore the basis for the demand for other forms of freedom, and for the desire to limit freedom. I base this analysis on our evolutionary background, and in particular on the evolution of political and economic preferences, as discussed in Rubin (2002 and 2003).

I begin with a discussion of individuality. I then discuss some specific forms of freedom: political freedom, religious freedom, crime, discrimination, and trade. I conclude with an organization scheme for measuring freedom.

Individuality

All individuals are different. This is not a casual observation, nor is it a new age "feel good" statement. Rather, it is a scientific statement based on evolutionary theory.

First is the difference between males and females. Males and females pursue different reproductive strategies, not just in humans, but in all sexual species. One important cause of this difference is that males have much more variance in their offspring than do females (though of course the means are, by definition, the same.) This difference in reproductive success then leads to important differences in behavior. In particular, males are more risk-seeking than females. This is because the potential payoff for a risky strategy is much greater for a male than for a female. This is because the maximum number of offspring for a female is limited because of the time and physiological cost of bearing children, while the number of offspring a male can father is virtually unlimited. This is particularly true for

---

* Paul H. Rubin is Samuel Candler Dobbs Professor of Economics, Emory University.

mammals because the cost of bearing and nurturing a child is quite high for female mammals. This means that there is a greater variance among males than females for most traits. More men than women win Nobel prizes, but there are more homeless men (e.g., Wikipedia has an entry on "Homelessness in the United States," which reports that about 25 percent of the homeless are women.) Since each child has one father and one mother, the mean number of offspring for males and females is the same

But there are differences other than gender between individuals.

Consider a simple evolutionary game, the hawk-dove game. The setup is this: There is some animal that may come in two types, a "hawk" and a "dove." The animals move about until they find some resource, such as food, which they then eat. If two doves find the food, they share it. If two hawks find the food, they fight and the winner eats the food (unless both are killed.) Fighting may lead to injuries for one or both animals. If a hawk and a dove find the food the dove leaves and the hawk eats the food.

Start with a population of all doves. Then allow a mutation creating a hawk. One hawk in a world of doves does very well since whenever he meets a dove he gets all the food. The hawk does so well that he is more "fit" than the doves. That is, the hawk has more offspring than the average dove, so that in the next generation there are more hawks. This continues for a while, but there are limits. As there are more hawks, the chance of two hawks meeting increases. If two hawks meet they injure each other. That is, the payoff to each hawk from meeting another hawk is less than the payoff to each dove from meeting another dove. So at some point, when the proportion of hawks increases enough, the payoff to being a dove and the payoff to being a hawk are the same. At this point the population is at equilibrium. The actual equilibrium will depend on relative payoffs and on the harm suffered by each hawk, but for our purposes it is enough to note that there is some equilibrium with both hawks and doves coexisting in the population.

This is an example of what is called "frequency dependent selection." That is, the direction of selection depends on the relative frequency of each type in the society. Should the number of hawks increase to too high a proportion, there are pressures to reduce the number of hawks, and similarly for doves. But the key point is that at equilibrium there will be both types in society as a result of natural forces. Even this simple model requires two types of animals. If there are more strategies, then there can be more types. For example, by adding a third strategy, the "bourgeois" strategy, which is to fight when you are first to arrive, but run if you are second, then there are three types. We can also modify each strategy quantitatively. For example, fight for 10 seconds and then quit if you haven't won. This leads to many more potential types in society.

Now consider this: Humans play a lot of games which are similar, but not identical, to the hawk-dove game. We can tell the truth or we can lie.

If everyone tells the truth, then a liar can successfully invade, just like a hawk. But if there are too many liars, then no one believes anyone, and there is no payoff from being a liar. Thus, there should be some proportion of honest people in society and some proportion of liars. The possibility of detecting lying adds another dimension: we try to determine if someone is a liar or not because no one (either honest or a liar) wants to do business with a liar. Then we become better or worse at detecting liars, and both the skill at lying and the ability to detect lying can increase over time in a type of evolutionary arms race. But at any given time there are some liars (some better and some worse), some honest people, some who are better than average at detecting liars, and some who are worse.

In a direct analogy to the hawk-dove game, think of bargaining strategies. One can be a hard bargainer or an easy bargainer. Hard bargainers get more when dealing with easy bargainers, but if two hard bargainers meet, they may not reach an agreement and so both lose. Easy bargainers might "split the difference" and so do well when pitted against each other, but fare poorly against a hard bargainer. Again, this would lead to equilibrium, with some people being hard bargainers and some easy bargainers. Moreover, as in the case of the hawk-dove equilibrium, we are not limited to two possible types. Some can bargain "really" hard and some less so. If we think of indexing bargaining by the number of offers one is willing to make, then we can get a large number of types in equilibrium.

Think of desire for dominance. Again, some people are more eager to dominate than others. At equilibrium there would be some individuals who would be more dominant and some who would be more submissive. Other examples include honesty or willingness to cheat, and selfishness or generosity. People may be more introverted or more extroverted. There is evidence that sociopathy follows similar principles, with 1 or 2 percent of the population being sociopaths. (Mealey, 1995). All of these strategies can be broken down further, and there are many more dimensions on which individuals can vary. Reiss (2000) identifies 14 dimensions; Arnhart (1998) identifies 20.

Moreover, this variation is merely genetic. There is also environmental variation. Identical twins, for example, share all their genes and have very similar preferences, but are not actually identical. Other than identical twins, all individuals have different genomes, and no two individuals share the same environment. Moreover, environments will affect different individuals differently. The bottom line is that individuals differ from each other. Any effort to treat all individuals the same will perforce fail, and will lead to great losses in utility or happiness as some individuals will suffer from this attempt. Think, for example, of previous efforts to force all children, including left-handed children, to write right-handed.

Because all individuals are different, there are gains from allowing individuality. These are both private and public gains. Privately, people are happier if left alone to do what they desire, subject to constraints involving harm to others. The left-handed children who were forced to write with their right hand suffered from this forced behavior.

There are also social gains from some (though not all) individuality. In general, if we allow individuals to specialize in what they do best (subject to market prices) then society will be richer because individuals will be more productive than if they could only do what they were told to do. Of course, some specialties will be socially counterproductive, and we try to deter these by punishment. For example, sociopaths are generally not productive, nor are cheaters or robbers. Nonetheless, as a general rule, allowing individuals to express their individuality will generally benefit society. Moreover, as markets become larger (due to increased wealth and greater possibilities for trade) there is more room for division of labor and specialization. This increased specialization allows each individual to choose an occupation that more naturally matches his or her preferences and abilities.

Political freedom

Humans are hierarchical, as are many other species. Males particularly seek to become dominant. Dominant males have greater sexual access and so leave more offspring. This in turn means that the genetic basis for seeking dominance remains strong. This pattern precedes our becoming human; it is common to most mammalian species, and perhaps even reptiles.

Nonetheless, the best evidence we have is that our human (male) ancestors were quite free throughout most of our evolutionary existence and the power of dominants was limited. This may seem counterintuitive. History as studied in school is full of dictators and kings, and most individuals seem to have had little freedom. However, most of our existence as humans and all of the existence of our pre-human ancestors occurred before there was writing, and so before "history." Indeed, the most important division in human existence is between the long period during which our ancestors were nomadic hunter-gatherers and the period when sedentary agricultural societies came into existence (Kelly, 1995.) During the hunter-gatherer phase of existence, humans were non-hierarchical and relatively egalitarian (Boehm, 1999.) This egalitarianism was maintained in spite of tendencies for males to want to dominate. It was maintained because coercion by dominants was limited. A group of individuals could resist anyone who attempted to obtain too much power (what Boehm calls an "upstart"). Moreover, societies had little or no fixed capital and were nomadic, so that it was possible for a group of individuals to simply leave a would-be dominant behind, and move elsewhere. This led to what is called "reproductive leveling" (Bowles and Gintis, 2011).

About 10,000 years ago, this changed. With the rise of agriculture, societies settled down and became sedentary. With the beginning of sedentary societies, kings and other rulers arose and were able to dominate others. This was partly because the move-away option was lost with the origin of fixed capital. It was also because societies became wealthy enough to support a group of specialists in violence who could support and defend a king or dictator. Because writing began during this period, it is also the beginning of history. This is the period of the beginning of the empires and kingdoms studied by historians.

One important biological characteristic of dominants is the number of wives and concubines available to them. Betzig (1986) has described in detail the sexual access available to dominants. Many kings and emperors had a very large number of wives and therefore descendants. Zerjal and others (2003) have shown that Genghis Khan is apparently the ancestor to 8 percent of the men in the area of Asia conquered by the Mongols. This ability of dominants to engross many women can perhaps explain the desire of our nomadic ancestors to limit the power of dominants and the wisdom of doing so.

Modern western societies have greatly increased political freedom relative to the kingdoms and dictatorships which have dominated human history. Indeed, these societies are the freest that have ever existed. This is because our hunter-gatherer societies provided a lot of freedom for men, but were generally oppressive for women. Modern contemporary western societies provide freedom for both men and women.

Political freedom is fragile and can be lost; consider the example of Nazi Germany. Even without such an extreme example, it is possible for those in power to abuse their position. This may be to unjustly enrich themselves or their relatives or followers. It may also be possible to illegitimately manipulate the political system to maintain power.

While democracy does not guarantee freedom, it is unlikely that there will be long term freedom without democracy. This is because in a non-democratic society the amount of freedom will be subject to the will of the particular dictator in power. One ruler may allow much freedom, but his successor may not. An unrestricted democracy may also restrict the freedom of minorities, whether they are religious, ethnic, or income-based minorities. For example, a majority may impose confiscatory taxes on a wealthy minority. The best system is probably a democracy with binding constraints on the power of government.

Many aspects of political freedom are useful in themselves, but are especially useful for protecting political freedom and avoiding political abuse. That is, these limits can serve as the binding constraints on the power of government, and of majorities (Mialon and Rubin, 2008). Freedom of the press enables people to learn about the behavior of government, including any efforts by government to expand its power. Freedom of speech enables people to communicate with each other and to protest efforts by government to increase its power. Freedom of assembly enables people to congregate in order to organize protests if government should misbehave. An important issue is captured in the answer to the question: Is everything that is not prohibited, allowed, or is everything that is not allowed, prohibited? That is, is the default that people have rights unless there is explicit authority to limit rights, or is the default that the government must explicitly allow individual actions? The former is consistent with freedom; the latter is not. Probably the most freedom that is possible is a democracy constrained by limits such as these.

The ultimate limit on the power of government is the right of citizens to have arms for self-defense and defense against an overly intrusive government. Of course, what is relevant for freedom is not the statement of these rights; rather, what is needed is actual enforcement of the rights.

Religious freedom

Humans are by far the most intelligent species on earth, by a wide margin. The main evolutionary driving force behind our enormous intelligence undoubtedly has been competition with other humans. Our distant ancestors were probably about as smart as chimpanzees, but with successive populations of humans, for unknown reasons, competition became more intense, and this competition led to increasing intelligence. This competition provides the only potential positive feedback mechanism that would have been necessary to increase intelligence to the level we observe.

This means that our brains evolved to deal with other intelligent beings. As a result, the default when we observe some event is that it is the product of intelligence (Boyer, 2001; Guthrie, 1993; Shermer, 2011). This is the ultimate source of religious belief: we look for intelligence to explain events and we call that intelligence "God" or gods. Once belief in supernatural beings and some sort of religion became established in our minds, it became a tool available for other uses. Two of these uses were the strengthening of morality (Burkert, 1996) and the strengthening of group solidarity. Moreover, we can compare religions in terms of their ability to strengthen or weaken particular groups.

An important feature of religion is that it is totally non-testable. That is, there is no objective or scientific way of determining if a set of religious beliefs is "true." If things go well, then the gods like us. If things go badly, then we have done something to annoy the gods. There is nothing that can happen that is inconsistent with any conceivable set of religious beliefs, and so no way telling if a religion is correct or not, and no way of telling if one religion is better than another. Thus, Tribe A can have one set of beliefs and Tribe B can have another, and these beliefs can be inconsistent. In particular, each tribe can believe that its god(s) are stronger than those of other tribes.

But although there is no way of measuring any truth value to religion, some religions may "work" better than others, in the sense that they lead societies that hold those beliefs to be more successful than others. For an extreme example, a religion that believes in complete celibacy will not do well, and will last only one generation. For an even more extreme case, a religion that believes in drinking poisoned Kool-Aid will not even last one generation.

There are less extreme examples. I mentioned that religion can enforce morality. Consider two possible moral tenets associated with different tribal religions: "The gods want you to keep your promises to other members of the tribe"; or, "The gods want you to lie to other members of the tribe whenever it is possible." While there is no way of telling what the gods really want, the first religion will have more followers than the second simply because followers of the first religion will be more successful and so biologically more fit. That is, keeping promises within the group will lead to increase possibilities for cooperation and so increased wealth and thus increased survival of children, and so increased fitness. Moreover, members of the second tribe, observing the success of the first tribe, will be more likely to try to join that tribe, also leading to faster growth. This may explain why all surviving successful religions advocate reasonably efficient moral values.

Humans are by nature a tribal species, and we easily define in-group and out-group members. When religions were tribal, then religion and tribe would have been mutually enforcing ways of defining group membership. One function of modern religions is to expand the in-group beyond the level of the tribe. In particular, Christianity and Islam both allow and encourage (and sometimes force) conversion of non-tribe members into the religion. While it appears that there is and has been much conflict between different religions and sub-religions (Sunni versus Shiite, Protestants versus Catholics, Christians versus Muslims) nonetheless, by increasing inclusivity and thus increasing group size, religion has probably had the net effect of reducing human conflict.

The key point, however, is that there is no objective way of determining that any religion is more true than another. Moreover, people are often strongly attached to their particular religion. Also, some religions may be more successful than others (in the sense mentioned above) and so competition between religions can lead to increases in efficiency or happiness. Therefore, it would be better if no one attempted to control religion, and the costs of such control can be very high because of the attachment people have to their religion. Thus, religious freedom is a net good for society. This is a two-part freedom. Government should not persecute or forbid particular religions. It should also not promote one religion over another, but should be neutral with respect to religion. Of course, some may believe that their religion is the only true one, and that everyone should follow that religion. Religious freedom is an important component of freedom, but one which is often under attack.

Crime

Some individuals will always find crime to be a privately useful activity. For some, crime is an efficient way to accumulate resources. Some males may not have access to females for consensual sexual services, and may find rape to be the best substitute. Some may find murder the best way to eliminate rivals (Daly and Wilson, 1988). For reasons having to do with risk-seeking, most crime is committed by young males, although others also commit crimes (Rubin and Paul, 1979). Crime interferes with the efficient functioning of society, and so societies make efforts to reduce the amount of crime, either by deterrence or by incapacitation.

Crime has two adverse effects on freedom. On the one hand, crime or the threat of crime can directly reduce freedom. If I am afraid to visit certain places because of crime, then I am not free to visit those places. If my money is stolen through force or fraud, then I am not free to spend that money. If I fear that my money will be stolen, then I will have reduced incentives to work hard and accumulate wealth. If I am the victim of physical crime (assault, rape, or even murder), then my freedom is clearly compromised. As a result, one of the first duties of government is to protect citizens from criminal victimization.

On the other hand, freedom can also be reduced when government efforts to control crime are excessive. If citizens are subject to random searches, or even to arbitrary arrest and conviction, or if punishments are disproportionate to the harm caused by crime, then again, their freedom is compromised. Thus, crime leads to an inescapable tradeoff: that between security from criminal victimization and security from government overzealousness in preventing crime. There are several dimensions to this tradeoff (which are discussed in Mialon and Rubin, 2007).

First, what rights do the police have in attempting to catch criminals? (Though every society must address these tradeoffs, I discuss mainly the case of the United States since I am most familiar with it.) Some restrictions on the police in the US are as follows. In most cases, police must have a warrant to search. If police conduct a search without a proper warrant, the evidence is "excluded." Police must refrain from questioning a suspect if he asks for a lawyer, and must inform suspects of the right to have an attorney present. While these particular rights are specific US rights, some limit on the power of the police is necessary and all societies must address the same tradeoffs.

Once a suspect is formally accused, there are several rights associated with the trial process. The most important two rights have to do with the burden of proof and the standard of proof. Perhaps the most fundamental issue is the burden of proof, enshrined in the phrase "innocent until proven guilty." That is, the burden of proof is on the prosecution (the government) which must prove that the accused committed the crime. It is difficult to conceive of a truly free society that does not honor this principle. Second is the standard of proof needed for conviction —the probability that the accused did commit the crime. In the US that standard is "beyond a reasonable doubt," enshrined in the maxim, "Better that 10 guilty men go free than that one innocent man is convicted" (Volokh, 1997). Other principles have to do with rules regulating trials: freedom from self-incrimination, the speed of the trial, freedom from double jeopardy, right to a jury trial, and similar procedural rights. If one is convicted, then issues of permissible punishment become relevant. Again, in the US "cruel and unusual punishment" is forbidden. This issue is most relevant today in debates about the legitimacy of capital punishment. Other societies still rely on corporal punishment: whipping or even mutilation.

Again, the key is the set of tradeoffs. Any additional rights granted to accused persons will of necessity lead to more guilty people being freed, which will lead to reduced deterrence and increased crime. Different governments may make this tradeoff on different terms, but all must confront the tradeoffs, and these tradeoffs will always have implications for freedom.

Two additional issues are associated with crime and freedom. One is the ability of individuals to protect themselves from crime. In the US, this is bound up with the right of individuals to possess guns and with rules about their permissible use in self-defense. Many other societies forbid individual gun ownership. (As mentioned above, this right is also associated with political freedom.)

An additional issue is the scope of the criminal law. One concern is the regulation of private behavior, and in particular regulation of the use of drugs. In much of the world, certain drugs (marijuana, heroin, cocaine) are illegal. Libertarians view these laws as being illegitimate. Again, the treatment of these issues is an aspect of freedom. A desire to ban the use of these substances may be related to the evolutionary role of young males in society. Specifically, a society depends on young males to protect it from other societies, but young males themselves are competitive with each other. It is important to limit this competition and to direct the energy of young males away from their own society. Drug consumption may be a form in inter-male competition, where individuals show that they can consumer harmful substances and still remain strong. (This is called "handicap" competition (Zahavi and Zahavi, 1997).)

Even where drugs are illegal, societies must make many additional decisions that affect freedom: decisions about methods of prosecution, whether the use of those drugs will be treated as a felony or misdemeanor, severity of sentencing, resources devoted to policing this issue. Moreover, making drugs illegal can affect other aspects of freedom (Miron and Zweibel, 1995). If drugs are illegal, then extralegal methods will be used for enforcement, and this can lead to increases in crime. For example, if the terms of a drug exchange are violated, the aggrieved party cannot use the courts for enforcement, and may instead rely on violence. Increasing the price of drugs by making them illegal can also induce drug users to commit crimes to obtain resources to purchase drugs.

Drug laws in one society can also export crime to another. For example, the US drug laws seem to lead to massive crimes in Mexico as gangs compete for the right to serve the illegal US drug market. While this aspect of drug laws may not have a direct impact on most US citizens, it should be a consideration is deciding on domestic policy.

Discrimination

In an ideal world, all rights would adhere to individuals as individuals, not to individuals as members of a group. Any violation of this principle, by private citizens or by governments, may be viewed as an infringement of freedom because some individuals will be denied some rights due to their birth. However, as discussed below, there are limits to discrimination by individuals, so there is greater danger of government violation of individual rights. Governments may discriminate against minorities or against majorities. There is also gender discrimination. All three types interfere with freedom.

Private versus government discrimination

If there is private discrimination, then there are market forces that will reduce or eliminate this discrimination. For example, consider employment discrimination. If it exists, then employers will pay more for workers than they would pay absent the discrimination. This is because discrimination essentially reduces the supply of workers, and a reduction in supply leads to higher wages. This creates an incentive for some employers to ignore the discrimination and hire the victims. Even if no current employer is willing to do so, new employers can enter the market and still make a profit, as when northerners opened textile firms in the US south and hired black workers who were discriminated against by southern employers. Similar forces work to reduce or eliminate discrimination against certain customers. Note that it only requires that some firms be willing to break the pattern of discrimination; it need not be a unanimous or even a majority decision. It might be possible to maintain a private system of discrimination if there are terrorist groups willing to enforce the discrimination (e.g., the Ku Klux Klan) and if the public authorities do not interfere, but otherwise the amount of such discrimination is limited.

On the other hand, government can enforce discrimination because competition for government services is limited and because government has access to tax revenues to finance losses. . For example, again in the US south, it was possible to maintain a racially segregated school system as long as white voters wanted this system and African-Americans were disenfranchised. There was no internal constraint on the ability of government to engage in this behavior. There was no possibility of a competing publicly financed school system to break down this discrimination.

Discrimination: minorities or majorities

Some societies discriminate against minorities, as the US did with respect to blacks before the Civil Rights era. Minorities may be denied employment rights or government services (e.g., provided with no or inferior education.) This may be because majorities do not want to associate with minorities (Becker's "taste for discrimination" (Becker, 1956, 1971)) or because majorities save money by discriminating (inferior schools are cheaper). Majorities may also want to eliminate the competition that minorities present; this has been a common motive for anti-Semitism and other forms of discrimination, including some aspects of apartheid in South Africa.

Societies may also discriminate against majorities. For example, affirmative action as practiced in the US and elsewhere (Sowell, 1990) is basically a form of discrimination against majorities. Part of the explanation for this form of discrimination is standard public choice analysis. Once minorities are no longer disenfranchised, then members of the minority group have a stronger interest in favorable discrimination than the interest of majority members in avoiding discrimination. That is for standard reasons. If blacks are 10 percent of the population, then on average, the benefits of affirmative action are nine times as large for each beneficiary as the cost to each majority member. Moreover, programs such as affirmative action will create a body of bureaucrats with an interest in enforcement, and these individuals will also act as a special interest group.

Public choice analysis is not sufficient to explain such discrimination, however. This is because there is discrimination in favor of some, but not all, minorities. For example, in the US, there is discrimination in favor of African-Americans and Hispanics, but not Asians or Jews. Some additional element is needed to explain this discrimination. This is probably some guilt on the part of majorities regarding the past or present treatment of the favored minority.

Discrimination by government may be particularly pernicious. That is because, as mentioned above, humans are a naturally tribal species. When members of one group perceive that they are being discriminated against in favor of members of some other group, this can lead to dislike of the favored group.

Gender discrimination

Most societies have discriminated against women and such discrimination is still common. In most Islamic societies women are denied many rights. In much of Asia there is even prenatal discrimination, with selective abortion against female fetuses so that more children will be male. Wife-beating has been a feature of every pre-literate society (Edgerton, 1992). In the West, women were only granted the vote in the late nineteenth or early twentieth century (e.g., New Zealand, 1893; US, 1918); other rights came even later.

As for other aspects of freedom, there are two benefits to gender equality. There is a utility benefit, as women clearly are less happy when discriminated against. There is also an economic benefit. Countries that deny economic rights to women are losing about one half of their labor force, and so they have greatly reduced productivity. Women who are forced to remain at home can produce some economic output, but not nearly so much as can be produced in the labor force.

Trade

International trade can increase freedom by increasing the set of goods available to consumers. Trade does this both by expanding the physical set of goods available and by reducing prices of goods that may already be available. Thus, such trade is an important component of freedom. While free trade is perhaps a component of economic freedom, I mention it here because views on trade are closely bound up with our evolved preferences, and because attitudes towards trade are also closely related to attitudes about immigration and treatment of foreigners.

There are two reasons related to human information processing as to why international trade is a politically difficult issue. First, our natural way of thinking is zero-sum. That is, our minds are not well adapted to thinking about positive-sum interactions. This is because for most of our evolutionary history our ancestors lived in a zero-sum world with little in the way of technological change or investment, and only small gains from trade (Rubin, 2003). As a result, we do not easily perceive that trade, and particularly international trade, benefits both parties. Moreover, zero-sum thinking also applies to the issue of jobs, so our natural way of thinking is that when we buy something made by foreigners, someone from our own society must lose a job.

Second, as mentioned above, we are a tribal species. This means that we put much more emphasis on our own welfare than on the welfare of those outside the tribe, which would include citizens of other countries. This combination means that when untrained people think of trade, they think of our tribe members losing jobs to foreigners, and find this thought repugnant. Of course, training in economics can teach people that their first thought is incorrect, and economists have done a remarkable job of convincing citizens that trade is beneficial and tariffs are harmful, but people must be convinced. Understanding the benefits of trade does not come without some effort at learning.

The freedom project

As mentioned above, there is an effort to develop a set of measures of non-economic freedom to complement the Economic Freedom of the World project. The analysis here suggests a classification scheme for this project. This is based in part on categories discussed in Vasquez and Stumberger, 2012. While the individual items suggested by Vasquez and Stumberger will fit into the categories discussed below, the organization of these categories is somewhat different.

Individuality and personal freedom

Some measures would apply to human individuality and to personal freedom. These would include measures of sexual freedom, such as rights of homosexuals and of sex workers. Restrictions on behavior, such as limits on gambling and pornography, and on drug use, would also fit into this measure (but perhaps in the section on crime), as would abortion restrictions. Perhaps a measure of the availability of private schools would be appropriate here as well. There is also the issue of military conscription, a restriction on freedom that leads to a mismatch between people and skills.

Political freedom

One measure would apply to political freedom. There are various direct measures, such as measures of government turnover (a measure of actual political competition) and measures of democratic institutions. Items such as actual government oppression (e.g., political imprisonment) would belong in this category. There are also measures of the inputs to political freedom, such as freedom of the press and freedom of assembly. These are the constraints on government political power. Rights to gun ownership would also be in this category.

Religious freedom

Religious freedom comes in two parts. First is the freedom of religion. That is, are people allowed to worship in whichever way they desire? This issue might overlap with the issue of discrimination, if some discrimination is religious. Second is freedom from religion: Is there a state religion, and are people taxed to support a religion that may not be theirs?

Crime

There are two issues with respect to crime and freedom. First is the degree of victimization: What are crime rates? How likely is the average person to be a victim of crime? Second is the measures governments take to control crime, and the impact of these on individuals. What are the rights of the accused? What restrictions are there on the state in fighting crime? How powerful are the police and what restrictions are there on police power? For many people who may not have an interest in politics these freedoms (from crime and from police) are likely to be the most important. Because regulation of some aspects of behavior (drugs, pornography, gambling) are criminally enforced, some of these issues might fit here instead of in the personal freedom section.

Discrimination

Issues of discrimination are complex. We must first distinguish types of victims of discrimination: minorities, majorities, and women. We must then distinguish between private and government discrimination. Then there are various forms of discrimination. Is there employment discrimination? Educational discrimination? Political discrimination? Restrictions on consumption (e.g., "ride in the back of the bus" rules, or segregated public facilities, such as restaurants)?

International trade

To what extent are people allowed to purchase goods that are made in other countries? Are there tariffs or non-tariff trade barriers? Are there other restrictions on the international movement of people or goods? Is emigration allowed? We might also include rights of non-citizens in this category. Are non-citizens allowed civil rights? Allowed to work? Subject to random deportation?

Summary

Our evolutionary background has caused us to value freedom. However, this same background has meant that we have tendencies that also cause us to limit freedom. Individuals want to become dominant, and institutions of political freedom are necessary to prevent this from happening. Crime can limit our freedom, and efforts to control crime can also limit freedom, so a careful balance is necessary. Although it is not possible to test religious beliefs, many are convinced that they have seen the "truth," and so may want to restrict the ability of others to worship as they may desire. We may dislike members of other "tribes" and want to deny them freedom. Most human societies have limited the freedom of women, harming both the women themselves and also limiting the wealth of society. International trade can increase our freedom by providing cheaper and more varied goods for consumption, but our natural way of thinking does not understand these benefits. For these reasons, some in society try to limit freedom. Vigilance to prevent these limits is important. Moreover, understanding of these evolved interferences with freedom can help us decide what to measure in an effort to devise freedom indices.

References

Arnhart, Larry, (1998). *Darwinian Natural Right: The Biological Ethics of Human Nature.* State University of New York Press.

Betzig, Laura L. (1986). *Despotism and Differential Reproduction: A Darwinian View of History.* Aldine de Gruyter.

Becker, Gary S. (1956/1971). *The Economics of Discrimination,* 2d ed. University of Chicago Press.

Boehm, Christopher (1999). *Hierarchy in the Forest: The Evolution of Egalitarian Behavior.* Harvard University Press.

Bowles, Samuel, and Herbert Gintis (2011). *A Cooperative Species: Human Reciprocity and its Evolution.* Princeton University Press.

Boyer, Pascal (2001). *Religion Explained: The Evolutionary Origins of Religious Thought.* Basic Books.

Burkert, Walter (1996). *Creation of the Sacred: Tracks of Biology in Early Religions.* Harvard University Press.

Daly, Martin, and Margo Wilson (1988). *Homicide.* Aldine de Gruyter.

Edgerton, Robert B. (1992). *Sick Societies: Challenging the Myth of Primitive Harmony.* Free Press.

Guthrie, Stewart (1993). *Faces in the Clouds: A New Theory of Religion.* Oxford University Press.

Kelly, Robert L. (1995). *The Foraging Spectrum: Diversity in Hunter-Gatherer Lifeways.* Smithsonian Institution Press.

Mealey, Linda (1995). The sociobiology of sociopathy: An integrated evolutionary model. *Behavioral and Brain Sciences,* 18 (3): 523-599.

Mialon, Hugo, and Paul H. Rubin (2008). The economics of the Bill of Rights. *American Law and Economics Review,* Spring, 10 (1): 1-60.

Miron, J, and J. Zwiebel (1995). The economic case against drug prohibition. *Journal of Economic Perspectives,* 9 (4): 175-192.

Reiss, Steven (2000). *Who Am I? The 16 Basic Desires That Motivate Our Actions and Define Our Personalities.* Tarcher/Putnam.

Rubin, Paul H. (2002). *Darwinian Politics: The Evolutionary Origin of Freedom.* Rutgers University Press.

Rubin, Paul H. (2003). Folk economics. *Southern Economic Journal,* July, 70, (1): 157-171.

Rubin, Paul H., and Chris Paul (1979). An evolutionary model of taste for risk. *Economic Inquiry,* 17 (4): 585-96.

Shermer, Michael (2011). *The Believing Brain: From Ghosts and Gods to Politics and Conspiracies—How We Construct Beliefs and Reinforce Them as Truths.* Times Books.

Sowell, Thomas (1990). *Preferential Policies: An International Perspective.* W. Morrow.

Tatiana Zerjal, et al. (2003). The genetic legacy of the Mongols. *American Journal of Human Genetics,* March, 72 (3): 717-721.

Vásquez, Ian and Tanja Štumberger (2012). An Index of Freedom in the World. In Fred McMahon (ed.), *Towards a Worldwide Index of Human Freedom* (Fraser Institute): 55-112.

Volokh, Alexander (1997). *n* guilty men. 146 *University of Pennsylvania Law Review* 173. <http://www2.law.ucla.edu/volokh/guilty.htm>, as of October 19, 2011.

Zahavi, Amotz, and Avishag Zahavi (1997). *The Handicap Principle: A Missing Piece of Darwin's Puzzle.* Oxford University Press.

CHAPTER EIGHT

Liberty in Comparative Perspective

China, India, and the West

Erich Weede *

Introduction

Until about 200 years ago, most of mankind was desperately poor. Then the great transformation happened. Global population increased seven-fold, global production more than 60-fold, and manufacturing industry at least 75-fold (Goklany, 2007: 19, 41). During the nineteenth and twenti-eth centuries, Europe and its North American and Australasian daughter societies overtook the great Asian civilizations and overcame mass pov-erty (Collins, 1986; Jones, 1981; Landes, 1998; Maddison, 2001; North, 1990; North, Wallis, and Weingast, 2009; Weber, 1923/1981; Weede, 1996, 2000). Ferguson illustrates Western dominance before World War I in these terms: "In 1500 the future imperial powers of Europe accounted for about 10 percent of the world's land surface and at most 16 percent of its population. By 1913, 11 Western empires controlled nearly three-fifths of all territory and population and more than three-quarters (a staggering 79 percent) of global economic output. Average life expec-tancy in England was nearly twice what it was in India" (2011: 5). Japan was the first Asian country to experience catch-up growth. Since the 1960s, Singapore, Hong Kong, Taiwan, and South Korea followed. Now,

* Professor Dr. Erich Weede was born 1942 and taught sociology at the University of Bonn until his retirement in fall 2004. He earned academic degrees in psychology and politi-cal science. In 1982/83 he was president of the Peace Science Society (International), and in 1985/86 was vice-president of the International Studies Association. He has pro-duced 11 books and more than 200 other publications in German or English. His topics include the causes and prevention of war, the rise and decline of nations, Asian civiliza-tions, the invention of capitalism, the spread of economic freedom, economic growth, and income inequality. His books include *Economic Development, Social Order and World Politics* (Lynne Rienner, 1996) and *The Balance of Power, Globalization, and the Capitalist Peace* (for the Friedrich-Naumann Foundation, Liberal Verlag, 2005)..

mainland Asia is catching up. According to Maddison, in 1950 the Asian share of world population was 54.7 percent, but the Asian share of world GDP was only 18.6 percent (2007: 378, 381). Until 2003, the Asian share of global population had increased to 59.4 percent, and the Asian share of world GDP had more than doubled and increased to 40.5 percent. In 2003, the West still commanded 43 percent of world GDP, but contained only 12 percent of global population (Maddison, 2007: 71).

In general, global growth has been good for the poor (Dollar and Kraay, 2002).[1] The rise of Asia is documented by the fact that China has become the world's biggest manufacturer over the USA (*Economist*, 2011, June 25: 3). Neither the so-called "great seven" nor the "great eight" of the global economy constitute what the names suggest. Including Canada or Italy but excluding China and India may have had historical or political reasons, but the decision certainly does not reflect the current and even less likely the future weight of these economies. According to data published by the World Bank, the rank order of gross national incomes *in purchasing power parity terms* is: first, the United States; second, China; third, Japan; fourth, India; fifth, Germany; sixth, Russia; seventh, Britain; and eighth, France (2011: 344-345). Three among the top five are Asian economies. Moreover, the Chinese economy might become equal to the American in size (but not, of course, in living standards) before 2020 (Maddison, 1998: 17, 96). *The Economist* once speculated that not only in purchasing power terms, but even in dollar terms, both economies might be equal in 2019 (2010, December 18: 129). According to Maddison's estimates, in 2030 China might control about 23 percent, the USA 17 percent, and India 10 percent of gross world product (2007: 343). Fogel (2010) dares to make an even more extreme prediction. In his view, China might control 40 percent and the West, i.e., the US and the EU together, about half as big a share of global GDP by 2040. Although Chinese per capita GDP will remain lower than America's income per head, income levels in China might become twice as high as European ones.

The purpose of this paper is to explain the divergent economic performance of Asia's giants and the West with special reference to economic

---

1   Although Anand and Segal (2008: 63-64) doubt whether we know how the global distribution of income is changing, six of the analyses in their compilation of studies that cover the last three decades of the twentieth century report a decrease, but only three report an increase in inequality. So, there is more, albeit inconclusive evidence, in favor of an equalizing trend than of a change for the worse. Nevertheless, 41.6 percent of all Indians had to survive on less than $1.25 a day, and 75.6 percent on less than $2.00 a day in 2005. By contrast, only 15.9 percent of Chinese live below the lower threshold and only 36.3 percent below the higher threshold (World Bank, 2011: 346).

freedom[2] and the roots of limited government in political fragmentation and interstate competition. In a subsequent section of the paper I will summarize why both China and India were overtaken by the West. In doing so, I shall introduce some factors that might explain why China could outperform India when both economies started to grow faster than the global economy and began their catch-up growth spurts. The third and fourth sections of the paper analyze Chinese and Indian growth in the latter half of the twentieth century. The final sections of the paper examine Western civilization's future prospects and summarize the theoretical approach elaborated in this paper.

Property rights, incentives and their consequences in Eurasia

Until the end of the twentieth century, neither China nor India had made much progress in overcoming mass poverty. Why did these great Asian civilizations stand still when the West grew rich? Although explanatory debates are by no means settled, I favor an approach focusing on institutions (Weede, 1996, 2000, 2011a). Alternative theories underline the importance of technological progress and innovation (Goldstone, 2008; Huff, 2011; Paldam and Grundlach, 2008). It is frequently claimed that technology accounts for about 50 percent of economic growth and 80 percent of productivity growth. Despite the plausibility of the link between technological progress and growth, Niskanen provides a useful warning against exaggerating the impact of technology: "'Technology' is one of economists'... favorite code words for what they do not understand.... All these estimates of technology are residuals, estimates of the percentage of economic growth that economists cannot explain by the measured increase in conventional inputs. Any underestimate of the increase in the quantity or quality of labor or capital, for example, increases the magnitude of the residual, attributed without any direct evidence to an increase in technology. Similarly, any condition that improves the allocation of resources, such as economies of scale or a reduction in the distortive effects of taxes, tariffs, regulation, and litigation, is also attributed to an increase in technology" (2008: 15).

---

2 Since the concepts "freedom" and "liberty" are frequently misunderstood, it is necessary to point out that my understanding of freedom requires "that the individual be allowed to pursue *his own* ends" (Hayek, 1988: 63). In philosophical discourse this type of freedom is frequently called "negative freedom." Although "open access" is related to liberty, the two concepts differ. North, Wallis, and Weingast's (2009) "open access societies" are not only characterized by equality and the rule of law, but also by big government and universal social insurance programs. Like Hayek, I regard big government as a threat to liberty. For a comprehensive review of concepts of liberty, see McMahon (2012).

Ultimately, institutions matter because they structure permissible actions and incentives. They affect technological progress as much as they have an impact on economic performance. Individual liberty to theorize and to experiment as well as decentralized instead of collective decision-making have been background conditions of progress. Rosenberg and Birdzell explain why even the requirement of consent is harmful: "A society which delayed innovations by the amount of time required to reach a political consensus would fall further and further behind a society which did not … It implies the substantive criterion that the benefits of the innovation are sufficiently understood and predictable that they can be persuasively verbalized in advance of its adoption—that is, that everything is too clear to need the test of experiment" (1986: 310). In research as elsewhere in the division of labor, individual liberty permits the exploitation of human diversity for the benefit of all (Hayek, 1988: 80).

The institutional account is as useful for the explanation of why China could overtake India in the second part of the twentieth century as it is for explaining the rise of the West. It focuses on the liberating benefits of institutional competition which are ultimately rooted in interstate rivalry and geopolitics.[3] One may contend that limited government and the rule of law are underwritten by balances of power within and, even more importantly, between states. In the West such power balances arose because of interstate rivalry (Jones, 1981; Weber, 1923/1981), because of the competition between church and state (Berman, 1983), and because of the tensions between cities and territorial rulers in the Middle Ages (Weber, 1922/1964, 1923/1981).[4]

In my account of the rise of the West, there is a causal chain running from institutional competition via safe property rights and individual liberty to economic growth. Whether the safety of property rights or the freedom to trade had been much better in Europe than, say, in Asia, or whether it had dramatically improved before the industrial revolution and the take-off of European economies has been strongly disputed (Angeles, 2011; Hobson, 2004; Pomeranz, 2000). In this paper I cannot even attempt to discuss alternative historical approaches in any detail. It

---

3 According to Vaubel (2008), eighteenth century thinkers, including Ferguson, Hume, Montesquieu, Kant and Smith, preempted most of the arguments applied by contemporary writers.

4 Sally has pointed to the fact that no single power controlled the ports surrounding the Indian Ocean before the arrival of the Portuguese, the Dutch, and the British (2011: 9). Although this lack of political centralization may have protected the property rights of traders there as it did in Europe, the littoral of the Indian Ocean was not the core area of the land-based empires in India, and even less in China, which gave up the exploration of the oceans and restricted overseas trade in the fifteenth century.

may suffice to admit that almost all the details about property rights and incentives, taxes, and commercialization are disputed. Although I elaborate on the mechanisms or reasons which I believe to be important for leading from political fragmentation via economic freedom to prosperity, I do not provide much historical evidence about the intervening variables in my account. This would require at least a book, if not multiple volumes.

Whether property rights dramatically improved during the eighteenth and nineteenth centuries partly depends on the indicators of property rights accepted. Like North or Weingast (1989), but in contrast to Angeles (2011), I would accept high interest rates on public debt as an indicator of insufficiently safe property rights. Nevertheless, the growth of taxation over centuries, including the period when European economies dramatically increased their growth rates, fits oddly with the argument that safe property rights for producers or traders are essential ingredients of the European miracle.[5] Sufficiently safe property rights and sufficient incentives might be enough. If the rewards of effort and work are sufficiently great (because of rising productivity), it might do ever less harm if the government taxes away a growing piece of the pie. Net returns and taxes may increase together. The necessity to defend the core of the research program about institutional competition and property rights by this kind of deliberation rather than by reference to unambiguously supporting historical data necessitates a look for other types of evidence in order to corroborate the theory. First, one should consider econometric evidence from the late twentieth century. Of course, this econometric evidence presupposes the availability of measures of economic freedom for cross-national studies. Thanks to the efforts of the Fraser Institute and its affiliates in lots of countries, such data are available for recent decades. Second, the contrast between both parts of divided nations after World War II (China, Germany, Korea) demonstrates that a strong rejection of capitalist institutions leads to impoverishment (Paldam and Grundlach, 2008: 80-82). Furthermore, the well-documented destruction of property rights and incentives during the great leap forward (1959-1962,

---

5   Of course, one should also consider what taxes pay for. Heavy taxation should be less harmful if invested in the procurement of public goods. Here, Goldstone, for example, admits that British taxes were spent in an economically useful way during the industrial revolution: "The big difference in Britain's economy was not the level of taxes or tariffs, but how they were spent… these high tax revenues were not squandered on palaces and playthings for the king and queen, but were instead directed to payment on state debts and funding for the Royal Navy. … The Royal Navy, swollen to become the largest and most formidable force in the world, was then able to protect British shipping and give British merchants secure passage around the world. The result was a virtuous circle ('virtuous' in the sense of self-reinforcing), in which taxes paid on trade were used for naval and military expenses that cleared the way for safer and more extensive trade" (2008, pp. 113-114).

to be analyzed below) in China delivers much starker evidence about the impact of insufficiently safe property rights and the corresponding destruction of incentives than European economic history. My claim is that no competing theory is compatible with (or even relevant for) all three types of evidence at the same time.[6]

Although econometric evidence on the impact of economic freedom is essentially cross-sectional rather than longitudinal, although it covers the most recent decades only, econometric studies do support the idea that economic freedom promotes economic growth and wealth (Chauffour, 2011; de Haan and Sturm, 2000, 2009; Doucouliagos and Ulubasoglu, 2006; Farr, Lord, and Wolfenbarger, 2003; Gwartney and Lawson, 2004; Gwartney, Holcombe, and Lawson, 2006; Liu, 2007; Norton and Gwartney, 2008; Vega-Gordillo and Alvarez-Arce, 2003; Weede, 2006).[7] The continuing debates among econometricians mostly concern three issues: whether the level of economic freedom or the rate of its improvement is more important; whether the relationship is approximately linear or whether the first steps toward economic freedom (or away from socialism) are much more important than later steps or approaching perfect economic freedom; and whether "size of government" should remain part of the economic freedom index or be treated separately.

One may raise the following objection against the claim that econometric evidence about the impact of economic freedom on growth and economic history support essentially the same argument about the institutional sources of growth: Although the effects of economic freedom or its growth are usually significant, they are dwarfed by the much stronger effects of the initial level of economic development or appropriate measures of human capital formation (Weede, 2006). But one must not conclude from these econometric findings that modest support for cross-sectional effects of economic freedom should lead one to expect only moderately strong freedom effects in the long run. What we observe as the most robust effect in cross-sectional growth regressions from recent decades, namely, the strong impact of the initial level of economic

---

6   Pomeranz's (2000) explanation of the great divergence between China and the West illustrates this perfectly. In his theory, the configuration of natural resource deposits (coal, iron) in China and Britain plays a major role. Even if this is true, such a proposition is not useful in understanding the misery produced by the great leap forward or econometric findings about the impact of economic freedom. The wider the applicability of a theory, the better its testability, and the more confidence we should place in it, if most test results support the theory.

7   The benefits of economic freedom are not limited to better growth rates. Economic freedom also reduces macroeconomic volatility (Dawson, 2010), unemployment (Feldmann, 2010) and even homicide rates (Stringham and Levendis, 2010).

development on growth rates or catch-up opportunities for poor countries, must have been fairly weak before modern economic growth in the nineteenth and early twentieth centuries made the West much richer than the rest of the world. As long as average incomes across the world were about equally close to the subsistence level, catch-up opportunities could hardly exist. Catch-up opportunities for the poor presuppose the existence of rich countries. That is why one may regard the current catch-up opportunities that Asian societies have exploited so skillfully as an external benefit of the *earlier* establishment of limited government, safe property rights, economic freedom, and the resulting prosperity in the West. In this account, institutions and incentives drive economic development. Technological progress is part of economic development. But the technological progress made possible by free institutions in the West also makes it possible for emergent economies to benefit from technologies invented elsewhere, i.e., in the West.

Since the fourteenth century, China was a unified empire for most of the time, first under the Ming, and then under the Manchu or Qing dynasties, which lasted for some centuries each. Imperial China succeeded in monopolizing authority to a much greater degree than did European states. As Jenner notes, "The success with which the Chinese state prevented any religion from becoming a rival source of authority across the empire was one of many factors preventing the emergence of a doctrine that the monarch's rights were limited by the rights of groups and individuals" (1998: 78). There were no autonomous cities in China. In Weber's (1922/1964) terms, the traditional Chinese empire was patrimonial. Under patrimonialism, the state does not need to respect the rights of its subjects. Chinese merchants suffered from arbitrary, high, and discriminatory taxation as well as from frequent confiscation. By harassing merchants, the imperial bureaucracy impeded the development of markets and commercialization and indirectly the division of labor and productivity growth (Yang, 1987).[8]

Whereas China suffered the consequences of political unity, Western Europe benefited from cultural unity and political fragmentation. Conflict between European kingdoms or principalities contributed to the limitation of governmental power over subjects. If political units are small, it is much easier to run away from arbitrary officialdom and confiscation than in huge empires. In medieval Europe, even peasants could run away and find refuge in autonomous cities. Rivalry between small political units and early trade in mass consumption goods forced European rulers to

---

8 Although de Bary, Chan, and Watson (1960) do not analyze the actual economic order in imperial China, they document that Chinese writers recommended promoting agriculture at the expense of commerce.

concede relatively safe property rights to merchants. If merchants were robbed by some European prince, they could avoid and circumvent his territory in future. Merchants preferred routes through safe territory over alternative routes. Income from protection fees or taxes strengthened less kleptocratic rulers over their more kleptocratic rivals. Successful strategies of taxation and rule provide an example for other rulers to imitate. That is why safe property rights could spread through time and space in Western Europe.

As underlined by Weber (1922/1964), Europe differed from the great Asian civilizations by having a large number of autonomous cities where individual liberty, economic freedom, and even political freedom were established earlier and for the benefit of a larger part of the population than elsewhere in traditional societies. European cities were fortresses of liberty. Schmidt und Dirlmeier make the following comment on southern German and northern Italian cities in the Middle Ages: "Towns attracted unskilled workers from the countryside and skilled workers from other towns with the guarantee of personal liberty, fiscal incentives and superior income chances" (1998: 158). Communities defended individual liberty in European cities. In Asia, inhabitants of big cities remained subservient to rulers. The existence of autonomous cities in Europe also improved the conditions of life for peasants. The possibility of exit limited abuse by rulers. According to Volkart, "Peasants simply did not have to go that far to find an authority which offered a different and possibly better set of rights, and rulers had to grant favourable conditions if they did not want to lose them. In my opinion it was therefore not by pure chance that in Renaissance Germany prosperity grew with political fragmentation, especially where this became greatest, that is, in the southwest. And it was not by chance either that it was just this area where peasants were sometimes represented at the local diets" (1998: 178).

Palmer also summarizes the importance of cities for the evolution of the West very well: "The cities of Europe were islands of freely organized production and exchange protected by walls that were built to exclude the practitioners of violence and theft. As a fortified place—a *Burg*—a city made possible the freedom of the Bürger. The new cities of Europe were generally places of trade and commerce, rather than administrative centers of vast empires, centers of religious cults, or centers of exploitative rule over subject peasant populations.... Serfs or vassals who could make it to a city and live there for a year and a day were freed of feudal obligations and would be defended by the city" (2009: 18). Jenner compares the situation in Europe with China: "The weakness of medieval European monarchies that allowed cities to select their own governments and to bargain with the king would have shocked a Song official's sense of a well-ordered world" (1998: 78).[9] As cities were scattered across the densely populated parts of central and west Europe, they provided exit opportunities for common people since the Middle Ages.

The Chinese state was not only strong enough to subordinate religious communities and cities. Simultaneously, it was strong enough to constrain the growth of knowledge, for example the exploration of the oceans. As Jones observed: "The record of Chinese exploration which was halted in 1430 and prevented by fiat from resuming in 1480 shows what could happen in a centralized empire that could not happen, or be enforced, in a decentralized system of states, like Europe…. Columbus did eventually find a sponsor. The other large societies in Eurasia that might potentially have developed as Europe did develop, tended to suffer from various disabilities including political centralism and whimsicality" (1981: 67).

As opportunities for exit and circumvention are so important for the establishment and protection of freedom, it can be added that exit opportunities were at least as good in the United States as in Europe. Until the Civil War, the United States was a decentralized federation where the states had to compete for people and capital. This was "market-preserving federalism" (Weingast, 1995). During the nineteenth century Americans enjoyed another option. Whoever felt some grievances in the increasingly crowded east of the country could go west and settle in sparsely populated lands. Given such exit opportunities, oppression simply was no option for ruling classes.[10] Moreover, the possibility of mass emigration from Europe to the United States or Canada or Australia also strengthened the common man against officialdom and employers. The exit option forced officials to treat subjects more respectfully than would have been necessary without it. Moreover, the emigration of about 60 million Europeans also contributed to the convergence of Western European and North American incomes (Hatton and Williamson, 2006: 3, 114, 121).[11] It might be more than a pure coincidence that North, Wallis, and Weingast (2009)

---

9 The Song (or Sung) dynasty ruled China at the beginning of the second millennium, before the Mongol conquest and much before the Ming dynasty.

10 I do not claim that ruling classes in America ever tried to establish a repressive regime. But infeasibility of such a project provides a stronger protection of freedom than political attitudes ever can.

11 Since the gap in purchasing power terms was much smaller between North American and European incomes before World War I than it is today between North America or Europe on the one hand, and poor countries like India on the other, obstacles to international migration condemn millions of people to persistent poverty (Hatton and Williamson, 2006: 215, 372). Chauffour criticizes this disgrace from a human rights perspective (2009: 43-44, 75). Palmer points out that restrictions of migration are typical of welfare states (2009: 245).

date the transition to "open access societies" or the extension of safe property rights from the elites to the masses in Britain, France, and the United States to the mid-nineteenth century when lots of exit opportunities for Westerners existed.

Unless people enjoy fairly safe property rights in the fruits of their labor, there are insufficient incentives to work. This insight can be found in Adam Smith (1776/1976) who recognized that shirking becomes the rule and hard work becomes the exception without property rights. The most fundamental cause for the divergence between China and India on the one hand, and the West on the other, is safer property rights and thereby better incentives in the West than in Asia (see Jones, 1981; Landes, 1998; Weede, 1996, 2000; and Yang, 1987, for evidence).[12] By contrast to China, Indian empires tended to be short-lived and less successful in uniting the entire civilization. Even the Mughal Empire never ruled all of India. Many Indian states engaged in war against each other. If the absence of a unitary empire contributes to safe property rights and limited government and ultimately to economic growth, then India does not fit with the theory, as argued by Lal (2004). In my view, however, one should not exaggerate the misfit between the Indian case and the argument that limited government, safe property rights, and incentives are prerequisites of economic development. By contrast to fairly persistent political units in Europe, Indian principalities and kingdoms disappeared fairly frequently. Indian rulers could not expect their sons and grandsons to be rulers of the same territory. Therefore, they had less reason to respect the property rights of their subjects for the long-term benefit of the ruling dynasty as well as of the economy. As North, Wallis, and Weingast (2009) elaborate for the West, there is some connection between the longevity of organizations and states—"perpetually lived" organizations and states in their terms—and the safety of property rights or the rule of law.

India also lacked other background conditions of limited government. Indian artisans and merchants did not acquire political power within self-ruling cities as European artisans or merchants did. According to Weber (1921/1978), this can be explained by Hinduism and the caste system. For orthodox Hindus, war-making and defense were assigned to warrior castes. Since artisan or merchant castes were not permitted to bear arms and to fight, they could not acquire political power. During the first millennium CE many inhabitants of Indian cities, in particular merchants, were not Hindus, but Jains or Buddhists. These religions disarmed their adherents, too. They were prohibited by their faith even from killing animals and this extended to humans, too. In contrast to European princes,

---

12   Hayek has also endorsed the view that the "certainty of law" contributed significantly to Western prosperity (1960: 208).

Indian rulers were safe from urban challenges to their prerogatives. Whereas a strong Catholic church during the Middle Ages contributed to containing the secular power of rulers in medieval Europe (Berman, 1983; North, Wallis, and Weingast, 2009), no comparable counterweight to political power can be found in Indian history.

An analysis of Indian history has to consider the fact that huge parts of India have been ruled by Muslims for most of the second millennium. In Weber's (1922/1964) terms, Muslim rule in India qualifies as "sultanism." Sultanism is the most extreme subtype of patrimonialism. Rulers were assisted by foreigners and slaves who enjoyed no support in society. They absolutely depended on the ruler and his grace. The more dependent on his grace the staff of the ruler is, the more reliable an instrument of arbitrary rule it becomes. That is why sultanism provides the weakest protection of property rights for subjects. As elaborated by North, Wallis, and Weingast (2009) or Pipes (1999), the first step towards safe property rights and the rule of law in the West has been elite privileges and their legal protection. Neither patrimonialism in China, where the emperor claimed to be the ultimate owner of all land (Yang, 1987), nor sultanism in Muslim-ruled India, provided a good starting point for the evolution towards the rule of law.

Whereas by the late eighteenth century Smith had already recognized the importance of property in providing incentives for hard work,[13] the special incentive problems arising with team production and firms were recognized only about 200 years later (Alchian and Demsetz, 1972). Wherever it is difficult to say or to measure who contributes how much to the productivity of the team, someone has to become the team leader and to specialize in coordinating and monitoring the work of the team members. The responsibility of the team leader includes the prevention of shirking by ordinary team members. If everyone shared equally in the output or profit of the team irrespective of effort and productivity, then incentives to shirk rather than to work would be tremendous. But if the team leader becomes the residual claimant of the profit, i.e., if the leader can keep whatever is left after paying for all the inputs, including the labor of the other team members, then the leader has an incentive not to shirk in his duty to control the others. Thus, efficient team production requires something like a capitalist firm, i.e., the private appropriation of the residual income. The value of residual claims becomes more useful if enterprises can outlive their owners, if ownership shares can be transferred

---

13 Here I do not want to claim that Smith was the first one to recognize the importance of property rights, but being the founding father of economics he was more influential than others. In China, for example, by the 4th century BC, Mengzi had pointed to the need for clear property rights in land (Mencius, 2003: 109).

within and between generations. In North, Wallis, and Weingast's (2009) terms, a productive economy requires "perpetually lived organizations." According to Jenner, "neither the state nor custom allowed large and permanent private companies to emerge" in China (1998: 80). As documented by Kuran (2010), Muslim civilization also made the establishment of permanent private companies difficult or impossible. Only under Western influence did Muslim civilization develop the idea of a legal person, which is essential for large and durable corporations to do business.

Capitalism is characterized not only by the existence of residual claimants and "perpetually lived" enterprises, but also by private property in the means of production and scarcity prices. In the early twentieth century, Mises (1920, 1927/2005) argued that socialism is bound to end in economic failure because of a lack of scarcity prices for production inputs. Under socialism all factories or means of production are at the disposal of the political leadership. Since there is no competition for land, workers, raw materials, machines, or other production inputs between different owners of the means of production, there is no information about the demand for and scarcity of these inputs. Opportunity costs remain hidden. Without competition and scarcity prices, however, there can be no rational allocation of resources. In a later book about bureaucracy, Mises (1944) made another argument against administrative guidance of the economy. In his view, economic and technological progress never result from following laws, orders, rules, or traditions. Whatever the virtues of bureaucratic dominion may be, the results cannot include innovation and progress.

Under which conditions can free or scarcity prices, i.e., the prerequisites of a rational allocation of resources, ever arise? Almost all traditional or pre-capitalist societies generated the idea of "just" or "fair" prices. Since "just" or "fair" prices actually depended on habits or traditions, they had to lack flexibility. Overcoming inflexible prices which do not respond to changing patterns of demand and supply is a prerequisite of a rational allocation of resources. Traditional prices are most easily overcome in cross-border trade where nobody has the necessary authority to enforce the terms of trade on both sides of the border. After people get used to flexible or scarcity prices in cross-border trade, this type of pricing is likely to spill over into domestic trade. Given the political fragmentation of Europe, cross-border trade had to be much more important in Europe than in Asia with its huge empires. Political units with the geographical area and population of Spain, France, or England would have been a mere province within China or India.[14]

The final basic component of my theoretical account concerns the exploitability of knowledge. This concept can be traced back to Hayek

---

14   At different periods in history each of these nations was a contender for supremacy in Europe.

(1945, 1960). In his view, human knowledge refers not only to academic or book knowledge, which can be acquired at universities. It also consists of practical knowledge to be acquired by experience, whether in farming or in an artisan's workshop. It may refer to what grows best on a particular field or to where there is a lot of demand for a certain product. Some of this knowledge is necessarily local. Other knowledge might be tacit. Nobody ever tried to make it explicit. The bearers of knowledge, especially of tacit and local knowledge, include illiterate peasants. Hayek's main argument is that knowledge can never be centralized by some authority. In order to exploit the knowledge dispersed among thousands of heads, people need the freedom to make decisions for themselves and the incentive to arrive at beneficial decisions. If one accepts Hayek's views on knowledge and his requirements for using it, then it follows that Europe could outgrow China and India because of a greater degree of economic freedom due to its more decentralized economic decision-making.[15] Economic freedom implies independent decision-making arising out of the fact that property owners are free to invest their property as they see fit, within the constraints of the law.

It is also possible to reconcile the Hayekian focus on the productivity of economic freedom with a Weberian analysis of the Indian caste system (Weber, 1921/1978; Weede, 2000). Although Hayek did not specifically refer to Indian civilization in the following quotation, it seems to fit the case perfectly: "Religious prophets and ethical philosophers have of course at all times been mostly reactionaries, defending the old against new principles. Indeed in most parts of the world the development of an open market economy has long been prevented by those very morals preached by prophets and philosophers" (1979: 165). The caste system makes one's rights and duties dependent on the caste one is born into (Dumont, 1970; Weber, 1921/1972; Weede, 2000, 2010). Individual liberty and economic freedom have been severely restricted, as long or wherever caste norms have been enforced, whether by social pressure from below or by rulers from above. In principle, albeit not always in practice, the caste system prohibits innovation and vertical mobility.[16] Since

---

15 Such a summary statement fits much better with Yang's (1987) analysis of China than with Chan's (2010). Chan's views, however, defy a brief summary. On the one hand, Chan refers to laissez-faire attitudes of the officialdom and light taxes (2010: 472), on the other, he refers to bureaucratic domination, low esteem of merchants, and incentives to keep the business small in order to avoid confiscations (Chan, 2010: 475-482). In my view, neither bureaucratic domination nor confiscation is compatible with laissez-faire or economic freedom. Moreover, low esteem made merchants vulnerable, as discussed by Yang.

16 In India, vertical mobility is often group mobility rather than individual mobility. One may distinguish Westernization and Sanskritization (Srinivas, 1959). Whereas Westernization is typical of more privileged castes, Sanskritization refers to the attempt of lower castes to

deviation from traditional caste duties might magically hurt even the reincarnation prospects of fellow caste members, it has usually been punished. Lower castes have frequently resorted to excommunication. Certainly, the caste system has made upward mobility by economic success less likely in India than either in China or Europe. Religious constraints on economic freedom had to interfere with profit-maximization and economic growth. In particular, entrepreneurship was much more accessible to members of the traditional trading castes than to others. While their members enjoyed superior access to opportunity, most Indians did not.[17]

Economic backwardness in India and elsewhere is sometimes explained by colonial exploitation. There is no doubt that exploitation has happened, but exploitation does not usually lead to development in the exploiting countries. Iberian rule over Latin America illustrates this point. It helped neither Spain nor Portugal to develop. Moreover, ruling classes other than Western colonialists have exploited their subjects, too. Maddison provides a quantitative estimate of the exploitation of India by the Mughals and their British successors: "The income which the Mughal elite, native princes, and zamindars managed to squeeze from the rural population was proportionately quite large. It amounted to about 15 percent of national income … But, by the end of British rule, the successors of the old elite got only 3 percent" (2007: 123).

In sum, the rise of the West and the stagnation of China or India can be explained by divergent institutional developments. In the West, political fragmentation and competition forced even autocratic (or "absolutist") rulers to respect the private property rights of producers and traders much earlier and to a greater degree than Asian rulers did. Because of better exit opportunities for common people, there was more economic freedom in the West than in Asia. Without economic freedom, incentives for hard work suffer. Political fragmentation in the West also contributed to scarcity prices and a rational allocation of resources as well as to decentralized decision-making and the application of knowledge that is dispersed among millions of heads.

Socialism in Asia

Although Europeans invented socialism, i.e., a program to roll back economic freedom, the West suffered much less from it than did Asia. From the 1950s to 1980, per capita incomes in China and India were fairly

---

improve their status by leading a "purer" form of life. If this implies giving up dirty work, Sanskritization may reinforce poverty.

17 According to the 1931 census in British India, trading castes, like the Baniya, had much higher literacy rates than even the higher-ranking Brahmins. Obviously, literacy is useful in business (Wolcott, 2010: 463).

similar to each other. Per capita incomes in both countries still grew more slowly than globally (Maddison, 1998: 40-41); both neglected comparative advantage and pursued "leap-forward strategies" that focused on heavy industries in spite of capital scarcity and labor abundance (Lin, Cai, and Li, 2003: ch. 2). China and India were afflicted with socialism and an emphasis on planning. The choice of planning and import substitution by many poor countries, including China and India, had two roots. One was the spirit of the 1950s and 1960s, or the tendency of development economists to exaggerate market failure and to overlook state failure. The second was the desire to achieve national security by heavy industrialization, autarky (a policy of national self-sufficiency), and, at least in the Chinese case, building a strong army. A comparative-advantage-defying development strategy would have been impossible in a market economy where private investors suffer the consequences of their misjudgments. Government's large scope makes big and persistent mistakes possible. Whereas China suffered from the repressive and radical variety of socialism, India tried the democratic variety. Both countries, even democratic India, more or less disengaged from the global economy. Between the early 1950s and the late 1970s, the ratio between trade and output in China fell from more than eight to less than six percent (Lin, Cai, and Li, 2003: 83). In the late 1940s, when India became independent, its share of global exports was 2.4 percent. In the early 1990s, it was only 0.4 percent (Bhagwati, 1993: 58).

Although China and India should have enjoyed the "advantages of backwardness" and should have benefited from "conditional convergence" (Barro and Sala-i-Martin, 1995; Levine and Renelt, 1992; Olson, 1996; Weede, 2006), both of them grew slowly from the 1950s to 1970s. It depends on other factors whether or not a backward economy develops. Without investment and human capital formation, it is unlikely that they can catch up. Insufficient amounts of investment cannot explain why neither India nor China succeeded in realizing the advantages of backwardness in the 1950s to 1970s. Instead, the productivity of investment left much to be desired (Bhagwati, 1993: 40ff.). Human capital formation is another candidate for explaining this. Here, China and India differ. Already by 1950, the Chinese had benefited from a little bit more schooling than Indians had received (Maddison, 1998: 63). By the late 1970s, about 90 percent of all Chinese in the 15-to-19-year age group knew how to read and to write. Even in 2008, China scored much better in adult literacy than India, i.e., 94 against 63 percent (World Bank, 2011: 344). What holds Indian education back is not inadequate pay, but teacher absenteeism (Panagariya, 2008: 365 and ch. 20).[18] So, human

---

18 Absenteeism is even worse in Indian public health services than in Indian schools (Panagariya, 2008: ch. 19).

capital formation and its difference between Asia's giants may help us to understand why China outperformed India in the late twentieth century. In the early twenty-first century the Chinese advantage persisted. According to the World Bank and the *Economist,* Chinese workers were 50 percent more productive than Indian workers, but cost only 25 percent more (*Economist,* 2005, March 5: 10). Complementing the cross-national comparison with a look a trends in Chinese labor costs again delivers good news about the Chinese economy. Although labor costs in big enterprises tripled between 1995 and 2004, productivity quintupled, thereby cutting unit labor costs by 43 percent (*Economist,* 2010, July 31: 47).

Compared to the global economy China *and* India did poorly in the 1950s to 1970s. Advantages of backwardness were not realized in spite of sufficient investment and, at least in China's case, sufficient human capital formation. This poor economic performance was to be expected, if the explanation of the great divergence between Europe and Asia provided above and inspired by Weber (1923/1981) and Jones (1981), by Smith (1776/1976), Alchian and Demsetz (1972), Mises (1920), and Hayek (1945, 1960) is true. Take the case of China first. Under communism and central planning, incentives were poor. Egalitarianism prevented special material rewards for those who worked hard, carefully, and effectively. Since the means of production were nationalized, too, there were neither residual claimants to a firm's profits nor scarcity prices, least of all in input markets for production. Finally, few people enjoyed the opportunity of exploiting their knowledge for the benefit of themselves, their families, and their exchange partners. Obeying commands from above killed private initiative. Since economic freedom is productive, its abolishment under central planning guaranteed slow growth rates and persistent poverty. It was possible to use valuable inputs for the production of shoddy goods.

After the Communists had acquired political power, they confiscated land from larger landlords, murdered many of them, but provided small farmers with full private property rights. Their "land to the tiller" reforms contributed to rising farm incomes; by 85 percent in the first few years (Zhu and Prosterman, 2007: 3). In the middle of the 1950s, however, collectivization began, at first slowly, but then ever more radically. Mao Zedong's "Great Leap Forward," from 1959-1962, is a perfect illustration of the suffering socialism causes (Dikötter, 2010). The previously small collectives were combined into huge people's communes that often encompassed a few villages and tens of thousands of people. Agricultural property rights were further diluted. Incentives to work hard without permanent supervision were eliminated and replaced by threats of violence against those who shirked or disobeyed orders. Since the leaders of people's communes were not residual claimants of the commune's income, after paying for all the inputs including labor, they faced few incentives to carefully monitor the effort and work of commune members. Shirking at the leadership level complimented shirking by the peasants. The local and tacit knowledge of peasants (for example, what grows best when and where) was no longer applied. Political indoctrination wasted a lot of time. Changing political priorities (for example, a temporary focus on dam building or establishing rural industries) interrupted harvests so that grain sometimes rotted in the fields. Cadre arrogance prevailed. Close cropping, deep plowing, and mis-application of fertilizer did not produce the intended abundance of crops. In order to impress superiors, many cadres inflated reported harvests. Thereafter the state took a rising share of the harvests leading to short-ages and famine in the countryside. For a while the government seemed to believe the inflated reports of miracle harvests and signed agreements with other communist countries to export grain and to import machinery or military equipment. Grain exports continued as promised after the fam-ine had begun, even after many top leaders suspected how desperate the situation in many provinces was.

Efforts at achieving the industrialization of the countryside were aimed at local autarky. From a geopolitical point of view, local or regional autarky would have made sense if the Soviet Union had ever invaded China.[19] It made less sense, however, to cut down trees or to confiscate house-hold implements and farming tools in order to feed small and primitive rural furnaces which produced extremely poor iron or steel. Because of a lack of experience many work accidents happened. But cadres insisted on rising output irrespective of cost. The Great Leap Forward became a great disaster. Whereas older sources estimate that more than 30 million people starved to death (Fu, 1993: 235, 304; Lin, Cai, and Li, 2003: 58), more recent research based on local and provincial sources arrives at an estimates of at least 45 million out of about 650 million Chinese in those days (Dikötter, 2010: 324-334). Not all of these victims starved to death. Some of them took their own lives, and others were murdered by cadres and militias. Dikötter estimates that about 2.5 million were tortured or otherwise murdered, whereas between 1 and 3 million committed suicide (2010: xi and 304). China paid an extremely high price for running the economy on the foundations of Marxism and Maoism instead of being guided by the principles elaborated by Smith, Mises, and Hayek.

Although the immediate consequences of Mao's policies were often disastrous, some of his policies can be interpreted more positively. According to Bardhan, one may credit Mao's policies (except for the disas-ters of the Great Leap Forward and the Cultural Revolution) with the

---

19   As Soviet and Chinese troops clashed along the Ussuri border in the late 1960s, the Chinese had some reason to fear the Soviets.

provision of a "launching pad" for later economic growth: by establishing some minimum, but broad-based education and health standards; by rural electrification; by making a highly egalitarian land distribution possible; by regional decentralization; and by high female participation in education and work (2010: 8).

India became and remained a democracy after its independence. Although it never nationalized all the means of production, it was inspired by the Soviet model for a long time (Lal, 1998: 129). As Maddison pointed out, "Ghandian pressures in favor of self-sufficiency" had a similar impact (2007: 130). Slow growth and persistent poverty were the results of this inspiration. Bureaucratic controls and interventions weakened incentives, severely restricted entrepreneurial decisions on hiring and firing, and distorted prices. Import substitution and protectionism contributed to weak competition. Favored enterprises, cartels, and even monopolies enjoyed an easy and profitable life at the expense of consumers. The political economy of India was characterized by "license-permit raj" (FICCI, 1999: 165). Instead of unifying Indian markets by improving infrastructure, political interference reinforced their fragmentation by erecting internal barriers to trade. In doing this, the state limited the size of Indian markets and the potential productivity benefits of lager markets (Nilekani, 2009: 242-243, 250). Moreover, taxation cut incentives for hard work and entrepreneurship. For a long time, marginal income tax rates in India had been above 90 percent. Later they came down to about 30 percent (Panagariya, 2008: 336-342).

By contrast to the private sector, the public sector expanded. Its share in gross domestic product increased from eight to 26 percent between 1960 and 1991 (Yergin and Stanislaw, 1998: 216). In the late 1980s, the Indian public sector was responsible for about 70 percent of all workers employed by big enterprises (Bhagwati, 1993: 64). Except for the impoverished informal sector and agriculture, public enterprises were dominant in India. As in China, public enterprises in India tended to be less efficient than private enterprises (Majumdar, 1998; *Economist*, 2011, September 3). Labor market policy made little sense. Firing workers was next to impossible before the enterprise went bankrupt (Bhagwati, 1993: 65, 86; Joshi and Little, 1998: 211ff.). Strong job protection in the formal sector, however, came at a price. Employment in the formal sector was reduced by at least 18 percent (World Bank, 1995: 90). The size of the unorganized sector in India matters because it depresses productivity. According to Luce, "the average labor productivity of the worker in the private organized sector was six times that of his counterpart in the unorganized sector [in 1983, E.W.]. By 2000, that had risen to nine times. The disparity in earnings was similar" (2006: 49). Although Indian socialism benefited a minority of workers, the poorest stratum of society was denied all access to formal employment. Luce summarizes the effects of democratic socialism in India on the poor by reference to a state that is "never absent from your life, except when you actually need it" (2006: 64).

Creeping capitalism in Asia

After Deng Xiaoping's final rise to power as well as under his successors, the Chinese government switched from radical communism to creeping capitalism. Reforms began in the countryside. Incentives to work were reestablished. Peasant judgment replaced cadre decision-making again. As implied by the label of the new policy, "Household Responsibility System," those who made the decisions had to suffer the consequences again. Although the state retained ownership of the land, the communists returned rights to work the land to small groups, to families, and even to individuals.[20] Peasants had to pay rent and to sell part of the harvest to the government at fixed prices. Since surplus products could be sold in free markets, even scarcity prices got a toehold in the Chinese country-side. Chinese peasants responded forcefully to the reforms. From 1978 to 1984 agricultural output grew about 42 percent (Lin, Cai, and Li, 2003: 145). Within less than a decade, per capita incomes in the countryside doubled. Since the mid-1980s, however, the rural-urban income dispar-ity has widened again. In 2006, urban per capita income was about 3.3 times the rural income (Zhu and Prosterman, 2007: 2). By and large, the urban-rural gap is wider in the western interior than in the coastal prov-inces. The wider it is, the more investment is discouraged and the more provincial growth rates suffer (Wan, Lu, and Chen, 2008). According to Bardhan, these early rural reforms have been even more important than urban reforms, exports, or globalization for China's economic develop-ment: "Much of the high growth in the first half of the 1980s and the asso-ciated dramatic decline in poverty happened largely because of internal factors, not globalization. These internal factors include an institutional change in the organization of agriculture, the sector where poverty was largely concentrated, and an egalitarian distribution of land-cultivation rights, which provided a floor on rural income-earning opportunities, and hence helped to alleviate poverty" (2010: 6).[21]

---

20 Most rural households do not even now have certificates stating which land they farm and which residential property they occupy. A completed land registry might become the first step towards private property in farmland, which some day might permit the consolida-tion of tiny plots into more efficient farms. Although rural residents are discriminated against when they work in cities, as tens of millions of them do, rural registration also has some advantages, including access to cheaper medical insurance, a residence, and some farmland (*Economist*, 2010, May 8).

21 Huang makes the same point about the timing of significant poverty reduction (before) and foreign direct investment (later) in China (2008: 26).

In the 1980s, urban and industrial reforms complemented agricultural reforms. The comparative-advantage-defying strategy was replaced by a comparative-advantage-exploiting strategy (Lin, Cai, and Li, 2003: 101). The preferences for heavy industry and import substitution were overcome. Township and village enterprises (TVEs) were established. In the first two reform decades they enabled 120 million peasants to move from agricultural to industrial employment (Lin, Cai, and Li, 2003: 199). In the absence of the rule of law, or even legitimacy of private property ownership in the means of production, Western-style property rights would have been insecure (Rodrik, 2007: 24). Entrepreneurs could not yet become owners of the means of production. Instead they were forced into some kind of partnership with the local administration, i.e., with those who might be tempted to expropriate them and who had the power to do it. But local governments lost interest in expropriation because they could share TVE profits. Although the necessity to reward entrepreneurship was respected, private property in the means of production was legalized only after the reforms had already succeeded. At the beginning of the reform process TVEs were an efficient institution.

TVEs had to compete with each other. The reach of "their" local government was not long enough or strong enough to protect them. Even if the ownership was still public or collective, most TVEs had to compete, *as if* they were private enterprises. Although not protected by law, managers and local cadres became de facto residual claimants of profits and therefore had an incentive to monitor the workforce and to prevent shirking. Later, truly private enterprises were tolerated. Prices were permitted to reflect supply and demand. By the early 1990s, most prices were determined by scarcities rather than political fiat (Lin, Cai, and Li, 2003: 172). Only 6 percent of the Chinese farm produce was sold in open markets in 1978; that proportion rose to 80 percent in 1993 (Bardhan, 2010: 44).[22] By contrast to TVEs and the increasing number of truly private enterprises, state-owned enterprises (SOEs) incurred losses for a long period without suffering bankruptcy.

While making SOEs profitable has been difficult and elusive for a long time, China had succeeded in quickly reducing their weight and importance. In the late 1970s when the reform process began, they accounted for more than three-quarters of the industrial output. Two decades later, their share was down to about one-quarter of it (Lin, Cai, and Li, 2003: 187). Of course, the transition from a state-dominated economy to a more capitalist one was costly. During the late 1990s about 30 million workers lost their jobs in state-owned or collective-owned enterprises. Whereas

---

22 Agricultural productivity is better in China than in India, about twice as high per hectare for rice, and one-and-a- half times as high for wheat (Bardhan, 2010: 43).

SOEs controlled about two-thirds of fixed capital in Chinese industry in 1990, now it is down to about one-third. "The Chinese economy is primarily privately owned or controlled today" (Bardhan, 2010: 68, 80, and 98). According to the *Economist*, enterprises that are *not* majority-owned by the state contribute 70 percent to Chinese GDP, 67 percent to industrial output, but 75 to 80 percent of the profits of Chinese industry (2011, March 26: 72). Huang is more cautious. In his view, just above half of the Chinese economy is privately controlled, with more of it controlled by foreigners than by indigenous entrepreneurs (2008: 15). Whereas foreign investors frequently established joint ventures with the Chinese in the late 1980s and early 1990s, since the beginning of the twenty-first century, wholly foreign-owned enterprises dominate (Walter and Howie, 2011: 7). Foreign investment is an essential background condition of Chinese export successes. According to the *Economist*, the biggest exporters are foreign invested enterprises (2010, July 31: 46).

Small and medium enterprises in China get little help from the government. According to the *Economist*, there were a million of them by 1990, eight million by 2001, and around 60 million in 2009 (2009, September 12: 68). Ninety-five percent of them are privately owned. They account for more than half of China's tax revenues, about 60 percent of China's GDP, 66 percent of its patent applications, 68 percent of the country's exports, and 80 percent of China's new products. They find it hard to get formal loans. Worse still, pooling private funds outside of official channels may be treated as a crime and can even lead to the death penalty (*Economist*, 2011b, April 16: 63). If environmental regulations are enforced at all, then small and medium firms are much likelier targets than state-owned enterprises. In general, political connections still count in China. According to Du and Girma, such "connections enhance firms' growth and survival prospects, even if politically neutral start-ups enjoy faster efficiency improvements" (2010: 543). Since politically less well connected businesses demonstrate better productivity growth than "red hat" enterprises,[23] the impact of political connections on resource allocation and economic performance tends to be negative.

It is hard to understand how the Chinese economy could do so well since the late 1970s without a full commitment to private property rights rather than the ambivalence about the degree to which they might be tolerated that actually exists. One answer to this conundrum has been provided by the theory of "market-preserving federalism" (Montinola, Qian, and Weingast, 1995; Weingast, 1995). By delegating much economic decision-making authority to provincial and local governments,

---

23 If one factors in the low cost of borrowing for SOEs and their preferential access to land, the real return to equity for SOEs might even be negative (*Economist*, 2011, June 25: 12).

the Chinese have invented a partial and preliminary substitute for the rule of law. If regional governments arbitrarily interfere with business or impose more arbitrary taxation than other provinces do, if they are more corrupt than others, then they lose capital, business, and even qualified labor to other areas. "Federalism, Chinese-style" imposes effective constraints on politicians and thereby generates opportunities for growth. Competition among themselves forces local and regional governments to act *as if* they wanted to respect private property rights. Whoever succeeds in making his county or province grow faster than comparable political units is likely to be rewarded by markedly better promotion and career prospects within the Communist Party or governmental hierarchy. An indicator of the strength of local government in China (and its weakness in India) is the fact that more than half of all public expenditure is made at the sub-provincial levels in China, but only about five percent at those levels in India (Bardhan, 2010: 38). Local decision-making in China is reminiscent of the political fragmentation that propelled Western Europe toward modernity and helped it to overcome mass poverty.

Experimentation by regional and local governments complements entrepreneurial experimentation from below. Since the 1990s, about 150,000 businesses have been formed per year and about 100,000 have been closed down (Chan, 2010: 492). But the modernization of the Chinese economy is not only promoted by market-preserving federalism or competition between local and regional governments, but also by what Huang calls "access to efficient institutions outside of China" (2008: 6). This institutional access ranges from laws and regulations that copy Western models and tend to favor foreign-invested firms over domestic private enterprises, or registering some enterprises (for example: Lenovo) in the more liberal legal environment of Hong Kong, to importing education (by sending Chinese students abroad) or overseas Chinese entrepreneurship. Walter and Howie make a similar, but much more radical argument: In their view, American and other Western investment bankers deserve much of the credit for restructuring China's fragmented and moribund state-owned enterprises and turning them into national champions (2011: chs. 6 and 7). Although these enterprises dominate Chinese stock markets, Walter and Howie point to three persistent shortcomings: first, the state and the party still control these enterprises and appoint their managers; second, because of majority state ownership, most of the shares are not available for trade; third, therefore Chinese stock prices cannot reflect fundamentals as well as Western stock prices do.

Instead of pursuing autarky as China did under Mao, Deng and his successors proceeded to exploit the opportunities of export-led growth and globalization. Chinese exports in 2009 were nearly ten times as high as Indian exports, if one includes Hong Kong with China. Without

Hong Kong, they were nearly eight times as high. Moreover, 94 percent of Chinese exports resulted from manufacturing, compared with only 67 percent of Indian exports (World Bank, 2011: 352). China has become a magnet for foreign direct investment. In 2009, China (excluding Hong Kong) attracted more than twice as much foreign investment as India. Even Hong Kong alone attracted more than did India (World Bank, 2011: 352). In 2010, China still attracted more than four times as much FDI as India (*Economist*, 2011, March 26: 68). By as early as 2004, China had overtaken Japan to become the third largest trader in the global economy behind the US and Germany. In 2009, China overtook Germany to become the largest exporter in the world (*Economist*, 2010, February 13: 74). China's trade-to-GDP ratio has risen from 21 percent in 1982 to about 65 percent in recent years. By contrast, in recent years, India's ratio has risen from 16 percent in 1990-91 to 45 percent (Bardhan, 2010: 25).[24]

By the time China was the third most important exporter in the world, India's rank as an exporter was not even equal to that of Taiwan (*Economist*, 2005, April 23: 101). Of course, trade in manufactured goods is China's comparative advantage. India might have a comparative advantage in services, particularly in software exports.[25] Moreover, the approximately 3-million-strong affluent Indian-American community of doctors, engineers, businessmen, and software experts (Dhume, 2008: 27; Feigenbaum, 2010: 79) may link India at least as closely to the United States as Sino-American trade does China. Conceivably, Indian expatriates might contribute to India's future globalization as much as Chinese expatriates have already done for China through past direct foreign investment. Certainly, there is little reason to doubt that more trade openness and globalization will help India. Its per capita growth rate was 6.2 percent in 2008-2009, by contrast to China's 8.5 percent (World Bank, 2011: 344).

Although recent data suggest that previous analyses have underestimated China's poverty rate, new data show that the country's poverty rate has fallen even more dramatically than older data indicate (Chen and Ravallion, 2008). In 1981, 84 percent of Chinese had to survive on less than US$1.25 a day (in 2005 prices); by 2005, that proportion was cut to only 16 percent. By contrast, the proportion of India's population that was below the same poverty threshold was lower (60 percent) in 1981, but the country was much less successful in cutting the ratio down: it dropped to 42 percent by 2005 (*Economist*, 2009, November 28: 68). Although

---

24 There is some disagreement about these data. According to Panagariya, the Indian trade-to-GDP ratio increased from 25 to 43 percent between 1990 and 2006 (2008: 109).

25 According to Bardhan, information technology (IT) and IT-enabled services employ less than one-half of one percent of the Indian labor force. Two thirds of India's service output remains in traditional and "unorganized" activities (2010: 6).

China's income inequality seems to be greater than India's, it is worth noting, first, that "the bottom quintile in China experienced a significant 3.4 percent growth rate in mean per capita expenditure between 1993 and 2004; the corresponding figure for the bottom quintile group in India is only 0.85 percent" (Bardhan, 2010: 138); and second, that equality of opportunity is better in China than in India because of a more egalitarian distribution of land cultivation rights, better access to schooling in the countryside, and a lack of caste barriers (Bardhan, 2010: 12, 16).

For decades there has been a debate about the importance of export orientation in accounting for growth (Dollar, 1992; World Bank, 1993). Recently, Rajan examined the benefits of a focus on exports for emerging economies: "One way to both discipline inefficient firms and expand the market for goods is to encourage the country's largest firms to export. Not only are firms forced to make attractive cost-competitive products that can win market share internationally, but the larger international markets offer them the possibility of scale economies. Moreover, because they are no longer constrained by the size of the domestic market, they can pick the products for which they have the greatest comparative advantage" (2010: 58). As Rajan suggested, a focus on exports fits a number of economic miracles very well: Germany and Japan after World War II, Hong Kong, Singapore, South Korea, and Taiwan since the 1960s, or Mainland China since the 1980s. Bhalla (2010) agrees that its export orientation explains China's growth, but adds that undervaluation of the currency helps. In Bhalla's view, the yuan has been more than 60 percent undervalued (2010: 15). Exports and a surplus in the balance of trade may be useful for some countries, but too many successful exporters, or those that are too big may generate problems at the global level.

Whereas China reformed its economy ahead of the bankruptcy of the Soviet model, India was a late and slow convert to capitalism. As Panagariya (2008: 96) and Lal (2008: 15) point out, there is a link between earlier Chinese and later Indian reforms. It was much easier for Indians to deny the policy relevance of the South Korean or Taiwanese economic miracles than of the Chinese miracle. Since independent India's economy grew much better even under Nehru than in the colonial period before it, Indians did not expect much growth (Cohen, 2001: 95; Panagariya, 2008: ch. 2). As in China, economic growth rates and productivity picked up in India during the 1980s. Growth in the 1980s has sometimes been explained by growing aggregate demand driven by soaring government deficits and a build-up of external debt which led to the crisis of the early 1990s and thereafter to liberalizing reforms (Ahluwalia, 2002; Lal, 2008). It has also been explained by "the suspension of the government's hostility to the private sector" in the 1980s (Rodrik and Subramanian, 2004: 3), by the government's pro-business orientation, which resulted in fewer restrictions on capacity expansion for established industries, fewer price controls, and lower corporate taxes. In essence the reforms were "liberalization by stealth" (Panagariya, 2008: ch. 4) or creeping capitalism.

These early reforms and the favorable growth record in the 1980s were not sufficient to prevent the crisis in 1991. Public sector deficits rose. Foreign currency was in short supply and became ever more so. After the dissolution of the Soviet Union, the main source of foreign aid disappeared. The reforms abolished most of the industrial licensing system. The dream of autarky was given up. Foreign investment was reluctantly welcomed. The Indian currency was devalued. Tariffs were cut dramatically. The average tariff rate was reduced from 125 percent in 1990-91 to only 71 percent three years later. The peak rate fell from 355 percent in 1990-91 to only 12.5 percent in 2005-2006 (Joshi and Little, 1998: 70; Nilekani, 2009: 71). Although the Indian economy did not switch as vigorously from inward to outward orientation and export promotion as China did, it moved significantly in the right direction. Since growth rates improved in the early 1990s, especially in manufacturing, and since the current account deficit fell and foreign exchange reserves strongly recovered while the primary deficit of the central government fell, the liberalizing reforms paid off (Joshi and Little, 1998: 17, 35). Given the poor record of Indian administrations in large scale policy implementation, liberalization made sense because it implies some economizing on limited state capability (Pritchett, 2009: 33). As Olson (1987) had recognized long ago, an efficient administration is not the comparative advantage of most developing countries. Therefore, planning is least likely to work in poor countries like India.

But the Indian development pattern does not offer sufficient job opportunities to its labor force, which is dominated by low-skilled workers (Bosworth, Collins, and Virmani, 2006: 34). Most of India's labor force is not even employed in the formal economy or the so-called "organized sector." According to Bardhan, 94 percent of the Indian labor force works in the informal sector (2010: 79). Frequently, workers are self-employed. Enterprises are tiny. Work is quite unproductive. Indian firm structure is characterized by a "missing middle." Nearly half of all Chinese workers are employed by enterprises with between 10 and 500 workers, but very few Indians are. This is an important difference, because productivity in 500-plus worker enterprises in India has been about ten times as high as in tiny enterprises (Bardhan, 2010: 35-36). Whereas manufacturing employs more than a hundred million Chinese workers, it employs just seven million Indians (Luce, 2006: 48-49). According to the *Economist*, foreign-invested enterprises in China alone employ more Chinese in manufacturing than the seven million Indians similarly employed (2010, July 31: 46).

Whereas China's economic development started with agricultural reforms, then moved to low-cost manufacturing before climbing the value-added chain, India grows from the other end with a strong emphasis on capital- and human-capital-intensive products and services (Luce, 2006: 38). Nevertheless, even in the service sector, total factor productivity could grow faster in China than in India (Bardhan, 2010: 29). According to Panagariya, "the key barrier to the emergence of large-scale, unskilled-labor-intensive firms is the complex set of labor laws they face in India" (2008: 288). Indian labor laws privilege insiders, but deny opportunities to outsiders. Neither much higher pay in the formal part of the economy, nor perfect job security helps those who cannot find a formal job in rigid labor markets. Within the formal economy, pay for people with modest skills may be three times as high in the public sector as in the private sector (Bardhan, 2010: 133).

In contrast to China, India had never abolished private property in land and private farming.[26] Nevertheless, Chinese rice yield per hectare has always been higher than India's. It still is about twice as high (Bardhan, 2010: 42-43). For a long time, Indian agriculture suffered from serious distortions. According to Joshi and Little, "the prices of all major agricultural products have been largely determined by the central government's total control of foreign trade in them. The prices of cereals—rice, wheat, and coarse grains—and cotton have been held below world prices in most years by controlling exports" (1998: 89). Although this specific problem has been mitigated or even overcome, subsidies for food, fertilizer, electricity, or water are still more likely to assist well-to-do farmers than the poor. Moreover, half of the value of the subsidies supports inefficient fertilizer producers (Bardhan, 2010: 46). The money could be better spent in building up rural infrastructure. According to Panagariya's estimate, only between 4 and 18 percent of the food subsidies reach the poor (2008: 361). Since subsidies, like labor market rigidities, distort market signals and reduce growth rates, one should concur with Panagariya's conclusion that a focus on equity has had harmful effects on poverty alleviation in India (2008: 77).

Compared to China, India *seems* to possess some advantages. Because of the British legacy, India seems much closer to the rule of law than China. As Kohli (2004) points out, the British built a much more effective administrative service in India than they did in some of their African colonies, such as Nigeria. Unfortunately, however, "affirmative action" for the benefit of backward tribe, low-caste, and untouchable (or dalit) Indians must have undermined the quality and effectiveness of the bureaucracy.

---

26 Legal titles to land are poorly documented in India. Records are incomplete and fragile (Panagariya, 2008: 323). This is also true in China (*Economist*, 2010, May 8).

In 1990, 49 percent of central government positions were set aside for these groups (van Praagh, 2003: 201). According to Peerenboom "violations of physical integrity rights in India appear to be more severe" (2007: 166) than in China—quite in contrast to what one might expect concerning the differential human rights performance of democracies and autocracies. Unfortunately, the application of the law in India leaves much to be desired. Relations between some politicians and criminals are simply too good (Cohen, 2001: 115). Even in big cities, property conflicts may still be "settled" by gangs of bullies rather than by courts of law (Kakar, 1996). In 2006, 27 million legal cases waited for a judgment, murder cases included. About US$75 billion was tied up in these legal disputes (Luce, 2006: 94-95). Problems of law enforcement also reduce the impact of this presumed Indian advantage. Bardhan bemoans that "India's overpoliticized administration and decision-making process, its clogged courts and corrupt police and patronage politics frequently make mockery of the rule of law for common people" (2010: 159).

Since Indian states are on the way to becoming more assertive, enterprising, and powerful, it is conceivable that they may also become engaged in a "race to the top," where they will compete with each other in providing a good business environment. "Federalism, Indian-style" may provide some hope for the future. As Bihar, one of the bigger and poorer states of India, has recently demonstrated, catch-up growth of poorer regions is possible (*Economist*, 2010, January 30). So far, however, India benefits little from its putative advantage in the rule of law, but it still suffers from the legacy of 'license-permit raj' (FICCI, 1999: 165). According to the *Economist*, "Indian bureaucracy continues to slow things down… it takes 89 days to receive all the permits needed to start a business in India, compared with 41 in China. Insolvency procedures take ten years, compared with 2.4 in China" (2005, March 5: 14). Tardiness of administration and endemic corruption undermine the advantages of the rule of law (Quah, 2008). As Palmer reminds us: "There is also a strong connection between the scourge of governmental corruption and the extent of governmental intervention into the market. The more obstacles the state places in the way of willing buyers and sellers, for example, the more opportunities for bureaucrats to exact a toll"[27] (2009: 213). On the legal system and property rights part of the economic freedom scale, China received a somewhat better rating than India (for 2008) (Gwartney, Hall, and Lawson, 2010: 9).

Both Asian giants face severe problems and vulnerabilities, albeit not exactly the same ones. Chinese savings and investment ratios are very high. Whereas Chinese profits are rising, wages and private consumption

---

27 For econometric evidence on economic freedom, corruption, and economic performance, see Graeff and Mehlkop (2003) and Blasius and Graeff (2009).

as shares of GDP have been falling since about 2000 (Hale and Hale, 2008: 65). But capital is frequently not used productively. State banks in China prefer to provide loans to state-owned enterprises (SOEs). Until some years ago, they were least likely to invest the money productively. By contrast, private entrepreneurs sometimes pay more than 200 percent interest per year on the black market (*Economist,* 2011, March 12: 74). Chinese banks fail to channel the savings toward productive investment. It has even been questioned whether the earlier problem of non-performing loans has been solved or merely been swept under the rug and transferred to the future. Moreover, there are reasons to fear that the stimulus spending in 2009 will generate new and additional non-performing loans in the near future (Walter and Howie, 2011). Nevertheless, Chinese total factor productivity growth has been excellent: "one-third of China's growth is coming from rising productivity" (Anderson, 2009: 20-21). Whereas the total factor productivity growth rate in the United States, Japan, or Germany was not much better than one percent per year in between 1990 and 2008, China achieved four percent (*Economist,* 2009, November 14: 88). But India did well, too. It achieved nearly 3 percent productivity growth.

India should raise its investment rate. Since household savings have strongly increased, the savings rate could support more investment (Bosworth, Collins, and Virmani, 2006). Actually, India seems to be well on the way towards raising investment. By contrast to China, there is little financial repression in India. But in infrastructure development, India might lag a full decade behind China (Lal, 2008: 28-29). Since the Indian public sector is already deeply in deficit, financing infrastructure will be difficult; 44 percent of recurrent public expenditures in India service the public debt (*Economist,* 2005, March 5: 14). So, the legacy of past profligacy undermines India's capability to improve its infrastructure. Chinese public debt *might* be as little as 17 percent of GDP.[28] But India's is as high as 75 percent (Bardhan, 2010: 127). Whereas China's government might have been

---

28 China's government accounts, its banks, and their debts are still opaque and leave room for radically divergent evaluations. Chang arrives at an estimate of public debt that is about seven times as high as that of the *Economist* by including bad bank debts in the public debt (2008: 34). Recently, the *Economist* reported estimates of Chinese public debt ranging from 20 to 50 percent of GDP (2010, January 16: 65). According to Walter and Howie, 75-77 percent is a good estimate for the 2009-2011 period (2011: 201). The higher estimate includes local public debt and asset management companies which took over non-performing bank loans which seem to be rising again. Even the highest estimates of Chinese public debt compare not unfavourably with public debt in rich Western countries, which averages close to 90 percent. Certainly, central government finances are much healthier than local government finances in China. Whereas local governments receive only 46 percent of tax receipts, they account for 77 percent of public spending.

in surplus in 2007, India's total government deficits might be close to seven percent of GDP (*Economist*, 2008, February 16: 72). In 2008-2009, the Indian deficit was about 10 percent of GDP (Bardhan, 2010: 70). Given India's scarcity of capital, the country should welcome foreign direct investment. In 2010, however, the country received only US$24 billion, about one third less than in the previous year (*Economist*, 2011a, April 16: 14).

Although Indian public spending is frequently rationalized by the need to serve the poor, in fact, the poor benefit little.[29] Subsidies on fuel or fertilizer are most useful for those who own vehicles or farm large plots of land. In Luce's evaluation, two thirds of the nominally "pro-poor" subsidies in India benefit better-off groups (2006: 89). Moreover, even a few years ago, India's government depended to a significant degree, i.e., for about one sixth of its revenue (*Economist*, 2005, March 5: 15), on customs duties, or barriers to trade and globalization. Poor infrastructure, poor productivity, and bigger barriers to trade make it unlikely that India can repeat China's success in attracting foreign capital in order to compensate for the weakness of domestic investment. Although difficult, China's problems with investing capital productively still look more amenable to a solution than India's problems. But attitudinal obstacles against capitalism, free markets, and globalization seem to be weak in both countries. According to a Pew survey (*Economist*, 2009, May 30: 26), in no major country did faith in free markets exceed the Indian level or increase as much between 2002 and 2007. Although faith in free markets increased less in China than in India, China still is number two out of 11.[30] Whether politicians translate this permissive opinion into pro-growth policies or prefer to service rent-seekers remains to be seen.

As China is graying rapidly, demography will become less benign than it was. One may argue that there still is sufficient underemployed rural labor for years to come (Anderson, 2009).[31] Anderson adds that some reduction in China's enormous capital exports might be sufficient to plug the gap which a lower savings rate might generate in future. So, neither demography, nor lower savings and investment rates should do too much harm to China's growth prospects. One should consider

---

Local governments make up much of the shortfall up selling land to developers without adequately compensating previous users (Sender and Anderlini, 2011, June 2: 5).

29 A corresponding statement applies to China where transfers focus on the better-off urban population rather than on the rural poor (Wang, 2008).

30 Of course, survey findings depend on specific questions. If one asks about increasing profits and the responsibility of business, then Indians demonstrate much more faith in unadulterated capitalism than Americans or Chinese (*Economist*, 2011, January 29: 57).

31 According to the *Economist* (2010, July 31), another 70 million rural Chinese might be willing to migrate to urban factories.

another source of growth, i.e., conditional convergence or the potential advantages of backwardness.[32] Since China remains poor compared to the West or Japan, this potential source of growth will last for some more decades. Thus, the future economic development of China seems to be at the mercy of two factors: whether a global depression and a wave of protectionism can be avoided, and whether the government of China will continue market-enhancing reforms instead of relapsing into social- ist dead ends. The more China restricts economic freedom, the poorer its prospects will become. In this context, it may be important to note that about one-third of Chinese entrepreneurs have become members of the ruling party (Bardhan, 2010: 80). On the one hand, this may reinforce corruption and crony capitalism. On the other hand, this reconciliation of economic and political elites in China may help to improve Chinese economic policy-making.

For the sake of growth, government concessions of freedom to the people should not be restricted to a narrowly defined economic sphere. Freedom of technological and scientific research is obviously important for innovation and progress. Moreover, tolerance for severe criticism of the economic order or political institutions might be important for overcoming institutional obstacles to growth and the correction of pol- icy errors. One might argue that generalized liberty instead of narrowly defined economic freedom becomes more important once the advan- tages of backwardness have been exploited.[33]

India's demographic future looks much more benign than China's (Eberstadt, 2010). Although India will not suffer from a scarcity of young people and an abundance of older ones in the near future like China or the West, the Indian problem is that the economically more successful regions already suffer from below replacement fertility, whereas the less successful regions are still above replacement level fertility. Therefore, human capital development remains a challenge in India. If one adds poor infrastruc- ture, the remnants of the caste system, still overregulated labor markets, and corruption undermining administrative efficiency and the rule of law, then it becomes hard to be optimistic about India's prospects. If, how- ever, India could overcome the legacy of permit-license-quota raj, which

---

32 A superficial comparison of provincial growth rates in China seems to be incompatible with advantages of backwardness. By and large, the more prosperous coastal provinces benefit from better growth rates than the interior provinces. According to Lin and Liu (2008), this results from the interior suffering more than the coast from comparative-advantage-denying development strategies. If this factor is controlled, then advantages of backwardness can be demonstrated within China.

33 It is sometimes argued that Chinese tradition is hostile to criticism. As de Bary (1983) elaborates for Neo-Confucianism and the Sung dynasty, this is an exaggeration.

provided so fertile a ground for corruption, and if India could expand economic freedom, then it might benefit from the optimism typical of young and growing populations. Since India is much poorer than the West and even China, it enjoys much greater advantages of backwardness and therefore potentially faster growth prospects than the other big civilizations.

Creeping socialism in the West?

Whereas developing countries and emerging markets tend to score a little better on economic freedom scales than on personal freedom scales, the opposite is true for Western democracies (Vasquez and Stumberger, 2012). Although personal freedom and political freedom still look safe in the West, economic freedom is under attack. As will be argued below, Western Europe seems to be even more at risk than the United States. Even "post-materialists" who care little about growth or prosperity (because they already tend to be prosperous) should worry about the attack on economic freedom for the following reasons: The ultimate consequences of economic freedom are prosperity and political liberty. Economic freedom is a prerequisite of political liberty. In Western and Central Europe, economic freedom was established before political democracy, if you define the latter by a franchise covering the entire adult population. Applying such a definition of democracy, the statement is even true for the United Kingdom or Switzerland, the oldest and most stable accountable governments in Europe.

Without economic freedom or capitalism[34] and the prosperity it promotes, democracy or political freedom might not be viable.[35] This view is corroborated by econometric evidence (Burkhart and Lewis-Beck, 1994; Lipset, 1994; Inglehart and Welzel, 2009).[36] Acemoglu et al. (2008)

---

34 In my view, "economic freedom" and "capitalism" are synonyms.

35 Although capitalism is essential for the preservation of democracy, democracy might undermine capitalism. Olson (1982) had suggested that older democracies grow more slowly than younger ones which, in the long run, must undermine their prosperity. There are some econometric studies to support this view (Bernholz, 1986; Weede, 1991). Unfortunately, contemporary researchers seem to have lost interest in Olson's proposition. One reason might be that Olson (2000) himself has become more optimistic about the impact of democracy on economic performance in his later work. Another reason might be that the Anglo-Saxon economies did better than the losers of World War II since the 1990s. The contrast between them had been the inspiration behind Olson's (1982) theorizing. Although North, Wallis, and Weingast (2009: 140ff.) do not persuade me that the older public choice literature on the pernicious impact of organized interest groups and their rent-seeking activities in democracies is misleading, there is a need to develop appropriate research designs to find out which point of view fits better with the data.

36 Przeworski et al. deny a causal link between prosperity and democracy and assert that "economic circumstances have little to do with the death of dictatorships" (2000: 117).

provide the most serious challenge to the idea that prosperity promotes democracy. Although the challenge itself has already been rebutted and the income democracy nexus has been reestablished (Benhabib, Corvalan, and Spiegel, 2011), the criticism itself implied only a minor modification of the relationship. Acemoglu et al. (2008) looked for factors that affect prosperity *and* democracy. They analyzed the long-run development paths where some countries have grown rich and become democracies, versus others that have remained poor and autocratic. Although they did not use my preferred labels for the common determinants of prosperity and democracy, I think that their analysis is compatible with calling them limited government, secure property rights, or economic freedom. North, Wallis, and Weingast would call it "open access order" (2009: 13). Under this interpretation, the causal link between prosperity and democracy becomes replaced by one linking free or capitalist institutions and democracy where prosperity still may *indicate* that the institutional prerequisites for democratization are in place. But capitalism contributes to democracy not only (or even primarily) because of prosperity. Private ownership of newspapers, radio, and TV stations provides sources of information for citizens that are not under the control of ruling politicians. Moreover, the private economy provides opportunities for defeated politicians to prosper, whereas in a socialist economy the loss of political power is likely to lead to impoverishment, too. For democracy to persist, electoral defeat should be tolerable for office-holders. Otherwise, defeated politicians might not quit their offices peacefully.

European economic success was rooted in political failure and disunity. Whereas military and political leaders in Asia succeeded in conquering huge territories and imposing imperial rule for centuries again and again, Europe remained politically fragmented. There was interstate rivalry between principalities and kingdoms, but cultural unity. In the Middle Ages, this unity resulted from Christianity; later from the enlightenment and science. As early as the seventeenth century, when Europeans invented the telescope and progressed from a geocentric to a heliocentric view of the universe, the Dutch, Italians, Germans, and English contributed to this evolution (Huff, 2011). Given the small size of most European principalities compared to Asian empires, there was more trade between politically independent territories in Europe than in Asia. Independent cities, the rivalry between church and state, later the reformation and competition between the Catholic and Protestant churches also contributed to the dilution of authority in the West. In a nutshell, political fragmentation in Europe and the West provided individuals with exit opportunities and some degree of liberty. Competition

---

Boix and Stokes (2003), however, have rebutted this assertion and demonstrated that economic growth promotes transitions to democracy.

between governments for capital and trade, for talent and people forced European governments to respect private property rights and individual liberty much earlier and to a greater degree than in Russia or Asia. European success rests on providing less room for government error than elsewhere. That is why Europeans and Westerners, i.e., Europeans and Americans, had become undisputed masters of the world at the beginning of the twentieth century (Ferguson, 2011).

Political fragmentation within the West or European disunity was not only a prerequisite for the establishment of the institutional package of limited government or individual liberty, private property rights and capitalism, but also the background condition of the wars which devastated much of Europe during the first half of the twentieth century. Except for the radical shift of power *within the West*, from European nation-states like Britain, France, or Germany to the United States of America and transiently to the Soviet Union, the catastrophe of two world wars killing between 70 and 80 million people, most of them Europeans, did not suffice to finish Europe and even less Western civilization. By about 1970 Western Europe, at least, had risen like a phoenix from the ashes. Western nations still dominated the global economy (Maddison, 2007; Ferguson, 2011). Neither the Chinese nor the Indian economies had grown faster than the global economy. Although the Soviet bloc constituted a military challenge until about 1990, it never was remotely able to grow rich and to challenge the superior quality of Western consumer goods. For the roots of the contemporary Western malaise we have to look elsewhere.

At the beginning of the twentieth century limited government was still a reality in the West. Now it has become a romantic memory of a past golden age or a distant ideal.[37] Since the beginning of the twentieth century, government expenditures as a share of GDP grew from less than 10 percent in the most austere states to more than 50 percent in the most profligate ones during the 1980s (*Economist*, 2011, March 19; Tanzi, 2011; Tanzi and Schuknecht, 2000). The United States always lagged Western Europe in taxation and government expenditure. Although some of the older democracies, including the US, Switzerland, or the UK, are less affected by this than some younger democracies, such as Germany, or countries where German military occupation during World War II interrupted democratic government, like France or Belgium, one may still argue that democratization and the universal franchise has driven the expansion of the tax and welfare state (Tanzi, 2011: 66). At the end of the century, state shares in GDP were about one third in the US and close to one half in most of Western Europe. The lower government revenue as a percentage of GDP or

---

37 Whereas North, Wallis, and Weingast (2009) argue that limited government and big government (or welfare states) are compatible, I disagree with them.

the level of taxation is, the higher the growth rate of the economy is (Bergh and Karlsson, 2010; Bernholz, 1986; Romer and Romer, 2010; Vedder and Robe, 2009; Weede, 1991).[38] Not all taxes are equally harmful. Corporate taxes and progressive income taxes are worst; consumption and property taxes are less harmful (Arnold, 2008).[39] The only hope to limit the tax burden comes from globalization and tax competition (Tanzi, 2011: 140-145).

Limited government in the West suffers from erosion, in pacific Western Europe more than in the United States. Whereas democracy depends on the prior establishment of economic freedom and prosperity, democracy might nevertheless undermine its prerequisites. In Europe, transfer payments have become the dominant element of government budgets. The new focus of European governments on transfers and the provision of welfare must lead to unfortunate consequences. First, the tax and welfare state cannot avoid punishing hard work by taxing workers and rewarding the lack of economic success by transfers. Such reinforcements undermine incentives. Second, the welfare state looks self-destructive. It gets more costly, if more and more people are ready to claim benefits fraudulently. An empirical analysis of World Value Survey data supports the view that generous welfare states encourage illegitimate claims and deteriorating ethics (Heinemann, 2008). Third, the welfare state also undermines the willingness of parents to discipline and educate their children (Lindbeck and Nyberg, 2006). It hardly affects one's living standard whether one is an unskilled worker or lives on income support at the taxpayer's expense. So, why should parents of modestly gifted children teach them discipline and a willingness to work hard? Fourth, the welfare state stimulates the wrong kind of migration. Look at high tax and welfare states. There are incentives for high earners to migrate to lower tax states and incentives for would-be welfare recipients to immigrate. All of these developments undermine the long-run viability of European welfare states.

Worse still, most European welfare states have not been capable of financing their persistent expansion out of current taxation (Tanzi, 2011: 98, 232). Deficits and government debt have been growing for decades. With an explicit debt-to-GDP ratio close to 80 percent, Germany still counts as solid and attracts the envy of other states. Assuming that public debt continues to grow at the same speed as during the last decades, however, German public debt will be nearly three times as large as its gross domestic product in 2030 (Simon, 2011: 69). But the German welfare state, like other Western democracies, including the United States, has made lots of unfunded promises concerning health care as well as pensions (Peterson,

---

38   Unfortunately, this view is not unanimously accepted. For example, see Lindert (2004).

39   Although Arnold (2008) does not make much of it, his regressions are compatible with the view that high tax burdens as such also decrease economic growth rates.

2004). Since retired people are the main beneficiaries of Western welfare states, one may raise Hayek's question about when "the physically stronger will rebel and deprive the old of both their political rights and their legal claims to be maintained" (1960: 297). If one includes unfunded promises, then Germany's government debt is already about three times as large as its GDP. The worst estimates of government debts which I have seen have been published by the *Financial Times* (2010, February 16). These estimates of government liabilities (pension promises and health benefits included) are about four times GDP in Germany and the UK, about five times in France and the US, and more than eight times in Greece.

The two wings of the West seem to suffer from different afflictions. In Europe, especially on the continent, the tax and welfare state is the main threat. While many Europeans believe that the state is responsible for the provision of welfare and even for equalizing incomes, fewer Americans share such views. Whereas 78 percent of Americans ascribed American economic success to "American business," fewer Europeans would assign business and capitalism a similar degree of legitimacy (Lipset, 1996: 72, 146, 287). Nevertheless, the United States became a welfare state, too (Voegeli, 2010). In addition, the US made lax monetary policy and easy credit a means of pacifying those who had been left behind in the market economy (Eckert, 2010: 79-80; Rajan, 2010: 31). In the United States, Keynesianism and the demand for stimuli still dominate. The recent financial and economic crisis illustrates this. In essence, the cure to the crisis consisted of three components. The first component has been to rescue system-relevant banks and other major financial market participants, such as the American International Group (AIG). Since no one can know for sure what the consequences of a financial market meltdown would have been, politicians can argue that there was no reasonable alternative. Although Austrian economists and libertarians do not concur, many economists accept the argument. With the benefit of hindsight at least, one may argue that the taxpayer did not suffer too much from those governmental actions that targeted banks or big financial market players like AIG. Much of the taxpayer money that went to them has already been paid back. According to estimates by Deutsche Bank Research (2010), the American taxpayer will almost certainly suffer losses below two percent of GDP (which includes money diverted to saving the auto industry in Detroit, and Fannie Mae and Freddy Mac), and the German taxpayer no more than one percent of GDP. French and possibly even British taxpayers still can hope to avoid significant losses that will come from stabilizing their banks during the crisis.[40] Wherever the state rescued the

---

40 The *Economist's* evaluation is even more optimistic (2011, June 11: 69). The Troubled Assets Relief Program may even turn a profit. Fannie Mae and Freddie Mac are responsible

banks and other big players on financial markets, it suffered the consequences of its poor performance in regulation. Unfortunately, the financial crisis and the response to it has done nothing for mitigating the "too big to fail" problem, which got worse rather than better. Worse still, rescuing banks and AIG has reinforced moral hazard.

The second component has been the continuation of the cheap money policy which was a prerequisite of the crisis in the first place. Possibly, there was no better alternative to low interest rates and quantitative easing, i.e., central banks buying government bonds and financing public deficits by the equivalent of printing money.[41] But it should be emphasized that the extraordinary fear of deflation and its consequences that politicians, central bankers, and most economists demonstrated rests on a tenuous empirical basis (Atkenson and Kehoe, 2004). Given the high (and, because of the crisis, more rapidly growing than ever) indebtedness of most Western democracies, and given the resulting incentive for governments to lighten the debt burden by inflation, the long-run problem will be inflation rather than deflation (Bagus, 2011; Bernholz, 2003; Hayek, 1960).[42] The question is less whether central banks know when and how to tighten monetary policy than whether the politicians shall let them do what is necessary sooner or later. Here, I must admit deep pessimism. As Friedrich August von Hayek (1976/2008) recognized in the 1970s, money might be too important to leave it to the politicians. We might need to wrest control of monetary aggregates from politicians and politically appointed central bankers by either returning to some kind of commodity-based money or by the privatization of money. According to Hayek, the future of individual liberty and economic freedom might depend on it.[43]

---

for the lion's share of the losses, but relief for the banks was quite profitable. Of course, the financial crisis also affected growth rates and government revenue and therefore public debts. According to Reinhart and Rogoff, the real stock of debt tends to come close to doubling within three years after financial crises (2009: 170).

41 Hummel argues that Bernanke's Federal Reserve (Fed) did not flood markets with liquidity in response to the financial crisis, but that it redirected it, thereby becoming something like a central planner of the American economy (2011: 509). In the summer of 2008, the Fed's lending to banks was sterilized by its selling of Treasury securities.

42 Not only politicians, but even some economists (for example, Rogoff, 2011, August 9: 9) favor a higher rate of inflation in order to lighten the debt burden of democratic governments. Assuming that such a policy is a lesser evil than any alternative, the advice to politicians to confiscate part of people's savings implies an indictment of politicians and a strong verdict about government failure.

43 The most detailed proposal has been made by Huerta de Soto (2009). In his view, the limited reserve requirements in banking or the creation of credit out of nothing by banks, which are supported by central banks, are the main culprits for recurrent crises. That is

The third component of the rescue package has been Keynesian deficit spending.[44] In contrast to most Austrian or libertarian economists (such as Huerta de Soto, 2009), I can at least imagine that insufficient demand exists and that some deficit spending is desirable under some exceptional circumstances. I shall sidestep important technical issues such as the size of the multiplier. The smaller the multiplier is, the less effective deficit spending becomes. Suffice to say that there is disagreement about its size as well as about which kind of deficit spending is most effective (Barro, 2009; Cogan and Taylor, 2011). I shall also sidestep the related issue of crowding out. Possibly deficit spending is more effective in replacing private demand and private investment than in increasing aggregate demand. What really worries me is a different and more fundamental issue. Most Western governments almost always perceive the need to stimulate demand, but almost never see the need to renew the war chest for coming crises by accumulating government savings or at least paying back most of the excessive public debt accumulated through boom and bust. Most politicians behave as if running deficits were a free lunch and *always* good for the economy. Keynesian economists are much better in explaining the need for running deficits given insufficient demand than in urging politicians to reduce public debt during booms. The politically effective part of Keynesianism is nothing but pandering to the unfortunate inclination of politicians to spend almost without limits.[45] According to Buchanan and Wagner, the political legacy of Keynesianism in Western democracies amounts to a denial of scarcity: "Scarcity is indeed a fact of life, and political institutions that do not confront this fact threaten the existence of a free and prosperous society" (1977: 184).

Politicians have generated a framework where private actors, ranging from the poor desiring to become homeowners to overpaid bankers, have committed lots of errors which ultimately brought Western economies close to a collapse (Sowell, 2010; Taylor, 2009; Woods, 2009). In

---

why he demands 100 percent reserves, free banking, and abolition of central banks as well as a return to gold.

44 See Krugman (2008) for a recent explanation and defense of it. Other endorsements of the American stimulus are provided by Posner (2009) or Roubini with Mihm (2010).

45 As Tanzi underlines, high public spending and increasing public debt are not objectives of Keynesian economics, but by-products of demand management and stabilization policies (2011: 126). By contrast to some of his disciples, Keynes was not in favour of tax burdens above 25 percent of GDP. Some academics call for "hard Keynesianism," i.e., the requirement that governments run budget surpluses in good years so that they have resources to spend on stimuli in bad years (Farrell and Quiggin, 2011: 100). In theory, this is a good idea. In practice, it cannot work. If public choice economics comes even remotely close to reality, then it will remain impossible to persuade politicians to implement such recommendations.

order to contain the crisis, politicians expanded the scope of the state, increased deficits even more rapidly than before, and continued loose monetary policies which were a prerequisite of the last crisis. They did nothing effective against the "too big to fail" problem. By bailing out big players on financial markets, they increased moral hazard and put the Federal Reserve on the road to become a central planning agency. They have not worried about bankruptcy or the next generation in greying welfare states. They have not worried about individual liberty and economic freedom, i.e., about the ultimate source of Western prosperity.

Currently, Europeans are on the road towards a continental version of the tax-and-transfer state. The original idea behind the European Union (EU) was commendable: No more fratricidal wars between Europeans. Since Franco-German rivalry had resulted in three wars between 1870 and 1945, the special focus of the European unification project was always the prevention of another Franco-German war that might escalate into a larger European conflagration. Of course, we should be grateful that the risk of war in Europe is extremely low. Adherents of European integration credit the EU, even the euro and a process of achieving ever greater integration with the peaceful state of European affairs. I partially agree with this view. A free market in goods, services, capital, and labor, i.e., economic integration, does contribute to the prevention of war. I label this effect "peace by trade" or "the capitalist peace." The EU undoubtedly contributed to it. Furthermore, capitalism and free trade made Western Europe prosperous enough in the decades following World War II to support democratic governments. Thus, the democratic peace can complement "peace by trade" (Gartzke, 2005; Weede, 2011b).

But obviously the capitalist peace, and even the democratic peace, rests on a capitalist foundation. As soon as the European integration project undermines capitalism and the prosperity that can only be provided by capitalism, it will no longer serve the cause of European peace. From the beginning some economists doubted whether Europe was sufficiently close to being an optimal currency area for introducing a common currency,[46] or whether the inclusion of comparatively weak economies, like Greece or even highly indebted Italy, made sense. The frequent devaluations of other European currencies against the Deutsche Mark during the 1980s as well as the critical pronouncements by German economists should have provided warnings (Bagus, 2011: 46; Eckert, 2010:

---

46 Feldstein predicted adverse effects of the euro on inflation and unemployment as well as tensions within Europe and between Europe and the US (1997: 60, 67-68). He also pointed out that more centralized decision-making in Europe would lessen the opportunity for European countries to find out which policies succeed and which ones fail. Therefore, Europe would become less competitive with the rest of the world.

154, 173). At least political leaders in the late 1990s still insisted on combining the common currency with a "no bailout" principle and the prohibition for the European Central Bank to contribute to the financing of government deficits. These two prohibitions served the purpose of preventing an expansion or deepening of the European transfer union.[47] Governments still had to face the consequences of their profligacy. Of course, a European transfer union cannot avoid resulting in negative consequences just as transfer payments within Western welfare states do. In a transfer union, responsible governments that avoid the debt and deficit trap will be punished by having to help others, whereas irresponsible governments with high and growing deficits will be rewarded by receiving assistance. Government irresponsibility within a transfer union will spread, and deficits and debts will grow. Sound money will become a victim. The higher debt and deficits become, the more attractive inflationary policies become. Furthermore, current attempts to save the euro are likely to undermine the respect for international treaties and the legitimacy of the European project (Issing, 2011, August 9: 9).

Europe is in peril. The welfare state has undermined incentives for more than a generation. Debt and deficits have been growing for more than a generation. Although a greying Europe might need skilled immigrants, Europe certainly does not need immigration that will add to its welfare support system. Although rich European countries cannot hope to match the growth rates of China or India which benefit from the advantages of backwardness, there is little excuse for European politicians to be satisfied with the poor growth record of the last two decades. Why shouldn't Germany or France be capable of American growth rates (before the financial crisis); why shouldn't Greece or Portugal be able to rival the South Korean performance? Now the Euro-zone, the core of the EU, has added another problem: an extension of the transfer union or a second tier to the welfare state. The European Central Bank has been buying Greek and Irish and Portuguese government bonds—and recently even Spanish and Italian bonds. German, French, Austrian, and even Slovak taxpayers are picking up some of the unpaid bills left behind by the weaker Euro-zone governments.[48] The ruling elites of Europe are determined to achieve

---

47 According to Willeke (2011), the EU has been a transfer union for a long time. Germans, Dutch, and Swedes are the biggest losers, whereas the Mediterranean periphery of the EU comprises the biggest winners.

48 Instead of burdening the taxpayers of still solvent European states, one might have imposed a haircut on the creditors of Greece, Ireland, and Portugal. This would have been the lesser evil than providing guarantees amounting to 923 billion euros until the beginning of November 2010. Germany's share has been 215 billion, France's share 165,3 billion (Sinn and Carstensen, 2011: 1). One has to ask whether rescuing weaker euro

Continental unity. The preservation of individual liberty and economic freedom against state interference is not as high on their agenda.

European politicians want to become more powerful and thereby capable of enforcing truly grand errors: first, a deepening of the transfer union, which might later result in the inflationary union. Of course, non-members of the European Union with rapidly growing public debts, like United States, run similar inflationary risks. According to Bernholz, "Inflation has been the higher the greater the influence of politicians on monetary policy" (2003, 2010: 3). Before World War I, the gold standard established a hard budget constraint. Later some independent central banks remained obstacles against inflation. But the gold standard has gone and the responses to the financial crisis as well as rescue packages for the European periphery have undermined central bank independence. Democratically elected politicians seem to dislike hard budget constraints as much as central planners did. They are on the way to liberating themselves from such chains. The higher the mountain of public debt grows, the greater the temptation for elected officials to overcome the debts by inflation.

The early Keynes understood well what inflation does to property rights and a free society: "By a continuing process of inflation, governments can confiscate, secretly and unobserved, an important part of the wealth of their citizens. By this method they not only confiscate, but they confiscate *arbitrarily*; and, while the process impoverishes many, it actually enriches some.... There is no subtler, no surer means of overturning the existing basis of society than to debauch the currency. The process engages all the hidden forces of economic law on the side of destruction..." (1919/1988: 235-236). Whereas Keynes' negative view of inflation[49] implies an awareness of how easily inflation might get out of control, Western governments seem to remember the postwar period when inflation, together with financial repression, forced savers to accept negative interest rates for long periods of time and thereby permitted governments to reduce their debts (*Economist*, 2011, June 18: 80). Even the slow confiscation of savings by moderate inflation, however, is a frontal attack on private property rights. The fruits of centuries of European disunity are

---

countries overburdens the seemingly strong states. It has been estimated that the euro rescue package might add 18 percent to German indebtedness (Blankart, 2011: 46). Since the rescue operation has a tendency to expand, no end is in sight. The final effect might be overburdening the strong so that all of us can collapse later, but together.

49 Since Hayek (1960) disagreed a lot with Keynes, it is noteworthy that he quoted Keynes' statement about inflation approvingly at the beginning of the twenty-first chapter of his book. By contrast to most economists, Hayek does *not* believe that deflation is a greater threat to prosperity than inflation. Exaggerated fear of deflation is not supported by empirical research (Atkenson and Kehoe, 2004).

at risk: limited government and individual liberty, private property rights and capitalism, and in the long-run, even prosperity and peace.

Conclusion: Geopolitics, evolution and the expansion of liberty

Three hundred years ago, most of mankind was poor. Chinese, Indian, and European shares of world product were about equal. Then the West overtook Asian societies. Three decades ago, China and India were about equally poor in purchase power parity terms. Since then, China has left India behind. Chinese per capita income in purchase power parity terms is about twice as high as Indian per capita income. This history of economic performance raises two explanatory challenges. Why did China and India fall behind Europe or the West? Why did China do better than India recently? Here, an explanatory sketch has been suggested for answering both questions. While stagnation is blamed on restrictions of economic freedom, conversely, growth and prosperity have been explained by the expansion of economic freedom. Asia's giants grew much more slowly than the West because of weaker property rights, lack of scarcity prices, and insufficient mobilization of dispersed knowledge or deficiencies in economic freedom. Europe and the West benefited from better institutions than Asia because of interstate rivalry resulting in limited government and comparatively free markets. China could outperform India and start its attempt to catch up with the West only after climbing out of the socialist trap by a de facto improvement of personal freedom and property rights and implementing some economic freedom, by "market-preserving federalism" and joining the capitalist global economy. The extraordinary growth of both Asian giants would have been inconceivable without the advantages of backwardness. These advantages result from the earlier Western establishment of economic freedom or capitalism and the prosperity coming out of it. China did better than India because it moved away from socialism earlier and more forcefully than India did.

This account of Western, Chinese, and Indian economic performance is driven by geopolitics. Rivalry between European kingdoms and principalities, between territorial rulers and autonomous cities produced the checks and balances, as well as the exit opportunities for ordinary people, which contributed to the establishment of safe property rights and the European miracle. European states had to concede limited instead of absolutist government and therefore initiated the commercial and industrial revolutions in the West. During the twentieth century, the United States overtook Western Europe and established a transient hegemony at the end of the century.[50] Nevertheless, international rivalries still

---

50 The libertarian element in American political culture (Lipset, 1996) made American hegemony less burdensome than other types of hegemony would have been (Mandelbaum, 2005).

implied checks and balances against political power. Rivalry between the People's Republic of China on the Mainland and the Republic of China on Taiwan, the hostile competition between Communist China and the Soviet Union, the historical conflict between China and Japan, and the geographical closeness of US military deployments to China forced the PRC leadership to consider the consequences of falling further and further behind the economies of the West, Japan, and Taiwan. The more privileged geopolitical location of India compared with China, and the fact that Indian relations with America and the Soviet Union were never as bad as Chinese relations with these powers sometimes were, may explain the lateness and half-hearted character of Indian economic reforms.

The rise of Asia, in particular of China, constitutes a challenge to Western ideals of individual liberty. The appeal of political freedom is likely to suffer. A rhetorical question by Kaplan explains why: "Is a chaotic democracy better than the rule of autocrats who have overseen GDP growth rates of 10 percent annually over the past three decades?" (2011: 55). But the Chinese challenge is deeper. It concerns not only the selection of rulers, but also their decision latitude. It might ultimately be rooted in the Confucian heritage of China. Jenner points to "the unfree nature of the Confucian gentleman's place in the political order... An official could no more switch his allegiance to another regime than a married woman could leave home... It is as unusual to come across challenges to the principle of authoritarian rule (as opposed to misrule) in Chinese written records as it is to find the institution of the family questioned" (1998: 69).[51] Although economic freedom is less severely restricted than personal freedom in China, the Chinese economic miracle remains an intellectual as well as a political challenge to the defenders of liberty. Is as little freedom as currently exists in China enough for prosperity and growth? Or will China face the choice between dramatically expanding liberty or renewed stagnation once the advantages of backwardness are exhausted?

In the theory suggested above, liberty is the fruit of evolution, not of human planning. Rulers and ruling classes never can be interested in expanding liberty. Liberty for ordinary people rests on limited government or constraints for rulers.[52] Under some circumstances, rulers had to concede limited government, but they never desired to establish it. Although freedom is desirable and productive, we know little about how to fortify and extend it. But we do know that extending the territorial scope or the duties of government undermine liberty.

---

51 Bell (2006) has made an interesting suggestion about how to combine Confucianism and democracy. Members of the upper house might be selected according to academic merit.

52 In previous centuries, ordinary people were labelled "subjects."

References

Acemoglu, Daron, Simon Johnson, James A. Robinson, and Pierre Yared (2008). Income and democracy. *American Economic Review* 98(3): 808-842.

Ahluwalia, Montek S. (2002). Economic reforms in India since 1991: Has gradualism worked? *Journal of Economic Perspectives* 16(7): 67-88.

Alchian, Armen A., and Harold Demsetz (1972). Production, information costs, and economic organization. *American Economic Review* 62(5): 777-795.

Anand, Sudhir, and Paul Segal (2008). What do we know about global income inequality? *Journal of Economic Literature* 46(1): 57-94.

Anderson, Jonathan (2009). Beijing's exceptionalism. *The National Interest* 100: 19-26 and 28-30.

Angeles, Luis (2011). Institutions, property rights, and economic development in historical perspective. *Kyklos* 64(2): 157-177.

Arnold, Jens (2008). *Do Tax Structures Affect Aggregate Economic Growth? Empirical Evidence from a Panel of OECD Countries.* OECD Economics Department Working Paper No. 643. Organisation for Economic Co-operation and Development.

Atkenson, Andrew, and Patrick J. Kehoe (2004). Deflation and depression: Is there an empirical link? *American Economic Review* 94: 99-103.

Bagus, Philipp (2011). *Die Tragödie des Euro. Ein System zerstört sich selbst.* FinanzBuch.

Bardhan, Pranab (2010). *Awakening Giants, Feet of Clay: Assessing the Economic Rise of China and India.* Princeton University Press.

Barro, Robert J. (2009). Voodoo multipliers. *The Economist's Voice* 6(2): article 5.

Barro, Robert J., and Xavier Sala-i-Martin (1995). *Economic Growth.* McGraw-Hill.

Bell, Daniel A. (2006). *Beyond Liberal Democracy: Political Thinking for an East Asian Context.* Princeton University Press.

Benhabib, Jess, Alejandro Corvalan, and Mark M. Spiegel (2011). *Reestablishing the Income-Democracy Nexus.* NBER Working Paper 16832. National Bureau of Economic Research.

Bergh, Andreas, and Martin Karlsson (2010). Government size and growth: Accounting for economic freedom and globalization. *Public Choice* 142(1-2): 195-213.

Berman, Harold J. (1983). *Law and Revolution: The Formation of the Western Legal Tradition.* Harvard University Press.

Bernholz, Peter (1986). Growth of government, economic growth and individual freedom. *Journal of Institutional Economics (Zeitschrift für die gesamte Staatswissenschaft)* 142: 661-683.

Bernholz, Peter (2003). *Monetary Regimes and Inflation: History, Economic and Political Relationships.* Edward Elgar.

Bernholz, Peter (2010). *Politics, Financial Crisis, Central Bank Constitution and Monetary Policy.* Paper presented at a Frankfurt conference (Nov. 15). Universität Basel.

Bhagwati, Jagdish N. (1993). *India in Transition.* Clarendon.

Bhalla, Surjit S. (2010). *The New World Order: Importance of China and India.* Paper delivered at the meeting of the Mont Pelerin Society, Sydney, Australia (Oct. 15).

Blankart, Charles B. (2011). Europäischer Stabilitätsmechanismus: Wie weit umschulden, wie weit aushelfen? *Orientierungen zur Wirtschafts und Gesellschaftspolitik* 127: 46-51.

Blasius, Jörg, and Peter Graeff (2009). Economic freedom, wealth and corruption. In Peter Graeff and Guido Mehlkop (eds.), *Capitalism, Democracy and the Prevention of War and Poverty* (Routledge (Taylor and Francis)): 135-155.

Boix, Carles, and Susan C. Stokes (2003). Endogenous democratization. *World Politics* 55(4): 517-549.

Bosworth, Barry, Susan M. Collins, and Arvind Virmani (2006). *Sources of Growth in the Indian Economy.* Brookings.

Buchanan, James M., and Richard E. Wagner (1977). *Democracy in Deficit: The Political Legacy of Lord Keynes.* Academic Press.

Burkhart, Ross E., and Michael S. Lewis-Beck (1994). Comparative democracy: The economic development thesis. *American Political Science Review* 88(4): 903-910.

Chan, Wellington K. K. (2010). Chinese entrepreneurship since its late imperial period. In David S. Landes, Joel Mokyr, and William J. Baumol (eds.), *The Invention of Enterprise* (Princeton University Press): 469-500.

Chang, Gordon G. (2008). The end of the Chinese miracle? *Commentary* 125(3): 32-36.

Chauffour, Jean-Pierre (2009). *The Power of Freedom: Uniting Development and Human Rights.* Cato Institute.

Chauffour, Jean-Pierre (2011). *On the Relevance of Freedom and Entitlement in Development.* World Bank Policy Research Working Paper 5660. World Bank.

Chen, Shaohua, and Martin Ravallion (2008). *China is Poorer than We Thought, But No Less Successful in the Fight against Poverty.* World Bank Policy Research Paper 4621. World Bank.

Cogan, John F., and John B. Taylor (2011). Where did the stimulus go? *Commentary* 131(1): 23-26.

Cohen, Stephen Philip (2001). *India: Emerging Power.* Brookings.

Collins, Randall (1986). *Weberian Sociological Theory.* Cambridge University Press.

Dawson, John W. (2010). Macroeconomic volatility and economic freedom. In James Gwartney, Joshua Hall, and Robert Lawson, *Economic Freedom of the World: 2010 Annual Report* (Fraser Institute): 175-185.

De Bary, William T. (1983). *The Liberal Tradition in China.* The Chinese University Press.

De Bary, William T., Wing-Tsit Chan, and Burton Watson (comps.). (1960). *Sources of Chinese Tradition* (Vol. 1). Columbia University Press.

De Haan, Jacob, and Jan-Egbert Sturm (2000). On the relationship between economic freedom and economic growth. *European Journal of Political Economy* 16: 215-241.

De Haan, Jacob, and Jan-Egbert Sturm (2009). Is the IMF right? How robust is the relationship between market-oriented institutions and policies and economic growth? In Peter Graeff and Guido Mehlkop (eds.), *Capitalism, Democracy and the Prevention of War and Poverty* (Routledge): 108-134.

Deutsche Bank Research (2010). Direkte fiskalische Kosten der Finanzkrise. *Deutsche Bank Research* (July 1).

Dhume, Sadanand (2008). Is India an ally? *Commentary* 125(1): 25-30.

Dikötter, Frank (2010). *Mao's Great Famine: The History of China's Most Devastating Catastrophe, 1958-1962.* Bloomsbury.

Dollar, David (1992). Outward-oriented developing economies really do grow more rapidly. *Economic Development and Cultural Change* 40(3): 523-544.

Dollar, David, and Aart Kraay (2002). Spreading the wealth. *Foreign Affairs* 81(1): 120-133.

Doucouliagos, Hristos, and Mehmet Ulubasoglu (2006). Economic freedom and economic growth: Does specification make a difference? *European Journal of Political Economy* 22(1): 60-81.

Du, Jun, and Sourafel Girma (2010). Red capitalists: Political connections and firm performance in China. *Kyklos* 63(4): 530-545.

Dumont, Louis (1970). *Homo Hierarchicus: The Caste System and Its Implications.* University of Chicago Press.

Eberstadt, Nicholas (2010). The demographic future. *Foreign Affairs* 89(6): 54-64.

Eckert, Daniel D. (2010). *Weltkrieg der Währungen.* FinanzBuch Verlag.

The Economist (2005, March 5). Survey: The tiger in front. *The Economist* 374 (8416).

The Economist (2005, April 23). Top exporters. *The Economist* 375 (8423): 101.

The Economist (2008, February 16). Asian budget finances. Poles apart. *The Economist* 386 (8567): 72.

The Economist (2009, May 30). Government versus market in America. The visible hand. *The Economist* 391 (8633): 25-27.

The Economist (2009, September 12). China's struggling smaller firms. Small fish in a big pond. *The Economist* 392 (8648): 68-69.

The Economist (2009, November 14). Economic focus. Secret sauce. *The Economist* 393 (8657): 88.

The Economist (2009, November 28). Fighting poverty in emerging markets. The gloves go on. *The Economist* 393 (8659): 68.

The Economist (2010, January 16). China's economy. Not just another fake. *The Economist* 394 (8665): 63-65.

The Economist (2010, January 30). Bihar's remarkable recovery. *The Economist* 394 (8667): 59-60.

The Economist (2010, February 13). Settling trade disputes. When partners attack. *The Economist* 394 (8669): 74.

The Economist (2010, May 8). Migration in China. Invisible and heavy shackles. *The Economist* 395 (8681): 24-26.

The Economist (2010, July 31). The next China. *The Economist* 396 (8693): 46-48.

The Economist (2010, December 18). The world's biggest economy. Dating game. *The Economist* 397 (8713): 129.

The Economist (2011, January 29). Attitudes to business. Milton Friedman goes on tour. *The Economist* 398 (8718): 57.

The Economist (2011, March 12). Entrepreneurship in China. Let a million flowers bloom. *The Economist* 398 (8724): 71-74.

The Economist (2011, March 19). Taming Leviathan. A special report on the future of the state. *The Economist* 398 (8725): after p. 44.

The Economist (2011, March 26). Business in India. The price of graft. *The Economist* 398 (8726): 66-68.

The Economist (2011a, April 16). India and foreign investment. Fling wide the gates. *The Economist* 399 (8729): 14.

The Economist (2011b, April 16). Chinese business. When fund-raising is a crime. *The Economist* 399 (8729): 63.

The Economist (2011, June 11). America's bail-out math. Hard-nosed socialists. *The Economist* 399 (8737): 69.

The Economist (2011, June 18). Economics focus. The great repression. *The Economist* 399 (8738): 80.

The Economist (2011, June 25). Special report: China. Rising power, anxious state. *The Economist* 399 (8739): after p. 50.

The Economist (2011, September 3). Privatisation in China. Capitalism confined. *The Economist* 400 (8749): 58-60.

Farr, W. Ken, Richard A. Lord, and J. Larry Wolfenbarger (1998). Economic freedom, political freedom, and economic well-being. *Cato Journal* 18(2): 247-262.

Feigenbaum, Evan A. (2010). India's rise, America's interest. *Foreign Affairs* 89(2): 76-91.

Farrell, Henry, and John Quiggin (2011). How to save the euro—and the EU. *Foreign Affairs* 90(3): 96-103.

Feldmann, Horst (2010). Economic freedom and unemployment. In James Gwartney, Joshua Hall, and Robert Lawson, *Economic Freedom of the World: 2010 Annual Report* (Fraser Institute): 187-201.

Feldstein, Martin (1997). EMU and International Conflict. *Foreign Affairs* 76(6): 60-73.

Ferguson, Niall (2011). *Civilization: The West and the Rest.* Allen Lane (Penguin).

Federation of Indian Chambers of Commerce and Industry [FICCI] (1999). *Footprints of Enterprise: Indian Business through the Ages.* Oxford University Press.

Financial Times (2010, February 16). Sovereign fret. (The Lex Column.) *Financial Times:* 12.

Fogel, Robert (2010). Why China's economy will grow to $123 trillion by 2040. *Foreign Policy* 177: 70-75.

Fu, Zhengyuan (1993). *Autocratic Tradition and Chinese Politics.* Cambridge University Press.

Gartzke, Erik (2005). Freedom and peace. In James D. Gwartney and Richard A. Lawson, *Economic Freedom of the World: 2005 Annual Report* (Fraser Institute): 29-44.

Goklany, Indur M. (2007). *The Improving State of the World. Why We Are Living Longer, Healthier, More Comfortable Lives on a Cleaner Planet.* Cato Institute.

Goldstone, Jack (2008). *Why Europe? The Rise of the West in World History, 1500-1850.* McGraw-Hill.

Graeff, Peter, and Guido Mehlkop (2003). The impact of economic freedom on corruption: Different patterns for rich and poor countries. *European Journal of Political Economy* 19: 605-620.

Gwartney, James D., and Robert A. Lawson (2004). Economic freedom, investment, and growth. In James D. Gwartney and Robert A. Lawson, *Economic Freedom of the World: 2004 Annual Report* (Fraser Institute): 28-44.

Gwartney, James D., Joshua Hall, and Robert A. Lawson (2010). *Economic Freedom of the World: 2010 Annual Report.* Fraser Institute.

Gwartney, James D., Randall D. Holcombe, and Robert A. Lawson (2006). Institutions and the Impact of Investment on Growth. *Kyklos* 59: 255-73.

Hale, David D., and Lyric Hughes Hale (2008). Reconsidering revaluation: The wrong approach to the US-Chinese trade imbalance. *Foreign Affairs* 87(1): 57-66.

Hatton, Timothy J., and Jeffrey G. Williamson (2006). *Global Migration and the World Economy.* MIT Press.

Hayek, Friedrich August von (1945). The use of knowledge in society. *American Economic Review* 35(4): 519-530.

Hayek, Friedrich August von (1960). *The Constitution of Liberty*. University of Chicago Press.

Hayek, Friedrich August von (1979). *Law, Legislation and Liberty. Vol. 3.* University of Chicago Press.

Hayek, Friedrich August von (1988). *The Fatal Conceit*. Routledge.

Hayek, Friedrich August von (1976/2008). *Denationalisation of Money*. Institute of Economic Affairs.

Heinemann, Friedrich (2008). Is the welfare state self-destructive? A study of government benefit morale. *Kyklos* 61(2): 237-257.

Hobson, John M. (2004). *The Eastern Origins of Western Civilisation*. Cambridge University Press.

Huang, Yasheng (2008). *Capitalism with Chinese Characteristics: Entrepreneurship and the State*. Cambridge University Press.

Huerta de Soto, Jesus (2009). *Money, Bank Credit, and Economic Cycles* (2nd ed.). Ludwig von Mises Institute.

Huff, Toby E. (2011). *Intellectual Curiosity and the Scientific Revolution: A Global Perspective*. Cambridge University Press.

Hummel, Jeffrey Roger (2011). Ben Bernanke versus Milton Friedman: The Federal Reserve's emergence as the U.S. economy's central planner. *The Independent Review* 15(4): 485-518.

Inglehart, Ronald, and Chris Welzel (2009). How development leads to democracy. *Foreign Affairs* 88(2): 33-48.

Issing, Otmar (2011, August 9). Slithering to the wrong kind of union. *Financial Times*: 9.

Jenner, W. J. F. (1998). China and freedom. In David Kelly and Anthony Reid (eds.), *Asian Freedoms* (Cambridge University Press): 65-92.

Jones, Eric L. (1981). *The European Miracle*. Cambridge University Press.

Joshi, Vijay, and I.M.D. Little (1998). *India's Economic Reforms 1991-2001*. Oxford University Press.

Kakar, Sudhir (1996). *The Colors of Violence: Cultural Identities, Religion, and Conflict*. University of Chicago Press.

Kaplan, Robert D. (2011). The good autocrat. *The National Interest* 114: 51-58.

Keynes, John Maynard (1919/1988). *The Economic Consequences of the Peace*. Penguin.

Kohli, Atul (2004). *State-Directed Development: Political Power and Industrialization in the Global Periphery*. Cambridge University Press.

Krugman, Paul (2008). *The Return of Depression Economics*. Penguin.

Kuran, Timur (2010). The scale of entrepreneurship in Middle Eastern history: Inhibitive roles of Islamic institutions. In David S. Landes, Joel Mokyr, and William J. Baumol (eds.), *The Invention of Enterprise: Entrepreneurship from Ancient Mesopotamia to Modern Times* (Princeton University Press): 62-87.

Lal, Deepak (1998). *Unintended Consequences: The Impact of Factor Endowments, Culture, and Politics on Long-Run Economic Performance.* MIT Press.

Lal, Deepak (2004). India. In Peter Bernholz and Roland Vaubel, *Political Competition, Innovation and Growth in the History of Asian Civilizations* (Edward Elgar): 128-141.

Lal, Deepak (2008). An Indian economic miracle? *Cato Journal* 28(1): 11-34.

Landes, David S. (1998). *The Wealth and Poverty of Nations.* Norton.

Levine, Ross, and David Renelt (1992). A sensitivity analysis of cross-country growth regressions. *American Economic Review* 82: 942-963.

Lin, Justin Yifu, Fang Cai, and Zhou Li (2003). *The China Miracle: Development Strategy and Economic Reform.* Chinese University Press.

Lin, Justin Yifu, and Liu Peilin (2008). Development strategies and regional income disparities in China. In Guanghua Wan (ed.), *Inequality and Growth in Modern China* (Oxford University Press): 56-78.

Lindbeck, Assar and Sven Nyberg (2006). Raising children to work hard: Altruism, work norms, and social insurance. *Quarterly Journal of Economics* CXXI: 1473-1503.

Lindert, Peter H. (2004). *Growing Public Social Spending and Economic Growth Since the 18th Century.* Cambridge University Press.

Lipset, Seymour M. (1994). The social requisites of democracy revisited. *American Sociological Review* 59(1): 1-22.

Lipset, Seymour M. (1996). *American Exceptionalism: A Double-Edged Sword.* Norton.

Liu, Lirong (2007). *Wirtschaftliche Freiheit und Wachstum.* LIT.

Luce, Edward (2006). *In Spite of the Gods: The Strange Rise of Modern India.* Little and Brown.

Maddison, Angus (1998). *Chinese Economic Performance in the Long Run.* OECD Development Centre, Organisation for Economic Co-operation and Development.

Maddison, Angus (2001). *The World Economy: A Millennial Perspective.* Organisation for Economic Co-operation and Development.

Maddison, Angus (2007). *Contours of the World Economy, 1-2030 AD.* Oxford University Press.

Mandelbaum, Michael (2005). *The Case for Goliath.* Public Affairs Press.

Majumdar, Sumit K. (1998). Assessing comparative efficiency of the state-owned, mixed and private sectors in Indian industry. *Public Choice* 96(1-2): 1-24.

McMahon, Fred (2012). Human Freedom from Pericles to Measurement: A Literature Review and Analysis. In Fred McMahon (ed.), *Towards a Worldwide Index of Human Freedom* (Fraser Institute): 7-54.

Mencius (2003). *Mencius: A Bilingual Edition.* (D.C. Lau, trans.). Chinese University Press.

Mises, Ludwig von (1920). Die Wirtschaftsrechnung im sozialistischen Gemeinwesen. *Archiv für Sozialwissenschaft und Sozialpolitik* 47(1): 86-121.

Mises, Ludwig von (1944). *Bureaucracy.* Yale University Press.

Mises, Ludwig von (1927/2005). *Liberalism.* Liberty Fund.

Montinola, Gabriella, Yingyi Qian, and Barry Weingast (1995). Federalism Chinese style: The political basis of economic success in China. *World Politics* 48(1): 50-81.

Nilekani, Nandan (2009). *Imagining India: Ideas for the New Century.* Penguin (Allen Lane).

Niskanen, William A. (2008). *Reflections of a Political Economist.* Cato Institute.

North, Douglass C. (1990). *Institutions, Institutional Change and Economic Performance.* Cambridge University Press.

North, Douglass C., John Joseph Wallis, and Barry R. Weingast (2009). *Violence and Social Orders.* Cambridge University Press.

North, Douglass C., and Barry R. Weingast (1989). Constitutions and commitment: The evolution of institutions governing public choice in 17th century England. *The Journal of Economic History* 49(4): 803-832.

Norton, Seth W., and James D. Gwartney (2008). Economic freedom and world poverty. In James D. Gwartney and Robert A. Lawson, *Economic Freedom of the World: 2008 Annual Report 2008* (Fraser Institute): 23-40.

Olson, Mancur (1982). *The Rise and Decline of Nations.* Yale University Press.

Olson, Mancur (1987). Diseconomies of scale and development. *Cato Journal* 7(1): 77-97.

Olson, Mancur (1996). 'Big bills left on the sidewalk: Why some nations are rich, and others poor. *Journal of Economic Perspectives* 10(2): 3-24.

Olson, Mancur (2000). *Power and Prosperity: Outgrowing Communist and Capitalist Dictatorships.* Basic Books.

Paldam, Martin, and Erich Grundlach (2008). Two views on institutions and development: The grand transition vs the primacy of institutions. *Kyklos* 61(1): 65-100.

Palmer, Tom G. (2009). *Realizing Freedom, Libertarian Theory, History, and Practice.* Cato Institute.

Panagariya, Arvind (2008). *India: The Emerging Giant.* Oxford University Press.

Peerenboom, Randall (2007). *China Modernizes: Threat to the West or Model for the Rest?* Oxford University Press.

Peterson, Peter G. (2004). *Running On Empty. How the Democratic and Republican Parties are Bankrupting Our Future and What American Can Do about It.* Farrar, Straus and Giroux.

Pipes, Richard (1999). *Property and Freedom.* A. A. Knopf.

Pomeranz, Kenneth (2000). *The Great Divergence.* Princeton University Press.

Posner, Richard A. (2009). *A Failure of Capitalism.* Harvard University Press.

Pritchett, Lant (2009). *Is India a Flailing State? Detours on the Four Lane Highway to Modernization.* HKS Faculty Research Working Paper Series RWP09-013. Harvard Kennedy School, Harvard University.

Przeworski, Adam, Michael E. Alvarez, Jose Antonio Cheibub, and Fernando Limongi (2000). *Democracy and Development: Political Institutions and Well-Being in the World, 1950-1990.* Cambridge University Press.

Quah, Jon S. T. (2008). Curbing corruption in India: An impossible dream? *Asian Journal of Political Science* 16(3): 240-259.

Rajan, Raghuram G. (2010). *Fault Lines: How Hidden Fractures Still Threaten the World Economy.* Princeton University Press.

Reinhart, Carmen M., and Kenneth S. Rogoff (2009). *This Time is Different: Eight Centuries of Financial Folly.* Princeton University Press.

Rodrik, Dani (2007). *One Economics, Many Recipes: Globalization, Institutions, and Economic Growth.* Princeton University Press.

Rodrik, Dani, and Arvind Subramanian (2004). *From Hindu rate of Growth to Productivity Surge: The Mystery of the Indian Growth Transition.* HKS Faculty Research Working Paper Series RWP 04-013. Harvard Kennedy School, Harvard University.

Rogoff, Kenneth (2011, August 9). The bullets yet to be fired to stop the crisis. *Financial Times*: 9.

Romer, Christina D., and David H. Romer (2010). The macroeconomic effects of tax changes: Estimates based on a new measure of fiscal shocks. *American Economic Review* 100: 763-801.

Rosenberg, Nathan, and L.E. Birdzell (1986). *How the West Grew Rich.* Basic Books.

Roubini, Nouriel, with Stephen Mihm (2010). *Crisis Economics: A Crash Course in the Future of Finance.* Penguin (Allen Lane).

Sally, Razeen (2011). *Liberty Outside the West.* Paper delivered at the Hayek Tage (June 10). Freiburg.

Schmidt, Fritz and Ulf Dirlmeier (1998). Rise and decline in Italy and Upper Germany in the Middle Ages and Early Modern Times. In Peter Bernholz, Manfred E. Streit, and Roland Vaubel (eds.), *Political Competition, Innovation and Growth* (Springer): 145-175.

Sender, Henny, and Jamil Anderlini (2011, June 2). Land price fall threatens local finances. *Financial Times*: 5.

Simon, Hermann (2011). *Die Wirtschaftstrends der Zukunft.* Campus Verlag.

Sinn, Hans-Werner and Kai Carstensen (2010). Ein Krisenmechanismus für die Eurozone. *Ifo-Schnelldienst* 23 (November). Institut für Wirtschaftsforschung an der Universität München.

Smith, Adam (1776/1976). *An Inquiry into the Nature and Causes of the Wealth of Nations.* Oxford University Press.

Sowell, Thomas (2010). *The Housing Boom and Bust.* Basic Books.

Srinivas, M.N., Y.B. Damle, S. Shahani, and A. Beteille (1959). Caste: A trend report and bibliography. *Current Sociology* 8(3): 135-151.

Stringham, Edward Peter, and John Levendis (2010). The relationship between economic freedom and homicide. In James Gwartney, Joshua Hall, and Robert Lawson, *Economic Freedom of the World: 2010 Annual Report* (Fraser Institute): 203-217.

Tanzi, Vito (2011). *Government versus Markets: The Changing Economic Role of the State.* Cambridge University Press.

Tanzi, Vito, and Ludger Schuknecht (2000). *Public Spending in the 20th Century.* Cambridge University Press.

Taylor, John B. (2009). *Getting Off Track: How Government Actions and Interventions Caused, Prolonged, and Worsened the Financial Crisis.* Stanford University Press.

Van Praagh, David (2003). *The Greater Game: India's Race with Destiny and China.* McGill-Queen's University Press.

Vaubel, Roland (2008). A history of thought on institutional competition. In Andreas Bergh and Rolf Höijer (eds.), *Institutional Competition* (Edward Elgar): 29-66.

Vásquez, Ian, and Tanja Štumberger (2012). An Index of Freedom in the World. In Fred McMahon, ed., *Towards a Worldwide Index of Human Freedom* (Fraser Institute, 2012): 55–112.

Vedder, Richard, and Jonathan Robe (2009). *Taxes and Economic Growth: Implications for German Tax Reform.* Taxpayers' Association of Europe.

Vega-Gordillo, Manuel, and Jose L. Alvarez-Arce (2003). Economic growth and freedom. *Cato Journal* 23(2): 199-215.

Voegeli, William (2010). *Never Enough: America's Limitless Welfare State.* Encounter.

Volckart, Oliver (1998). Comment. In Peter Bernholz, Manfred E. Streit, and Roland Vaubel (eds.), *Political Competition, Innovation and Growth* (Springer): 177-181.

Walter, Carl E., and Fraser J.T. Howie (2011). *Red Capitalism: The Fragile Financial Foundation of China's Extraordinary Rise.* Wiley (Asia).

Wan, Guanghua, Ming Lu, and Zhao Chen (2008). The inequality-growth nexus in the short and long run. In Guanghua Wan (ed.), *Inequality and Growth in Modern China* (Oxford University Press): 1-17.

Wang, Xiaolu (2008). Income inequality in China and its influencing factors. In Guanghua Wan (ed.), *Inequality and Growth in Modern China* (Oxford University Press): 18-32.

Weber, Max (1921/1978). *Gesammelte Aufsaetze zur Religionssoziologie: Band 2.* Mohr Siebeck.

Weber, Max (1922/1964). *Wirtschaft und Gesellschaft.* Kiepenheuer und Witsch.

Weber, Max (1923/1981). *Wirtschaftsgeschichte.* Duncker und Humblot.

Weede, Erich (1991). The impact of state power on economic growth rates in OECD countries. *Quality and Quantity* 25: 421-438.

Weede, Erich (1996). *Economic Development, Social Order, and World Politics.* Lynne Rienner.

Weede, Erich (2000). *Asien und der Westen.* Nomos.

Weede, Erich (2006). Economic freedom and development. *Cato Journal* 26(3): 511-524.

Weede, Erich (2010). The rise of India: Overcoming caste society and permit-license-quota raj, implementing some economic freedom. *Asian Journal of Political Science* 18(2): 129-153.

Weede, Erich (2011a). Long-run economic performance in the European periphery: Russia and Turkey. *Kyklos* 64(1): 138-156.

Weede, Erich (2011b). The capitalist peace. In Christopher J. Coyne and Rachel L. Mathers (eds.), *The Handbook on the Political Economy of War* (Edward Elgar): 269-280.

Weingast, Barry R. (1995). The economic role of political institutions: Market-preserving federalism and economic development. *Journal of Law, Economics, and Organization* 11(1): 1-31.

Willeke, Franz-Ulrich (2011). *Deutschland, Zahlmeister der EU.* Olzog.

Wolcott, Susan (2010). An examination of the supply of financial credit to entrepreneurs in Colonial India. In David S. Landes, Joel Mokyr, and William J. Baumol (eds.), *The Invention of Enterprise* (Princeton University Press): 443-468.

Woods, Thomas (2009). *Meltdown: A Free-Market Look at Why the Stock Market Collapsed, the Economy Tanked, and Government Bailouts Will Make Things Worse.* Regnery.

World Bank (1993). *The East Asian Miracle.* Oxford University Press.

World Bank (1995). *World Development Report 1995.* Oxford Univ. Press.

World Bank (2011). *World Development Report 2011: Conflict, Security, and Development.* World Bank.

Yang, Tai-Shuenn (1987). *Property Rights and Constitutional Order in Imperial China.* Ph.D. dissertation. Department of Political Science, Indiana University.

Yergin, Daniel, and Joseph Stanislaw (1998). *The Commanding Heights: The Battle between Government and the Marketplace that is Remaking the Modern World.* Simon and Schuster.

Zhu, Keliang, and Roy Prosterman (2007). *Securing Land Rights for Chinese Farmers.* Center for Global Liberty and Prosperity, Cato Institute.

CHAPTER NINE

The Eviseration of Liberty in Canadian Courts

Karen Selick, Derek From, and Chris Schafer *

The classical liberal philosopher, J.S. Mill, said of liberty:

> The only [liberty] which deserves the name is that of pursuing our own good, in our own way, so long as we do not attempt to deprive others of theirs, or impede their efforts to obtain it. (Mill, 1859/1974: 72)

Mill's concept of liberty is powerful and robust. It protects the so-called "negative" freedom of individuals, permitting them to be self-determining, free *from* state interference of any kind, unless it is to prevent harm to another.

Unfortunately, this concept of liberty is almost completely foreign to Canadian constitutional law jurisprudence. Our courts are out of step with the classical liberal philosophical foundations of our own political system. In fact, the courts in Canada have eviscerated the concept of liberty.

---

* Karen Selick, L.L.B., is the Litigation Director for the Canadian Constitution Foundation. Since her call to the Bar in 1978, she has practiced in the areas of tax planning, civil litigation, wills and estates, and matrimonial law. Ms. Selick's legal and public policy commentary has been published in the Globe and Mail, National Post, Lawyers Weekly, Canadian Lawyer, and other publications.

Derek From, B.R.S., B.A. (Hon), J.D., is Legal Counsel for the Canadian Constitution Foundation. After graduating with a Bachelor in Religious Studies from Briercrest College, he completed a degree in philosophy at the University of Waterloo. As a musician who has worked with many different record labels in the last ten years, he is interested in copyright law.

Christopher Schafer, B.A. (Hon), M.A., LL.B., is Executive Director of the Canadian Constitution Foundation. Prior to this, he was an associate at Gowling Lafleur Henderson LLP in Ottawa, where his practice areas included constitutional and regulatory law. A published author, Mr. Schafer has written several studies and numerous articles on public policy and legal issues for think tanks, journals, and newspapers.

The Canadian Charter of Rights and Freedoms was adopted in 1982. The Charter is a constitutional document that is the supreme law of Canada. It is the standard by which all federal and provincial laws are measured. Most importantly, it limits the authority of government. It does this by prohibiting the government from enacting laws that violate individual freedoms without justification. This is one of the chief purposes of the Charter.

The Charter offers explicit protection for liberty. Section 7 reads:

> Everyone has the right to life, liberty and security of the person and the right not to be deprived thereof except in accordance with the principles of fundamental justice.

Having a cursory understanding of the structure of the Charter is important for understanding how the courts have treated liberty. Legal analysis under section 7 of the Charter has three important and distinct steps. And when a Charter right or freedom has allegedly been violated by legislation or other government action, the Court will come to one of four possible conclusions.

First, the court inquires whether the right to life, liberty, or security of the person is affected by a government's action. If none of these rights are affected, then the government's action has not breached section 7 and legal analysis stops. But if the courts determine that an individual's right to life, liberty, or security of the person is affected by the government's action, legal analysis proceeds to the next step.

Step two is for the court to inquire into whether the government's action accords with the principles of fundamental justice. If the government has acted in accordance with the principles of fundamental justice, the government's actions have not breached section 7 and legal analysis stops. But if the government's actions have not accorded with the principles of fundamental justice, the government has violated section 7.

Third, once a section 7 violation is established, the legal analysis will proceed to section 1 of the Charter to determine if the government's action or legislation was demonstrably justified as a reasonable limit prescribed by law. Section 1 of the Charter reads:

> The Canadian Charter of Rights and Freedoms guarantees the rights and freedoms set out in it subject only to such reasonable limits prescribed by law as can be demonstrably justified in a free and democratic society.

If the court finds the government action that violated section 7 is justified as reasonable, then the government action is vindicated as legitimate. But if the court finds both that the government's action has violated section 7 and that the violation is not justified under section 1, the government's action will be considered an unconstitutional breach of a Charter right.

A constitutional guarantee of liberty, to be consistent with J.S. Mill's description, should ensure that everyone has the right to freely pursue their own happiness as long as their actions do not harm others. Such a constitutional guarantee would protect individuals from unjustified state inference with their chosen way of life. But there are many ways in which the courts in Canada have permitted the government to impede individual liberty.

For example, the government may confiscate your property without compensation (*R. v. Tener*). It can force you to have your photo taken even if it conflicts with your deeply held religious beliefs (*Alberta v. Hutterian Brethren of Wilson Colony*). It can force parents to educate their children in a particular fashion (*R. v. Jones*). It can force individuals to pay union fees even if they are not union members (*Lavigne v. Ontario Public Service Employees Union*). It can punish you for putting certain substances in your body (*R. v. Malmo-Levine; R. v. Caine*). And it can prohibit you from entering into mutually agreeable contracts with other individuals (*Reference re ss. 193 & 195.1(1)(c) of Criminal Code (Canada)*).

In each of these instances, the government may take these steps regardless of whether anyone is harmed.[1] And the government has demonstrated no hesitancy about arguing that its coercive actions further a public good or that it is advancing your interests—whether you recognize it or not. Government acts of this type are an affront to individual liberty. And if section 7 of the Charter had a robust and meaningful guarantee of liberty, each of these government acts would be constitutionally suspect.

By way of illustration, Michael Schmidt, a client of the Canadian Constitution Foundation, has operated a cow-share in rural Ontario since the early 1990s. Cow-shares are contractual arrangements between individuals who co-own cows in common with other owners, and farmers who tend to the cows. The farmer will typically provide food, land, and other necessities of life to the cow, and make the cow's milk accessible to the owner. In the English Common Law, this arrangement is known as a contract of agistment, with the farmer being called the agister.

As expected, Schmidt, acting as an agister, not only tended the cows in his care, he also provided raw milk from the cows to the cows' owners. It is not illegal to consume raw milk in Ontario. It is illegal, however, to "sell, offer for sale, deliver or distribute" unpasteurized milk. As a

---

1 The Supreme Court of Canada rejected J.S. Mill's harm principle as a principle of fundamental justice in *Malmo-Levine*. By so doing, the court held that the government may curtail the liberty of individuals whose actions cause no harm to others.

result, the Government of Ontario charged Schmidt with 19 violations of Ontario's Health Protection and Promotion Act and Milk Act. If Schmidt were convicted under these acts, he would face probation or a fine under the Ontario Provincial Offences Act.

The fines Schmidt was exposed to were potentially ruinous. Under these Acts he could be ordered to pay $10,000 per day for each day he is found to have violated Ontario law.

The government's actions against Schmidt cannot be reconciled with Mill's concept of liberty. Schmidt and the owners of the cows he tends have willingly entered into a mutually agreeable contractual arrangement. The cows' owners believe that consuming raw milk is beneficial to their health. And there is no evidence of anyone becoming sick or suffering any ill-health as a result of drinking the raw milk from Schmidt's farm. If liberty under the Charter were a robust and powerful concept like Mill's, there would be no obvious justification for charging Schmidt.

But it is worse yet. Not only does the Charter guarantee of liberty fail to protect Schmidt from an unjustified, coercive, and paternalistic law, the courts do not acknowledge that exposing individuals like Schmidt to financial ruin has an impact whatsoever upon their liberty.

Section 7 of the Charter is recognized to be relevant in circumstances where a government action has placed an individual's life, liberty, or security of the person in jeopardy. An individual may therefore successfully advance a section 7 Charter argument if his right to life, liberty, or security of the person has the potential of being infringed. How have the courts understood the terms life, liberty, and security of the person?

The right to life is easily understood. Any government act that endangers the life of an individual will engage the Charter. Security of the person is less obvious, but it has been recognized to include, among other things, an individual's psychological integrity. For example, security of the person is affected when the government threatens to remove a child from a parent's care (*New Brunswick (Minister of Health and Community Services)*). But what about the right to liberty? Under what circumstances do the courts recognize that the government has violated an individual's right to liberty?

The Canadian courts have recognized that a potential restriction on an individual's freedom of movement triggers the section 7 right to liberty (*Re B.C. Motor Vehicle Act*). But liberty may protect more than this. In *Blencoe v. British Columbia*, Chief Justice McLachlin said,

> The liberty interest protected by s. 7 of the Charter is no longer restricted to mere freedom from physical restraint.

And in *B. (R.) v. Children's Aid Society*, Justice La Forest said,

> ... the liberty interest protected by s. 7 must be interpreted broadly and in accordance with the principles and values underlying the Charter as a whole and that it protects an individual's personal autonomy ...

Even though the courts have said they are willing to interpret the right to liberty broadly, they have been reluctant to recognize that being exposed to ruinous financial penalties should trigger section 7. Sufficiently large monetary penalties can have a more severe, longer-lasting impact on a convicted individual's liberty than short-term imprisonment. And it is contrary to good reason that the possibility of imprisonment triggers the section 7 right to liberty while the possibility of financial ruin cannot. Yet that is how our courts have interpreted section 7.

It has become almost a mantra for legal commentators and the courts to intone that section 7 rights do not include economic or business-related liberty. However, during the early years of Charter jurisprudence, the Supreme Court of Canada was generally careful not to completely close the door to interpretations of section 7 that might include economic components. In *Irwin Toy v. Quebec*, the case most often cited by lawyers, law-students, politicians, and the like, as standing for the legal proposition that section 7 does not protect economic liberty, the court said,

> This is not to declare, however, that no right with an economic component can fall within "security of the person." Lower courts have found that the rubric of "economic rights" embraces a broad spectrum of interests, ranging from such rights, included in various international covenants, as rights to social security, equal pay for equal work, adequate food, clothing and shelter, to traditional property—contract rights. To exclude all of these at this early moment in the history of Charter interpretation seems to us to be precipitous. We do not, at this moment, choose to pronounce upon whether those economic rights fundamental to human life or survival are to be treated as though they are of the same ilk as corporate-commercial economic rights. In so stating, we find the second effect of the inclusion of "security of the person" to be that a corporation's economic rights find no constitutional protection in that section. (*Irwin Toy v. Quebec* at para. 95.)

As can be seen, although the Supreme Court is confusing "claim" rights such as a right to social security and adequate food that can only be realized by violating another person's freedom, with economic liberty, *Irwin Toy v. Quebec* did not definitively conclude that economic rights, which includes protection of property rights and contract rights, are excluded from section 7 protection. Yet there is an overwhelming tide of opinion that the Charter does not and should not protect economic liberty. This tide includes Peter Hogg, a widely quoted scholar of Canadian Constitutional Law. Hogg asserts that "there are good reasons for caution in expanding the concept of liberty in s. 7" (2009: 1,080) to include economic liberty. However, the reasons he sets out in his textbook would not likely persuade anyone who agrees with J.S. Mill.

Mill's definition of liberty aside, according to a wide variety of dictionaries, two of the most important definitions of the word "liberty" revolve around the notions of freedom of choice and the absence of external constraints. In the economic realm, "liberty" is often taken to mean the right to earn an honest living in the occupation of your choice.

The definition of "liberty" was unencumbered by judicial interpretation when the Charter became part of Canada's constitution in 1982. But the courts have virtually eviscerated it since then. The earliest instance of this curtailment of the scope of "liberty" occurred in 1985, when Justice Bertha Wilson wrote:

> Indeed, all regulatory offences impose some restriction on liberty broadly construed. But I think it would trivialize the Charter to sweep all those offences into s. 7 as violations of the right to life, liberty and security of the person even if they can be sustained under s. 1. (*Re B.C. Motor Vehicle Act*)

In other words, Justice Wilson deliberately chose to curtail the plain, broad meaning of the word "liberty." Instead of applying the test contained in section 1 of the Charter to determine when legislative violations of liberty were justified in a free and democratic society, she simply defined away a vast portion of the word "liberty." Subsequent courts have followed this example, reluctant to engage in section 1 analysis (perhaps out of fear of being accused of usurping the role of the legislature).

The current state of section 7 jurisprudence sets the bar extremely high for section 7 violations. It is exceedingly difficult to demonstrate to a court's satisfaction that section 7 has been violated. But in the rare instance that a section 7 violation is found, the courts find scant justification for it under section 1.

And as a result of this reluctance to find violations of section 7 or to rely on section 1, Canadian courts have ruled that a wide variety of activities which would certainly fall within the dictionary definition of "liberty" do not fall within the concept of "liberty" for the purposes of section 7. For instance, liberty in section 7 of the Charter "is not synonymous with unconstrained freedom" does not include "an unconstrained right to transact business whenever one wishes," according to the court in *R. v. Edwards Books and Art Ltd*. But by any standard dictionary, that is precisely what liberty does include: an absence of external restraint, and freedom of choice.

Likewise, the courts have held that section 7 liberty does not include the right to smoke marijuana for recreational purposes in the privacy of one's own home (*R. v. Malmo-Levine; R. v. Caine*), or even the right for a doctor to practice his profession (*Mussani v. College of Physicans and Surgeons of Ontario*). It would have made much more sense, and would have accorded far better with the plain use of language, for the courts to have acknowledged that the laws restraining business hours, drug use, and medical licensing were indeed restrictions on liberty but were justified under section 1 of the Charter.

By tightly circumscribing the scope of section 7, what the courts have effectively accomplished is not the trivialization of the Charter so feared by Justice Wilson in 1985, but the far worse trivialization of Canadians' liberty (*Re B.C. Motor Vehicle Act*). What, indeed, remains within section 7 liberty after the courts have finished emptying it out? Not much. By the time of the *R. v. Morgentaler* decision in 1988, liberty had been boiled down to the highly subjective catch-phrase, "decisions of fundamental personal importance."

> Thus, an aspect of the respect for human dignity on which the Charter is founded is the right to make fundamental personal decisions without interference from the state. This right is a critical component of the right to liberty. Liberty, as was noted in Singh, is a phrase capable of a broad range of meaning. In my view, this right, properly construed, grants the individual a degree of autonomy in making decisions of fundamental personal importance. (*R. v. Morgentaler*)

At times, even the Supreme Court of Canada has ignored its own cautionary stance taken in *Irwin Toy v. Quebec* and joined in reciting the "no economic liberty" mantra. The issue in *Siemens v. Manitoba* was whether the Province of Manitoba had the constitutional authority to pass legislation making municipal plebiscites on video gaming terminals legally binding. The town of Winkler had earlier held a plebiscite banning video lottery terminals (VLTs). The appellants operated a business in Winkler and challenged the legislation as an unjustified impediment to liberty. In the end, the constitutional challenge was unsuccessful because,

> … the appellants' alleged right to operate VLTs at their place of business cannot be characterized as a fundamental life choice. It is purely an economic interest. The ability to generate business revenue by one's chosen means is not a right that is protected under s. 7 of the Charter. (*Siemens v. Manitoba* at para. 46)

The *Morgentaler* decision and those that follow from it seem to indicate that the Charter protects us from violations of our liberty regarding the big, important decisions in our lives—decisions that may perhaps come along once in a lifetime—yet does not protect us from the minor, day-to-day violations of our liberty that occur routinely, over and over. This reasoning is problematic in several respects.

First, the dividing line between a "decision of fundamental importance" and one that is insignificant or trivial is highly subjective. Why does the legal permission to abort a foetus (*R. v. Morgentaler*) qualify as more important than the ability of a doctor to practice his profession (*Mussani v. College of Physicans and Surgeons of Ontario*)? There is no scale, and no units, by which such things can be measured, and it is unlikely that any two people would ever rank the vast panoply of lifetime decisions in the same order of importance.

Second, it is absurd to think that minor violations of liberty, aggregated together, do not eventually add up to a full-blown case of totalitarianism. Suppose, for instance, that the state decided to prescribe what time we must rise in the morning, what colour clothing we must wear, how often we can visit the toilet, how many hours of television we can watch, and how many times we must chew our food before we swallow. Each of these rules in itself might be described as a trivial regulation not worthy of constitutional protection. But could anyone honestly believe we would still be living in a free country? How many trivial violations of liberty can the state heap upon us before we are forced to admit that this is stifling authoritarianism and not freedom at all?

Third, it seems logically backwards to have liberal rules for decisions of fundamental importance, and restrictive rules for decisions of trivial importance. If citizens are so unintelligent or irresponsible that they cannot handle minor decisions without direction from the state, how can they ever be expected to acquire the wisdom and character to handle the big, momentous decisions that occasionally intrude into their lives?

Fourth, who are the lawgivers with the wisdom and intelligence to decide all those little matters for us, when they themselves are citizens who likewise cannot be trusted to make little decisions for themselves? How does being elected to office suddenly elevate political candidates from the status of ignoramuses who cannot be trusted to make everyday decisions about their own lives, into sage lawmakers who can make such decisions not only for themselves but for everyone in the country?

The courts in Canada have defined away a vast portion of the word "liberty" to avoid applying the test contained in section 1 of the Charter. As such, the country's governments are not called upon to defend intrusive legislation under section 1 of the Charter because the Supreme Court of Canada has decided that what are in fact infringements of liberty are not infringements of liberty for the purposes of section 7 of the Charter. If Mill is correct and "the only [liberty] which deserves the name is that of pursuing our own good, in our own way, so long as we do not attempt to deprive others of theirs, or impede their efforts to obtain it" (Mill, 1859/1974: 72), it is not hyperbole to say that our courts have eviscerated the concept of liberty.

References

Hogg, Peter (2009). *Constitutional Law of Canada*. Student Edition. Thomson Reuters Canada.

Mill, John Stuart (1859/1974). *On Liberty*. Penguin Books.

Legislation cited

B.C. Motor Vehicle Act, [1985] 2 S.C.R. 486

The Constitution Act, 1982, being Schedule B to the Canada Act 1982 (UK), 1982, c 11.

Criminal Code (Canada), [1990] 1 S.C.R. 1123.

Provincial Offences Act, RSO 1990, c P.33.

Health Protection and Promotion Act, RSO 1990, c H.7.

Milk Act, RSO 1990, c M.12.

Legal cases cited

Alberta v. Hutterian Brethren of Wilson Colony, [2009] 2 S.C.R. 567.

Blencoe v. British Columbia (Human Rights Commission), [2000] 2 SCR 307.

B. (R.) v. Children's Aid Society of Metropolitan Toronto, [1995] 1 S.C.R. 315.

Irwin Toy Ltd. v. Quebec (Attorney General), [1989] 1 S.C.R. 927.

Lavigne v. Ontario Public Service Employees Union, [1991] 2 S.C.R. 211.

Mussani v. College of Physicians and Surgeons of Ontario, 2004 CanLII 48653 (ON CA).

New Brunswick (Minister of Health and Community Services) v. G. (J.), [1999] 3 SCR 46.

R. v. Edwards Books and Art Ltd., [1986] 2 SCR 713 at para. 155.

R. v. Jones, [1986] 2 SCR 284.

R. v. Malmo-Levine; R. v. Caine, [2003] 3 S.C.R. 571.

R. v. Morgentaler, [1988] 1 S.C.R. 30.

R. v. Tener, [1985] 1 S.C.R. 533.

R. v. B.C. Motor Vehicle Act, [1986] 2 SCR 486.

Siemens v. Manitoba (Attorney General), [2003] 1 SCR 6.

CHAPTER TEN

From Fighting the Drug War to Protecting the Right to Use Drugs

Recognizing a Forgotten Liberty

Doug Bandow *

Introduction

The battle to control the definition of freedom has long permeated philosophical discourse and political campaigns. Common are arguments over negative and positive liberty, as well as discussions of liberty versus license. Should individuals be "free" to do wrong and should a community be "free" to act collectively? The definition of freedom can determine the policy outcome.

---

*   Doug Bandow is a Senior Fellow at the Cato Institute. Previously he was the Bastiat Scholar at the Competitive Enterprise Institute, the Cobden Fellow at the Institute for Policy Innovation, and a Visiting Fellow at the Heritage Foundation. He also served as a Special Assistant to President Ronald Reagan. He is a weekly columnist for *Forbes online* and contributes regularly to the *Huffington Post, National Interest online, American Spectator online*, and other online publications. Previously a columnist for *antiwar.com*, a nationally syndicated columnist with Copley News Service, and editor of the monthly political magazine *Inquiry*, he has been widely published in such periodicals as *Time, Newsweek, Fortune, Harper's, National Interest, Christianity Today, National Review, New Republic*, and *American Conservative*, as well as leading newspapers including the *New York Times, Wall Street Journal*, and *Washington Post*.

    Bandow has written and edited several books, including *Foreign Follies: America's New Global Empire* (Xulon Press), *The Korean Conundrum: America's Troubled Relations with North and South Korea* (Palgrave/Macmillan; co-author), *Perpetuating Poverty: The World Bank, the IMF, and the Developing World* (Cato; co-editor), *The Politics of Envy: Statism as Theology* (Transaction), *The Politics of Plunder: Misgovernment in Washington* (Transaction), and *Beyond Good Intentions: A Biblical View of Politics* (Crossway).

    He has appeared on numerous television and radio programs. Bandow received his B.S. in Economics from Florida State University in 1976 and his J.D. from Stanford University in 1979. He is a member of the California and D.C. Bars.

So it is with drug use. Drugs are merely one kind of product which people ingest, and there are many different drugs with many different effects.[1] Indeed, the word "drugs" is routinely used in three ways: 1) substances having a notable physical or mental effect, ranging from caffeine to cocaine; 2) substances having ill effects which are banned, such as cocaine; and 3) substances officially sanctioned for use in medical treatment, such as penicillin. Today there are three different drug markets involving legal, prescription, and illegal products (Szasz, 1992: 18).

The presumption of this paper is that individual liberty is the paramount political value. There is more to life than the freedom to act without political constraint, but that liberty underlies the rest of human action, including the pursuit of the transcendent. Steven Wisotsky, a law professor at Nova Southeastern in Florida, argued that "the fundamental moral premise of our political, economic, and legal systems" is "that the individual is competent to order his life to vote, to manage his own affairs and be responsible for whatever results he produces in life" (1986: 201).

Some argue that the majority of people are not capable of self-governance, that only a minority of people make rational decisions (see, e.g., Bakalar and Grinspoon, 1984: 28). This argument proves too much, however, for why should such people be allowed to choose political leaders and why should officials so chosen be allowed to make decisions for others? One might not trust the decisions made by individuals with dubious reasoning ability, but one should not casually assume that collectives including the same people would make better decisions.

Of course, there always will be some legal limits on human conduct. After all, laws against murder, theft, and fraud impair "freedom" in one sense, yet are required to protect liberty, properly understood. Nevertheless, human beings, as the basic moral agents in any society, should be generally free to act so long as they accept the consequences of their actions.

One of the freedoms that should be treated as a legal right is drug use. Making this argument is not to encourage drug use. Rather, it is to hold that government may not properly criminalize drug use. The basic moral case was famously articulated by John Stuart Mill (Bakalar and Grinspoon, 1984: 1).[2] Adults are entitled to ingest substances even if a majority views that decision as foolish.

Drug use can have negative social consequences, but that does not set it apart from other products and activities. After all, most any human action—smoking cigarettes, driving cars, climbing mountains—may

---

1 For a discussion of the definition of "drugs," see Husak, 2002: 27-43; and Husak, 1992: 20-37.

2 Mill's arguments and qualifications have attracted the attention of other participants in this intellectual battle. See, e.g., Zimring and Hawkins, 1991: 3-13.

have some negative impact on someone. To justify government regulation, harms must be serious and direct. Moreover, any restrictions must be crafted to minimize the violation of liberty. In criminalizing substance use, wrote dissident psychiatrist Thomas Szasz, then "Like medieval searchers for the Holy Grail, these modern seekers look for the correct answer to an absurd question, namely: How can we reduce or eliminate the risks and undesirable consequences of liberty, while retaining its rewards and benefits?" (Szasz, 1992: 12).

A right to ingest?

The use of drugs should be seen as a freedom, just like most human actions. Choosing to go hang-gliding is a freedom (of recreation). Choosing to have surgery is a freedom (of medical treatment). Choosing to use drugs is a freedom, usually of recreation or medical treatment, depending on the substance and intention.

To label an action a freedom does not automatically determine its appropriate legal status. While autonomous individuals are presumed to be best judges of their own behavior, actions that cause harm are judged differently. Some are banned; others are restricted; many are left unconstrained.

Few personal acts more closely implicate the life and dignity of the human person than deciding what to put into one's own body. Choices of food and medicine are largely left to individuals, not government. Similarly, most decisions to alter one's mental and physical states are vested in individuals, not politicians, hence the almost universal use of caffeine and alcohol. Despite laws imposing some limits on the use of these substances, as well as tobacco, people still are widely believed to possess a basic moral right to consume what they want.

Illicit drugs are seen differently—today. Recreational drug use once was accepted, just as recreational alcohol use remains not just common, but pervasive. Now the same substances are treated as unusually dangerous, irresistibly addictive, and inevitably harmful. The criminal justice system even treats drug use as a disease, thereby obscuring "the morality of choice" (Wisotsky, 1986: 200). Perceptions dominate policy. Argued Richard E. Vatz of Towson University and Lee S. Weinberg of the University of Pittsburgh, "the dominance of scenic rhetoric, combined with a set of public fantasies and perceptions that fail to differentiate the impact of drugs from the impact of their illegality, makes it unlikely that the policy of prohibiting drug use will change in the near future" (1998: 69-70).

Unsurprisingly, the reality differs substantially from the rhetoric. As Douglas Husak of Rutgers wrote: "too much of our policy about illegal drug use is based on generalizations from worst-case scenarios that do not conform to the reality of typical drug use" (1992: 51).

What about addiction?

One reason drugs are treated differently is because they are considered to be "addictive." Some critics contend the entire concept is artificial, though common experience suggests that there is a physical and psychological dimension that makes some decisions seem less voluntary. Nevertheless, even intense physical and psychological attraction does not eliminate the ability to choose.[3]

Moreover, different people appear to be more or less susceptible to the attraction of variously destructive behaviors, such as alcohol and tobacco use, as well as gambling and sex. That some people abuse instead of just use is a dubious justification for a universal government ban.

Indeed, despite the fearsome reputations acquired by some illicit drugs, the addiction rate of different substances appears to be relatively constant, between 10 and 15 percent (Sweet and Harris, 1998: 448). The US government's own data indicate that the vast majority of drug users consume intermittently, even rarely (see, e.g., Eldredge, 1998: 3).

Patricia Erickson of the Addiction Research Foundation and Bruce Anderson of Simon Fraser University concluded in one assessment of the literature regarding cocaine use: "the evidence reviewed here indicates that the likelihood that cocaine users will become addicted has been greatly overstated." In fact, "most human cocaine users never use it immoderately" (Erickson and Alexander, 1998: 283; see also Erickson and Weber, 1998: 291-305). A study of cocaine users found that most consumed only "infrequently" (Erickson and Weber, 1998: 291; see also Mugford, 1991: 41). A survey of US soldiers who used heroin in Vietnam found that later they were no more likely than other soldiers to be heroin addicts (Winick, 1993: 151; Zinberg, 1987: 264-67). American society would not be economically productive if the tens of millions of people who have used drugs all were "addicted."

Harm to others

The classic justification for regulating individual behavior is that it violates the freedoms and especially the legal rights of others. (If an action is not legally protected, interference with that action is less likely to be penalized by government.) Prohibitionists routinely tie drugs to crime. However, no drug appears to be strongly crimogenic, that is, a trigger for criminal behavior, and especially violent criminal behavior, against others.

Drug use may impair judgment and reduce inhibition, making some people more likely to commit crimes. That certainly is the case with

---

3 For detailed discussions of this issue, see Husak, 1992: 100-30; Bakalar and Grinspoon, 1984: 35-67.

alcohol. But since drugs vary greatly in their effects, at most this would justify selective prohibition, and no substance appears to generate crime in a high number of its users. In fact, the drug laws do far more than drugs to create crime, creating victims far and wide (see, e.g., Ostrowski, 1991: 304-05, 314-15).

Of course, drugs have other impacts on other people (see, e.g., Moore, 1993: 232-33; Taubman, 1991: 97-107; Hay, 1991: 200-25; Kleiman, 1992: 46-64). However, the criminal law normally applies to direct rather than indirect harm, that is, when individual rights (to be secure in one's person or property, for instance) are violated. The criminal must *cause* the harm to others, rather than engage in otherwise legal conduct which causes incidental loss.[4] Moreover, only some drug use some of the time hurts others. Observed Robert J. MacCoun of the University of California (Berkeley) and Peter Reuter of the University of Maryland, "it is likely that many if not most drug users never do wrongful harm to others as a result of their using careers" (2001: 61).

In any case, this argument for prohibition proves far too much. Most human activities create "externalities," that is, impose costs on others. The same surely can be said of alcohol abuse, heavy tobacco use, excessive gambling, extreme consumerism, and short-sighted careerism. In fact, there is little conduct that does not affect others. Ironically, since drugs act as imperfect substitutes for one another, drug prohibition may increase alcohol use, doing more to transform harm than to eliminate harm.

Despite reliance on this argument, the increasingly violent Drug War never has been driven by social problems.[5] Noted sociologist Jerry Mandel, "the war on drugs preceded any drug use problem except alcohol" (1998: 212). Indeed, the problems of opium and marijuana use at the time they were banned were far less serious than today.

It seems particularly odd to leave alcohol use legal if "social costs" is the chief criterion for a government ban. The failure to reinstitute Prohibition demonstrates that even those inclined towards prohibition believe the mere existence of social problems does not warrant a government ban. That famous enforcement effort failed to eliminate the problems from use while adding the problems created by turning drinking into a crime (see, e.g., Levine and Reinarman, 1998a: 264-70). In fact, noted Harry Levine of Queens College (City University of New York) and Craig Reinarman of the University of California (Santa Cruz), "prohibitionists were utopian moralists; they believed that eliminating the

---

4   For a discussion of this issue, see Husak, 1992: 164-68.

5   Restrictions on drug use began more than a century ago, and advanced intermittently in succeeding years, though the greatest leap in intensity of enforcement dates to the Nixon administration. For the early years, see, e.g., Szasz, 1992: 37-57.

legal manufacture and sale of alcoholic drink would solve the major social and economic problems of American society" (1998a: 261). Alas, the utopians were sadly disappointed.

On almost any social measure, today's ban on drug consumption appears to increase net adverse social impacts. Modern prohibition is particularly problematic if the objective is to maintain a society that can accurately be called free. As noted later in this paper, the more brutal the tactics in the War on Drugs, the more the government undermines the essentials of a free society.[6]

Response to externalities

Although externalities—the various impacts (which in theory could be positive as well as negative) on others—do not justifying banning drugs, users should be held accountable for the direct consequences of their actions. Even Thomas Szasz pointed to areas where government restrictions, such as driving while intoxicated, are entirely appropriate. So are employer restrictions on drug use which impair job performance (Szasz, 1992: 161-62). Moreover, people should be liable when they hurt others or fail to live up to their legal obligations, whatever the cause.

In contrast, individuals should not be punished for simply taking substances which might make some of them more likely to hurt others or fail to live up to their legal obligations. And some harms are too idiosyncratic or diffuse—such as emotional distress to family and friends of drug abusers, lost productivity of drug users—to warrant government regulation.

Harm to users

Advocates of criminal enforcement also resort to paternalism, claiming that prohibition is necessary to protect users. Drug use obviously can be harmful, though advocates of government control, including public officials attempting to justify their activities and budgets, often have exaggerated the risks of illicit drugs, especially compared to the problems created by legal drugs (Husak, 2002: 93-108; Miller, 1991: 1-23).

In any case, government should not attempt to protect people from themselves. Drug users generally are aware of the real (as opposed to imagined) dangers (Bakalar and Grinspoon, 1984: 170). In this way, drug use reflects an informed choice—at least as informed as most choices made by most people.

The government should not override these decisions simply because it (or a popular voting majority) employs a different calculus of costs and benefits (see the discussion at Husak, 1992: 88-89). A free society allows people to make what most people believe to be mistakes. If nothing else,

---

6 One brief but sobering survey is available in Sweet and Harris, 1998: 448-49.

jailing the alleged victims is a particularly odd way to "protect" people from themselves (see, e.g., Husak and Marneffe, 2005: 41-53).

Moreover, most users are not abusers. Contrary to popular assumptions, the vast majority of drug users enjoy productive, balanced lives. Noted Charles Winick of the City University of New York, "the conventional picture of uniformly negative consequences of regular drug use is not supported by the data" (1993: 136). The United Nations estimates that there are 250 million drug users worldwide, less than 10 percent of whom are considered to be "problem drug users" (Global Commission on Drug Policy, 2011: 13).

Rejecting paternalism requires erasing the line between medical and recreational drug use (see, e.g., Husak and de Marneffe, 2005: 17-24). Controversial though this might seem, recreation normally is seen as a positive good. People rarely make a pretense of using alcohol or tobacco for medical or other "serious" purposes. The difference between using Viagra to treat erectile "dysfunction" and to enhance an otherwise normal sexual experience is small.

Moreover, when it comes to non-drug forms of recreation, even potentially dangerous activities that participants sometimes describe as "addictive," the government leaves people alone. Explained Steven Wisotsky, "Society simply defers to the freedom of the individual. It takes individual rights seriously insofar as it is willing to accept a high risk of injury or death as the natural or inevitable price of such freedom" (1986: 208-09).

Yet, observed Douglas Husak, "For reasons that are deep and mysterious, many persons become apologetic and defensive about arguing in favor of a right to engage in an activity simply because it is pleasurable. Apparently the pursuit of fun is perceived to be so shallow and trivial that many persons feel obliged to find some other basis to defend their choice" (1992: 46).

Of course, special measures are warranted to protect children. However, this does not justify treating the entire population like children. Moreover, prohibition for all makes it harder to concentrate enforcement on kids. "Leakage" to children also is more dangerous from an illegal black market than from a legal adult market.

Does morality trump liberty?

Proponents of jailing drug users and sellers deploy morality as their trump card. Never mind the costs of prohibition—drug use is wrong, and, *ipso facto*, should be prohibited (see Husak and de Marneffe, 2005: 71).

Even granting that for some people to use some drugs for some purposes might be immoral, in a liberal society they should remain free to act, that is, they should have a legal right to engage in an immoral act where the immorality is directed at themselves, not others. In essence, "the *right* of the individual to do as he pleases takes precedence over the *good* of the individual, where 'good' is measured by some standard external to the agent's own wishes" (Hill, 1992: 104). Most people at one time or another have grave doubts about the behavior of family and friends. Nevertheless, rarely does anyone call forth the power of the state to limit the other person's choices.

Peter de Marneffe of Arizona State University curiously denied "that someone's moral rights are violated whenever the government burdens the many for the benefit of the few" (Husak and de Marneffe, 2005: 163). However, government cannot rightly sacrifice basic liberties just to advantage some people. If it is moral for individuals to seek pleasure through drug use, then prohibition violates their freedom without due cause. Their moral right should be treated as a legal right as well. One might argue that the violation nevertheless is justified to promote a larger good. But responsible individuals are being prevented from engaging in non-coercive activities which harm no one else—and in most cases not even themselves. A utilitarian justification for prohibition should not supersede the moral calculus. An individual freedom is still being circumscribed. Given the importance of protecting individual liberties, those freedoms should not be abrogated except for a very significant benefit.

The assertion that use of all drugs by everyone in every circumstance is immoral is rarely supported by argument (Husak, 1992: 65-68). Advocates of criminalization prefer to assume rather than demonstrate the moral case for their policy (see, e.g., Husak,1992: 61-63). Douglas Husak contended: "I am not insisting that no good reason *can* be given for concluding that the recreational use of illicit drugs is immoral. Again, a negative is notoriously hard to prove. I am only saying that no good reason *has* been given in support of this moral conclusion" (2002: 117).

The problem is not that government cannot legislate morality. Most laws, at least most criminal laws, do so. The critical question is: what kind of morality? Inter-personal morality, that is, the conduct toward others, offers a clear basis for legislation. Murder, theft, assault, rape, and fraud are all prohibited because they violate the freedoms as well as legal rights of others—the impact on others *is what makes them wrong*. Prohibiting such conduct is the very purpose of government.

As noted earlier, use of drugs does not fall into this category. If morality is involved, it is of a different kind: intra-personal morality, or soul-molding. To the extent that harm occurs, the criminal and victim are one.

By this standard, is drug use immoral? There is nothing inherent to the act of using drugs that is wrong.[7] Even the Bible, the fount of morality in the Western world, treats alcohol use as normal and inveighed only against intoxication. There is no criticism of the simple desire to gain pleasure.

---

7   For one argument on this issue, see Husak and de Marneffe, 2005: 73-82.

Sociologist James Q. Wilson declared: "drug use is wrong because it is immoral and it is immoral because it enslaves the mind and destroys the soul" (quoted in Husak and de Marneffe, 2005: 71).[8] A behavior that "enslaves the mind and destroys the soul" would seem to be wrong, an affront to the value and dignity of the human person. But even if so, such behavior is not the proper province of government and especially the criminal law.

Criminalizing violations of inner morality would invite government regulation of most aspects of human life. After all, Christian theology indicates that sin grieves God, damages the soul, and risks damnation. And there is much sin in the world. Yet Peter de Marneffe would go even further, worrying about "the risk to some individuals of losing important opportunities, the loss of which would significantly dim their life prospects" (Husak and de Marneffe, 2005: 133). Government is not well-equipped to judge sin, assessing which behaviors are most likely to enslave the mind and destroy the soul, let alone decide on economic potential.

Moreover, does drug use enslave the mind and destroy the soul? Maybe it does for a few people. Some drug abusers—like alcoholics and gamblers—lose themselves to the perceived pleasures of their activities. But for most people, like most alcohol users and gamblers, the answer obviously is no.[9]

Researchers have hunted in vain for evidence that moderate drug use causes individual or social ills. Most drug users appear to suffer little if any serious harm. Indeed, despite claims of debased and destroyed lives, studies have found little damage from moderate drug use (Husak, 1992: 97). The findings of one study of cocaine use called "into question many of the prevailing assumptions about cocaine's inevitably destructive power over lives, careers, and health, and provide empirical evidence about a different reality" (Erickson and Weber, 1998: 291).

Still, undoubtedly there are drug users who harm themselves. They have wasted their money and risked their health. They have not fulfilled their life's potential. They may ultimately look back on their drug use with regret. But they still did not enslave their minds and destroy their souls, or done anything else to warrant the attentions of the criminal law.

And why would the consequences Wilson fears be worse than the ill consequences of other activities? He considered cocaine to be worse than nicotine because the former "debases" life while the latter merely

---

8 Former "drug czar" William Bennett has made similarly extravagant yet unsupported claims. See, e.g., Husak, *Drugs and Rights*, p. 71.

9 Even Peter de Marneffe, who advocates heroin prohibition, acknowledges that "it is arguable that a majority of heroin users now use heroin responsibly as a way to relax and enjoy, even though its use is illegal" (Husak and de Marneffe, 2005: 156).

"shortens" it (quoted in Husak and de Marneffe, 2005: 80). Yet is the occasional cocaine sniffer really more debased than the chain smoker dying from lung cancer?

What of "abusers," those who "get into patterns of heavy chronic use, which they did not anticipate and would prefer not to continue" (Kleiman, 1992: 28)? UCLA Professor Mark Kleiman argued that "all of the widely used drugs—including heroin and cocaine, even smoked cocaine—can be used safely if they are used in small and infrequent doses and at times and places where an intoxicated person is unlikely to do or suffer injury" (1992: 27-28). However, too often, in his view, this is not the case (causing "failures of self-command") (Kleiman, 1992: 30-41).

Even for drug users with severe problems, substance abuse may be more a consequence than a cause. Wrote James Bakalar and Lester Grinspooon: "Most differences between drug users and nonusers apparently precede the drug use" (1984: 132). Researchers studying heroin addiction have observed: "People who use heroin are highly disposed to having serious social problems even before they touch heroin" (Robins, 1988: 264).

Unfortunately, people are capable of damaging their lives without drugs. Indeed, individuals have found an infinite number of methods of harming themselves, sometimes irrevocably. The Global Commission on Drug Policy stated: "The factors that influence an individual's decision to start using drugs have more to do with fashion, peer influence, and social and economic context, than with the drug's legal status, risk of detection, or government prevention messages" (2011: 13). Indeed, if the government only reduces the availability of drugs, alcohol will remain available as a potentially destructive alternative.

Attempting to nevertheless aid the immoral few still would not justify a "war" on drug use by all. Improving opportunities for and decision-making by a small minority would make far more sense than threatening to imprison a much larger number of people (and a majority of drug users). Even those who worry about drugs recognize the difference. Kleiman, for one, wrote of being "somewhat more paternalistic when it comes to choices about drug use" (1992: 45). That is a long way from militarized criminal law enforcement in what purports to be a free society.

Respecting a moral right to use drugs

Individuals should have a legal as well as moral "right," grounded in their status as free, consenting adults, to use drugs recreationally. Treating drug use as a morally legitimate freedom, or a moral right, is more than an abstract philosophical exercise. Attorney John Lawrence Hill argued simply: "If the state may not rightfully use the coercive sanction of the criminal law to prohibit the ingestion of any of a variety of psychoactive substances, then these other [practical] considerations are rendered moot" (1992: 102).

This means that people have a moral right vis-à-vis the government to use drugs, even if their particular decision to use drugs is immoral in terms of their lives. Treating drug use as a morally legitimate freedom is important because doing so would shift the burden of proof in the legal debate.[10] If it is moral for individuals to use substances recreationally, then the state must deploy a compelling justification to regulate their behavior. In short, "the best reason to *de*criminalize drug use is that the reasons to *criminalize* drug use are not good enough" (Husak and de Marneffe, 2005: 38).

Normally people are viewed as the best judges of their own circumstances and interests. In any particular case, people may make a mistake, but that is not inherent to drugs. Noted Bakalar and Grinspoon: "The 'force' of the argument against state interference with sexual acts between consenting adults is said to be enormously powerful because sex comes within the proper 'range' of the principle; but outside that range, in the territory of drug use or consumer protection, the principle may have no force at all. This is a statement of preference, not an argument" (1984: 14).

There is no reason to treat drugs as different from most everything else. One can speak of "the value of drug use" even if most people do not believe that the benefits justify the costs (Husak and de Marneffe, 2005: 84-91). Individuals best assess costs and benefits for themselves, while collective decisions inevitably disregard unique personal characteristics and emphasize majority prejudices.

Argued Thomas Szasz: "Why do we want drugs? Basically, for the same reasons we want other goods. We want drugs to relieve our pains, cure our diseases, enhance our endurance, change our moods, put us to sleep, or simply make us feel better—just as we want bicycles and cars, trucks and tractors, ladders and chainsaws, skis and hang gliders, to make our lives more productive and more pleasant" (1992: xv).

Some drug users cite relaxation and alertness as reasons for moderate drug use (Miller, 1991: 152-54). Moreover, the desire to alter mental and physical states is ancient and has existed in every culture. Wrote James Bakalar and Lester Grinspoon: "altering consciousness does not have to be conceived as something abrupt, unusual, and mysterious" (1984: 145). Even many avid drug prohibitionists cheerfully drink alcohol, smoke tobacco, and seek adrenalin highs through sports or gambling. Far from being uncontrolled, drug users usually appear to choose their drugs with care, seeking to achieve a certain kind of physical or mental change (Husak and de Marneffe, 2005: 91). The majority of people may view engaging in these activities to be foolish, even reckless, but that alone is irrelevant.

---

10 Today advocates of criminalization embrace the status quo, pushing advocates of reform to bear the burden of proof. See, e.g., Husak and de Marneffe, 2005: 25-40.

Anyway, changing one's physical and mental state is among the most personal of decisions. Some legal analysts contend that drug use should be viewed as part of the "zone of privacy" or "personal autonomy" that most Americans have come to expect (Hill, 1992: 103-05). Four years ago the Argentine supreme court ruled unconstitutional the prosecution of people for possessing drugs for personal use. Explained the judges: "adults should be free to make lifestyle decisions without the intervention of the state" (quoted in Jenkins, September 3, 2009). Szasz put it another way: "How can a person lose the right to his body? By being deprived of the freedom to care for it and to control it as he sees fit" (Szasz, 1992: 6).[11]

The same argument applies to the use of substances which are provisionally legal, that is, legal with a prescription. The issues often are related: prohibition sometimes influences prescription access, such as to pain medication, and interferes with use of marijuana for medical purposes. But more broadly, people should have the same legal right to use drugs for self-medication as for recreation (see, e.g., Szasz, 1992: 125-43). The limited prohibition for medicine has had its own perverse and counterproductive consequences, including limiting access to life-saving products and slowing the spread of needed medications to market (see, e.g., Trebach and Zeese, 1992: 25-33; Howley, 2005). (Of course, there may be an argument for some limited controls, such as over the distribution of antibiotics to reduce the rise of drug-resistant strains of bacteria.[12])

Legalization versus decriminalization

Just as people have a moral right to make other lifestyle choices, despite the potential negative impacts, they have a moral right to consume drugs, despite potentially harmful effects.[13] For this reason, drugs should be legalized, not just decriminalized.[14] Even some advocates of prohibition prefer to direct criminal penalties at producers and sellers rather than users (see,

---

11 Szasz grounds the right to use drugs in property rights (Szasz, 1992: 13-14). However, the right to own property is merely one of many specific rights that any free individual possesses.

12 Moreover, Douglas Husak of Rutgers argues that there may be a greater argument for government paternalism in the latter because the likelihood of mistake, as in misjudging the efficacy of treatment, may be higher. That is, most illicit drug users know such substances can cause harm (Husak, 1992: 137).

13 Positing a moral right does not necessarily yield a constitutional right, as some contend. See, e.g., Sweet and Harris, 1998: 451-60.

14 These terms sometimes are confused. Decriminalization, as implemented by a dozen American states, is a vast improvement over prohibition. See, e.g., Husak and de Marneffe, 2005: 3-14. Nevertheless, decriminalization presumes some *government-imposed* legal and economic sanction on use per se, in contrast to even the most restrictive state regimes governing alcohol use, which merely restrict access to alcohol in time and form. Legalization would not, however, prevent legal punishment of drug use with direct consequences on

e.g., Husak and de Marneffe, 2005: 129). However, if consumption does not warrant jail, why should those who make it possible for people to consume face jail? And the standards for imposing criminal penalties always should be high, much higher than for imposing civil penalties.[15]

Legalization would not mean viewing drug use as a positive good. Rather, seeking pleasure through drug use should be treated as a legitimate activity, one involving the often complex trade-offs evident with other aspects of human life.

Still, legal drug use would have both bad and good consequences, just like other activities. To view drug use as a moral right does not mean there would be no proper collective response, irrespective of circumstances.[16] To the contrary, most societies have adapted to drug use by creating social controls, whatever the substance or product.

Consider alcohol. Argue James B. Bakalar and Lester Grinspoon of the Harvard Medical School: "We all know that alcohol abuse produces disease, accidents, crime, family conflict, and social chaos" (1984: 79). Yet countries such as Great Britain tamed what once was a great social scourge. Alcohol abuse has waxed and waned in the US. Ironically, Prohibition created a more relaxed, less controlled atmosphere for alcohol consumption. Argued psychiatrist Norman Zinberg: "Although repeal provided relief from excessive and unpopular legal control, the society was left floundering without an inherited set of social sanctions and rituals to control use" (1987: 250).

Modern prohibition is one reason the US today lacks adequate social controls over drug use. Socialization is a complex process involving family, peers, culture, and more (Zinberg, 1987: 260-61). It is less likely to occur, and occur effectively, if the activity is underground: "The furtiveness, the suspicion, the fears of legal reprisal, as well as the myths and misconceptions that surround illicit drug use, all make the exchange of information that leads to the development of constraining social sanctions and rituals more difficult" (Zinberg, 1987: 266; see also Wisotsky, 1986: 213). Noted Szasz, "after generations of living under medical tutelage that provides us with protection (albeit illusory) against dangerous drugs, we have failed to cultivate the self-reliance and self-discipline we must possess as competent adults surrounded by the fruits of our pharmacological-technological age" (1992: xvi).

---

others (e.g., driving while under the influence) as well as private restrictions on drug use (e.g., airlines banning use by pilots).

15 For a detailed discussion of this issue, see Husak, 1992: 170-95.

16 Douglas Husak criticizes libertarians who believe that "the best moral and political theory disables the state from coping with social problems that are truly horrendous" (Husak, 1992: 87).

Nevertheless, the problems likely to result from legal drug use appear manageable. Wrote Bakalar and Grinspoon: "In the United States today, despite easy availability of cheap alcohol, a third of the adult population does not drink at all, and another third drinks three times a week or less. Most people do not find it hard to exercise self-restraint in using drugs. Attitudes towards tranquilizers, for example, are very conservative in all racial, social, and economic groups, but are especially among the poorest and least educated… Most people disapprove of using drugs to enhance normal functioning; by association, they tend to be suspicious of antidepressants and drugs for energy or alertness [source omitted]. Volunteers allowed to regulate their own intake of amphetamines for weight loss used less than the amounts usually prescribed. The picture of drug abuse as a potentially uncontrollable epidemic is vastly overdrawn" (Bakalar and Grinspoon, 1984: 144).

Utilitarian arguments

The issue of illicit drug use most often is fought on utilitarian, consequentialist grounds. Are the benefits of prohibition worth the cost? The issue is important, and would be decisive if the issue of drug use was one of moral indifference.

Assume that drug prohibition could be justified morally. Even so, it still must pass the test of practicality. Nobel Laureate Milton Friedman criticized the moral basis of the War on Drugs, but went on to argue: "I readily grant that the ethical issue is difficult and that men of good will may well disagree. Fortunately, we need not resolve the ethical issue to agree on policy. Prohibition is an attempted cure that makes matters worse for both the addict and the rest of us. Hence, even if you regard present policy toward drugs as ethically justified, considerations of expediency make that policy most unwise" (May 1, 1972).

War on Americans

As Prof. Douglas Husak of Rutgers has pointed out: "The war, after all, cannot really be a war on drugs, since drugs cannot be arrested, prosecuted, or punished. The war is against persons who use drugs. As such, the war is a civil war, fought against the 28 million Americans who use illegal drugs annually. And unlike previous battles in this apparently endless war, current campaigns target casual users as well as drug abusers" (1992: 2).

Robert J. MacCoun and Peter Reuter suggested that one can imagine prohibition differently implemented that would cause less damage. However, with today's American model "it is reasonable to conclude that tough enforcement is responsible for much of the observed damage. The extraordinary prices of cocaine and heroin, the massive involvement of young minority males in center cities, foreign corruption, and the violence of the drug trades are all plausibly much increased by the nation's decision to be highly punitive toward these drugs" (MacCoun and Reuter, 2001: 127).

The costs of drug prohibition

Banning drugs raises their price, creates enormous profits for criminal entrepreneurs, thrusts users into an illegal marketplace, encourages users to commit property crimes to acquire higher-priced drugs, leaves violence the only means to settle disputes within the drug trade, forces government to spend lavishly to curtail drug sales and use, and results in widespread corruption of public officials and institutions. All of these effects are evident today in the US, with its huge appetite for illicit substances and a harsh enforcement regime. Today's experience is reminiscent of Prohibition (of alcohol) in the early 20th century (Thornton, 1991; Levine and Reinarman, 1998b: 43-61).

Perhaps the most obvious cost of enforcing the drug laws is financial. Government must hire police, court, and prison personnel; prosecute and jail millions of drug offenders; and underwrite a variety of other anti-drug efforts, including foreign aid to foreign governments and military action abroad. At the same time, government must forgo any tax revenue from a licit drug market.

According to Harvard lecturer Jeffrey A. Miron and New York University doctoral candidate Katherine Waldock, in the US alone "legalizing drugs would save roughly $41.3 billion per year in government expenditure on enforcement of prohibition" and "drug legalization would yield tax revenue of $46.7 billion annually" (2010: i). Although an extra $90 billion a year wouldn't end America's financial crisis, it is foolish for Washington to toss away so much money.

The drug war also has corrupted private and public institutions wherever it has reached. Pay-offs commonly go to employees in private companies able to help transport drugs, such as the airlines. Worse are bribes to police, border control officials, Drug Enforcement Agency agents, and even military personnel when involved in interdiction efforts. The taint also reaches prosecutors, judges, and politicians.

The problem is serious enough in the US, where it began decades ago during the early years of the War on Drugs (see, e.g., Wisotsky, 1986: 141-50; Eldredge, 1998: 53-59). The issue is a crisis overseas, where militarized enforcement, relentlessly pushed by Washington, has helped corrupt entire nations, such as Colombia, Afghanistan, and Mexico. Indeed, drug production has become a tool of Communist guerrillas in Peru and Columbia, left-wing governments in Venezuela and North Korea, and both insurgents and government in Afghanistan (see, e.g., Naim, 2011).

Prohibition is advanced as a means to protect users from themselves. And there are excellent reasons for people, especially adolescents who are still developing physically and mentally, to eschew consumption of most drugs, including some which are legal today.[17] (Indeed, risk assessments have held alcohol and tobacco to be more dangerous than many prohibited substances, such as cannabis (Global Commission on Drug Policy, 2011: 12).)

However, the illegal marketplace makes drug use more dangerous. Noted economists Daniel K. Benjamin and Roger Leroy Miller, "Many of the most visible adverse effects attributed to drug use… are due not to drug use per se, but to our current public policy toward drugs" (1991: 131). Products are adulterated; users have no means of guaranteeing quality. Given the threat of discovery, dealers prefer to transport and market more potent (and thus both more concealable and valuable) drugs (Cussen and Block, 2005: 103-104; Benjamin and Miller, 1991: 113-31; Morgan, 1991: 405-23). As a result, the vast majority of "drug-related" deaths are "drug law-related" deaths (Husak, 2002: 137; Glasser, 1991: 271-74).

Moreover, AIDS is spread through the sharing of needles by intravenous drug users, who are more likely to engage in the dangerous practice in an underground world created by prohibition (Eldredge, 1998: 126-36; Glasser, 1991: 276; Global Commission on Drug Policy, 2011: 6). John Morgan of the City University of New York Medical School said simply that the increasing incidence of AIDS and HIV "is a direct result of prohibition" (1991: 409). In the same way, the War on Drugs has helped spread hepatitis and other blood-borne diseases (Miron, March 24, 2009).

Not only does the War on Drugs make people sick, it interferes with the treatment of the sick and dying. A number of people suffering from a variety of maladies believe that cannabis and other drugs offer helpful treatments. There is substantial disagreement among medical researchers and professionals, but additional research would help determine if and how marijuana use might have value (Grinspoon, 1991: 379-89; Grinspoon and Bakalar, 1987: 183-219). However, America's national government remains steadfastly opposed to providing a compassionate option for anyone (see, e.g., Annas, 1988: 120-29). The result may be to leave vulnerable people in great pain, even agony.

The drug laws also threaten the basic liberties of all Americans, whether or not they use drugs. The erosion of basic constitutional liberties in America is years, even decades, in the making (Benjamin and Miller, 1991: 122-49). As a classic "self-victim" crime, drug prohibition requires draconian enforcement techniques: informants, surveillance,

---

17 For one discussion of the dangers of different substances, see Goldstein and Kalant, 1993: 78-86.

wiretaps, and raids. Television commentator John Stossel noted that the drug war is being used to "justify the militarization of the police, the violent disregard for our civil liberties, and the overpopulation of our prisons" (Stossel, June 17, 2010).

In the United States, police work has taken on military attributes, with 100-plus SWAT raids every day. Those guilty of even minor, nonviolent offences have suffered disproportionately, while innocent people routinely have been harmed or killed in misdirected drug arrests and raids (Husak, 2002: 4-5; Balko, March 23, 2010; Balko, April 6, 2006).

Lawyers openly speak of the "drug exception" to the Fourth Amendment, which is supposed to limit government searches. Jack Cole, a former New Jersey policeman who co-founded Law Enforcement Against Prohibition (LEAP), talked of "a war on constitutional rights." He explained: "We would illegally search people all the time, because we felt like 'we're fighting a war, we're the good guys, and no matter how we get these guys, it's worthwhile because we're taking them off the streets and that's our job.' So that's why so many get involved in not telling the truth on the stand when they're testifying about drug cases. And you almost never find that in other cases. All these violations come from drug cases" (Cole, 2006: 45).

Drug prohibition also skews law enforcement priorities. Property forfeitures have turned into big business. Police departments routinely seize property without criminal convictions (Eldredge, 1998: 77-82; Fraser, July 4, 2010). Indeed, in many cases the government doesn't bother to file criminal charges. The lure of "free" cash has distorted police decisions. Noted an *amicus* brief filed in one Supreme Court case by the Cato Institute, Goldwater Institute, and Reason Foundation: forfeiture "provides powerful, dangerous, and unconstitutional financial incentives for law enforcement agencies and prosecutors' offices to overreach."[18] In effect, there is a direct financial benefit for the government to violate people's liberties.

Even more extreme authoritarian practices, including executions and maimings, used abroad have been endorsed by some US officials (Husak, 1992: 13). Moreover, the so-called Rockefeller drug laws in New York State (implemented by an alleged liberal) as well as federal mandatory minimum sentences have imposed draconian penalties on even low level drug operatives.

---

18 Brief for the Cato Institute, Goldwater Institute Scharf-Norton Center for Constitutional Litigation, and Reason Foundation as Amici Curiae Supporting Respondents, in the Supreme Court of the United States, *Anita Alvarez, Cook County State's Attorney v. Chermane Smith*, et al., No. 08-351, August 2009, p. 6. <http://www.cato.org/pubs/legal-briefs/alvarez-v-smith.pdf>, as of May 3, 2012.

The explosion of the drug trade, combined with promiscuous jail time, has increasingly turned America into a prison state. There were 13.7 million arrests in 2009, more than 10 percent of which (1.7 million), were for drug offenses. Nearly half of the latter for were marijuana. In comparison, just 590,000 people were arrested for violent crimes. Overall, 80 percent of the drug arrests are for possession. More than half of federal prisoners are serving time for drug offenses. About 20 percent of state prisoners are incarcerated for drug crimes.

According to Bryan Stevenson of the Equal Justice Initiative, "in the United States, the prison population has increased from 300,000 in 1972 to 2.3 million people today. One in 31 adults in the United States is in jail, prison, on probation or parole" (Stevenson, 2011: 2; see also www.drugwarfacs.org/cms/Crime). Lisa Trei at Stanford University makes a broader analysis: "In 1980, about 2 million people in the United States were under some kind of criminal justice supervision, said [Professor Lawrence] Bobo, the director of Stanford's Center for Comparative Studies in Race and Ethnicity. By 2000, the figure had jumped to about 6 million—and the United States had become the country that incarcerated its citizens more frequently than any other major western industrialized nation. The jump is largely attributed to the government's ongoing war on drugs" (Trei, May 25, 2005).

Although the US is by far the worst offender internationally, increased enforcement efforts have increased prison populations elsewhere. A total of 10 million people currently are in jail around the world for drug offenses (Stevenson, 2011: 2).

The irony is tragic. The self-proclaimed "land of the free" is most likely to throw more of its citizens into jail for an act of self-harm. Over the last two decades more people have gone to jail for drug offenses than for violent crimes. Arrests and imprisonment disproportionately affect African-Americans, who make up only about 13 percent of the population but account for 34 percent of drug arrests and 45 percent of state prisoners convicted of drug offences (Law Enforcement Against Prohibition, n.d). This exacerbates problems in a community where families are less often intact and job opportunities are less available. American cities have suffered as a result (Staley, 1991: 63-74).

Finally, the negative social impact of the drug laws includes creating crime. Drugs obviously are related to crime, but rarely are "crimogenic" themselves. That is, many illicit substances, such as marijuana and heroin, encourage passivity. (There is a much better argument that alcohol makes crime more likely, loosening inhibitions of would-be perpetrators and victims alike.)

Some addicts steal to fund their habits, but that often reflects high prices resulting from prohibition. Most of the crimes attributed to cocaine and even crack result from turning drugs over to an illegal market.

As Prohibition spurred the growth of the traditional mob, drug prohibition has spurred the growth of newer forms of organized crime, many competing gangs and organizations (Benjamin and Miller, 1991: 8-112). Wrote David Boaz and Timothy Lynch of the Cato Institute: "Addicts commit crimes to pay for a habit that would be easily affordable if it were legal. Police sources have estimated that as much as half the property crime in some major cities is committed by drug users" (Boaz and Lynch, 2006: 11).

More dramatically, because drugs are illegal, participants in the drug trade cannot go to court to settle disputes, whether between buyer and seller or rival sellers. Explain Boaz and Lynch, "When black-market contracts are breached, the result is often some form of violent sanction, which usually leads to retaliation and then open warfare in the streets" (Boaz and Lynch, 2006: 11). Benjamin and Miller wrote: "If you want to establish an unmistakable, unbreakable link between drugs and crime, the surest way to do it is to make drugs illegal" (1991: 112).

Rutgers Professor Douglas Husak estimated that such "systemic" crimes account for three-quarters of "drug-related" crime (2006: 32). Even prohibition advocate James Q. Wilson acknowledged that "It is not clear that enforcing the laws against drug use would reduce crime. On the contrary, crime may be caused by such enforcement" (quoted in Husak, 2006: 32). The Global Commission on Drug Policy reached the same conclusion: "increased arrests and law enforcement pressures on drug markets were strongly associated with increased homicide rates and other violent crimes" (2011: 15). Thus, more crime is primarily the price of drug prohibition, not drug use (Cleveland, 1998: 179-80). Even more so the veritable wars that have broken out in foreign nations, such as Mexico (Chapman, March 29, 2010).

Failure to end drug use

Despite all this effort, drug prohibition seems to have accomplished little. Obviously, the law is only one factor affecting drug use. Noted Mary M. Cleveland: "Most people choose not to use illicit drugs even when they have cheap and easy access to them. Enforcement can have some effect on light users; regular and problem users will get their drugs even in prison. Drug treatment and changes in social norms have far more influence on drug use than enforcement because they affect individuals' attitudes" (Cleveland, 1998: 182).

Government drug seizures rise and fall, with records constantly broken. Street prices rise and fall. Yet people continue to use drugs, their consumption more affected by social and cultural factors than enforcement campaigns. For years drug use rose even among teens, the vast majority of whom told government researchers that it was easy to find and purchase drugs. Government figures indicate that 118 million Americans above the age of 12, or 47 percent, have used illegal drugs (Law Enforcement Against Prohibition, n.d.). A similar percentage of high school students have tried illegal drugs before graduation (Law Enforcement Against Prohibition, n.d.).

Mike Trace, Chairman of the International Drug Policy Consortium, has concluded that despite receiving "unequivocal political support and massive financial investment," the campaign to suppress drugs "has not achieved the desired control and constriction of wholesale markets." Moreover, "efforts to stifle the flow of drugs from points of production to retail markets (generally described as interdiction), have also met with fundamental problems" (Trace, n.d.: 4). Demand reduction efforts have been no more successful. Indeed, "Various mixtures of these strategies and tactics have been implemented around the world over the last 50 years, but there is no evidence that any national government has been able to achieve anything like the objective of a controlled and diminished drug market, let alone a drug free world" (Trace, n.d.: 6).

In fact, enforcement often appears to correlate with *increased* use. Attorney and author Glenn Greenwald noted that, "the prevalence rate for cocaine usage in the United States was so much higher than the other countries surveyed that the researchers formally characterized it as an 'outlier'" (Greenwald, 2009: 24). Other countries with an emphasis on enforcement, such as Australia and Canada, also exhibit higher than average drug use. The *Economist* magazine stated simply that, "There is no correlation between the harshness of drug laws and the incidence of drug-taking: citizens living under tough regimes (notably America but also Britain) take more drugs, not fewer" (Will, October 29, 2009).

The costs of the War on Drugs are felt throughout the world, starting with America's closest neighbors. The terrible price has sparked growing interest in Latin America in decriminalization/legalization. Leading politicians, including former Mexican presidents Vincente Fox and Ernesto Zedillo, Brazilian president Fernando Henrique Cardoso, and Colombian president Cesar Gaviria, have begun pressing for Drug Peace.

In a paper prepared for the Global Commission on Drug Policy, Martin Jelsma of the Transnational Institute observed: "Some of the consequences resulting from the escalation of the last two decades were a nearly worldwide rapid increase in the prison population; human rights violations; restricted access to essential medicines; criminalization of users creating obstacles for health care, including strategies for HIV/AIDS prevention" (Jelsma, 2011: 8). In its June report the commission concluded: "The global war on drugs has failed, with devastating consequences for individuals and societies around the world." Yet despite global enforcement efforts, consumption of cocaine, marijuana, and opiates increased by 27 percent, 8.5 percent, and 34.5 percent, respectively, from 1998 to 2008 (Global Commission on Drug Policy, 2011: 4). The commission stated that "fundamental reforms in national and global drug control policies are urgently needed" (2011: 2).

What kind of reform?

Legalization could take different forms. One could imagine anything from open commercial sales, with only age-related restrictions (the traditional cigarette model) to sales through restricted, perhaps even government stores backed by limits on marketing and advertising (the traditional alcohol model) (Bandow, January 1, 1992; Evans and Neustadter, 1998: 129-48; Fish, 1998: 163-71; Duke and Gross, 1998: 201-21; MacCoun and Reuter, 2001: 310-17; Benjamin and Miller, 1991: 166-204; Frazell, 1992: 293-96; Branch, 1992: 297-308; Trebach, 1992: 308-19; Eldredge, 1998: 160-79; Ethan A. Nadelmann, 1991: 241-50; Husak, 1992: 209-51). Individual drugs could be treated differently, depending on assessments of harm and other factors (see, e.g., Kleiman, 1992: 203-382).

Obviously, the strongest individual rights position would indicate no restrictions on adult drug use. Indeed, Thomas Szasz contended: "the drug legalizers' opposition to the drug prohibitionists is so unprincipled that it makes the differences between the two parties illusory. Both groups accept that drugs denominated as dangerous *are* dangerous, and that 'drug use' *is* 'bad'" (1992: 103). Szasz overstates the case, but any restrictions should not turn into prohibition *sub rosa* and should be carefully tailored to ameliorate the impact of drug abuse on others.

Of course, advocates of both decriminalization and legalization would maintain restrictions on drug use by children. Total prohibition does not protect them (Husak, 2002: 67-83). In fact, today's enforcement efforts push youthful experimentation into criminal black markets rather than into less harmful gray markets, actually endangering children. In contrast, legalization for adults would allow greater emphasis on reducing leakage to kids.

Overall drug use likely would increase, but perhaps not as much as commonly assumed. Given the porous nature of drug prohibition, at least Western-style prohibition where users and sellers are not executed, the most likely abusers already have access to drugs. In their careful and detailed book, Robert MacCoun and Peter Reuter conclude that "Reductions in criminal sanctioning have little or no effect on the prevalence of drug use (i.e., the number of users)" and that "if relaxed drug laws increase the prevalence of use... the additional users will, on average, use less heavily and less harmfully than those who would have also used drugs under prohibition" (2001: 326, 327).

In fact, MacCoun and Reuter noted, America itself had "a smaller drug problem when cocaine and heroin were legal," though the results still were "unattractive" (2001: 204). The challenges then look minor compared to today, and much media-driven misinformation spurred the campaign to outlaw drugs a century ago (Miller, 1991: 85-99). Moreover, consumption of both alcohol and especially tobacco has fallen without a "war," and even before politicians began dramatically hiking tobacco taxes (Husak, 2002: 160).

Indeed, legalization would not be a step into the unknown. Great Britain, the Netherlands, and Switzerland all allow some use of some drugs without criminal prosecution (see, e.g., MacCoun and Reuter, 2001: 205-99; MacCoun and Reuter, September 20, 1999: 28-30. See also Levine and Reinarman, 1998b: 68-71; McVay, 1998: 13-16; MacCoun and Reuter, 2005: 121-241; Oppenheimer, 1993: 194-225; Miller, 1991: 125-31; Turner, 1991: 175-90; Global Commission on Drug Policy, 2011: 7). (The approach of some nations often seems contradictory: Britain, for instance, was famed for permitting regulated heroin use, but limited that option in recent years and is harsh in other ways.) Many nations, as well as a dozen US states, have effectively decriminalized marijuana use.

Such systems are not without problems because drug use is not without problems. In particular, a small country liberalizing its laws is likely to draw in users from other nations, creating difficulties unrelated to drug liberalization per se. Nevertheless, countries that have liberalized and states that have decriminalized their drug laws have suffered no great increase in consumption (Global Commission on Drug Policy, 2011: 410-11).

A particularly important example is Portugal, which decriminalized use of all drugs, including cocaine and heroin, a decade ago. The measure was advanced, wrote Glenn Greenwald, "as the most effective government policy for reducing addiction and its accompanying harms" by encouraging users to seek treatment and has proved to be politically popular (2009: 10).

Adult use has increased only modestly while consumption by minors actually has fallen: "None of the parade of horrors that decriminalization opponents in Portugal predicted, and that decriminalization opponents around the world typically invoke, has come to pass" (Greenwald, 2009: 11). More people are in treatment as users no longer fear criminal sanction. Drug-related HIV infections and mortality rates are down. Drug use in Portugal remains low compared to the rest of the European Union (Greenwald, 2009: 22).

Conclusion

Liberty—protecting individual freedom of action—is important because of its practical value, dramatized by the collapse of collectivism in its many forms in the 20th century. But liberty is even more important because it reflects the essence of the human person. Individuals are moral actors, responsible for themselves, their families, their communities, and their nations. Only liberty allows them to act on that responsibility, while holding them accountable for their actions.

Drug use may not be wise—indeed, some drugs inevitably will be abused by some people. However, free individuals must be allowed to make mistakes. To have meaning, liberty must protect the freedom to act in ways which may offend individuals and even majorities. So it is with "drugs" currently banned by the US and other governments.

The issue is most often fought on practical grounds. And, despite the brutal determination of avid supporters of prohibition, the policy seems doomed for practical reasons. Explained Mike Trace: "What is now common knowledge—that prohibition and harsh enforcement cannot control the basic human impulse to use psychoactive substances, and the immutable rules of commodity markets—was hypothesized by a small number of voices through the 20th century, and has been repeatedly indicated by all respectable academic and policy analysis conducted in recent years" (Trace, n.d.: 13).

Equally important, the War on Drugs has turned into a broad assault on a free society. Argued law professor Steven Wisotsky: "the War on Drugs actually is a war on the American people—their values, needs and choices, freely expressed in the marketplace of consumer goods" (1986: 198). To an astonishing degree, drug enforcement has targeted the very liberties which to most people are inherent in a free society.

Thus, any analysis of liberty should include protection of the freedom to take drugs. Such a freedom need not be treated as absolute, given the negative impact of drug abuse. However, a free society should affirm and protect individuals who choose to ingest substances which alter their mental and physical states. Contrary to conventional wisdom, drug use should be treated as a protected liberty.

References

Annas, George J. (1988). Reefer Madness—the Federal Response to California's Medical-Marijuana Law. In Jeffrey A. Schaler (ed.), *Drugs: Should We Legalize, Decriminalize or Deregulate?* (Prometheus Books): 120-29.

Bakalar, James B., and Lester Grinspoon (1984). *Drug Control in a Free Society.* Cambridge University Press.

Balko, Radley (2006, April 6). No SWAT. *Slate.* <http://www.slate.com/articles/news_and_politics/jurisprudence/2006/04/no_swat.html>, as of February 24, 2012.

Balko, Radley (2010, March 23). Another Senseless Drug War Death. Reason online. <http://reason.com/archives/2010/03/23/another-senseless-drug-war-dea>, as of February 24, 2012.

Bandow, Doug (1992, January 1). Dealing with Legalization. *American Prospect.* <http://prospect.org/cs/articles?article=dealing_with_legalization>, as of February 24, 2012.

Benjamin, Daniel K., and Roger Leroy Miller (1991). *Undoing Drugs: Beyond Legalization.* Basic Books.

Boaz, David, and Timothy Lynch (2006). Federal drug prohibition should be repealed. In Stuart A. Kallen (ed.), *Legalizing Drugs* (Thomson Gale).

Branch, Taylor (1992). Let Koop Do It: A Prescription for the Drug War. In Rod L. Evans and Irwin M. Berent (eds.), *Drug Legalization: For and Against* (Open Court): 297-308.

Chapman, Steve (2010, March 29). In the Drug War, Drugs Are Winning. *Reason online.* <http://reason.com/archives/2010/03/29/in-the-drug-war-drugs-are-winn>, as of February 24, 2012.

Cleveland, Mary M. (1998). Economics of Illegal Drug Markets: What Happens If We Downsize the Drug War? In Jefferson M. Fish (ed.), *How to Legalize Drugs* (Jason Aronson, Inc.).

Cole, Jack (2006). The War on Drugs is Destroying Lives. In Stuart A. Kallen (ed.), *Legalizing Drugs* (Thomson Gale).

Cussen, Meaghan, and Walter Block (2005). Drugs Should be Legalized. In Karen F. Balkin (ed.), *Drug Legalization* (Greenhaven Press).

Duke, Steven B., and Albert C. Gross (1998). Issues in Legalization. In Jefferson M. Fish (ed.), *How to Legalize Drugs* (Jason Aronson, Inc.): 201-21.

Eldredge, Dirk Chase (1998). *Ending the War on Drugs: A Solution for America.* Bridge Works Publishing Co.

Erickson, Patricia G., and Bruce K. Alexander (1998a). Cocaine and Addictive Liability. In Jeffrey A. Schaler (ed.), *Drugs: Should We Legalize, Decriminalize or Deregulate?* (Prometheus Books).

Erickson, Patricia G., and Timothy R. Weber (1998b). Cocaine Careers, Control and Consequences: Results from a Canadian Study. In Jeffrey A. Schaler (ed.), *Drugs: Should We Legalize, Decriminalize or Deregulate?* (Prometheus Books): 291-305.

Evans, Richard M. and Stanley Neustadter (1998). Legalization: An Introduction. In Jefferson M. Fish (ed.), *How to Legalize Drugs* (Jason Aronson, Inc.): 129-48.

Fish, Jefferson M. (1998). Proposals for De-Escalating the War on Drugs. In Jefferson M. Fish (ed.), *How to Legalize Drugs* (Jason Aronson, Inc.): 163-71.

Fraser, Ronald (2010, July 4). Property Seizures Are Getting Out of Hand. *Winona Daily News.*

Frazell, Daryl (1992). Should Drugs be Legalized? The Perils at the Extremes. In Rod L. Evans and Irwin M. Berent (eds.), *Drug Legalization: For and Against* (Open Court).

Friedman, Milton (1972, May 1). Prohibition and Drugs. *Newsweek*, <http://www.druglibrary.org/special/friedman/prohibition_and_drugs.htm>, as of February 24, 2012.

Glasser, Ira (1991). Drug Prohibition: An Engine for Crime. In Melvyn B. Krauss and Edward P. Lazear (eds.), *Searching for Alternatives: Drug-Control Policy in the United States* (Hoover Institution Press): 271-74.

Global Commission on Drug Policy (2011). *War on Drugs: Report of the Global Commission on Drug Policy* (June). Global Commission on Drug Policy. <www.globalcommissionondrugs.org>, as of February 24, 2012.

Goldstein, Avram, and Harold Kalant (1993). Drug Policy: Striking the Right Balance. In Ronald Bayer and Gerald M. Oppenheimer (eds.), *Confronting Drug Policy: Illicit Drugs in a Free Society* (Cambridge University Press).

Greenwald, Glenn (2009). *Drug Decriminalization in Portugal: Lessons for Creating Fair and Successful Drug Policies.* Cato Institute.

Grinspoon, Lester (1991). Marijuana in a Time of Psychopharmacological McCarthyism. In Melvyn B. Krauss and Edward P. Lazear (eds.), *Searching for Alternatives: Drug-Control Policy in the United States* (Hoover Institution Press): 379-89.

Grinspoon, Lester, and James B. Bakalar (1987). Medical Uses of Illicit Drugs. In Ronald Hamowy (ed.), *Dealing with Drugs: Consequences of Government Control* (Lexington Books): 183-219.

Hay, Joel W. (1991). The Harm They Do to Others: A Primer on the External Costs of Drug Abuse. In Melvyn B. Krauss and Edward P. Lazear (eds.), *Searching for Alternatives: Drug-Control Policy in the United States* (Hoover Institution Press): 200-25.

Hill, John Lawrence (1992). The Zone of Privacy and the Right to Use Drugs: A Jurisprudential Critique. In Rod L. Evans and Irwin M. Berent (eds.), *Drug Legalization: For and Against* (Open Court).

Howley, Kerry (2005). Locking Up Life-Saving Drugs: Prescription Laws Make Us Sicker and Poorer. *Reason Magazine* (August/September).

Husak, Douglas N. (1992). *Drugs and Rights*. Cambridge University Press.

Husak, Douglas N. (2002). *Legalize This! The Case for Criminalizing Drugs*. Verso.

Husak, Douglas N. (2006). Legalizing Drugs Would Reduce Crime. In Stuart A. Kallen (ed.), *Legalizing Drugs* (Thomson Gale).

Husak, Douglas, and Peter de Marneffe (2005). *The Legalization of Drugs*. Cambridge University Press.

Jelsma, Martin (2011). The Development of International Drug Control: Lessons Learned and Strategic Challenges for the Future. Global Commission on Drug Policy working paper. Prepared for January 24-25, 2011 meeting.

Jenkins, Simon (2009, September 3). The War on Drugs is Immoral Idiocy. We need the Courage of Argentina. *Guardian*.

Kleiman, Mark A.R. (1992). *Against Excess: Drug Policy for Results*. Basic Books.

Law Enforcement Against Prohibition [LEAP] (n.d.). *The War on Drugs at a Glance*. Web page. LEAP. <www.leap.cc/for-the-media/the-war-on-drugs-at-a-glance>, as of February 24, 2012.

Levine, Harry G., and Craig Reinarman (1998a). The Transition from Prohibition to Regulation: Lessons from Alcohol Policy for Drug Policy. In Jefferson M. Fish (ed.), *How to Legalize Drugs* (Jason Aronson, Inc.): 264-70.

Levine, Harry G., and Craig Reinarman (1998b). Alcohol Prohibition and Drug Prohibition: Lessons from Alcohol Policy for Drug Policy. In Jefferson M. Fish (ed.), *How to Legalize Drugs* (Jason Aronson, Inc.): 43-61.

MacCoun, Robert J., and Peter Reuter (1999, September 20). Does Europe Do It Better? Lessons from Holland, Britain, and Switzerland. *The Nation*: 28-30.

MacCoun, Robert J., and Peter Reuter (2001). *Drug War Heresies: Learning from Other Vices, Times, and Places*. Cambridge University Press.

MacCoun, Robert J., and Peter Reuter (2005). Drug Policies Should Focus on Harm Reduction. In Karen F. Balkin (ed.), *Drug Legalization* (Greenhaven Press): 121-24.

Mandel, Jerry (1998). The Opening Shots of the War on Drugs. In Jefferson M. Fish (ed.), *How to Legalize Drugs* (Jason Aronson, Inc.).

McVay, Douglas A. (1998). Appendix 1a: The United States and the Netherlands. In Jefferson M. Fish (ed.), *How to Legalize Drugs* (Jason Aronson, Inc.): 13-16.

Miller, Richard Lawrence (1991). *The Case for Legalizing Drugs*. Praeger.

Miron, Jeffrey A. (2009, March 24). Legalize Drugs to Stop Violence. *CNN*.

Miron, Jeffrey A., and Katherine Waldock (2010). *The Budgetary Impact of Ending Drug Prohibition.* Cato Institute.

Moore, Mark H. (1993). Drugs, the Criminal Law, and the Administration of Justice. In Ronald Bayer and Gerald M. Oppenheimer (eds.), *Confronting Drug Policy: Illicit Drugs in a Free Society* (Cambridge University Press).

Morgan, John P. (1991). Prohibition Is Perverse Policy: What Was True in 1933 Is True Now. In Melvyn B. Krauss and Edward P. Lazear (eds.), *Searching for Alternatives: Drug-Control Policy in the United States* (Hoover Institution Press): 405-23.

Mugford, Stephen (1991). Drug Legalization and the "Goldilocks" Problem: Thinking About Costs and Control of Drugs. In Melvyn B. Krauss and Edward P. Lazear (eds.), *Searching for Alternatives: Drug-Control Policy in the United States* (Hoover Institution Press).

Nadelmann, Ethan A. (1991). Beyond Drug Prohibition: Evaluating the Alternatives. In Melvyn B. Krauss and Edward P. Lazear (eds.), *Searching for Alternatives: Drug-Control Policy in the United States* (Hoover Institution Press): 241-50.

Naim, Moises (2011). *The Drug Trade: The Politicization of Criminals and the Criminalization of Politicians.* Global Commission on Drug Policy working paper. Prepared for January 24-25, 2011 meeting.

Oppenheimer, Gerald M. (1993). To Build a Bridge: The Use of Foreign Models by Domestic Critics of US Drug Policy. In Ronald Bayer and Gerald M. Oppenheimer (eds.), *Confronting Drug Policy: Illicit Drugs in a Free Society* (Cambridge University Press): 194-225.

Ostrowski, James (1991). Answering the Critics of Drug Legalization. In Melvyn B. Krauss and Edward P. Lazear (eds.), *Searching for Alternatives: Drug-Control Policy in the United States* (Hoover Institution Press): 304-15.

Robins, Lee N., et al. (1988). Vietnam Veterans Three Years after Vietnam: How Our Study Changed Our View of Heroin. In Jeffrey A. Schaler (ed.), *Drugs: Should We Legalize, Decriminalize or Deregulate?* (Prometheus Books).

Staley, Sam (1992). *Drug Policy and the Decline of American Cities.* Transaction Publishers.

Stevenson, Bryan (2011). *Drug Policy, Criminal Justice, and Mass Imprisonment.* Global Commission on Drug Policy working paper. Prepared for January 24-25, 2011 meeting. <http://www.globalcommissionondrugs.org/wp-content/themes/gcdp_v1/pdf/Global_Com_Bryan_Stevenson.pdf>, as of May 3, 2012.

Stossel, John (2010, June 17). End the Drug War: Government Goes Astray When it Tries to Protect us From Ourselves. *Reason online.* <http://reason.com/archives/2010/06/17/end-the-drug-war>, as of February 24, 2012.

Szasz, Thomas (1992). *Our Right to Drugs: The Case for a Free Market.* Praeger.

Sweet, Robert W., and Edward A. Harris (1998). Moral and Constitutional Considerations in Support of the Decriminalization of Drugs. In Jefferson M. Fish (ed.), *How to Legalize Drugs* (Jason Aronson, Inc.).

Taubman, Paul (1991). Externalities and Decriminalization of Drugs. In Melvyn B. Krauss and Edward P. Lazear (eds.), *Searching for Alternatives: Drug-Control Policy in the United States* (Hoover Institution Press): 97-107.

Thornton, Mark (1991). *The Economics of Prohibition.* University of Utah Press.

Trace, Mike (n.d.). *Drug Policy—Lessons Learnt, and Options for the Future.* Global Commission on Drug Policies.

Trebach, Arnold S. (1992). Tough Choices: The Practical Politics of Drug Policy Reform. In Rod L. Evans and Irwin M. Berent (eds.), *Drug Legalization: For and Against* (Open Court): 308-19.

Trebach, Arnold S., and Kevin B. Zeese, eds. (1992). *Friedman and Szasz on Liberty and Drugs: Essays on the Free Market and Prohibition.* The Drug Policy Foundation Press.

Trei, Lisa (2005, May 25). Higher Incarceration Rates Harm Social Stability, Scholars Claim. *Stanford University News.* <http://news.Stanford.edu/news/2005/may25/inequality-052505.html>, as of February 24, 2012.

Turner, David (1991). Pragmatic Incoherence: The Changing Face of British Drug Policy. In Melvyn B. Krauss and Edward P. Lazear (eds.), *Searching for Alternatives: Drug-Control Policy in the United States* (Hoover Institution Press): 175-90.

Vatz, Richard E., and Lee S. Weinberg (1998). Rhetorical Dimensions of Decriminalization. In Jefferson M. Fish (ed.), *How to Legalize Drugs* (Jason Aronson, Inc.).

Will, George F. (2009, October 29). Gil Kerlikowske's Reality Check in the Drug War. *Washington Post.*

Winick, Charles (1993). Social Behavior, Public Policy, and Nonharmful Drug Use. In Ronald Bayer and Gerald M. Oppenheimer (eds.), *Confronting Drug Policy: Illicit Drugs in a Free Society* (Cambridge University Press).

Wisotsky, Steven (1986). *Breaking the Impasse in the War on Drugs.* Greenwood Press.

Zimring, Franklin E., and Gordan Hawkins (1991). The Wrong Question: Critical Notes on the Decriminalization Debate. In Melvyn B. Krauss and Edward P. Lazear (eds.), *Searching for Alternatives: Drug-Control Policy in the United States* (Hoover Institution Press): 3-13.

Zinberg, Norman E. (1987). The Use and Misuse of Intoxicants: Factors in the Development of Controlled Use. In Ronald Hamowy (ed.), *Dealing with Drugs: Consequences of Government Control* (Lexington Books).